Abortion Wars

ABORTION WARS

A HALF CENTURY OF STRUGGLE,
1950–2000

Edited by Rickie Solinger

UNIVERSITY OF CALIFORNIA PRESS
BERKELEY   LOS ANGELES   LONDON

University of California Press
Berkeley and Los Angeles, California

University of California Press, Ltd.
London, England

Grateful acknowledgment is made for permission to reprint
material from the following:
Faye Ginsburg, "Saving America's Souls: Operation Rescue's
Crusade Against Abortion," in *Fundamentalisms and the
State: Remaking Politics, Economies, and Militance,* edited by
Martin Marty and R. Scott Appleby (Chicago: University of
Chicago Press, copyright © 1993 by University of Chicago).
By permission of the publisher.
Warren M. Hern, "Life on the Front Lines," *Women's Health
Issues* 4 (1): 48–54, copyright 1994. By permission of the
Jacobs Institute of Women's Health.
Alison Jaggar, "Regendering the U.S. Abortion Debate,"
Journal of Social Philosophy 28, no. 1 (spring 1997). By per-
mission of the *Journal of Social Philosophy.*
Dorothy E. Roberts, "Punishing Drug Addicts Who Have
Babies," *Harvard Law Review* 104, copyright © 1991 by the
Harvard Law Review Association.

Library of Congress Cataloging-in-Publication Data

Abortion wars : a half century of struggle, 1950–2000 / edited
by Rickie Solinger.
    p. cm.
    Includes index.
    ISBN 0–520–20256–2 (cloth : alk. paper). —
ISBN 0–520–20952–4 (pbk. : alk. paper)
    1. Abortion—United States—History—20th century.
2. Women's rights— United States—History—20th century.
3. Abortion—Government policy—United States.   4. Abortion—Law and legislation—United States.   5. Pro-life movement—United States.   I. Solinger, Rickie, 1947–   .
HQ767.5.U5A2825   1998
363.46'0973—dc 21   97–12261

Printed in the United States of America
9 8 7 6 5 4 3 2 1

Contents

Acknowledgments   ix

Chronology of Abortion Politics   xi

Introduction: Abortion Politics and History
Rickie Solinger   1

Part One
COERCION, RESISTANCE, AND LIBERATION
BEFORE *ROE V. WADE*   11

1   Pregnancy and Power before *Roe v. Wade,* 1950–1970
Rickie Solinger   15

2   Beyond Safe and Legal: The Lessons of Jane
Laura Kaplan   33

3   Women versus Connecticut: Conducting a
Statewide Hearing on Abortion
Amy Kesselman   42

Part Two
STRATEGIC ARENAS   69

4   The Rule of Law, the Rise of Violence, and the Role
of Morality: Reframing America's Abortion Debate
Marcy J. Wilder   73

5   Legal Strategies for Abortion Rights
in the Twenty-first Century
Kathryn Kolbert and Andrea Miller   95

6 Electoral Politics and Abortion: Narrowing the Message
William Saletan   111

7 Punishing Drug Addicts Who Have Babies:
Women of Color, Equality, and the Right of Privacy
Dorothy E. Roberts   124

Part Three
ACTIVISM   157

8 African-American Women and Abortion
Loretta J. Ross   161

9 Abortion in the United States—Legal But Inaccessible
Marlene Gerber Fried   208

10 Rescuing the Nation: Operation Rescue and the Rise
of Anti-Abortion Militance
Faye Ginsburg   227

11 Toward Coalition:
The Reproductive Health Technologies Project
Marie Bass   251

Part Four
PHYSICIANS AND THE POLITICS OF PROVISION   269

12 "We Called It Kindness":
Establishing a Feminist Abortion Practice
Elizabeth Karlin   273

13 The Twentieth-Century Gender Battle:
Difficulties in Perception
Jane E. Hodgson   290

14 Life on the Front Lines
Warren M. Hern   307

15 The Crisis in Abortion Provision and
Pro-Choice Medical Activism in the 1990s
Carole Joffe, Patricia Anderson, and Jody Steinauer   320

Part Five
REINTERPRETING ABORTION RIGHTS OVER TIME   335

16   Regendering the U.S. Abortion Debate
    Alison M. Jaggar   339

17   Psychologies of Abortion:
    Implications of a Changing Context
    Sharon Gold-Steinberg and Abigail J. Stewart   356

18   Disability Rights and Selective Abortion
    Marsha Saxton   374

    Contributors   395

    Index   401

Acknowledgments

It is an honor to have worked with every contributor in this volume. Here I would like to express deepest respect and thanks to each of them for extraordinary efforts on behalf of women's rights.

A warm thank you to Liza Butler, whose expert assistance moved this project along. Thanks to Jennifer Heath, in general. And to Erika Doss, who opened my eyes, as usual. Naomi Schneider, Sue Heinemann, and Nola Burger at the University of California Press were extremely helpful, thoughtful, and supportive.

Jim Geiser was indispensable in every way as I worked on this book.

Late 1940s–early 1950s   Experts estimate 200,000 to 1.3 million illegal abortions in United States annually.

Rise of hospital abortion boards, formed to adjudicate women's appeals for permission to obtain legal "therapeutic abortions."

1953   Alfred Kinsey's *Sexual Behavior in the Human Female* reports that 9 out of 10 premarital pregnancies end in abortion and 22 percent of married women have had an abortion while married.

1955   Mary S. Calderone, medical director of Planned Parenthood, organizes high-profile conference, "Abortion in America"; conference volume published in 1958.

1960   American Medical Association observes that laws against abortion are unenforceable.

American Law Institute (ALI) endorses liberalization of abortion laws.

1962   In highly publicized incident, Sherri Finkbine, denied an abortion in Phoenix, goes to Stockholm to abort a fetus damaged by thalidomide; according to Gallup Poll, 52 percent of Americans approve.

In California, Pat Maginnis founds women's-rights-based Citizens for Humane Abortion Laws.

1965 *New York Times* endorses abortion law reform, February 13.

Rubella epidemic leads to abortions performed on grounds of "mental health crisis."

In *Griswold v. Connecticut* Supreme Court rules, 7–2, that Connecticut law banning contraception infringes on married couples' right to privacy.

Mid-1960s Abortion law repeal (vs. reform) efforts gain momentum.

1966 National Organization for Women (NOW) formed.

Association to Repeal Abortion Laws in California started.

1967 *Journal of the American Medical Association* prints pro-reform editorial.

Abortion reform bills considered by at least 25 state legislatures.

Colorado enacts ALI-style abortion reform law, followed by North Carolina and California.

Twenty-one New York clergymen establish Clergy Consultation Service on Abortion, an abortion referral network.

Federal government spends over $20 million a year on contraceptive programs in United States.

Modern Medicine magazine reports 87 percent of American physicians favor liberalization of country's anti-abortion policies.

1969 Jane, an underground abortion services network, formed in Chicago.

First National Conference on Abortion Laws held; National Association for Repeal of Abortion Laws (NARAL) founded there.

Radical feminist group Redstockings holds first speak-out on abortion.

1970 New York state legislature legalizes abortion; Hawaii and Washington follow.

1971 National poll shows that over half of Americans favor legalizing abortion.

American Bar Association officially supports a woman's right to choose abortion up to 20th week of pregnancy.

Supreme Court hears first round of oral arguments in *Roe v. Wade.*

Abele v. Markle filed in Connecticut; 858 plaintiffs.

Dr. Jane Hodgson convicted for performing in-hospital abortion; only U.S. physician ever convicted for this reason.

Feminist Women's Health Center set up in Los Angeles; teaches women how to perform "menstrual extractions."

1972 Connecticut's abortion law declared unconstitutional; Meskill bill reinstates law; Women versus Connecticut files new suit with 2,000 plaintiffs.

1973 Supreme Court's *Roe v. Wade* decision legalizes abortion, as does its ruling in companion case, *Doe v. Bolton.*

NARAL becomes National Abortion Rights Action League in response to anti-*Roe* backlash.

First edition of National Right to Life Committee's newsletter editorializes, "We must work for the passage of a constitutional Human Life Amendment."

Religious Coalition for Abortion Rights founded.

1975 National Women's Health Network founded.

1976 Hyde Amendment enacted, prohibiting Medicaid-funded abortions except "where the life of the mother would be endangered."

1980 Republican Party platform calls for appointment of anti-abortion-rights judges at every level of the federal judiciary.

In *Harris v. McRae* Supreme Court rules that although the government "may not place obstacles in the path of a woman's exercise of her freedom of choice, it need not remove those not of its own creation. Indigence falls within the latter category."

1983 National Black Women's Health Project founded.

1985 Women of Color Partnership Program created by Religious Coalition for Abortion Rights.

1987 Reproductive Health Technologies Project founded.

Randall Terry leads first "rescue."

1988   Operation Rescue formally established.

In *Bowen v. Kendrick* Supreme Court upholds Adolescent Family Life Act's denial of funding to programs that "advocate, promote, or encourage abortion."

1989   In *Webster v. Reproductive Health Services* Supreme Court upholds Missouri law stating "human life begins at conception" and placing restrictions on access to abortion; Court comes within one vote of overturning *Roe v. Wade.*

Teenager Becky Bell, afraid to obey parental-notification statute, dies after septic illegal abortion.

1989–1992   Over 700 anti-abortion-rights bills introduced in state legislatures across the country.

Late 1980s–early 1990s   Anti-abortion violence aimed at abortion clinics escalates.

1990   In *Hodgson v. Minnesota* Supreme Court upholds state law that no abortion should be performed on a minor woman for 48 hours after both parents are notified; statute also provides for "judicial bypass."

1991   RU 486 approved for use in Britain.

Operation Rescue stages massive blockades throughout summer in Wichita, Kansas.

In *Rust v. Sullivan* Supreme Court rules 5–4 that since the government had not discriminated on the basis of viewpoint, but had "merely chosen to fund one activity [childbirth] to the exclusion of another [abortion], the 'gag rule' prohibiting physicians and other employees of abortion-providing facilities from counseling pregnant women about abortion or engaging in activities that encourage, promote, or advocate abortion as a method of family planning" did not violate the free-speech rights of doctors, their staffs, or their patients.

1992   President Clinton lifts "gag rule."

National Network of Abortion Funds established.

Eighty-four percent of counties in United States have no physician willing to perform abortions.

In *Planned Parenthood v. Casey* Supreme Court rules, 5–4, to "retain and reaffirm" women's right to abortion but also upholds Pennsylvania restrictions.

In wake of *Casey* decision, Mississippi becomes first state to introduce a mandatory delay and biased-information requirement.

1993 NARAL changes name to National Abortion and Reproductive Rights Action League.

National Black Women's Health Project takes lead in fight against Hyde Amendment.

Dr. David Gunn, an abortion practitioner, murdered in Florida.

Congress expands Hyde Amendment to provide federal funding for abortions in cases of rape and incest.

1994 Supreme Court rules RICO may be used to prosecute perpetrators of abortion clinic violence.

FACE Act passed, restricting protest activity near clinic entrances.

After circulating his "justifiable homicide" petition, Paul Hill murders abortion provider Dr. John Britton and his volunteer escort, James Barrett, in Florida; Dr. Gary Romalis shot at his home in British Columbia.

Republicans attain majority in Congress; move quickly to bar health-insurance coverage of abortion for federal employees, outlaw use of U.S. military hospitals for abortions, ban federal funding of abortions for federal prisoners, and abolish federal subsidies for international family-planning agencies that provide abortions or abortion-related information.

Attorney General Janet Reno convenes grand jury to investigate clinic violence.

Medical Students for Choice founded.

1995 Two clinic employees, Shannon Lowney and Leanne Nichols, murdered in Brookline, Massachusetts.

Ohio bans abortions carried out by dilation and extraction method ("partial birth abortions").

1996 Both houses of Congress take the unprecedented step of passing a bill that criminalizes the performance of abortion by a specific method, so-called partial birth abortions. Legislation is vetoed by President Clinton and efforts to override veto fail; however, Congress and state legislatures continue attempts to ban this infrequently used method, properly called intact dilation and extraction.

FDA issues letter finding RU486 "approvable," but subsequent business and legal complications render U.S. distribution plans unclear.

Rickie Solinger

INTRODUCTION

Abortion Politics and History

Fifty years ago, politicians in this country did not speak in public about
abortion. Nor did priests or rabbis. Large groups of people did not
collect in Washington, D.C., to demonstrate their support for or abhor-
rence of abortion rights. Fifty years ago almost no one in the United
States imagined coupling the shadowy world of abortion with the concept of the civil rights of women. Abortion practitioners—and there
were hundreds of them working in our cities and towns then—did not
don bulletproof vests when they went to work in the morning. And
fifty years ago, hundreds of thousands of women sought and obtained
abortions, furtively keeping appointments with criminalized practitioners in venues on the wrong side of the law.

At the end of the twentieth century, the subject of abortion occupies
the dedicated space in public discourse for expressions of fear, outrage,
and hatred; for struggles over ideology and justice. This is the space
that forty to fifty years ago was filled by the subjects of civil rights and
communism. Clearly, a great deal has changed in the past half century
regarding abortion, and this volume aims to consider aspects of the
change.

There are pressing reasons to look at the abortion controversy in the
United States over time. But before discussing some of the reasons that
seem particularly pressing, I want to make the simple point that when
a subject is given its history—when the abortion controversy and abortion practice are examined within a historical framework—it becomes

1

unsettlingly impossible to think about the subject in a fixed, static way or to claim universalized, decontextualized meanings for abortion and its satellite issues.

The subject of abortion is a model example of this point. What would a contemporary reader make, for instance, of a 1966 letter in my files from a Portland, Oregon, parish priest in good standing who wrote to the Portland City Council imploring this body to quit harassing the city's most active, most successful, and most demonized abortion practitioner? In this letter the priest insisted that the council grant a permanent license for the motel the abortionist owned on the same block occupied by St. Michael's Catholic Church. The priest defined his defense of the abortionist clearly: "I sincerely trust that we are still living in an age when a person's property is respected." This letter directs the attention of today's readers to the very interesting fact that in 1966 a Catholic clergyman not only argued publicly that property rights trumped abortion wrongs but even portrayed the abortion provider as a hardworking, generous grandmother of four whose place of business was a respectable hostelry.

Keeping the priest from St. Michael's in mind, let's return to the important reasons for considering the subject of abortion in its historical context. To begin with, a historical framework makes clear that the meanings of the most fundamental terms associated with abortion— such as *life, choice, mother, fetal viability*—have shifted, contracting or expanding over the past half century. For both scholarly and strategic reasons, it is important to cultivate a heightened awareness of this process.

The fact is, when foundational terms—particularly those associated with politically charged matters—have fluid and mutable meanings over time, their usage is easily manipulated or distorted and politicized. An advocate can emphasize vestigial meaning in a way that subtly but powerfully eclipses contemporary usage. In the abortion arena, opponents of abortion rights often invoke terms such as *life* and *mother's destiny* as if they had fixed, enduring transcultural and transhistorical meanings. At other times, these same people imbue old terms with apparently modern significations. A demonstration that the meaning of many abortion-related terms has changed over time calls into question the claim of universal, unchanging truth advanced by the anti-rights forces.

The term *fetal viability* is a case in point. Fifty years ago, embryologists and neonatologists were in general agreement that viability—the capacity of the fetus to live outside the womb—was reached after approximately thirty-four weeks of gestation. Scientists and physicians also agreed that *fetal viability* was a technical term relevant mostly to obstetric emergencies. Over the decades, scientific advances have pushed the date of fetal viability back, so that today, in some cases, a fetus of twenty-seven or twenty-eight weeks' gestation can be rendered viable. New science has thus fractured old meanings and common usage. Today, anti-rights legislators all over the country and in Congress have appropriated the term from the medical domain and refashioned it as a legal status and a political rallying cry. For abortion rights opponents, the term now demarcates the beginning of a stage of pregnancy in which abortion is deemed *late,* and therefore notoriously and irredeemably wicked. *Fetal viability* has become an anti-rights strategy for demonizing women and disqualifying doctors.

In contrast, for abortion rights proponents, the term largely retains its original reference to the fetus *qua* fetus. People who support abortion rights are aware that the very small number of abortions performed after fetal viability are bound up with unavoidable tragedy. Many rights advocates have come to believe that, in practice, fetal viability is a socially constructed and not simply a scientifically predictable status; a woman's access to prenatal care, adequate diet, high-tech obstetric and neonatal services, and other resources has a decisive impact on when any given fetus achieves viability. Taking into account older meanings and usages of terms central to public discussion of abortion, and the ways these have changed over time, is not only an interesting intellectual pursuit. It is an aspect of building an effective political strategy.

A second benefit of placing abortion politics in time is that historical perspective pushes us to examine anti-rights and pro-rights activism in a context that includes other contemporaneous forms of activism and other social movements. The historical frame captures and helps us understand how the abortion issue in the United States has drawn in and interacted variably with a broad array of other social concerns. Loretta Ross's essay in this volume delineates the complex and changing relationship between civil rights and reproductive rights activists during much of the twentieth century. Faye Ginsburg's essay on Operation Rescue suggests that the demography, ideology, and activist trajectory of this anti-rights sect (and others like it) must be understood as part of the history of American fundamentalism.

Looking at abortion politics in a historical framework creates one more important opportunity: the historical evidence challenges and can even demolish the myths that have frozen much of the public discussion of abortion in a dangerous rhetoric outside of time and social context, obscuring and distorting what is at issue. For example, Randall Terry and Patrick Buchanan and other anti-abortion leaders speak of the blasphemous effect on the United States of the millions of abortions performed since legalization in 1973. Terry goes so far as to claim that the destructive flooding of the Mississippi River in the summer of 1993 expressed God's vengeance against abortion-seeking women and abortion-performing physicians. Terry, Buchanan, and others broadcast the untruth that before *Roe v. Wade*, the United States was a virtually abortion-free country and thus, they say, a country with stronger family values, closer to God. The historical evidence makes clear, however, that before legalization, hundreds of thousands of women obtained abortions each year. The historical evidence forces us to recognize that the laws against abortion did not come anywhere near ending or even effectively containing the procedure, though the laws did, of course, make being a woman more dangerous in this country.

A related myth, promulgated by a broad spectrum of people concerned about abortion and public policy, is that before legalization abortionists were dirty and dangerous back-alley butchers. In one recently released pro-rights documentary about the illegal era, women forced into the back alley by the law and determination to control their own fertility are portrayed as taking their lives into their hands because practitioners were all filthy mercenaries, sexual predators, or both. Again, the historical evidence does not support such claims. Rather, trial records and public health studies—two of the best historical sources for tracking a secret, criminal activity such as abortion—show astonishingly high rates of technical proficiency among criminalized abortion practitioners and surprisingly low rates of septic abortion caused by these persons. The widespread practice of self-induced abortion, on the other hand, did leave a horrible trail of morbidity and mortality. The enduring myth of the back-alley butcher has profound contemporary relevance. The anecdotal, unsubstantiated taint attached to old-time practitioners has a way of bleeding across time to infect the public and professional standing of contemporary practitioners, who, with the myth intact, are "justifiably" targeted by violent "pro-lifers," marginalized by the medical profession, and shunned by their own communities.

Two other commonly invoked myths are equally disingenuous and ahistorical. One claims that the 1973 Supreme Court decision legalizing abortion, *Roe v. Wade,* reflected only the determination of a few old men sitting on the court. The implications here are that Americans did not then and do not now want legal and easily accessible abortion and that recriminalization can be accomplished as smoothly as legalization, if efforts are directed wisely. The other myth, that abortion is a white middle-class women's issue, trades on historical divisions among women of different races in the United States. Amy Kesselman's essay vividly debunks the first of these historical distortions, and Marlene Fried, Loretta Ross, and Dorothy Roberts overturn the other, from a variety of perspectives. The work of addressing and discrediting the mythologies of abortion and abortion politics is an important aspect of the fight to preserve and extend women's rights to control their own bodies.

In this volume the commitment to examine abortion across time is enriched by multiple and interdisciplinary perspectives. The authors of the eighteen essays represent seven academic disciplines and the fields of journalism, medicine, and law. Many of the authors are activists, and all share a conviction about and a commitment to pro-rights politics.

This volume is unabashedly a pro-rights book. The perspectives collected here yield a complex picture of what has been at stake in abortion politics during the past fifty years. These essays help clarify why so many women consider abortion crucial to their lives and so bound up with full citizenship rights. They also help explain why opposition to abortion rights has persisted and become so violent today. Together, these essays illuminate a fundamental lesson about social change in the United States. The recent history of abortion has confirmed that judicial decisions that overturn restrictive laws and establish new rights (even in the context of widespread support from citizen-activists) do not settle social policy and, in fact, are likely to spark severe and long-lasting resistance. A quarter of a century after *Roe v. Wade,* abortion remains one of the most unresolved and violently contested issues in the United States. Beyond its scholarly value the material in this volume offers a rich base from which abortion rights activists can analyze the nature of abortion politics in the past and present and strategize for the future.

Aesthetics (and my personal obsessions) notwithstanding, there are several reasons why the band of time marked out by this collection begins in approximately 1950. In my judgment, the contemporary era of reproductive politics began soon after World War II. Five years after the end of the war, more women in this country—16.5 million—were employed outside of their homes than ever before, and that number was increasing by approximately one million each year, despite postwar reconversion policies that aimed to eliminate huge numbers of women from the workplace. At the same time, in a not unrelated development, a number of powerful cultural and political authorities began to mandate and enforce the vulnerability and relatively weak citizenship status of women. Tactics included unprecedented crackdowns on abortion practitioners and new laws and social practices that gave government entities and other social agencies the right to decide when and if a woman was a mother.

The lives of millions of women were adversely affected over several decades by this new postwar stringency. But at the same time, in the face of coercion, women began to resist the authorities who would define the conditions of maternity for them. Just as *Roe v. Wade* stimulated the rise of the anti-rights movement in the 1970s, twenty years earlier, females across the country were stimulated by new restrictive social policies to fight back. Early on, resistance was massive, if carried out on an individual basis: each year throughout the 1950s, hundreds of thousands of teenage and adult women got abortions. Doctors held conferences and published books and scores of professional papers on the abortion dilemma women presented them with. Some doctors quietly tucked a few more abortion-seeking patients into their weekly schedules. The rise in the late 1940s and early 1950s of hospital abortion boards—panels of doctors to which an unwillingly pregnant female could apply for permission to obtain an abortion—represented, in an odd way, a giant, if oblique, step toward reproductive rights. Even though the boards operated in a harshly coercive and authoritarian manner and made women into supplicants, these postwar panels were established in response to women's demands for safe abortion. In addition, the existence of abortion boards was predicated on the belief that women had a voice in the matter of their pregnancies, a right to *request* an abortion and, in some cases, a right to have one. It was not long before secret, individual resistance and the humiliatingly won right to ask a committee of doctors for an abortion evolved into collective public demands for abortion rights.

The millennium provides a dramatic, if artificial, end point for this collection. It is artificial because there is no evidence that important aspects of the abortion issue will be resolved by the end of the twentieth century. Yet the year 2000 provides us with an opportunity, perhaps a mandate, to assess the shape and content of abortion politics over the last half of the twentieth century. This assessment is important for predicting future scenarios and for mapping out strategies. As we move into the twenty-first century, pro-rights proponents realize, as they largely did not in 1973, that the struggle to establish fully legal and accessible abortion rights for all women is a long-term project.

In some ways, at the end of the twentieth century, abortion politics exists on paradoxical terrain. On the one hand, the status of abortion in the United States is more volatile than ever, dependent on a host of variables including presidential elections, the political complexion of the Supreme Court and the fifty state legislatures, and even on the political culture of thousands of municipal police departments. On the other hand, abortion has achieved a dailiness in the consciousness of Americans. Regular news reports of legislative hearings, protests, violence, legal challenges to restrictions, and other abortion-related events have kept the issue before the public in ways that were simply unimaginable a half century ago and that today push millions of Americans to consider their personal relation to the issue and take a stand. In part, the purpose of this volume is to offer readers historical and multidisciplinary perspectives that will deepen, enrich, and clarify the base of their participation in the national discussion of abortion and abortion rights, and their advocacy of these rights.

Abortion Wars is divided into five parts: (1) Coercion, Resistance, and Liberation before *Roe v. Wade*; (2) Strategic Arenas; (3) Activism; (4) Physicians and the Politics of Provision; and (5) Reinterpreting Abortion Rights over Time. Predictably, the essayists share preoccupations and concerns across these divisions. All are horrified by anti-rights violence. All are searching for effective strategies to safeguard women's rights to reproductive safety and autonomy. In one way or another, all of the contributors are abortion rights *activists* and are devoted to stimulating and channeling the activism of others. I believe that all of the contributors are committed to the position that "abortion rights" refers to one of a broad array of entitlements, services, and resources constituting *reproductive rights* that *all* women must possess in order to be full members of society. These themes are threaded across the sections, woven through essays with distinctive content.

Four additional themes stand out for their importance to more than one author. First, several of the essayists agree with the proposition that "the erosion of *Roe* was inevitable," as Kathryn Kolbert and Andrea Miller of the Center for Reproductive Law and Policy put it, in part because of the "privacy" doctrine the Supreme Court placed at the core of abortion rights in 1973. In various and fascinating ways, Kolbert and Miller, Alison Jaggar, Dorothy Roberts, and Marsha Saxton reassess the basis and the nature of abortion rights in light of post-1973 developments in law, feminist theory, and politics that have exposed dangerous loopholes, which threaten the rights of many groups of pregnant women, including the poor, the young, the drug-addicted (especially women of color), and the disabled.

Second, a number of the essayists illuminate the fact that the abortion struggle in the United States has been so protracted and become so violent because of the ways that abortion activates and engages with the most bedeviling cultural and political issues facing this country. These include the complex and contested relationship among femininity, feminism, sex, and fertility, and the widely perceived need at the end of the twentieth century to redefine the feminist movement so that race and class as well as gender considerations are at its core. Abortion politics also activates questions regarding the citizenship rights of poor women and women of color, especially questions about whether women in these groups have the same rights as other women to decide when and whether to become pregnant, to stay pregnant, to have abortions, to become mothers, and to keep and raise their children.

In addition, abortion politics presses us to reevaluate the role of violence in American history, specifically as a tool for individuals and groups frustrated by their lack of success in shaping the outcomes of social struggles. Essays by Amy Kesselman and Marlene Fried consider the problem of redefining and sustaining nonviolent movements in a receptive era (1970s) and during largely conservative and nonactivist times (1980s and 1990s).

Abortion politics interacts with and stimulates still other enduringly difficult and contested issues, including the questions dealt with by Marie Bass and Marsha Saxton concerning feminist strategies for integrating new technologies, including reproductive technologies, into a largely unprepared and uninformed consumerist society. All of the contributors in the section devoted to physicians and abortion provision face hard questions about the tortured and politicized relationship between law and medicine in the United States.

The third theme that surfaces again and again in this volume is the conviction that pro-rights advocates must draw on the movement's experience since legalization—and before—to set agendas and strategies for the twenty-first century. William Saletan, Marcy Wilder, and Laura Kaplan, along with Dorothy Roberts and others, argue that the way abortion rights proponents now define these rights (in many cases differently from how they were defined earlier) has an impact on legal and political strategies and outcomes. It is worth noting here that my own use of the term *abortion rights,* instead of the more commonly used term *choice,* reflects a growing recognition among advocates that "choice" is the ultimate marketplace concept. When we construct the abortion arena on the marketplace model, we justify the fact that millions of women in the United States cannot afford to purchase adequate or necessary reproductive health services. When we talk about *rights*— about reproductive rights, including abortion rights of all women—then we are constrained to reevaluate the kinds of efforts, in which venues we must pursue these rights, as Kathryn Kolbert and Andrea Miller put it, in order to secure a "new positive rights articulation of Roe" as well as to protect the abortion rights women currently have and win back the ones already lost.

Finally, a theme or undercurrent that runs through all the essays in *Abortion Wars* is that the rights advocates included here, and the organizations, constituencies, and causes they represent, have not lost their taste for the struggle. Despite the work and the pain involved in facing and facing down the violent opposition, despite the tragedies that has entailed, despite the harsh tasks of responding to hostile legislators while devising innovative strategies, despite the arduous efforts associated with applying the lessons of history to the process of redefining the issues that constitute the heart of the abortion rights struggle today, the voices in this volume are surprisingly energetic. At the end of the twentieth century, abortion rights—reproductive rights—remain a deeply worthy cause because achieving these rights will bolster the claim of all women to lives imbued with justice, safety, and dignity.

PART ONE

COERCION, RESISTANCE, AND LIBERATION BEFORE *ROE V. WADE*

I n recent years historians and activists have begun to write the history of abortion politics in the era before 1973. They have been motivated to reclaim this history in part to remind women and men in the United States how dangerous it was to be a fertile female in this country when the judiciary, the legislatures, and social agencies—but not vulnerable pregnant women—had the legal right to determine who was a mother and when. Historians of this era are also determined to analyze the factors that made legalization possible in 1973, including, prominently, a massive, organized pro-rights feminist movement. The writers of the three historical essays in this section believe that understanding the waning decades of criminal abortion is important for understanding contemporary abortion politics and the opportunities before us today.

Rickie Solinger shows how, even in the face of criminalized abortion and intensified coercion after World War II, millions of women were determined to control their own fertility by obtaining abortions. In addition, she argues that medical, municipal, and federal politics in the 1950s and 1960s make it clear, in a way often obscured today, that women's bodies and their fertility did then and continue to stimulate political opportunities for politicians and others committed to white supremacy and male supremacy.

Laura Kaplan demonstrates how the coercion and danger that accompanied illegal abortion, in an era when an emergent feminist movement was powerful, created the opportunity for feminist resistance in the form of Jane, a group of underground lay abortion providers in Chicago. Kaplan also shows how, in the context of a vibrant feminist movement, it is possible to develop a new feminist paradigm for medical care, a lesson that both she and Elizabeth Karlin (Part Four) believe needs relearning today.

Amy Kesselman confronts the myth of the context-free Supreme Court decision that legalized abortion. She demolishes the myth by providing dramatic evidence that feminist activists in Connecticut and elsewhere generated powerful analyses, mass movements, and effective strategies that succeeded in decriminalizing abortion even before *Roe v. Wade.*

1

Rickie Solinger

PREGNANCY AND POWER
BEFORE *ROE V. WADE*, 1950–1970

In the late 1980s, when the legal right to abortion seemed desperately
threatened, I decided to find out as much as I could about the experiences of single mothers and unwillingly pregnant girls and women in
the decades immediately preceding *Roe v. Wade*. I imagined that in un-
covering these experiences, I would find patterns reflecting literally millions of instances of danger, coercion, humiliation, and basic degradation of females in the United States. And indeed I did. I believed then
that writing about these patterns—laying out the proof of degradation—would help dissipate legislative and judicial efforts to reenslave
girls and women to their fertility.

Today, with the threat to reproductive freedom still a virulent strain
in our political culture, I am painfully aware of the romanticism of my
original intention, based as it was on the simple conviction that history
is transformative. Having had such high hopes for the evidence I found
in archives and trial transcripts, I neglected to consider how difficult
it is to communicate history, perhaps especially this recent, decidedly
unglamorous history of the politics of female fertility.

But even now that my perspective on the power of history is more
clear-sighted, in the sense that I know more about how hard it is to
bring history into the political and policy arenas, I remain just as certain
that knowledge of the history of reproductive politics in the United
States is crucial, for a number of reasons. One of the most important
reasons is that history does teach that most transformative lesson:

progressive social change is possible and occurs most surely and swiftly in eras of progressive activism. And, when we know the history of reproductive politics, we can better understand the roots of current conflicts in this arena. Then we who believe in women's reproductive rights can use this understanding to define our goals and shape our strategies.

In this essay I consider how reproductive politics in the immediate pre–*Roe v. Wade* decades illuminates the roots—and helps explain the persistence of—some of the more hideous impulses that bedevil reproductive politics today. Specifically, I look at why abortion practitioners were targeted and demonized in the postwar decades, an era when, of course, most of them operated outside of the law. Then I consider one of the many ways that women were coerced in the 1950s and 1960s to cede control over their bodies to "experts," in this case to doctors sitting on hospital abortion boards. And finally, I review how reproductive politics after World War II divided women against each other by race.

In addition to exposing the roots of contemporary conflicts, these historical aspects of the politics of female fertility, taken together, reveal the variety and complexity of the forces arrayed against women—including municipal, medical, and federal politics and policies. The material also points to the depth and force of women's determination to control their own fertility, even in the face of so many obstacles. It is important to note that this history most decidedly does not validate the central claim of Randall Terry and other leaders of the opposition to reproductive rights: that, before legalization, women did not seek and did not obtain abortions. The truth is that even when blocked by laws, institutions, and authorities, up to one million women a year sought and obtained abortions in the illegal era—though not without a struggle.

Women and the state have been engaged in a series of overlapping and ongoing struggles to determine who will control women's bodies and their fertility. In this regard three great struggles waged individually and collectively by women in the twentieth century have been for legalization of contraception, for legalization of abortion, and—most intractably— for nonracist and non-class-based policies supporting access to reproductive self-determination.[1] The history of these struggles reveals that women's bodies and their fertility have repeatedly provided rich opportunities for U.S. politicians and policy makers determined to preserve both male and white supremacy.

The contemporary history of reproductive politics in the United States begins immediately after World War II, after a period when women had joined the paid workforce in unprecedented numbers, and at a point when the issue of race was emerging as a central concern of the polity and its citizens. In the late 1940s and into the 1950s, cultural arbiters and authorities—psychiatrists, lawyers and judges, educators and employers, journalists and politicians, advertisers, the clergy, fashion designers, social service providers, and others—used the media as never before to address what had become a set of burning questions: Who is the American woman? What is a woman? Who is a mother?[2] Most prominently published responses to these questions claimed not just that motherhood was a defining attribute of womanhood, but that for motherhood to be an authentic expression of femininity (a postwar synonym for womanhood), it must occur within marriage. A woman, they claimed, must passively receive and submit to the "gifts" of marriage, especially pregnancy. Sensationalized public censure of females who got pregnant without being married or were otherwise unwillingly pregnant, combined with greatly increased prosecutions of illegal abortion practitioners, gave bite to prevailing definitions of womanhood and warned all women about the wages of transgression.[3] It was in this context that various power centers mobilized to clamp down on women seeking to control their fertility and on those willing to help them do so.

Today, abortion practitioners in the United States are targeted and reviled by the radical right and isolated by their communities. Many wear bulletproof vests in public, and almost all have unlisted home telephone numbers. The need for such precautions is relatively recent. During the illegal era (from the mid–nineteenth century until 1973), abortion practitioners operated with varying degrees of secrecy, but they did not fear for their lives. In fact, a number of abortionists in the illegal era provided their services for years—twenty, thirty, forty years, and more—completely unimpeded by the law. In many communities, the local abortion practitioner's name and address were well known, not only to women who might require the service but also to police and politicians, who generally regarded the presence of a good abortionist as a public health asset. For decades after the American Medical Association worked with state legislatures in the nineteenth century to outlaw abortion, abortion prosecutions were rare relative to the number of abortions performed. In most communities an unwritten agreement prevailed between law enforcement and practitioners: no death, no prosecution.[4]

But after World War II the old agreement was rather suddenly canceled, and practitioners—chiefly the female ones (presumed by law enforcement to be unskilled, untrained, and unprotected in comparison to their male counterparts, and therefore more likely to be convicted)—were arrested, convicted, and sent to jail in unprecedented numbers, even when there was no evidence of a botched abortion. Many of these practitioners were highly skilled and experienced, having performed twenty some abortions a day, year after year.

If we look at when and how these arrests were carried out and at how abortion trials were conducted, we can get a sense of what was at issue and begin to understand the agendas of the district attorneys, judges, and politicians who managed the postwar crackdowns. In many cities what stands out is that everything about these prosecutions—the sensationalized media coverage of police raids, arrests, and trials—transformed abortion from an everyday, if semi-secret, occurrence into a crime. Often scandal-tainted mayors and police forces were looking for opportunities to demonstrate that municipal governance and law enforcement were not ineffectual or corrupt, as charged. Many police chiefs, in concert with a district attorney's office, an eager crime-busting reporter, or a clutch of city fathers concerned with civil probity, scouted for fodder for municipal exposés. Theirs was a peculiarly postwar–cold war project: to root out the "hidden" enemy within and "cleanse" the city in the process. In Los Angeles, San Francisco, Cincinnati, St. Louis, Trenton, Portland, Oregon, and other cities, even though there was no expressed anti-abortion agenda (nobody raised the specter or even the subject of unborn babies), women abortionists and their clients became attractive targets. These women represented a political opportunity because they were vulnerable, with almost no recourse to credible defense. Moreover, given the associations of sex and secrecy, the arrests were exciting; the lurid headlines sold newspapers and made law enforcement appear well deployed.[5]

What one finds in the abortion courtroom is that in the postwar decades such trials became first-rate occasions for men—doctors, lawyers, judges, police, jury members—to gather in a public place and affirm their right to govern women's bodies, to define women's rights, and to enforce women's vulnerability. In addition, these trials were titillating dramas that pitted one woman against another—the alleged abortionist (cast most often as a perverse and mercenary harridan) against her putative client (the slut). The whole event was drenched in sex. Wherever it occurred, the trial emerged day by day as a species of pornography, a cryptoporn show in which, in the name of the law and public morality, men invoked women's naked bodies, their sexuality, and their vulnerability in a style that was both contemptuous and erotic.[6]

In the largest sense, the abortion trials became arenas to address the culturally crucial question: Who is not a "real" woman? By defining female abortionists and their clients as perverse and unwomanly, the qualities of real womanhood were reaffirmed. The lawyers, doctors, and judges in command of these trials met no resistance as they defined the female transgressors before them. The political context made it easy to interpret an act of "exposing deviance" as an act of concern for the safety of the community. The social context sanctioned efforts to reinforce rigid gender roles in the aftermath of the war. To promote their defensive ends, the men who ran the show almost always adopted an offensive mode: cryptoporn, titillating the crowd while at the same time provoking shame and repugnance.

The men in charge at the courthouse shared a dreadful sense that the gender roles and relations they had depended on were threatening to give way. That they conducted the proceedings so brutally indicates how strongly they felt this. Women were on trial; the script called for them to be degraded, humiliated, divided against each other, and exposed. The most private facts of their lives were publicly revealed and reviled: their bodies (even their wombs), their sexuality, the intimate sources of their personal dignity. At the same time, the script allowed for men—doctors, lawyers, judges, journalists, and myriad expert witnesses—to stand up, one by one, and reaffirm their prerogatives over women's bodies and lives.[7]

These scenarios were enacted against a backdrop of demands for the domestication of women after the Depression and war years, during which women had shouldered economic and social responsibilities outside their homes. Cultural arbiters of every sort ordered women to go back home, to be proper wives and mothers, to be content.[8] The incidence of abortion after the war provided distressing evidence that many women were resisting some parts—or all—of this prescription. The trials provided the opportunity to humiliate resisters, to reiterate the injunction, and to underscore an important source of cultural as well as legal authority.[9]

The politicians and the law enforcement officers who canceled the old arrangement that had tolerated abortion as long as nobody got hurt, together with the courthouse men in charge of naming women's guilt and setting their punishment, were fighting the prospect of a community in which women could decide when and whether to associate sex and marriage, sex and maternity, marriage and maternity. In the 1950s these men had the institutional power to mount their opposition by targeting individual women. And their leverage extended even farther: the newspaper headlines and the courtroom dramas carried powerful cultural messages to the general citizenry.

These spectacles announced the danger and the just desserts for any woman associated with abortion. They also announced that the law was predicated on a willingness to place women in danger and on a contempt for women's self-determination. Anyone could see that enforcing anti-abortion laws involved the degradation of women. Every woman, whether she ever had or ever would climb up on the abortionist's table, was endangered by the statutes that criminalized abortion.

The prosecutions (and our memories of them) also carried the message that abortion practitioners were vulnerable vermin—an attitude that lives on in the anti-abortionists' hit list, as well as in the pro-choice claim that the chief function of *Roe v. Wade* has been to protect women from the back-alley butchers of the past, despite the historical reality that most illegal abortions were performed by highly skilled and experienced practitioners, who compiled an astonishing record of successful procedures under extremely difficult conditions. In actuality, the power of *Roe v. Wade* has been, since 1973, to diminish the danger and the degradation of women mandated by the anti-abortion statutes of the criminal era.

At the same time that police and politicians were busy burnishing their reputations by cracking down on illegal abortionists, medical doctors were experimenting with opportunistic and oppressive supervisory structures of their own. In the late 1940s doctors designed these structures—hospital abortion boards—to govern the meaning and the course of the pregnancies of millions of women. The boards ensured that experts, not women themselves, had final control over the abortion decision.[10]

In the postwar era, after several generations of performing abortions themselves, looking the other way, or facilitating, through referrals, illegal abortions, a great many doctors adopted an aggressive position against abortion.[11] Before the war many women had found cooperative doctors, as evidenced by the vast number of approved medical indications for "therapeutic abortion" (a list that kept expanding through the 1930s).[12] Even a woman who did not have a medical problem had little

trouble finding one of the hundreds of illegal practitioners who practiced undisturbed, in the shadows of cities and towns across the country. One way or another, thousands and thousands of women each year
who wanted to end their pregnancies found a way.[13] But after the war
things changed. Many doctors said abortion was no longer necessary.

For one thing, the list of illnesses that doctors had defined as incompatible with pregnancy began to shrink year by year with the advent of
new therapies and technologies. By the early 1950s, influential physicians were standing up to make the claim that almost no medical con-
traindications to pregnancy remained.[14] Even a woman with breast cancer or cardiovascular disease, who could have gotten a routine hospital
abortion in the 1930s, was now told not to worry about having a baby.

The doctors' turnabout, however, did not stop the many women who
had grown accustomed to a certain degree of abortion availability from
coming to their offices, begging for abortions or referrals to abortionists. It was an awkward situation all around. Most doctors were simply
not willing to break the law, no matter what their private thoughts
might be about abortion. But they still had to find a way to deal with
the women in their offices seeking help.

Doctors dealt with these women by explaining to them and to each
other that pregnancy no longer represented an added burden or an increased strain on a woman, even on a woman with a preexisting illness.
In many cases, of course, this rationale had the effect of diminishing the
relevance of a pregnant woman's condition *and* her own assessment of
it. Doctors implied now that pregnancy was an event that transcended
a woman's body and had, in an odd way, ceased to be a medical issue.

In these postwar years, pregnancy became fundamentally a moral
issue. As new imaging technology allowed doctors to construct the fetus
as a "little person," they tended to describe pregnancy *first* as a process
of fulfillment and realization for the fetus, and to refer to the pregnant
woman's body in terms that suggested a safe reproductive container.
Now the pregnant woman, along with her physician, had the moral
duty to keep the container fit. As one obstetrician put it: "Woman is a
uterus surrounded by a supporting mechanism and a directing personality." Completely effaced, the woman-as-uterus simply housed the
child.[15]

As doctors adopted and promoted these ideas, the number and the
rate of therapeutic abortions performed in U.S. hospitals plummeted.[16]
But women did not necessarily accede to the new medical definition
of pregnancy. They did not stop seeking abortions. Underground

abortionists knew that. And so did hospital-affiliated obstetricians and gynecologists, whose dilemma was graver than ever.[17] In some ways the situation was paradoxical. On the one hand, many people believed that doctors were scientific and humanitarian heroes for subduing the dangers of pregnancy and for developing methods to conquer diseases that threatened pregnancy and the pregnant female. On the other hand, state laws still required that a pregnant woman's life had to be endangered for her to get an abortion. Medical advances had seemingly wiped out any legal grounds for demanding abortion—but they had not changed women's determination to get abortions, the law and their doctors' proscriptions notwithstanding.

There is no question that doctors were feeling the squeeze from all sides and from within their own ranks as well. Any two doctors might disagree about which woman should be given permission for an abortion, under which conditions.[18] Nevertheless, doctors still had a legal responsibility to make the decision. And they were still interested in holding on to their medical authority to do so. The result was that many physicians struggled to find new grounds for making medical decisions about abortions. To a significant extent, psychiatrists helped out in the crisis, providing myriad esoteric ways of selecting who should and who should not be permitted an abortion. It must be added that most of these ways were based on providing a clinical answer to the question, "Is this woman psychologically fit to be a mother?" Answers in the negative—those that gave women permission to abort—defined the petitioner as unfit, unwomanly, to some degree depraved. The means and the ends here were both degrading to women seeking to control their fertility.[19]

Beyond this help from psychiatrists, though, physicians felt a need to create institutional structures to strengthen their position as abortion decision makers. In the late 1940s and early 1950s, they began to assemble hospital-based abortion committees.[20] From these official groups, professional, expert diagnoses and decisions regarding individual women could be issued in one voice. The abortion committees gave doctors legal protection and ensured that the "right" ratio of births to abortions was maintained in the hospital. The ratio varied from hospital to hospital, but doctors everywhere believed that a high ratio of births to abortions would protect the reputation of their hospital.[21]

By associating abortion decisions with the scientific objectivity of the group of doctors, and with the probity of the profession, all committee members could disassociate themselves personally from widespread

concerns that an unreasonable number of abortions—legal and illegal—
were being performed. Through the committee, doctors could diminish
their individual vulnerability and perhaps their crises of conscience.
And they could promote the aura of medical solidarity and legal compli-
ance. For all these reasons, many doctors were satisfied that hospital
abortion committees were a good solution.

As might be expected, women seeking abortions were not so thrilled
with them. Imagine the physically exhausted pregnant woman, already
the mother of three little ones and determined to have no more children,
being told by her doctor that abortion was unnecessary and immoral.
Imagine that the woman was determined enough to persist and to make
an application to the abortion committee (a humiliating and coercive
innovation, from her point of view, which no one had even heard of the
previous year). What if she were turned down?

Today we can look back at how the committees functioned and understand the pain and humiliation with which women remember these
ordeals. At the time Dr. Alan Guttmacher, a great champion of these
committees, described how his committee worked at Mt. Sinai Hospital
in New York:

> The director of the obstetrical and gynecological service is chairman of the
> permanent abortion committee. The other members are the chief, or a senior
> attending, from the departments of medicine, surgery, neuropsychiatry, and
> pediatrics. The board has a scheduled weekly meeting-hour, and convenes
> routinely whenever a case is pending. No case is considered unless the staff
> ob-gyn desiring to carry out the procedure presents affirmative letters from
> two consultants in the medical field involved. Five copies of each letter must
> be filed at least forty-eight hours in advance of the meeting. The ob-gyn
> whose case it is, and one of the two consultants who made the recommenda-
> tion must make themselves available at the meeting for further information
> when desired. In addition, if the chairman feels that an expert from some
> other department would be helpful in arriving at a proper decision, this spe-
> cialist is requested to attend as a non-voting member. The case is then care-
> fully discussed and if any member of the five on the committee opposes
> therapeutic interruption, the procedure is disallowed.[22]

The fact is, many women whose unwanted pregnancies were vetted
by abortion boards in the 1950s and 1960s say that these experiences
were among the most awful of their lives. Many could not bring themselves to submit to such a process and went off on their own, in search
of an abortionist. Other women did apply to the board, were denied an
abortion, but emerged with their determination undiminished. These
women, too, often went into the so-called back alley.

It is a shocking fact that many women who were "successful" with the committee found out, to their horror, that they could have the abortion only if they agreed to be sterilized at the same time. One doctor explained, "A serious effort is made to control the need for dealing with the same problem in the same patient twice." A doctor who objected to this practice chose a pointed analogy to explain why: "For some while now, I have called attention to this irrational policy of insisting that a patient be sterilized at the time of the therapeutic abortion as a guarantee that the patient will not return again pregnant seeking another therapeutic abortion. Such an argument possesses hardly less logic to recommend it than one which advocates amputation of the penis along with routine leutic therapy because, unless this is done, the patient may return with another chancre sore." Another doctor, equally angry at his colleagues for their hostility to women seeking abortions, declared, "The fairly common practice of insisting on sterilization if an abortion is permitted may have arisen from dealing with epileptics or feeble-minded women. It carries on as a punishment or a threat—as if the physician is saying: 'All right, if you do not want this baby, you are not capable of having any.' "[23]

Studies conducted in the early 1950s showed that, indeed, sterilization had become a fairly common practice. Over 53 percent of teaching hospitals made simultaneous sterilization a condition of approval for abortion, and in all U.S. hospitals, the rate was 40 percent.[24] One doctor, unhappy that unwillingly pregnant women were being forced to accept sterilization, observed that the practice was driving women to illegal abortionists because dealing with law-abiding physicians was likely to entail the permanent loss of their fertility. He added, "I would like to point out because the package [therapeutic abortion/sterilization] is so frequent, I therefore consider them fortunate to have been illegally rather than therapeutically aborted and thus spared sterilization."[25]

This doctor had a good point, although it was a point rarely made at the time. Many of his colleagues knew it was true but proceeded, week after week, to gather in their abortion tribunals and warn each other that, as one put it, "The physician must have a high index of suspicion for the patient who tries to pull a fast one." Another doctor spoke for many committee members when he raised the specter of the "clever, scheming women, simply trying to hoodwink the psychiatrist and obstetrician" when they appealed for permission to abort.[26]

Despite what they could plainly see in their own offices and at the weekly committee meetings about the determination of ordinary women to make their own decisions, doctors bolstered their personal righteousness about intervention by referring to the hefty and growing body of literature affirming that women's role on earth was to have children and that a woman's healthy sex life was predicated on her desire to have children. Leading postwar experts in the psychology of women argued that women who insisted on separating sex and procreation, for example, by deciding to abort, were consigned to the hell of "sexual limbo." A Portland, Oregon, doctor expressed his pleasure when an illegal abortionist in town was arrested by explaining that he believed in stamping out abortion because the operation caused guilt complexes, frigidity, and divorce. Stamp out abortion, he said, and these neurotic symptoms would disappear naturally.[27] Many doctors told each other about women like "Laura," whose case exemplified the problem. After her abortion, Laura "lost her sexual desire and moved to a separate bedroom. So seriously was her marriage affected that Laura was sent to a psychiatrist for treatment. She was on the brink of divorce. And all this was caused by interrupting the most vital biologically sacred function of womanhood—conception." [28] In line with this 1950s orthodoxy, the committee doctors forced a woman who did not want to carry any given pregnancy to term to declare herself insane. That was what the structure demanded.

Doctors also justified their committee work by referring to the force of women's will to have children. They basically accepted the adage that nobody gets pregnant who doesn't want to be. In this way, any and every pregnancy became a choice. It may well have been an unconscious choice (a favorite Freudian explanation in the 1950s), but it was a choice nonetheless, despite what the woman herself might think she wanted. (A doctor said at the time, "If we have learned anything in psychiatry, we have learned to respect the unconscious far more than the conscious and we have learned not to take abortion requests at face value.") [29] In a cruel twist on the meaning of choice today, a woman who said she wanted an abortion could be understood to be proposing to violate her own choice to be pregnant.

As they made their way through this nightmarish maze of new psychological and cultural ideas about pregnancy and abortion, many pregnant women declined the opportunity to become suppliants before the abortion panels.[30] They did not accept the new definition of pregnancy that granted primacy to the fetus, nor did they give up the idea that a particular pregnancy could be dangerous to them, or damaging. So while abortion boards were sitting in hospitals around the country, hundreds of thousands of pregnant women each year did the only thing they could. They sought out abortionists elsewhere.

The physicians who developed hospital abortion committees were not, it should be noted, primarily concerned with the issue of when life begins. They were, however, very concerned with what they took to be their cultural mandate in postwar America to protect and preserve the links between sexuality, femininity, marriage, and maternity. They were also deeply concerned about their professional dignity and about devising strategies to protect and preserve the power, the prerogatives, and the legal standing of the medical profession.

An important strategy of many doctors in this era was to draw on the vulnerability of pregnant women to construct a definition of pregnancy that effaced the personhood of the individual pregnant woman. This definition created a safe place for the fetus and also for the doctor forced by law to adjudicate the extremely personal decisions of women, many of whom were resisting effacement. The subordination of the pregnant woman to the fetus revitalized medical participation in the abortion decision because the doctor was now required to make sure that the woman stayed moral, that is, served her fetus correctly. These postwar ideas are powerful demonstrations of the prevailing relationship then between scientific advances and ideological positions on women, pregnancy, and fetuses.[31]

While mayors and police chiefs and obstetricians and psychiatrists were using the abortion issue to resolve issues of municipal and medical politics in cities and towns across the country, the role of reproductive politics on the national political scene in the postwar years is in many ways even more terrifying. What we can learn from examining the point at which female fertility emerged as a national political preoccupation is that, from the start, reproductive politics provided legislators and the judiciary with rich opportunities to support agendas hostile to female autonomy and racial equality.

The postwar experiences of white and black females who were unmarried and pregnant make it clear, first of all, that when lawmakers take the right to regulate and control female fertility—to answer the question "Who is a mother?"—all women are degraded. And beyond that, when lawmakers take this right, they simultaneously and quite "naturally" take the additional right to treat different groups of women differently, in this case depending on the race of the woman and her "illegitimate" child.

I have written extensively in *Wake Up Little Susie: Single Pregnancy and Race before Roe v. Wade* about the different treatments and experiences of white and black unwed mothers in this country at midcentury. Briefly, after World War II tens of thousands of white girls and women who became pregnant outside of marriage each year were unable to determine either the course of their pregnancies or the conditions of their maternity. They were, in astonishing numbers, deeply shamed by their families, removed from school, diagnosed as psychologically disturbed, and defined as not-mothers without husbands.[32] They were pressed, even coerced, into giving up their "valuable" white babies for adoption to infertile, white, married couples prescreened and judged by social workers to be eager and proper parents.[33]

In contrast, black girls and women who were unmarried and pregnant kept their "illegitimate" children, often with the help of their families and community-based institutions.[34] But politicians in every region of the country began to blame unwed black mothers for producing "excessive" numbers of "unwanted" black babies. Politicians and journalists said these babies created burdens for white taxpayers. Worse, many politicians, policy makers, and ordinary citizens began claiming at midcentury that the wombs of poor black women, excessively and wantonly fertile, were the source of all problems in the black community (including poverty, juvenile delinquency, and urban disorders) and, by extension, in America as a whole.[35]

Consequently, beginning in the late 1940s and continuing with increasing determination throughout the postwar decades, politicians threatened unwed mothers of color with incarceration, sterilization, and removal from welfare rolls. Social scientists and social commentators of diverse political persuasions began—at a time when the whole country was a battleground in the war of integrationists versus segregationists—to use the out-of-wedlock pregnancies of some women of color to bolster policies of white supremacy. Many used these "illegitimate" pregnancies to justify stands against school integration and for restrictive public housing policies. Numerous politicians associated welfare with oversexed black women who had too many children, thus giving focus to white opposition to government aid to poor mothers and their children, especially African Americans.[36]

This review of some of the ways that players on the terrains of municipal, medical, and national politics opportunistically targeted, constrained, and degraded millions of American women on the basis of
their gender and reproductive capacity in our recent past illuminates
how deeply vulnerable fertile women may be in an era lacking a collective, vibrant, feminist political culture. To the degree that such a political culture is weakened or unrealized in the contemporary United
States, many politicians and others are seizing the same opportunities
today as they did in the 1950s.

We can find additional roots (and lessons) in this history. To begin
with, it seems to me that the poisonous attacks and deathly threats
against abortion providers today depend heavily on a continuing cultural hostility to women who take the right to separate sex and maternity. The attacks also depend, just as heavily, on a misreading of the
past, a misreading that says that cravenly greedy back-alley butchers
were the chief source of danger to helpless women in the criminal era.
Given the salacious and sensational prosecutions of illegal abortionists
in the postwar decades, it is easy to understand why so many people on
all sides of the abortion issue find it reasonable to marginalize or target
practitioners. They forget that it was *the law*, not illegal abortionists,
that created, even mandated, danger for all women before *Roe v. Wade*.

When we also consider the history and the projects of hospital abortion boards in the 1950s, we can clearly recognize the dangers fertile
women faced when male authorities (who often ignored these women's
perspective) had the right to control pregnancy-related decisions. The
history of hospital abortion boards strikes a particularly chilling note
at the end of the twentieth century when, for the first time since legalization, congressional Republicans, free from substantial opposition by the
medical establishment, are determined to legislate medical matters and
to start outlawing abortions by type, thus once again forcing women
(any woman, all women) into roles of supplication and obedience.

Perhaps most resonant today is the history of the ways that politicians have used race-based reproductive politics to shore up and advance a politics of male supremacy and white supremacy. It is sad, frustrating, and frightening that these politics are still dividing women
against each other.

The lessons of midcentury reproductive politics are not, however, all
cautionary and grim. For example, it is instructive to know that in the
late 1950s, among broadly middle-class white girls and women who
got pregnant while unmarried, over 95 percent gave their babies up for

adoption. Today the rate for all such girls and women is 3 percent. This is a startling change and suggests that with *Roe v. Wade,* women won more than the right to decide whether to stay pregnant. They also won the overlapping but distinct right to decide whether to become a mother. With the dramatic decline of coerced adoptions and the advent of legal abortion, many women in the United States have rights and choices that were virtually unimaginable in the recent past and certainly unobtainable. Social change is possible and, in the case of reproductive politics, was realized largely during the resurgence of the feminist movement from 1965 to 1980.

At the end of the twentieth century, racism, misogyny, and prejudice against poor people are factors that deeply stain our national culture and consequently stain the politics of female fertility. Against this culture, women have been and are determined, whenever and however they can, to control their own bodies and their lives, and to answer for themselves the questions: What is a woman? And who is a mother? In the future American women will continue to exercise the same determination. The task before us is to revitalize a vast feminist movement so that women's determination can be exercised in a climate that honors the relationship between reproductive autonomy and citizenship rights for each and every female.

NOTES

1. Some relatively recent—and excellent—treatments of these twentieth-century struggles include Carole Joffe, *Doctors of Conscience: The Struggle to Provide Abortion before and after Roe v. Wade* (Boston: Beacon Press, 1995); Leslie Reagan, *When Abortion Was a Crime: Women, Medicine, and Law in the United States, 1867–1973* (Berkeley: University of California Press, 1997); Laura Kaplan, *The Story of Jane: The Legendary Underground Feminist Abortion Service* (New York: Pantheon, 1995); Carole R. McCann, *Birth Control Politics in the United States, 1916–1945* (Ithaca, N.Y.: Cornell University Press, 1994); Ellen Chesler, *Woman of Valor: Margaret Sanger and the Birth Control Movement in America* (New York: Simon and Schuster, 1992); David J. Garrow, *Liberty and Sexuality: The Right to Privacy and the Making of Roe v. Wade* (New York: Macmillan, 1994); *From Abortion to Reproductive Freedom: Transforming a Movement,* ed. Marlene Gerber Fried (Boston: South End Press, 1990); *The Politics of Pregnancy: Adolescent Pregnancy and Public Policy,* ed. Annette Lawson and Deborah Rhode (New Haven: Yale University Press, 1993); *Conceiving the New World Order,* ed. Faye Ginsburg and Rayna Rapp (Berkeley: University of California Press, 1995). Also see Rickie Solinger,

Wake Up Little Susie: Single Pregnancy and Race before Roe v. Wade (New York: Routledge, 1992); and *The Abortionist: A Woman Against the Law* (New York: Free Press, 1994).

2. See Rickie Solinger, "The Smutty Side of LIFE: Picturing 'Babes' as Icons of Gender Difference in the 1950s," in *Looking at LIFE: Rethinking America's Favorite Picture Magazine,* ed. Erika Doss (Washington, D.C.: Smithsonian Press, forthcoming).

3. See Solinger, *Wake Up Little Susie* and *Abortionist.*

4. Solinger, *Abortionist,* 16.

5. Ibid., ch. 6 and 7.

6. Ibid., ch. 8.

7. See, for example, *State of California v. Geraldine Rhoades* (1948), Superior Court, Sacramento County, transcript in California State Archives, Sacramento, and *State of Oregon v. Ruth Barnett* (1966), no. 15959, transcript in Oregon State Archives, Salem.

8. See, for example, Robert Coughlan, "Changing Roles of Modern Marriage," *Life,* December 24, 1956, 109–18; and, of course, Ferdinand Lundberg and Marynia Farnham, *Modern Woman: The Lost Sex* (New York: Harper and Brothers, 1947).

9. This tendency can be found in almost all the abortion trials of the postwar era, including *State of North Carolina v. Geneva Phifer Hoover and Florence Stallworth* (1960), Superior Court, Mecklenburg County, transcript in North Carolina State Supreme Court Law Library, Raleigh.

10. Rickie Solinger, "A Complete Disaster: Abortion and the Politics of Hospital Abortion Committees, 1950–1970," *Feminist Studies* 19 (Summer 1993): 241–68.

11. See Dr. X as told to Lucy Freeman, *The Abortionist* (Garden City, N.Y.: Doubleday, 1962), and Joffe, *Doctors of Conscience.*

12. Quinten Scherman, "Therapeutic Abortion," *Obstetrics and Gynecology* 11(March 1958):323–35.

13. To get a sense of the flavor and frequency of abortion in the illegal era, see Rickie Solinger, "Extreme Danger: Women Abortionists and Their Clients before *Roe v. Wade,*" in *Not June Cleaver: Women and Gender in Postwar America, 1945–1960,* ed. Joanne Meyerowitz (Philadelphia: Temple University Press, 1994), 335–57.

14. Mary Calderone, ed., *Abortion in the United States* (New York: Harper and Brothers, 1958), 84.

15. Ibid., 118. Also see the images in "The Drama of Life before Birth," *Life,* April 30, 1965, 54 ff. For discussion of these images, see Solinger, "A Complete Disaster," 255–56.

16. Lawrence Lader, *Abortion* (Indianapolis: Bobbs-Merrill, 1966), 26–27.

17. Herbert L. Packer and Ralph J. Gampell, "Therapeutic Abortion: A Problem in Law and Medicine," *Stanford Law Review* 11 (May 1959): 417–55.

18. Keith P. Russell, "Changing Indications for Therapeutic Abortion: Twenty Years' Experience at Los Angeles Community Hospital," *Journal of the American Medical Association* 151 (January 10, 1953): 108; Myrna Loth and H. Close Hesseltine, "Therapeutic Abortion at the Chicago Lying-In Hospital,"

American Journal of Obstetrics and Gynecology 72 (August 1956): 304–11; Harry A. Pearse and Harold A. Ott, "Hospital Control of Sterilization and Therapeutic Abortion," *American Journal of Obstetrics and Gynecology* 60 (August 1950): 285.

19. Harold Rosen, "The Psychiatric Implications of Abortion: A Case Study in Hypocrisy," in *Abortion and the Law*, ed. David T. Smith (Cleveland: Press of Case Western Reserve University, 1967), 105.

20. Lewis E. Savel, "Adjudication of Therapeutic Abortion and Sterilization," in *Therapeutic Abortion and Sterilization*, ed. Edmund W. Overstreet (New York: Harper and Row, 1964); *Journal of the Indiana Medical Association* 40 (1947): 16; Pearse and Ott, "Hospital Control."

21. See, for example, John Johnson, "Termination of Pregnancy on Psychiatric Grounds," *Medical Gynecology and Sociology* 2 (1966): 2.

22. Dr. Alan Guttmacher described the Mt. Sinai committee in several places, including Calderone, *Abortion in the United States*, 92, 139; and Alan F. Guttmacher, "Therapeutic Abortion: The Doctor's Dilemma," *Journal of Mt. Sinai Hospital* 21 (1954): 111.

23. Johan W. Eliot, Robert E. Hall, J. Robert Willson, and Carolyn Hauser, "The Obstetrician's View," in *Abortion in a Changing World*, vol. 1, ed. Robert E. Hall (New York: Columbia University Press, 1970), 93; Kenneth R. Niswander, "Medical Abortion Practices in the United States," in *Abortion and the Law*, ed. Smith, 57. A Chicago study of 209 aborted patients showed that doctors at the Lying-In Hospital in that city determined, "In the majority of cases when therapeutic abortion is indicated, the patient's medical condition warrants the prevention of future gestations"; 69.4 percent of these women were sterilized. Loth and Hesseltine, "Therapeutic Abortion," 306; see also Pearse and Ott, "Hospital Control."

24. Eliot et al., "The Obstetrician's View," and Niswander, "Medical Abortion Practice."

25. Calderone, *Abortion in the United States*, 131.

26. Nicholson J. Eastman, "Obstetric Foreword," in *Therapeutic Abortion*, ed. Harold Rosen (New York: Julian Press, 1954), xx.

27. *Oregon Journal*, July 11, 1951.

28. Hans Lehfeldt, "Willful Exposure to Unwanted Pregnancy," *American Journal of Obstetrics and Gynecology* 78 (1959): 665; also see the statement of Dr. Iago Goldston defining the desire for abortion in a "so-called adult woman" as an indication of "a sick person and a sick situation . . . which could be relieved, or ameliorated [by the abortion] like cutting off a gangrenous foot" (Calderone, *Abortion in the United States*, 118–19).

29. Sidney Bolter, "The Psychiatrist's Role in Therapeutic Abortion: The Unwitting Accomplice," *American Journal of Psychiatry* 119 (September 1962): 315.

30. For estimates regarding the decline in the abortion rate after the institution of hospital abortion boards, see, for example, Niswander, "Medical Abortion Practices in the United States." Niswander lists a number of studies that also found a substantial decline.

31. See Edwin M. Gold et al., "Therapeutic Abortions in New York City: A

Twenty Year Review," *American Journal of Public Health* 55 (July 1965): 969; J. A. Harrington, "Psychiatric Indications for the Termination of Pregnancy," *Practitioner* 185 (November 1960): 654–58; J. G. Moore and J. H. Randall, "Trends in Therapeutic Abortion: A Review of 137 Cases," *American Journal of Obstetrics and Gynecology* 63 (January 1952): 28–40; Roy J. Heffernan and William Lynch, "What Is the Status of Therapeutic Abortion in Modern Obstetrics?" *American Journal of Obstetrics and Gynecology* 66 (August 1953): 335.

32. See Solinger, *Wake Up Little Susie,* ch. 3.

33. Ibid., ch. 5.

34. Ibid., ch. 2.

35. Ibid., ch. 6.

36. Ibid., see ch. 2, 6, 7.

2

Laura Kaplan

BEYOND SAFE AND LEGAL

The Lessons of Jane

In Chicago on the evening of the Supreme Court's decision in *Roe v. Wade*, the members of Jane: The Abortion Counseling Service of Women's Liberation celebrated. Our overwhelming feeling that night was relief. For the past four years we had been running an underground abortion service that, by early 1973, was providing between seventy-five and one hundred low-cost abortions a week for the most vulnerable women—teenagers and those with no financial resources. By the time Jane folded in the spring of 1973, we estimated that we had performed more than eleven thousand abortions.

But our relief that January night was tinged with apprehension. From four years of practical experience we had learned that a good abortion requires more than medical competence. Every woman, we believed, deserved to be respected for making an active choice. In Jane that respect was evident in the way we treated women before, during, and after their abortions. We educated women about their bodies and abortion; we included each woman in her abortion: talking to her during the procedure, explaining everything we did in detail, and fully informing her of every contingency. We viewed each woman as a participant, a partner, instead of a passive recipient of a service. Our approach gave her a sense of control over her abortion and helped her shed society's judgments of guilt and self-blame. We saw abortion as a potential catalyst for personal growth, an opportunity for a woman to take stock of her life. With abortion, through the *Roe* decision, legalized under medical control, not women's control, we worried that women would receive only an adequate medical procedure, a limited service that, we knew, would not meet their complex needs.

In 1969, when Jane was organized, it was part of the burgeoning women's liberation movement, whose antecedents were in the civil rights, antiwar, and student movements. All these movements shared a belief that people had to have power over their own lives. Women in these movements, however, discovered that "power to the people" did not include power to women, and they began questioning their second-class status. These women organized the first autonomous women's liberation groups. Groups of women gathered to explore their common problems and define themselves as a class. Out of these discussions, projects designed to solve women's problems emerged. Providing access to safe abortions was one task that these women's liberation groups took on.

The handful of women who came together to form Jane wanted to do something concrete to help women. One of the founders of the Chicago women's liberation movement, who had been counseling and referring women for abortions ad hoc, organized the group and trained its members. The women in Jane started with a feasible plan: to find doctors who were performing abortions, screen them to determine which ones were competent, and prepare women for their abortions. Group members realized immediately that unless they could lower the price of abortions (the going rate in Chicago then was between $500 and $1,000), few women would be able to afford them. Jane recognized that control over the abortion doctors was essential to keep the desperate women who turned to them from being emotionally, sexually, or financially exploited, as they often were in those pre-*Roe* years.

As members of the women's liberation movement, we in Jane identified the basic problem for women as a lack of control. To liberate ourselves we had to have the power to act on our own decisions. The ability to decide when and if we wanted to have children was integral to our freedom and full participation in society. We had to take that control. We had to control our reproduction; we had to control abortion.

From the activist who trained the original members of Jane and from women who had had illegal abortions, we compiled a list of fewer than half a dozen abortion practitioners. All were men; all said they were doctors. For leverage, we promised increased referrals if the doctor was willing to make concessions. That narrowed our options, since most of these doctors were not interested in negotiating. But one was willing to meet with us and form a working relationship. Eventually, a woman in Jane convinced him to let a few women in the group attend the abortions. With Jane women present, assisting the doctor, women felt less alone and were assured good treatment. After working successfully with this doctor for over a year, the group learned that he was not a physician. During a heated discussion after this revelation, one woman said, "If he can do abortions and he's not a doctor, then we can do them, too."

The news that our "doctor" was not a doctor was disturbing, even horrifying, to some of Jane's members, but the suggestion that women in the group could learn to do abortions was even more shocking. To accept that required a radical shift in consciousness. Up until then the approximately twenty-five members of Jane had adopted women's traditional and comfortable roles as counselors and assistants. It was one step, as members of the women's liberation movement, to assert women's need for independence; it was another actually to act independently. If Jane members did that, they would be totally responsible for whatever happened. Some women dropped out once they knew our doctor's true status; others left because the next step, for members to perform abortions, was more of a leap than they were willing to take. But for the few women who had been attending abortions and assisting, the technical aspects of the procedure had been demystified. Even though the idea had not previously occurred to them, now they realized: "This doesn't look so hard. We could learn to do it and charge a whole lot less."

Our abortionist taught a few women to perform abortions, and they taught other women. In less than two years, by mid-1971, the group shifted control from the illegal abortionists to the women in Jane. We lowered the price of an abortion to what a woman could afford (the maximum was $100). No one was turned down because she couldn't pay. Jane rapidly became a service for poor women, for women without resources, and for teenagers.

Because our work was based on a feminist political perspective, we attempted to use our service to raise women's consciousness, to turn an illegal abortion into a transformative experience, so that after their abortions women were in better shape, surer of themselves, than they had been before. Every contact with a woman subtly underscored our political message: You are a responsible decision-maker; you have a right to control your body; our job is to enable you to do that.

Over cups of tea in our living rooms in the evenings, we counseled women. During the counseling session we tried to alleviate women's fears by fully explaining the process, not only the technical part but where she would go, whom she could expect to see, what these people would say and do, what every step in the abortion would feel like. We answered her questions without judging, giving her a chance to talk about and resolve any lingering ambivalence. Our behavior was based on the respect we felt for the women's difficult choices. As one college student indicated after her counseling session: "These are people I can trust because they're being honest with me."

One of our most important functions as counselors was educational. We explained reproduction and contraception and handed out news-print copies of *The Birth Control Handbook* and *Our Bodies, Ourselves*. We included detailed aftercare instructions: what to do and expect during the recovery period, what complications might arise and how to deal with them, what symptoms warranted immediate medical attention. Being fully informed helped women feel in control. Every day we witnessed a simple truism: treat people as responsible and they will act responsibly. One woman noted, "I was treated like an adult who probably had some fears but was in control of my situation, and that sense helped me be in control."

Since we were breaking the law and could go to jail, we expected each woman to protect us as a condition of mutual responsibility: "Our safety is in your hands, just as yours is in ours." We hoped to build a sense of community among women involved in this essentially female process. We did not present ourselves as authorities to whom women had to turn over their power. Rather than having something done to them, they were the central actors: "We don't do this *to* you, but *with* you."

That sensibility was apparent during the abortions, which we performed in our apartments. To help the woman relax and include her in the process, one Jane member sat next to her, held her hand, and explained what was happening, connecting the medical procedure and the woman's sensations: "You may feel some cramping because we're dilating your cervix now. Do you feel that? Just try to breathe and relax." The person doing the abortion chatted with the woman throughout the procedure. The conversation might start with a casual question: "That's a beautiful pin you're wearing. What made you choose that one?" Relating to each woman as a full person, rather than as an object of medical care, was a way of underscoring that the abortion was part of her life, not separate from it. One woman says of her Jane abortion: "I did not feel alone. I was not treated like a patient, but like a human being going through a difficult experience."

We avoided systemic painkillers, which we felt complicated the medical situation. Women were awake, participating and interacting with the people performing the abortion, which furthered their sense of being in control. The pain women felt, which varied from woman to woman, was managed through personal attention. If a person was having a rough time, she was offered a chance to take a break and stretch her legs. How much pain a woman experienced was often a function of both her comfort level during the process and how comfortable she was with her decision. If a woman was ambivalent or was having an abortion at her husband's, boyfriend's, or parent's insistence, she often experienced the abortion as painful. Even when she had no doubts about getting an abortion, she might be violating deeply held beliefs, and that contradiction had to be acknowledged. This attention to the highly individual context surrounding each woman's decision reinforced the recognition that abortion is more than a medical procedure: it is a serious choice about her life.

Our intention was to provide an experience from which women could gain a stronger sense of themselves. We never knew if the women we served were actually affected in that way, but some of these women later spoke to me of a heightened self-awareness from their contact with us. One commented, "I felt that Jane was helping me to see my future and realize the seriousness of relationships, childbirth, and birth control. It isn't this momentary thing. It's about making this real solid decision: I choose to have an abortion because it's my body. I'm making this decision, nobody else is."

In the pre-*Roe* era, when abortions were illegal and access to birth control and health information was limited, women were stuck with bearing the responsibility for reproduction but having little power over it. Jane attempted to turn that position around by giving women control and expecting them to act responsibly. Our emphasis on educating women came from the belief that knowledge is power. As one Jane member commented, as much about herself as about the women she was counseling, "If you don't know things, you can't ask questions; you can't refuse. You're just taken advantage of or mistreated by professionals." Health education fostered independence; having information enabled women to assert themselves. One woman, pointing to a long-term effect of her Jane abortion, noted, "I'm more willing now to ask a doctor specific questions. I'm able to say to a doctor, 'I don't like the way you're treating me. I don't like what you're saying to me. I don't like that you're not saying anything to me.' "

I don't mean to suggest that we in Jane were superior people. Rather, because we were not medical professionals, we did not base our work on a medical model. Instead, we asked ourselves: How do we want to be treated? How can we design a service through which women can become empowered?

In contrast to Jane, the medical model is organized in a strict hierarchy with physicians at the top and patients at the bottom. A person, as patient, is the object of medical care, not the subject. Medical professionals are typically trained to deliberately distance themselves from patients. The patient is viewed solely through the lens of her illness: the broken bone, the disease to be fought. This model implies passivity on the part of the patient. We are supposed to trust doctors and comply with their orders, not because of a trusting relationship the physician has built, but because doctors are the authorities—only they have the expertise to make decisions about our health. If a physician has biases about race or class, toward particular treatments, or with regard to women in general, these biases are masked by his or her authority. The inequity in power is exacerbated by the vulnerability that people needing help naturally feel.

But people are more than their illnesses, and in any case abortion is not a treatment for a disease. Nor does it correct an injury, such as a broken bone. Rather, in asking for an abortion, the woman is making an active choice; she is not a passive patient. Every woman brings to her abortion a range of emotions: her fear of the procedure, her feelings about her relationships and her own life, her doubts—all in all, the same emotions felt by anyone who faces a crossroads. If these factors are not acknowledged she may leave a clinic depressed, angry, even doubting and punishing herself.

Several women who had abortions with Jane and then later had legal ones have compared their experiences. Overall they report that the Jane experience was less alienating than their later legal abortion. During one legal abortion, a woman was unnecessarily given a general anesthetic. She felt sick and depressed from the residual effects of the anesthetic, and those feelings triggered self-blame: How did I get into this mess again? What did I do wrong? Another woman described her legal abortion as more painful, even though it was performed by her own gynecologist at exactly the same point in pregnancy as her earlier Jane abortion. "The Jane experience," she said, "was one of a choice that I made and carried out and recognized the significance of, but don't regret or have bad feelings about. The second one—the whole thing was negative. The decision appears to have been wrong." She sums up: "If you make the choice to have an abortion, you need to have somebody say, 'All right, you've made the choice and this is your life and you're in control.' "

The medical setting—the body drapes, the perception of the patient as a series of body parts, the separation of the person from the procedure, the emotional distancing of professionals—heightened these women's feelings of isolation. Something was happening to them, to a part of them, but, somehow, they were not involved. "It was as though I wasn't even in the room," one young woman recalls, "or they thought of me as less than human and not worthy of being spoken to." Unfortunately, such feelings are easily internalized, and a woman may well feel that she is being punished, that she made the wrong choice, that she is at fault.

This is not to say that medical abortions are any worse than other forms of medical care. The problem, as I see it, is that they are provided in exactly the same manner as other medical care. Many of us dread going to the doctor because our previous contacts have left us feeling confused, humiliated, and helpless. Sometimes our complaints and perspectives were dismissed, our questions not only unanswered but unasked. It is not that health care providers are insensitive people but that the system, the professional training and the institution of medicine itself, tends to subvert their caring natures.

An abortion, because it is about more than the simple medical procedure, has the potential for serious negative emotional consequences. A woman who is torn by her abortion decision may transfer her negative impression of the medical experience to her decision and to abortion itself. Fortunately, there are many fine abortion providers whose services respect women and recognize the significance of abortion in women's lives. They have been able to temper their professional distancing and provide the kind of care women need at this critical time.

Those of us who are committed to reproductive freedom want to ensure that today's abortion services offer the best care. To do that we must reassert our feminist values and create a vision of what good care looks like. No one, least of all the women in Jane, would propose replicating our illegal service in the present. But I believe that we can find models for woman-centered health services in the past, in Jane and in the women's health movement of the 1970s.

Much has changed in the twenty-plus years since *Roe*. Although abortion is not illegal, it is available in less than 20 percent of the counties in this country. The ban on federal Medicaid funding and the restrictions imposed by many states, including parental consent laws, waiting periods, and mandatory counseling on fetal development, do not make abortion a realistic option for some women and girls. Many of these restrictions stem from the belief that women are not responsible decision-makers. They follow from *Roe*, which codified both the state's right to regulate abortion and the physician's responsibility for it. Within the medical profession itself, doctors who perform abortions are stigmatized. To compound these problems of access and attitude, abortion providers are being driven out by the high costs of protecting their clinics, their staffs, and themselves from violent attacks by abortion foes. The situation could hardly be worse for beleaguered clinics.

In society much has changed as well. In the 1960s and early 1970s broad social and political movements inspired large numbers of people to believe that they could change society. People joined together to create services that challenged institutional authority. A river of activism seemed to run through the country. A range of political projects and perspectives reached out to people through storefront offices. Women's liberation centers served as clearinghouses for activities pertaining to women.

It was in this climate that Jane and the women's health movement developed. The attempt to take back control of women's health through education and woman-run health centers forced changes in medical attitudes, just as the movement for home births forced hospitals to alter their birthing procedures. Today, every bookstore has a section devoted to self-help health books. Most doctors pay at least lip service to the idea that informing patients leads to better outcomes. But now the mass movements that fostered change have dissipated, and the challenge of the women's health movement, for women to control their own health care, has been co-opted, in part, by the growth of health "para" professions—physician's assistants and nurse practitioners.

Meanwhile, the medical profession is undergoing a major transformation. Cost containment measures, such as health maintenance organizations, provider networks, and the insurance industry's involvement in treatment decisions, act as a wedge between patient and practitioner. A physician is accountable to those who pay his or her fees, and that is rarely, any longer, the person needing care. These economic factors limit our input into health care decisions.

In an era when abortion providers are under physical, psychological, and financial attack, our natural response is to circle the wagons and defend these services. But I do not believe that we help our cause if we blindly repeat "Safe and Legal" and turn our backs on women's legitimate grievances. Instead, we need to restructure abortion services to reassert a feminist perspective and make women's needs central.

This will not be easy. Abortion clinics operate in a siege situation, and that mentality is not conducive to change. But that hostile climate could be used to create a community, a partnership, between clinic staff and the women who seek their services, much as we in Jane were able to use our illegality to build solidarity. An emphasis on health and reproductive education in abortion counseling would give women the tools they need to act responsibly. Training professional staff to respond to each woman as a full person not only benefits women but also makes the practitioners' work more rewarding and positively affects morale. Substituting responsive care for a reliance on drugs improves health outcomes and women's emotional recovery. Although we cannot expect provider associations to police their members, they could promote examples of quality care. In major cities, where a variety of abortion services exists, feminists could evaluate these services and make that information available to women.

These suggestions may seem simplistic, but I am well aware that what I am proposing requires a transformation of the doctor-patient relationship and runs counter to entrenched systems of authority. These dynamics are not exclusive to the medical profession but run throughout society. The expert, the professional, has societal sanction, enforced by laws and policies, to judge and determine. To pull at one thread threatens the whole garment. Because of this, it is imperative for activists, rather than merely reacting to the latest policy or legislative shift, to articulate, out of our politics, an alternative vision that moves beyond "Safe and Legal."

3

Amy Kesselman

WOMEN VERSUS CONNECTICUT

Conducting a Statewide Hearing
on Abortion

Writing in 1989, shortly after the Supreme Court heard oral arguments
in *Webster v. Reproductive Rights Services,* Nancy Stearns recalled her
involvement in the courtroom battles to legalize abortion before *Roe v.
Wade* and urged proponents of reproductive freedom to become politically active again. "We must never forget," she cautioned, "that *Roe v.
Wade* did not just 'happen.' That decision came only after the short but
intense political and legal efforts of women across the country."[1]

A sea change in attitudes toward abortion occurred during the five
years before *Roe v. Wade.* By 1971 over half the people questioned in
opinion polls favored legalizing abortion. Lawyers challenging abortion
statutes, who had previously emphasized the effect of unconstitutionally vague language on medical practitioners, began in the early 1970s
to argue on behalf of women's right to decide when to have a child.
Organizations that had been working to reform abortion laws changed
their goals, strategies, and often their names to reflect the new movement for repeal of all state abortion statutes, and after 1970 state courts
began ruling in favor of women's right to abortion.[2]

While many factors contributed to these rapid changes, the energy,
passion, and politics of women's liberation activists were crucial. By
transforming an abortion reform effort led by doctors and population
controllers into a movement that argued for abortion as an essential
ingredient of women's freedom, women's liberation activists brought

the devastating effects of the abortion statutes on women's lives into the public consciousness and legal discourse.[3] In addition to pressuring legislatures, participating in referenda, and organizing marches, demonstrations, and speak-outs throughout the country, women's liberation activists turned their attention to the courts. Teaming up with feminist lawyers and law students, they coupled litigation with grassroots organizing in a creative strategy that both stimulated public discussion of reproductive rights and brought women's experiences of the abortion laws to bear on what went on in the courtroom. A cluster of suits on their way to the Supreme Court when *Roe v. Wade* was decided had been brought by large groups of women who claimed that their constitutional rights were violated by their states' anti-abortion statutes. Recovering the stories of the campaigns that shaped these lawsuits enhances our understanding of how *Roe v. Wade* happened.

In 1969, when members of the New York City Women's Health Collective talked with Nancy Stearns of the Center for Constitutional Rights about ways to challenge New York's abortion law, Stearns remembered an article she had read in law school by Harriet Pilpel, legal counsel for Planned Parenthood, setting out constitutional arguments for legalizing abortion. Buoyed by the idealism that imbued the work of the Center for Constitutional Rights ("You may not know what you're doing, but you know you're right"), she agreed to work on a lawsuit against the New York abortion statute.[4] Drawing on the center's experience with the use of litigation as an organizing tool in the civil rights movement, Stearns helped the Women's Health Collective plan a campaign that would provide a focal point for abortion rights organizing while challenging the constitutionality of New York State's abortion law. Stearns put together a group of lawyers to work on the case, and the health collective began holding meetings around the city to recruit plaintiffs. They filed their complaint, collected depositions, wrote a brief, and made their motion for a three-judge court. Their case, *Abramowicz v. Lefkowitz* (whose plaintiff list includes many prominent New York radical feminists), was then consolidated with three other suits, but because the New York state legislature legalized abortion in March 1970, their case was never argued in court.[5]

The New York suit, however, became the model for lawsuits filed by groups of women in Connecticut, New Jersey, Rhode Island, Pennsylvania, and Massachusetts. The Connecticut case, *Abele v. Markle,* was particularly influential in framing the judicial opinions in *Roe v. Wade.* This essay examines the history of the organization that brought the

Connecticut suit, with a view toward assessing the impact of women's liberation politics on the abortion rights movement and on judicial opinions, both the immediate decisions handed down in their suit and the later decisions that drew upon it.

NEW HAVEN WOMEN'S LIBERATION
CONFRONTS THE ABORTION QUESTION

The origin of the New Haven abortion rights group illustrates the convergence of the two forms of resistance that endowed the women's liberation movement with its explosive power in the early 1970s. While women veterans of the movements of the 1960s were mining their experience for a political analysis of women's oppression, less political women were making decisions in their daily lives that pitted them against the mores of the culture and, in the case of abortion, the laws of society. A group of women who had been active in the American Independent Movement (AIM), a radical community organizing project in New Haven, began meeting in 1968 to engage in what New York feminists had recently dubbed "consciousness-raising." As they talked it became clear to them that controlling their reproductive lives was central to the liberation they were beginning to envision, but they didn't know what to do about it. In March of 1969 the New York radical-feminist group Redstockings held the first speak-out on abortion. Women, many of whom had never spoken above a whisper about their abortion experiences, testified in public to a large crowd of total strangers—rejecting "the pall of guilt which isolates women in crises." [6] News of the speak-out piqued the interest of the New Haven women's liberation activists, and they began to follow more closely the debates about the state abortion statutes occurring in the Connecticut legislature.

Enacted in 1860, the Connecticut anti-abortion statute was one of the strictest in the country—the woman herself was guilty of a felony for soliciting an abortion, permitting one to be performed on her, or attempting to perform one on herself. When a reform bill exempting women who had been raped was introduced in the Connecticut legislature in 1967, it received little support and never emerged from committee. In April 1969 the legislature considered a bill promoted by the Connecticut Medical Society that would "allow a doctor, after consultation with two other physicians, to perform an abortion" that he or she felt was medically indicated. [7]

When someone suggested that the women's liberation group go to the state capitol to lobby state representatives or testify at the hearing about the reform bill, the group's response was cool. Reforming the law to give decision making to the doctor was an uninspiring project, and several group members thought it would be "a complete waste of time to go up and talk to a bunch of male legislators."[8] A few women did go to the judiciary committee hearing, which was dominated by male experts on both sides of the issue. The women's liberation people did not get an opportunity to speak until the end of the day, and their testimony was not even recorded by the stenographer. "It was infuriating," recalls Ann Hill, one of the women who attended the hearing, "to have to sit through legislative hearings listening to doctors term abortion a 'medical decision,' while priests advocated the rights of the fetus and the liberal clergy represented the woman's rights to abortion. We were at the hearings—but we were invisible. We were not 'experts' or 'professionals.' We had no credentials, no degrees, and the lawmakers did not want to hear us."[9]

This expedition squelched any lingering thoughts among women's liberation activists about using legislative action to repeal Connecticut's abortion law. "The legislature," they concluded "was completely beholden . . . to the Catholic Church" and solidly against any reform in abortion laws, let alone their repeal. The reform bill died in the judiciary committee.[10]

Meanwhile, a woman in a suburb of New Haven began a search for an abortionist for her brother's fifteen-year-old girlfriend. Because she believed members of the women's liberation movement would know how to find one, she called the AIM office, whose phone was being used for the fledgling women's movement. The message reached Betsy Gilbertson, a member of the AIM women's group. Having no idea how to find an abortionist, she made many fruitless phone calls. Finally an Episcopal minister told her to send the young woman—alone—with $500 to "the fifth house on the left on Howard Avenue." "That flipped me out," Gilbertson recalls. "I communicated this information in positively tremulous tones. . . . I didn't have anything else to offer."[11]

Because Gilbertson had called so many people in the search for an abortionist, her name became associated with abortion in the minds of many. In the ensuing months, she received one or two phone calls a week from desperate pregnant women. Feeling uneasy about sending them to an unknown source on Howard Avenue, Gilbertson "suddenly felt like whatever I had thought about this before was not enough," and she called together a group of women to discuss abortion and related issues.[12]

The fifteen women who began meeting in February 1970 were all white, mostly in their mid-twenties, and college educated. Several were students at Yale Law School, and one was a graduate student in biology. They set up a "makeshift" referral system, took turns answering the ever-increasing calls from women seeking abortions, and began having "long, free-floating discussions about what having the capacity to make babies meant to us." After discovering that, highly educated though they were, they "didn't know diddly about their bodies," they began to educate themselves about female anatomy.[13] Because most of them were political activists, they looked for ways to involve other women and divided into two project groups. While one group offered courses on "women and their bodies," the other began to consider ways to challenge Connecticut's abortion law.

WOMEN'S LIBERATION
DECIDES TO USE THE SYSTEM

The abortion work group wanted a project that would both improve women's lives and provide a vehicle for talking to women about abortion and its connection to other aspects of women's oppression. Convinced that "courts were no less dominated by men and no more receptive to women than the legislature," the group approached the idea of a lawsuit with caution.[14] The activities of the New York Women's Health Collective—taking depositions at well-publicized open meetings; holding rallies, speak-outs, and meetings around the city; and stimulating discussions about abortion in a wide variety of organizations—made it clear to the New Haven women that a lawsuit could be a "wonderful organizing vehicle." "The objective," argued Betsy Gilbertson, "was not to change the law per se. The objective was to use the process of changing the law, which would be a good thing to do, to further the goals of the women's movement overall." [15]

It was particularly significant for the development of the case that the abortion work group found a lawyer who was sympathetic to this approach and committed to involving as many women as possible in the various aspects of the case.[16] Catherine ("Katie") Roraback, who had been practicing law in Connecticut since 1948, had litigated several civil liberties cases during the McCarthy era and was a member of the

National Lawyers Guild. She was the attorney for Planned Parenthood of Connecticut and was the principal lawyer for the Connecticut phase of the series of cases that culminated in *Griswold v. Connecticut.*

For years Roraback's anger about the indignities women suffered had simmered quietly. When she attended a meeting of the women's caucus of the National Lawyer's Guild in 1969, where women were talking about what it meant to be a woman in the legal profession, her long-buried anger surfaced: "I found that one of the most painful days of my life because . . . I had been practicing law for twenty years at that point and I realized how much I had acquired various habits— dissimulations, whatever you want to call it—in order to get by in what was a very nasty world. . . . It was as if you had very bad scabs on you from a burn or something, and you're just tearing the scabs off. To think of what you had made of yourself in the course of going along with things." [17]

The following year she became the lawyer for Ericka Huggins, one of eight New Haven Black Panther Party members charged with murder and conspiracy to commit murder. Roraback's anger about the sexism experienced by women lawyers was soon augmented by a new under- standing of what it meant to be a woman defendant. Huggins had a keen consciousness of women's invisibility in the court system (and in the Panther Party). Roraback recalls that when she first walked into the courtroom, Huggins commented on "what a male scene it was." Even though Roraback had discussed this issue in a women's caucus she be- longed to, the immediate experience was jarring: "I suddenly looked at that courtroom from the eyes of a woman defendant and I thought, my God, what do you do about this?" [18]

Although Roraback was very busy with the Panther defense when Gilbertson approached her in the fall of 1970, she was intrigued by the idea of a lawsuit that was in many ways a sequel to her earlier work on *Griswold.* She agreed to serve as counsel and to recruit other lawyers to work on the case.

IDEAS OF WOMEN VERSUS CONNECTICUT

As women's liberation activists, the members of the abortion work group brought to the campaign against Connecticut's abortion law sev- eral ideas that shaped their strategy and tactics. Two central tenets were that abortion was inextricably connected with other dimensions of an oppressive social system and that collective political activity on their own behalf would strengthen women's sense of their power to challenge this system. The lawsuit was to be a vehicle for stimulating discussion about abortion and its connection with other aspects of women's lives and bringing women together into political action.[19] Central to this process would be women talking about their lives, since it was women, they believed, who were the experts about the effects of abortion laws. Women speaking about their own experiences would reveal the political nature of private life.

Despite some opposition from members of the legal profession, who thought it violated legal ethics, the organizers set out to recruit as many plaintiffs as possible, using the recruitment process as an opportunity to stimulate discussion among women about reproductive freedom. This would not be a traditional class-action suit, with a few people representing a class, but a suit with many named plaintiffs, each representing herself and similarly situated women. The organizers felt that "the mere act of putting your name down and saying 'I want to be a plaintiff, I want to take this position,' was very important politically for the individual women who signed up as plaintiffs."[20]

The notion of the lawsuit as organizing tool reinforced the abortion work group's decision to reject the help of male experts. Unlike many of the cases being filed against state abortion laws, only women could be plaintiffs in the Connecticut suit.[21] The plaintiffs represented three groups of women who claimed to be injured by Connecticut's abortion law: women of childbearing age, women in a position to counsel other women about abortion, and women in the health care professions.

Even more controversial was the decision that only women could be lawyers and organizers. "The exclusion of men was necessary," the group felt, "to ensure free participation by all women and to build our own self-confidence as a group of people capable of winning our own struggles."[22] There was "a sense of unity and purpose," remembers Roraback, "that could never have been achieved if there had been both men and women involved."[23] Some of the doctors who had been involved in the birth control and abortion reform movements were shocked by their exclusion. "Where were you in the 1950s," one doctor complained to a member of the group, "when we needed women to support our efforts to open birth control clinics? We stood out front all alone and worked tirelessly for your benefit."[24] The members of the abortion work group stood fast on this issue. They did include some affidavits of male physicians as supporting evidence, but the actors in the suit were all women, a fact reflected in the name they chose for their organization: Women versus Connecticut.

In all the Women versus Connecticut literature in this early period, arguments for the legalization of abortion were embedded in a multifaceted analysis of women's oppression and a critique of capitalism. "We want control of our bodies," the plaintiff recruitment pamphlet declared. "We are tired of being pressured to have children or not to have children. It is our decision. But control over our bodies is meaningless without control over our lives. Women must not be forced into personal and economic dependence on men or on degrading jobs in order to assure adequate care for the children they bear. Our decisions to bear children cannot be freely made if we know that aid in child care is not forthcoming and that we will be solely responsible for the daily care of our children." The pamphlet argued against a society that put the needs of corporations before human needs, that exploited workers and polluted the environment. Its authors took pains to distinguish themselves from the population controllers: "We think the issue is not control of the world's population but control of the world's resources." [25]

Recognizing that making abortion legal would not guarantee that it was available and affordable for all women, Women versus Connecticut activists committed themselves to both goals. "We think that we must get rid of the law," Sasha Harmon told a reporter in October 1970, when members of Women versus Connecticut announced their plans to file the suit. "That's the necessary first step toward winning cheap and available legal abortions. Then we'll try to make sure that doctors and hospitals begin serving our needs, once the law doesn't stand in their way." [26]

By the time Women versus Connecticut was recruiting plaintiffs and preparing legal arguments, the legislatures of New York and Hawaii had legalized abortion, and federal courts in Wisconsin and Washington, D.C., had found anti-abortion laws unconstitutional. The Connecticut women felt that they had a good chance of winning their suit, and they believed that winning would strengthen the women's movement and give them a "voice to reckon with" as they mobilized women to work for "a health care system that was responsive to women." [27] They chose as their symbol the female silhouette that had decorated a popular women's liberation poster. To make the logo "proud and hopeful," they raised the woman's right hand in a gesture of defiance. [28]

RECRUITING PLAINTIFFS AND SPREADING THE WORD

After announcing the plans for a lawsuit, Women versus Connecticut approached women's organizations throughout the state, sending bright yellow pamphlets with carefully worded arguments and plaintiff coupons on the back and asking to make presentations about the lawsuit. Even though groups they contacted were often composed of women whose politics and lifestyles differed radically from those of the organizers, many groups invited speakers and most received them warmly. About thirty women served as speakers, many of them recruited at periodic orientation meetings. After the talk, speakers would distribute their pamphlets, urge people to fill out the plaintiff form on the back, and describe the varied ways one could be involved in the lawsuit: attending plaintiffs' meetings, court appearances, and other events; organizing forums in one's community; or volunteering to testify in court. "We'd always start out with a personal story," remembers Ann Hill:

> We thought that you went from the personal to the political, so everywhere we went, we told things that were hard to tell strangers, and they appreciated that. And they in turn told things that were hard to tell, so it was one major consciousness-raising thing that women were sharing secrets. . . . We broke down our feelings of isolation and said, "It's time that we did something about this—it's time that we stopped the suffering." Everybody had either had an abortion or had a friend who had had an abortion or went to school with somebody who suddenly wasn't in school anymore, and they'd heard they were in some home for pregnant teens and banished from society. . . . It was secret-sharing and experience-sharing.[29]

Women versus Connecticut activists were profoundly moved by the process of recruiting plaintiffs. While they had known intellectually about the devastating effects of the abortion law, talking to women around the state and reading the many letters that poured into their office at the law school made them understand "what it really meant to people with a lot less privilege than we had. Maybe at the beginning it seemed a little abstract, legal—something that wasn't right—a civil wrong that should be righted. I think the experience of talking to people—and the letters—educated us . . . about what a profound issue it was."[30]

Of the many "incredibly moving, terrible stories" she heard, Betsy Gilbertson remembers this one vividly:

> [One woman] became pregnant with twins when she was living in Boston alone; she was separated from her husband. They made love once in an

effort to make up. They didn't make up. She was living alone. She already had two children to support. She found herself pregnant the third time, knew she could not support a third child—they were barely eating as it was. She had an abortion in the public toilet in Harvard Square. The form of abortion was insertion of a foreign object, to induce labor. She ended up delivering at home in her toilet—twins, recognizable twins.[31]

The process of transforming personal secrets into resources for a political and legal campaign continued for the organizers as well as the women they recruited. A woman in the organizers' group talked for the first time in her life about having given her child up for adoption, after the group had looked for months for someone to testify about this in court. The shame and anguish surrounding what had been a common practice for young, unmarried white women who became pregnant in the 1950s and 1960s were so profound that most women never talked about that chapter of their lives.[32]

Although New Haven, where the group was based, had a sizable African-American and growing Puerto Rican population, the movement that Women versus Connecticut built, like the national abortion rights movement in the 1970s, was almost entirely white. While there were a few African-American plaintiffs, for a number of reasons the organizing group and most of the participants were white. The separatist direction that black organizations were moving in the late 1960s and early 1970s generated a conviction among many white radicals that white people were their logical constituency. Furthermore, the idea of connecting with women of color about reproductive rights raised particular problems. In Connecticut, as in the rest of the country, the racist policies and practices of population control groups had left a bitter legacy in communities of color.[33] Most black nationalist groups were hostile to both abortion and birth control, and white women were hesitant to talk with women of color about abortion.[34] According to Gail Falk, who had worked with the Black Panther defense as well as Women versus Connecticut, "the prevailing black male idea" was that abortion, like forced sterilization, was part of the genocidal war on African-American communities; Women versus Connecticut "wouldn't have asked a woman at that time to cross over and take on her black brothers on that issue. . . . It would have felt like undermining black solidarity to go try to talk about something that was so clearly labeled. So it was more hands off out of respect."[35] While there were certainly women of color who argued for women's right to an abortion, their voices were muted in the public discourse of the 1970s, and the white women in Women versus Connecticut had few social connections that would allow them to reach these women.[36]

The Women versus Connecticut message moved quickly throughout white communities in the state, and women joined the suit in numbers that astounded even the organizers. Between October 1970 and February 1971 they recruited eight hundred plaintiffs, who brought a wide variety of experiences to the lawsuit.[37] Some had had illegal or "therapeutic" abortions; some had carried a pregnancy to term against their will; still others had no direct experience with abortion but nevertheless felt profoundly affected by the unavailability of legal abortion.[38]

PREPARING THE LEGAL ARGUMENTS

By the beginning of 1971, six lawyers had agreed to work on the lawsuit: Katie Roraback and Barbara Milstein of New Haven, Kathryn Emmett of Bridgeport, Marjory Gelb and Marilyn Seichter of Hartford, and Nancy Stearns of New York.[39] Roraback, who had been practicing law longer than any of the others, played a leadership role, as did Stearns, who frequently traveled from New York to lend her expertise to the Connecticut case.

As they developed their legal arguments, the lawyers and law students drew on the New York case and other suits that had been filed against state abortion laws, but reworked arguments from those cases in close cooperation with the organizers to "integrate the legal arguments with the organizing effort and with the vision that infused the suit."[40] Each of the three counts of the lawsuit addressed the ways Connecticut's abortion law violated the constitutional rights of a different group of plaintiffs: women of childbearing age, medical personnel, and counselors. Count one, the most substantial portion of the complaint, claimed that Connecticut's abortion laws violated the "right to privacy" and the "right to life and liberty" of women of childbearing age, denied "equal protection of the law" to poor women, and constituted a form of sex discrimination and cruel and unusual punishment.[41] Counts two and three argued that the statutes violated the civil liberties and right to privacy of medical practitioners and counselors.

Women versus Connecticut organizers were determined that rather than emphasizing constitutional rights, their case would speak to the effects of the abortion laws on the lives of real women. At a plaintiffs' meeting in April 1971 Nancy Stearns reflected on her growing conviction that instead of a constitutional challenge, what was needed was a "flesh and blood" invocation of the issues: "I am fully convinced now, after listening to more and more judges, that if we present it as a matter of law, they are going to think we are daft. We have got to drum it into their heads what we are talking about so that they can't forget . . . they will know that it's flesh and blood people that they're talking about. . . . One of these days they'll even realize that it's their daughters and wives that we're talking about as well as all the other women they may or may not know."[42]

For these reasons the brief was constructed as a vehicle for describing the devastating emotional, physical, and economic effects of the abortion laws on women's lives. Combining constitutional arguments with a vivid panorama of the suffering caused by illegal abortion, the brief stated clearly that it was women whose cause they were defending—not members of the medical profession.

ABELE V. MARKLE IN COURT

On March 2, 1971, Women versus Connecticut filed its lawsuit, Abele (for Janice Abele, the first plaintiff on the lists) v. Markle (the Connecticut district attorney), with 858 plaintiffs. The suit asked for a three-judge district court to hear the case and render a judgment declaring Connecticut abortion laws unconstitutional. Women versus Connecticut turned the filing into a public event by demonstrating on the steps of the post office with posters and banners sporting their defiant logo and leaflets explaining the suit.[43]

On May 14, 1971, Judge Emmett Clarie dismissed the case on the grounds that the prosecutions of two people who performed abortions were in the process of being decided and that the plaintiffs lacked standing—that they had insufficient personal stake in the outcome of the case. Women versus Connecticut organizers saw this ruling as both a setback and an opportunity for involving more women in their battle. While the lawyers prepared an appeal, the organizers intensified their activity outside the courtroom, establishing regional plaintiff networks and urging plaintiffs to circulate petitions in support of the lawsuit at "supermarkets, hospitals, where you work, among friends."[44]

Despite the ruling on Abele v. Markle, there were significant breakthroughs for the proponents of abortion rights in 1970 and 1971. In November 1970 the New York Times reported that "a dramatic liberalization of public attitudes and practices regarding abortions appears to be sweeping the country."[45] A referendum in the state of Washington repealed that state's abortion laws, and four states' anti-abortion laws were voided by state courts. In February 1971 the American Bar Association officially supported a woman's right to choose abortion up to the twentieth week of pregnancy, and in December 1971 the Supreme Court heard the first round of oral arguments in *Roe v. Wade.*[46]

The Connecticut court participated in this shift of public attitude and practices. On December 13, 1971, an appeals court ruled that *Abele v. Markle* should in fact be heard by a three-judge court. The court, however, agreed with Judge Clarie's earlier ruling that nonpregnant women of childbearing age did not face sufficient personal harm to give them standing. Only pregnant women, medical personnel, and counselors were judged to face sufficient harm to have standing in the case.

In February 1972 Women versus Connecticut filed an affidavit on behalf of a pregnant plaintiff asking for a temporary restraining order to allow her to have an abortion. While only the pregnant plaintiff and the counselors and medical personnel were the official plaintiffs, the lawyers pursued their strategy of involving nonpregnant women of childbearing age in the lawsuit.

The court decided to make its decision on the basis of the lawyers' oral arguments and the written complaint, to the disappointment of Women versus Connecticut, who wanted very much to have women testifying about their lives in the courtroom. The affidavits submitted with the complaint, however, did describe the variety of hardships created by the abortion statutes. Women were also present in massive numbers for every public court event. At a time when only 4 percent of lawyers and less than 1 percent of judges were women, the sight of a team of women lawyers and crowds of women in the courtroom lives vividly in the memory of the participants.[47] According to Roraback:

> It was a wonderful scene. I mean . . . you can't even imagine what the scene was like back then. . . . When you practiced law, you go into court, the judges were men, the bailiffs, the marshals, the sheriffs were men; they were all male. The court reporters were men; the . . . clerks were men, . . . it was a very masculine courtroom. . . . In all of the abortion cases this was true. . . . The attorneys for the defendants, whether it was *Abele v. Markle* or later on, the Medicaid abortion cases . . . there were all these male attorneys. And they tended to have male witnesses. You know, you'd walk into the courtroom . . . I used to laugh and say, "We're friends of the bride," because the right-to-life movement was a male movement.[48]

On April 18, 1972, the three-judge district court, consisting of Judges Edward Lumbard, Jon O. Newman, and Emmett Clarie, declared Connecticut's abortion law unconstitutional. The opinion, written by Judge Lumbard, was, according to Roraback, "one of the best that was written. It . . . talked about women and what was really involved in this thing in a way that some of the others that got into legal theory and stuff just never quite did." [49]

According to Judge Lumbard, Connecticut's abortion statutes were a violation of the Ninth Amendment and the due process clause of the Fourteenth Amendment. "Due process as regards abortion," the court ruled, "requires that a woman be given the power to determine within an appropriate time after conception whether or not she wishes to bear a child." The statutes being voided represented an "over-reaching of police power" on the part of the state, which "trespasses unjustifiably on the personal privacy and liberty of its female citizenry." Judge Lumbard developed the liberty argument more fully than any abortion decision had before. Women, said Judge Lumbard, were "the equal to men" and "the appropriate decision-makers over matters regarding their fundamental concerns." Because there is no need to encourage population growth at this time, Lumbard ruled, the state no longer has a compelling social interest that would justify infringing on women's liberty. Because of the "extraordinary ramifications for a woman" of the decision to "carry and bear a child," such a decision, asserted Lumbard, was of "fundamental importance to a woman." [50]

The women of Women versus Connecticut were jubilant, not only because they had won, but because Judge Lumbard's opinion used stronger language than any previous rulings and he grounded his opinion "strongly in women's rights." Marilyn Seichter commented to the *Hartford Courant* that the "ruling was even more than she had expected of the court," and another spokesperson for Women versus Connecticut said that "the decision recognized the right of women to the privacy of their bodies in clear unequivocal language." [51]

Judge Newman's concurring opinion, according to his own appraisal, "covered less ground" than Judge Lumbard's. However, it was Newman's words that played a crucial role in events in Connecticut after the decision was announced. After examining the history of abortion statutes in Connecticut, Newman concluded that the main state interest behind the 1860 statute was concern for the health and morals of the mother. Since the *Griswold* decision had indicated that protecting women's morals was not a sufficient justification for intruding on her privacy, and recent medical developments had rendered abortion safer than childbirth, these state interests were no longer compelling. It was clear, according to Newman, that the legislature had not intended to protect the life of the unborn child in framing the abortion statute. "If," he said, "the Connecticut legislature had made a judgement on this issue and had enacted laws to accord such protection to the unborn child, the constitutionality of such laws would pose a legal question of extreme difficulty, since the legislative judgement on this subject would be entitled to careful consideration."[52]

In his lone dissent, Judge Clarie argued that the Connecticut statute was in fact intended to protect fetal life, a "state interest of compelling proportions," which should override the rights of pregnant women. The legislature, not the courts, he maintained, is the proper place to resolve the abortion question. Clarie's views were echoed by Catholic institutions throughout the state. The Hartford archdiocese immediately declared its hope that the state would appeal the case to "defend the absolute God-given right of the child," and Catholic hospitals made it clear they would not perform abortions.[53]

Local medical societies, however, began suggesting fee schedules for abortion immediately after the ruling, provoking the wrath of Governor Thomas Meskill, a staunch Roman Catholic, who fulminated that "the issue is not whether the murder is performed by a skilled surgeon or a lady wielding a hat pin in a back alley."[54] The state immediately appealed the ruling, which Meskill called "an amazing decision" that "read more like an academic, philosophical discourse than a judicial ruling," and it requested a stay to allow the abortion statutes to remain in effect pending the appeal. When on May 14 Justice Thurgood Marshall denied the state's request, Connecticut's abortion statute was off the books.[55]

WOMEN VERSUS THE CATHOLIC CHURCH

Governor Meskill sprang into action, calling the legislature into a special session to enact a new abortion law and making it clear that he wanted the toughest law possible. While the bills being considered ranged from granting women power to choose an abortion to allowing abortions only to save the life of the mother, the bill that had the governor's backing was essentially the same as the law that had been declared unconstitutional. The only new features were a preamble proclaiming that the intent of the law was to "protect and preserve human life from the moment of conception" and stiffer penalties for violators. Invoking Judge Newman's comment in the concurring opinion, Meskill insisted that this new language would render the measure constitutional.

The atmosphere at the hearing held by the Joint Committee on Public Health and Safety on May 19, 1972, was light-years away from the hearings held three years earlier on the reform bill sponsored by the Connecticut Medical Society. A broad coalition of twenty groups had formed to "fight any attempt to overturn" the court's decision, and three hundred people, most of them women, packed the hearing room.[56] "Many of them were women's rightists," the *New York Times* concluded, "to judge from the speeches they cheered, from their straight hair and shift dresses and sandals."[57] Women versus Connecticut was present in force, displaying signs and banners and performing a play before the hearing began. Feelings ran high; there was frequent applause by both sides, and the chair repeatedly inveighed against "uncalled-for demonstrations," reminding the audience at one point, "It's not a ball game; it's a public hearing."[58]

The rhetoric had also changed on both sides. The many doctors who spoke in favor of the liberal bills spoke less about their own professional prerogatives and more about the needs of their women patients. Dr. Michael Baggish, for example, chief of obstetrics and gynecology at Mt. Sinai Hospital in New York City and associate professor at the University of Connecticut, spoke against "compulsory pregnancy." The old law, he said,

> operated to treat women as chattel, as breeding animals without regard for their rights as human beings and with complete disregard of decent everyday respect. I think it is about time we had laws that are no longer sadistic and punitive. I would like to urge the view that everything else being equal, a woman ought to have control of her own body. In truth, disparate reproductive roles constitute the basic dichotomy between men and women. Unfortunately this difference has been exploited to support political, economic and sexual male supremacy.[59]

Several anti-abortion speakers felt it necessary to declare their respect for women's rights before speaking against abortion. Terry Pitt, for example, representing the Family Life Bureau of the diocese of Bridgeport, asserted that she was "fully aware of the inequity suffered by women in our society. The rights of a woman for her own body are very important, I believe, but they are not the supreme value in our society."[60]

The representatives of Women versus Connecticut continued their strategy of forcing the discussion to focus on women's experiences. When the lawyers spoke, they did so as women, not as lawyers. Katie Roraback, the only woman among the invited speakers, was repeatedly interrupted after she exceeded the five-minute limit. Noting that she was the first woman to speak, she continued her statement, which had been prepared by all the lawyers for the case. Describing the implications of enforced childbearing on women's lives in different situations, she declared, "Probably nothing but death itself can affect a woman's life more seriously than enforced bearing of children and enforced responsibility for them perhaps for the remainder of her and their lives."[61] The loud applause after her speech provoked a warning from the chair that "outbursts will not be tolerated."[62]

Throughout the hearing, supportive legislators, such as Wilbur Smith, an African-American state senator from Hartford, tried to call attention to the political manipulation that had gone on behind closed doors. "In the Senate as in the House," he disclosed, "the plan is . . . to introduce it [the Meskill bill]. Someone, already planned ahead of time, will get up and move the question, vote it, pass it, go home—to go fishing, golfing and the rest—when the public here will have been put through one of the biggest games they have ever been put through in their lives."[63]

This was, in fact, very much like what happened. After eight hours of public testimony, the assembly's Public Health and Safety Committee met for an hour in closed session. Although, in the opinion of one member, it went "completely contrary to the sentiments of the day-long hearing," the committee voted to present the Meskill bill to the assembly. On Sunday, petitions supporting the bill appeared at Catholic churches around the state and were presented to the legislature the next day. When the assembly debated the bill on May 22, spectators from both sides watched from the gallery, booing, hissing, and applauding with such vigor that the speaker repeatedly threatened to clear the gallery. After considering several amendments that would have softened the bill, both houses of the legislature approved the Meskill bill with no qualifications.[64]

The vote vividly illustrated the power of the Catholic Church over Connecticut politics and the power of the governor over the state legislature. "The impetus for the bill as it was drafted," noted one legislator, "came directly from the Hartford archdiocese. They didn't want any loopholes, and there weren't any." Another legislator, who switched his vote to support the bill, confessed that "the governor hands out all the goodies, and when he really wants to put the pressure on, it works."[65]

CHALLENGING THE NEW LAW

The events in Hartford, which Lawrence Lader, in his history of abortion politics, has called a "unique travesty of Federal court authority," brought abortion to the center of public debate in Connecticut. While the public controversy about the abortion bill polarized many communities, it broadened support for the abortion rights movement.[66] As Women versus Connecticut lawyers prepared their suit against the new law, more plaintiffs signed up, bringing the number to two thousand in June, when the case was filed. The coalition that was formed in the beginning of May offered its support, and several organizations, including Planned Parenthood Federation of America, Planned Parenthood of Connecticut, and the Connecticut Civil Liberties Union, prepared to file amicus briefs.[67]

Women versus Connecticut held meetings of plaintiffs throughout the state to organize local right-to-choose committees and participated in public forums with representatives of a range of groups that opposed the law. Emboldened by the public support they received from women throughout the state, the lawyers for Women versus Connecticut went on the offensive. They filed a memorandum not only asking for an injunction against the new law but also citing Governor Meskill for contempt for attempting to "circumvent the order of this court." To support this motion they brought two pregnant women who had been denied abortions by medical committees of a hospital. "Women from all over the state," read their press release, "have expressed their outrage at the Governor and the Legislature for their preoccupation with the unborn."[68]

In addition to arguing that the new law was unconstitutional for the same reasons that the old law was, the memo discussed at length the influence of the Catholic Church and argued that the preamble establishing the law as a means for protecting human life constituted "an enshrinement of religious doctrine in the law."[69] On June 9, the court granted a temporary restraining order for one of the pregnant plaintiffs;

the other, unable to wait, had obtained an abortion in New York. It dismissed the request that Governor Meskill be cited for contempt as "frivolous," and instead of granting the request for a continued injunction against the new law, it decided to hold a hearing.

Women versus Connecticut lawyers and organizers were delighted that they would finally be able to present live testimony. While the state brought photographs and films to support its claim that a fetus is alive and questioned witnesses about their unborn children, eight women from Women versus Connecticut testified about their lives. Interrupted repeatedly by attorneys encouraging them to speak up, three women described the experience of giving birth to children they couldn't afford to care for and the difficulties of finding work when they were pregnant or caring for young children. One spoke of the terror of becoming pregnant when she knew it would be physically hazardous, and another talked about her doomed marriage, which had resulted from one unwanted pregnancy and was haunted by the prospect of another. A fourth woman testified about her experience as an unwanted child who moved among various foster parents throughout her childhood, and another described the anxiety caused by her trip to New York for a legal abortion, where she faced a strange city and unfamiliar doctors. In addition, three women medical and social work practitioners contributed their observations about the effect of the abortion law on their women patients and clients. Marilyn Seichter, who gave the concluding argument for Women versus Connecticut, observed that "this court [made up of three men] can never understand what the fear of pregnancy means to women" but urged the judges to try.[70]

On September 20, 1972, the court announced its decision, with Judge Clarie again dissenting. The majority opinion, written this time by Judge Newman, held that the new Connecticut law imposed "a uniformity of thought about the nature of the fetus." "The fetus," concluded the court, "is not a person within the meaning of the fourteenth amendment," and therefore the state had no compelling interest that could justify unconstitutionally abridging women's "right to privacy and personal choice in matters of sex and family life."[71]

The state's appeal reached the Supreme Court when the justices were deciding *Roe v. Wade* and its companion suit, *Doe v. Bolton*. Both of the decisions made in *Abele v. Markle* played a significant role in the opinion that Justice Harry Blackmun framed that fall. As Nancy Stearns has noted, "Blackmun's description of the physical and emotional harm to women of an unwanted pregnancy, the stigma of an out-of-wedlock pregnancy, and the problems with bearing an unwanted child bears a striking resemblance to the language used by the Connecticut court" in the first *Abele v. Markle* decision.[72] Judge Newman's opinion on the status of the fetus vis-à-vis women's constitutional rights was influential as well.[73] "We won (again)," proclaimed the *Women versus Connecticut Newsletter* after *Roe v. Wade* was decided.[74] Although the state continued its appeal, the case was returned to a lower court, which voided the Connecticut statute (unanimously this time) in April 1973.

TRIUMPHS AND DISAPPOINTMENTS

The story of Women versus Connecticut illustrates the powerful contribution of women's liberation ideas to the pre-*Roe* abortion rights movement. While Women versus Connecticut activists were stunningly successful in putting some of these ideas into practice, other goals were more difficult to achieve. Their insistence on inserting the painful stories of women's thwarted attempts to control their reproductive lives into the public discourse gave vibrant meaning to that cardinal women's liberation notion: "the personal is political." By bringing women's experiences into the courtroom and organizing a movement that made itself felt throughout the state, Women versus Connecticut had a significant impact on the judicial process. As Katie Roraback commented:

> The judges who heard people testify, and saw the women in the courtroom as they came to court, knew that this was a group of people to whom this was important. . . . [It was] not just . . . lawyers making arguments, but . . . women sitting there and listening to [the case] and women testifying. . . . And in addition, quite frankly, the impact of the organization, since it was such a big group, came back to the judges in their own personal experience. One of the judges on that three-judge panel—his wife was sympathetic. You know, he wasn't just hearing about it in court. . . . A lot of people who were involved, even if they weren't named plaintiffs, . . . knew the named [plaintiffs]. . . . It was such a large group that . . . throughout the state . . . people knew what we were talking about and they had some sort of sense of relationship to it.[75]

But while the women's liberation activists who started Women versus Connecticut were pleased with the impact of their movement on the public and the courts, they were disappointed that they were unable to sustain the broader critique of women's position in the United States that they began with. They wanted to challenge, for example, the assumption that women should be more responsible for children than men and to provoke discussion of social responsibility for child-raising. "If there were systems of child care that were really good," commented Jill Hulton, "if there were systems in education that were really imaginative and exciting, if there were people that you were willing to trust your children to, it would be a different kind of choice, I think, for a lot of women who find themselves pregnant." To their consternation, the organizers found that it wasn't always easy to bring up these ideas when they were talking about their lawsuit.[76]

As they spoke to more and more groups that did not share their broader critique of society, they began to feel uneasy that their message about abortion was being cut off from their critique of patriarchy. "If you don't know about what's wrong with the whole political system in this state," said Ann Freedman, frustrated by her talk to a women's Democratic club in Darien, Connecticut, "then you can't change the fact that a legislator's going to screw around on abortion and women generally and also all the other things you believe in, because of the way that it's set up." Discussions of "how it all goes together" became more and more difficult to initiate. "I think women feel," Freedman commented, about the women they were recruiting, that "they can get into this as an abortion thing. When you contact people in a women's liberation way, it's very hard to move them into action on a specific issue. But when you contact people on a specific issue, it's very hard to move them to the point of questioning their own lives totally as women." The demands of the lawsuit on the organizers' time and energy exacerbated the single-issue trajectory of the movement they were building. "I feel like we're pulled in two directions—we have to keep the court satisfied, keep stuffing them paper. And in our spare moments we're trying to really talk to women about it," Harriet Katz commented.

In addition to the difficulty of sustaining a multifaceted analysis of women's position, Women versus Connecticut activists had trouble maintaining the momentum of their movement after *Roe v. Wade*. They repeatedly reiterated their commitment to continuing the struggle until doctors and hospitals were "responsive to women's needs" and abortions were available to all women, but after abortion became legal, they were unable to mobilize large groups of women against the attacks on the reproductive rights of women on welfare, attacks that, in Connecticut, began shortly after *Roe v. Wade*. Their newsletter cautioned that legislatures would use the trimester framework of *Roe* to limit women's access to abortion after twelve weeks. They argued strongly against such limitations, since birth defects often could not be detected until later, the shortage of hospital beds sometimes forced women to wait, and most important, because teenage women, paralyzed by fear and guilt, often delayed in seeking abortions. "Women versus Connecticut," they proclaimed, "will not be content with any laws or regulations which do not firmly recognize a woman's right to decide whether or not to bear a child. And once that right is established, we will not be content until it can be freely exercised by all women." They were not, however, able to keep large groups of women active on behalf of these concerns.[77] Their suit against Connecticut's welfare department, which refused to pay for the abortions of women on welfare two months after *Roe v. Wade,* never became the focal point of a public movement.[78]

While Women versus Connecticut's commitment to the struggle for humane health care for all women did not waver, it took different forms in the post-*Roe* period. Rather than organizing political activity and public demonstrations, as they had in the politicized atmosphere of the pre-*Roe* years, members addressed themselves to education and service. They taught "our bodies/ourselves" courses in various settings and bought an old school bus, which they used as a base for distributing literature and giving workshops on women's health. In cooperation with other community groups, they worked to establish a freestanding abortion clinic, Women's Health Services, which opened its doors in 1975 and grew into a full-service gynecological clinic over the next ten years. This movement from political action to alternative institutions characterized women's liberation groups throughout the country in the mid-1970s.

Women versus Connecticut brilliantly achieved its original goal of conducting a hearing on abortion outside the courtroom. For three years a handful of women's liberation activists brought the subject of abortion into households throughout the state, forced the conservative politics of the state government into the public spotlight, and involved thousands of women in political action on behalf of reproductive freedom. The combination of litigation and grassroots mobilization that they and women of other states engaged in was a crucial element in the making of *Roe v. Wade.*

NOTES

I would like to thank Betsy Gilbertson for introducing me to Women versus Connecticut, spending hours copying legal materials, and critically reading several drafts of this essay. The essay has also benefited enormously from the editorial assistance of Virginia Blaisdell and the comments of Katie Roraback, Rickie Solinger, and Nancy Stearns.

1. Nancy Stearns, "*Roe v. Wade:* Our Struggle Continues," *Berkeley Women's Law Journal* 4 (1988–89): 5.

2. For a full description of these changes, see David Garrow, *Liberty and Sexuality: The Right to Privacy and the Making of Roe v. Wade* (New York: Macmillan, 1994), ch. 8.

3. The first effort to organize a movement to repeal abortion laws was led by three California women, Patricia Maginnis, Lana Phelan, and Rowena Gurner, in the early 1960s. Arguing that abortion statutes were a form of sex discrimination, they taught courses on self-induced abortion, referred women to abortion providers in Mexico, mounted a legal challenge to California's abortion statute, and founded the Society for Humane Abortion. See Ninia Baehr, *Abortion without Apology* (Boston: South End Press, 1990), ch. 1, and Garrow, *Liberty and Sexuality,* ch. 5.

4. Nancy Stearns, interview with author, February 11, 1995.

5. Ibid. For a fuller description of the New York lawsuit and organizing project, see Diane Schulder and Florynce Kennedy, *Abortion Rap* (New York: McGraw-Hill, 1971). Women's liberation activists, despite their substantial contribution to the abortion movement, were still often regarded as objects of ridicule. Roy Lucas, for example, the lawyer for one of the suits being consolidated with *Abramowicz v. Lefkowitz,* noted in a letter to Clement Vose that a member of women's liberation was "breast feeding her child in the courtroom." "Please do tell me the schedule of any important hearings," Vose responded, "as I would like to attend especially if women liberators are to be on display" (Roy Lucas to Clement Vose, November 11, 1969; Clement Vose to Roy Lucas, November 17, 1969; box 25, Roy Lucas Papers, Wesleyan University).

6. Schulder and Kennedy, *Abortion Rap,* 3.

7. Hearing, Judiciary Committee of the State Legislature, Hartford, Connecticut, April 14, 1969, 394. The Connecticut League for Abortion Law Reform supported these bills but was a small group that did not generate much public support (telephone conversation with Donald Cantor, May 3, 1995). See also Garrow, *Liberty and Sexuality,* 340.

8. "Herstory of Women vs. Connecticut: Our Thoughts on Abortion and Ourselves" (transcript of discussion tape recorded in May 1971, in possession of author), 2.

9. Ann Hill, "Abortion, Self-Determination and the Political Process," paper dated May 22, 1971.

10. Ann Hill, interview with author, December 6, 1992.

11. Betsy Gilbertson, interview with author, August 6, 1991.

12. Ibid.

13. Ibid.

14. Ann Hill, speech at Women and Power Conference, New Haven, Connecticut, June 1973.

15. The *New York Times Magazine* (January 27, 1970, 29) featured a long article that described the New York case on January 25, 1970, and two days later described the testimony of Susan Brownmiller and others as the lawyers took depositions; Gilbertson interview.

16. The idea of using large numbers of plaintiffs in abortion suits was not universally accepted by lawyers involved in abortion litigation. Roy Lucas, for example, responded to an inquiry from a member of the New Haven abortion group with a letter advising her as follows: "Rather than spending weeks in gathering hundreds of plaintiffs, I would spend the time in a more productive way gathering concrete factual data and doing research on the legal and medical issues. Several plaintiffs are enough if their standing is amply demonstrated. Your time would be well spent in outlining the specifics of the case or controversy between plaintiffs and defendants" (Roy Lucas to Ann Hill, October 26, 1970, box 25, Lucas Papers).

17. Catherine Roraback, interview by author, January 20, 1992.

18. Ibid.

19. "Herstory" transcript; Gilbertson interview.

20. Stearns interview.

21. See Garrow, *Liberty and Sexuality*, ch. 6, for descriptions of cases that involved male plaintiffs, usually doctors.

22. Hill, "Abortion," 24.

23. Roraback interview.

24. Hill, "Abortion," 26.

25. Plaintiff recruitment pamphlet.

26. *Modern Times*, October 1970, 5.

27. Hill speech.

28. Gail Falk, interview with author, October 10, 1992.

29. Hill interview.

30. Falk interview.

31. Gilbertson interview.

32. Judy Robison, interview with author, October 9, 1992. See Rickie Solinger, *Wake Up Little Susie: Single Pregnancy and Race before Roe v. Wade* (New York: Routledge, 1992).

33. Planned Parenthood still called itself Planned Parenthood World Population, and in 1969 at its national convention a caucus of black workers organized against any statement on abortion as well as sterilization (Planned Parenthood, New Haven chapter, box 41, folder G, Planned Parenthood Papers, New Haven Historical Society). See also Thomas B. Littlewood, *The Politics of Population Control* (Notre Dame: University of Notre Dame Press, 1977), ch. 5. Connecticut Planned Parenthood had been criticized because all six of its outreach workers in the Hartford area were black (Planned Parenthood, New Haven chapter, board meeting, box 41, folder G).

34. The Black Panthers, who were the black nationalist voices that white radicals in New Haven were most familiar with in the late 1960s and 1970s, were divided on the questions of abortion and birth control. According to Loretta Ross, the Black Panther Party supported legalized abortion ("Abortion:

1800–1970," in *Theorizing Black Feminisms: The Visionary Pragmatism of Black Women*, ed. Stanlie M. James and Abena P. A. Busia [New York: Routledge, 1993], 153). Black Panther literature, however, often condemned it; see, for example, Brenda Hyson, "New York Passed New Abortion Law Effective July 1, 1970," *Black Panther*, July 4, 1970.

35. Falk interview.

36. Shirley Chisholm, Frances Beale, Patricia Robinson, and Florynce Kennedy were among the African-American activists who spoke out publicly for abortion in the late 1960s and early 1970s. See Ross, "Abortion," 155–56; Reva Polatnik, "Poor Black Sisters Decided for Themselves: A Case Study of Women's Liberation Activism," in *Black Women in America*, ed. Kim Marie Vaz (Thousand Oaks, Cal.: Sage, 1995), 113; Schulder and Kennedy, *Abortion Rap.*

37. Report to Plaintiffs, February 1971.

38. Information about plaintiffs is from a chart constructed by Women versus Connecticut organizers in the summer of 1971; the chart contained data on 848 plaintiffs.

39. After Ann Hill graduated from law school, she joined the legal team and participated in the court actions in 1972.

40. Gilbertson interview.

41. Plaintiff recruitment pamphlet, 9, 10; Complaint in Motion for a Declaratory Judgment, in *Abele v. Markle*, 5.

42. Quoted in Hill, "Abortion," 29, from a plaintiff meeting at the law school on April 22, 1971.

43. *New Haven Register*, March 2, 1971.

44. Letter to plaintiffs, May 21, 1971.

45. *New York Times*, November 29, 1970.

46. See Garrow, *Liberty and Sexuality*, ch. 7.

47. Plaintiff recruitment pamphlet.

48. Roraback interview.

49. Ibid.

50. 342 Fed. Supp. 800–802 (D. Conn. 1972). Lumbard's opinion built on the Supreme Court's decision one month earlier in *Eisenstadt v. Baird*, the Massachusetts case against Bill Baird, who distributed birth control and abortion information to a college audience. "If the right of privacy means anything," said the Court, "it is the right of the individual, married or single, to be free frounwarranted governmental intrusion into matters so fundamentally affecting a person as the decision whether to bear or beget a child" (Garrow, *Liberty and Sexuality*, 542).

51. See Lawrence Lader, *Abortion II: Making the Revolution* (Boston: Beacon Press, 1973), 192, for comparison with other decisions; *Hartford Courant*, April 19, 1972; *New Haven Register*, April 19, 1972.

52. 342 Fed. Supp. 805 (D. Conn. 1972).

53. *New Haven Register*, April 18, 1972.

54. *New Haven Register*, April 19 and 20, 1972.

55. *Hartford Courant*, May 14, 1972.

56. *New Haven Register*, April 22, 1972; *Meriden Record*, April 22, 1972.

57. *New York Times,* May 20, 1972, 13.

58. Transcript of the Hearings of Joint Committee on Public Health and Safety, May 19, 1972, 1.

59. Ibid., 8.

60. Ibid., 128.

61. Ibid., 19.

62. Ibid., 23.

63. Ibid., 26.

64. *New Haven Register,* May 20, 1972; *New York Times,* May 24, 1972.

65. *New York Times,* May 24, 1972.

66. Lader, *Abortion II,* 194.

67. *Women versus Connecticut Newsletter,* May 1972; *New Haven Register,* May 24, 1972.

68. Memorandum in support of motion for contempt, to enforce injunction and for other relief, May 25, 1972; press release, Women versus Connecticut, May 26, 1972.

69. Memorandum in support of motion for contempt.

70. *Abele v. Markle,* June 30, 1972, Civil Action No. B-521, Hartford, Connecticut, transcript; *New Haven Register,* July 1, 1972.

71. 352 Fed. Supp. 224, 228 (D. Conn. 1972).

72. Stearns, "*Roe,*" 5.

73. *New York Times,* January 23, 1973, 1, 20; *Time,* January 29, 1973.

74. *Women versus Connecticut Newsletter,* February 1973.

75. Roraback interview.

76. The ideas in this and the following paragraph are based on the "Herstory" transcript. The ten Women Versus Connecticut activists who participated in that discussion are Betsy Gilbertson, Ann Hill, Ann Freedman, Gail Falk, Harriet Katz, Jill Hulton, Marione Cobb, Sasha Harmon, Joan Gombos, and Michelle Fletcher.

77. Two months after *Roe v. Wade* the Connecticut state welfare department made its policy on abortions more restrictive than it had been before. Previously, the department had paid for abortions if a doctor had requested special approval, but the new policy denied payments for all abortions except to save the life of the mother.

78. Their suit received a series of positive decisions, but they lost their case in 1977 when the Supreme Court decided, in *Maher v. Roe,* that states could refuse to pay for the abortions of welfare recipients. Several years later, the Connecticut Civil Liberties Union, at the initiation of staff attorney Martha Stone, sued the state of Connecticut, arguing that the state Equal Rights Amendment required the state to pay for Medicaid abortions. Despite the widespread opinion that such a suit was a very long shot, it succeeded (Gilbertson interview).

PART TWO

STRATEGIC ARENAS

The four essays in this section provide beleaguered but clear-sighted views of the condition of the abortion rights movement today. They also set agendas and lay out tactics for the movement into the twenty-first century. Each essay considers various ways that anti-rights groups have shaped and misshaped pro-rights strategies, in many cases forcing abortion rights organizations, politicians, and other spokespersons into reactive postures. All stress the importance of learning from this history and devising new strategies, sometimes in new arenas, to carry the battle for reproductive rights successfully forward.

Marcy Wilder comprehensively describes the changing battlegrounds on which the struggle for reproductive rights has been waged and the varying stances the rights community has taken since the 1960s. She calls for a sharp focus beyond both the law and the violence, a focus on the reproductive health needs of all women, so the need for abortion in the United States will be radically reduced.

Kathryn Kolbert and Andrea Miller review legal strategies that have been employed since *Roe v. Wade* to secure, extend, and defend reproductive rights, and they describe the specific arenas in which this three-pronged effort will continue in the future.

William Saletan's essay concentrates on the 1980s, when the imperatives of electoral politics in the United States pressed pro-choice groups to "broaden their base by narrowing their message." In Saletan's analysis, this was a dangerous strategy because it placed the abortion debate at a perilous remove from the issue of women's rights and had the effect of sanctioning new legal restrictions on abortion rights.

Dorothy Roberts's contribution uses the new feminist and anti-racist jurisprudence to reconsider the discourse of reproductive rights and to advance insights concerning the struggles of women of color in this arena. Roberts analyzes the prosecution of pregnant, drug-using women of color to expose the racist foundation of the state's interest in motherhood and to reevaluate the principles of "privacy" and "equality" as sound bases for a just theory of reproductive rights.

4

THE RULE OF LAW, THE RISE OF VIOLENCE, AND THE ROLE OF MORALITY

Reframing America's Abortion Debate

As pro-choice advocates and abortion foes battle over the legal status of abortion, America's reproductive health crisis deepens. Every year our society faces three million unintended pregnancies, one and a half million abortions, one million teen pregnancies, and thirty-five thousand infant deaths.[1] The dialogue within the strict confines of the abortion debate has failed to address America's extraordinarily high rates of abortion, unintended pregnancy, teen pregnancy, sexually transmitted disease, and infant mortality. Moreover, until recently, the narrow strictures of the legal and political discourse have precluded a meaningful discussion that reflects the complex moral considerations inherent in the abortion decision. This chapter argues that the future of reproductive rights in America depends on the ability of the pro-choice movement to break out of a colloquy that has outlived its usefulness.

In the first section I chart the early battles over the legality of abortion, which were crafted largely by courts and lawyers in the language of legal rights. Abortion rights advocates fought for decriminalization with a passion fueled by the horrors of the back alley and a deep understanding that the decision of whether to have a child is so profound and life-altering that women will risk their lives in order to make it for themselves. After *Roe v. Wade* recognized the constitutional right to choose, abortion foes fought with equal intensity to ban all abortion, motivated by an unalterable belief that a fetus is a person and therefore abortion is murder. The constitutional framework was unable to accommodate the fact that a woman and the fetus she carries are one entity. As activists, courts, and legislatures argued over the proper balance among the competing interests within a pregnant woman's body, the abortion conflict became strictly defined as a contest between the rights of women and the "right to life" of a fetus.

The second section of this chapter documents the rise of confrontation, coercion, and violence in the anti-choice movement. In the early 1980s the number of clinic bombings, arsons, death threats, and acid attacks aimed at abortion clinics increased dramatically as a growing number of anti-choice activists, enraged at their inability to outlaw abortion, embraced more confrontational tactics. For more than a decade, traditional anti-choice leaders remained silent in the face of the rising tide of violence. They moved forward with their political work, turning to the state legislatures to restrict abortion and making sure that anti-choice President Ronald Reagan made good on his promise to pack the Supreme Court with justices willing to overrule *Roe v. Wade*. It was not until anti-choice activists began murdering physicians that political organizations like the National Right to Life Committee reluctantly spoke out against the use of violence to further their cause.

By the end of the 1980s, thanks in large part to the use of violent tactics, it appeared that the anti-choice movement would not need to make abortion illegal in order to make it unavailable to American women. In light of two new Supreme Court decisions expanding the scope of constitutionally permissible restrictions, more and more states were enacting laws that placed increasingly burdensome obstacles in the path of women seeking abortions. Mandatory waiting periods, biased counseling requirements, parental consent laws, and public funding were having a cumulative impact and making it more difficult for many women to obtain safe abortions. Compounding the problem, the number of providers nationwide was dwindling as many physicians—unwilling to work under the threat of death, behind bulletproof glass—abandoned their abortion practices. In addition, many medical schools stopped teaching the procedure.

The pro-choice movement's work throughout the 1980s was defined almost entirely by abortion foes. Defending the basic right to choose on so many fronts—in Congress, state legislatures, and the courts as well as on clinic sidewalks—left little time or thought for addressing the broader societal issues that could lead, if not to consensus, then at least to a peaceful resolution of the abortion conflict. In 1992 the political landscape changed dramatically. That year, the Supreme Court's decision in *Planned Parenthood v. Casey* made clear that although the government would be permitted to impose significant restrictions on abortion, the procedure could not be outlawed altogether. In addition, the election of a pro-choice president helped ensure that the next justice named to the Supreme Court would not provide the critical vote to overturn *Roe* completely. Pro-choice advocates finally had breathing room to recover from years of defensive action and to lay the groundwork for the movement's next stage.

The third section of this chapter suggests that the pro-choice movement now has an unprecedented opportunity to make profound and fundamental changes in the terms of the abortion debate. Recent anti-choice efforts to focus the debate on the morality of abortion are an invitation for the pro-choice movement to break out of the defensive posture it assumed following *Roe* and to stop talking past a large number of rhetoric-weary Americans who are looking for a more substantial public discussion of abortion. Pro-choice leaders have just begun to articulate clearly the moral framework that underlies the pro-choice position. They must continue to expand the debate to emphasize the importance of the right to choose, how and why this country should reduce the need for abortion, and the moral capability of women to make their own reproductive decisions.

The evolution of the pro-choice movement and, indeed, of the abortion debate can be seen through the changes in name and mission assumed by the leading political organization on the issue, NARAL. Since its founding in 1969, NARAL has modified its name three times, each time reflecting a significant and substantive shift in both the abortion debate and the pro-choice position. The organization began as the National Association to Repeal Abortion Laws, dedicated to revoking the criminal laws banning abortion that were endangering women's lives throughout the country. After the great pro-choice victory in *Roe v. Wade,* the organization retained the NARAL acronym but called itself the National Abortion Rights Action League. The new name signified the group's political orientation and its single-minded focus on defending women's newly recognized constitutional right to choose abortion.

The organization changed again in 1994, adopting the longer and somewhat cumbersome name of National Abortion and Reproductive Rights Action League. For the first time in its history, NARAL expanded its mission beyond abortion and made a commitment to use the political process to help ensure that women have a full range of reproductive choices, including preventing unintended pregnancy, bearing healthy children, and choosing legal abortion. In an editorial applauding the name change and expanded mission, the *Washington Post* wrote that "helping women avoid unwanted pregnancy *is* a key element of the abortion debate, not just because many people who are troubled by abortion have no such qualms about contraception but also because large numbers on both sides can agree that a smaller number of abortions is a desirable outcome." [2] Under its broadened mission, the organization continues to defend the right to choose abortion but also works to make abortion less necessary.

The name change and expanded mission reveal a deeper change within the pro-choice movement. Trying to break out of single-issue politics and to shed an agenda that helped anti-choice forces isolate the procedure and demonize abortion providers, the pro-choice movement is beginning to articulate clearly the values and vision that underlie its political program. A campaign to promote pro-choice values and access to a full range of reproductive health services will reduce the need for abortion and significantly improve reproductive health across the country. Failure will mean more of the same sorry abortion war that has let America's reproductive health crisis fester. Success at promoting the information and services women and men need to make informed, responsible decisions about childbearing will advance the health of families, society, and our nation.

THE RULE OF LAW:
THE FIGHT TO MAKE ABORTION LEGAL

Abortion rights activists of the late 1960s knew with certainty that the problem they faced was illegal abortion and that legalizing the procedure was the solution. They marched, demonstrated, protested, sued, and lobbied, looking first to state legislatures and then to the federal courts for relief. Anti-choice activists, even after the devastating defeat they suffered in *Roe v. Wade,* also fought within the legislative and legal systems. They sought a constitutional amendment that would punish abortion as murder and, failing that, state restrictions that would limit access to the procedure. The debate, if not always civil, was rarely violent And though discussion on both sides was passionate and polemic, all agreed that ultimately victory would be achieved through the rule of law.

From the late nineteenth century until the 1960s, virtually every state had laws prohibiting abortion unless the procedure was absolutely necessary to save a woman's life. Women who had money traveled abroad to obtain safe abortions in countries where the procedure was legal. Women who could not afford to leave the country ventured into back alleys for clandestine illegal abortions. Women too poor or afraid to seek any assistance resorted to coat hangers, knitting needles, solutions of bleach and lye, and other "home remedies." Many paid with their lives.

As early as the 1940s, physicians who had experience treating the victims of illegal abortion began to see the issue as a public health problem. In 1942, at the annual meeting of the Birth Control (soon to be Planned Parenthood) Federation of America, Dr. Alan Guttmacher expressed his belief that abortion should be legal whenever a woman's health might be at risk.[3] However, twenty years would pass before the drive for legal reform began in earnest.

Initial suggestions for reform by the legal community were conservative and modest. Most proposals involved crafting limited exceptions to existing criminal bans. The American Law Institute (ALI), a highly regarded professional organization of legal scholars and practicing attorneys, legitimized the notion of statutory reform of abortion laws in 1959, when it revised the widely accepted Model Penal Code to include a provision permitting abortion under extremely limited circumstances. The model statutory language permitted abortion if the pregnancy was the result of rape or incest, if the fetus suffered from grave abnormalities, or if a woman could find two doctors willing to certify that continuing the pregnancy would gravely impair her health.[4]

Lawyers, physicians, and activists lobbied state legislatures to adopt abortion law reform, but early legislative victories were extremely disappointing. The narrow exceptions added to the criminal abortion statutes failed to cover the circumstances of most women who needed safe abortions, and even those who qualified under the law often had trouble finding a legitimate doctor willing to perform the procedure. Governor Richard Lamm of Colorado, who as a legislator had sponsored the state's 1967 reform law, soon publicly expressed his frustration with its minimal impact and wrote in the *Denver Post* that "the right to control her fertility is a right every woman should have."[5]

It was not until the idea of "women's liberation" took hold in the late 1960s that grassroots momentum for abortion rights surged. Young feminists educated in the civil rights and antiwar movements saw the fight for abortion rights as part of a broader movement for social change. Their demands for equality broadened, deepened, and radicalized the debate, bringing a harder edge that was reflected in slogans such as "Abortion on Demand and Without Apology" and "Get Your Laws Off My Body." When feminists joined doctors and lawyers, the political alliance that would ultimately legalize abortion finally emerged.

Frustrated with the slow pace of reform, feminists were the first to embrace the notion that access to safe and legal abortion required repeal, not just moderate liberalization, of existing criminal bans. Assemblywoman Constance Cook, sponsor of a bill that would completely repeal the New York abortion ban, captured this change in the political climate when she said, "I knew that women did not want reform, at least not enough to go out and work for it, whereas I suspected they would work for repeal, and they did."[6] Abortion rights leaders finally made an unconditional and unapologetic commitment to repealing criminal bans at the First National Conference on Abortion Laws in Chicago in 1969. Identifying an intense and urgent need, they called for the creation of a national single-issue group that could help advance and coordinate local efforts at a national level. The name of the organization—the National Association for the Repeal of Abortion Laws (NARAL)—could not have stated the movement's goal more clearly.

Initially, NARAL and other pro-choice groups organized grassroots activists to lobby in statehouses across the country. Their commitment to abortion law repeal, however, was not well served by the state legislative process. The pace was far too slow and the compromises required untenable. As legal abortion became available in a few states, activists grew increasingly dissatisfied with allowing a woman's ability to obtain a safe procedure to depend entirely on which state she called home. It seemed that nothing less than a federally recognized constitutional right would ensure that safe and legal abortion was available to women throughout the country. Movement lawyers commenced a search for a plaintiff, and in late 1969 attorneys Linda Coffee and Sarah Weddington met the woman who would be known as Jane Roe. They filed a challenge to a Texas criminal ban on abortion that would ultimately lead to the most important legal victory for women since achieving the right to vote.

On January 22, 1973, the Supreme Court handed down the *Roe v. Wade* decision, and for a brief moment, it appeared as though abortion rights advocates had won the war. Overnight, every criminal ban on abortion in the United States had been overturned, and every woman in America was free to exercise her constitutionally protected right to choose legal abortion. NARAL executive director Lee Gidding asked rhetorically in a personal letter, "How many people do you know who have actually won, in total, the objective they set for themselves?"[7] The *New York Times* editorial following the decision predicted that *Roe v. Wade* would provide "a sound foundation for final and reasonable resolution" of the abortion debate.[8] Unfortunately, that forecast turned out to be less than prophetic.

The anti-abortion backlash following *Roe* was immediate and intense. Reeling from their stunning defeat, abortion opponents flooded congressional offices with mail calling for a measure more extreme than anything before: a constitutional amendment to criminalize abortion nationwide. Recognizing the need for a political counterforce to the burgeoning anti-choice movement, the National Association for the Repeal of Abortion Laws changed its name to the National Abortion Rights Action League and adopted a new mission statement. Pledging "to develop and sustain a constituency which effectively uses the political process at the state and national level to guarantee every woman in the United States the right to choose and obtain a legal abortion," NARAL organized its grassroots supporters into state affiliates charged with fighting the onslaught of state and federal anti-choice legislation.

Although anti-choice strategists did develop an abundance of legislative measures designed to restrict access to abortion, their undisputed priority was to amend the United States Constitution. In November 1973 the first edition of the National Right to Life Committee's newsletter editorialized: "We must work for passage of a Constitutional Human Life Amendment in Congress."[9] In August 1974 Mildred Jefferson, chairperson of the board of the National Right to Life Committee, testified before Congress that "we are committed to achieving an amendment to the Constitution which will protect human life from its beginning to its natural end." Jefferson accurately predicted both the rise of the anti-choice movement and the enduring nature of the abortion controversy when she testified: "With the necessity for ratification of such an amendment and securing as well as defending enabling legislation within the States, right-to-life organizations will become a permanent part of the political scene."[10]

Almost a decade later, anti-choice advocates moved their human life proposals to a congressional vote. The first proposal to reach this benchmark was not a constitutional amendment, but a bill sponsored by Senator Jesse Helms that would have prohibited federal funding for any abortion-related use and put Congress on record as declaring that "life begins at conception." In 1982 the bill was defeated by a vote of 46 to 47. A year later the Senate rejected Orrin Hatch's proposal to amend the Constitution to permit—but not require—states to ban abortion. The vote was 49 to 50, eighteen votes short of the two-thirds majority necessary for approval.[11] Having finally brought a measure to a vote in a Republican-controlled Senate and having failed, congressional efforts to overturn *Roe* ground to a halt, and the "human life" amendment was relegated to the realm of rhetoric.

Recognizing the apparent futility of attempts to amend the Constitution, traditional anti-choice institutions, including the National Conference of Catholic Bishops, the National Right to Life Committee, and Americans United for Life, prepared to fight the battle against *Roe* in increments. Abortion opponents recognized that apart from a constitutional amendment, the only way to overrule *Roe v. Wade* completely was to secure five solid anti-choice votes on the Supreme Court. Shifting strategies, anti-abortion leaders mapped out a plan to transform the federal judiciary and eventually to secure a majority on the nation's highest court willing to overrule *Roe*. In 1980 a plank was added to the national Republican Party platform calling for the appointment of anti-choice judges at every level of the federal judiciary. Shortly thereafter, Ronald Reagan was elected president and enthusiastically implemented the policy. During his eight years in office, using a strictly enforced anti-abortion litmus test, Reagan appointed more than half of the members of the federal bench and three new Supreme Court justices, each of whom replaced a member of *Roe*'s seven-member majority.

Reconstructing the Supreme Court, however, fulfilled only half of the battle plan to overturn *Roe*. Anti-choice lobbyists and legislators also set to work to enact carefully drafted statutes that would create "test cases," offering an increasingly sympathetic judiciary the opportunity to cut back constitutional protection. Participants in a March 1984 conference sponsored by Americans United for Life (AUL), "Reversing *Roe v. Wade* Through the Courts," advised designing legislation that would exploit opportunities presented by the *Roe* decision itself.[12] *Roe* had held that some state abortion restrictions could be justified by the state's interest in maternal health and others by an interest in fetal life. The anti-choice movement hoped to expand the scope of permissible state restrictions by gaining judicial approval of, for example, mandatory waiting periods, biased and inflexible "informed consent" provisions, and bans on specific abortion methods. According to one anti-choice legal scholar attending the AUL conference, "Once these [restrictions] . . . are achieved, the abortion privacy right would be drained of content, lose its significance, and could be directly attacked."[13]

Although the anti-choice movement could claim substantial success in achieving its incremental goals for legislation and judicial appointments, a growing number of anti-choice activists were infuriated by their inability to criminalize abortion outright. Opting for a direct and frontal assault, new and more radical leaders rejected what they saw as the movement's obsession with the legal status of abortion and instead promoted direct action steeped in coercion and intimidation.

FROM SIDEWALK COUNSELING TO MURDER: THE RISE OF CONFRONTATION AND COERCION

The tactics of the anti-choice movement grew increasingly confrontational: what began as picketing in front of clinics turned into "sidewalk counseling" and then escalated to full-fledged blockades. Death threats against physicians became commonplace, and arson and bombings more frequent. By the mid-1980s there had been a perceptible shift in anti-choice tactics from the rule of law to the reign of lawlessness.

In his 1990 book, *Accessory to Murder,* Operation Rescue leader Randall Terry disavowed the legislative and legalistic strategies of more traditional leaders, proclaiming: "For so many years, those in the pro-life movement had been saying abortion is murder and then writing a letter or carrying a sign once a year at a march. If you were about to be murdered, I'm sure you would want me to do more than write your congressman! . . . We are acting, to some degree, as if abortion is really murder. The logical response to murder is to physically intervene on behalf of the victim."[14]

Under Terry's direction Operation Rescue's unofficial slogan became, "If you think abortion is murder, act like it!"[15] It was only a matter of time before anti-choice activists would heed that call literally, take up arms, and begin shooting abortion doctors.

On March 10, 1993, forty-seven-year-old physician David Gunn was shot in the back with a .38-caliber revolver during an anti-abortion demonstration outside the clinic where he practiced in Pensacola, Florida. At the time many anti-abortion leaders insisted that the murder was the act of a lone, sick extremist. That claim became more difficult to defend a year and a half later, when another "pro-life" activist fired a 12-gauge shotgun into the truck of volunteer clinic escorts James and June Barrett, a seventy-four-year-old retired air force lieutenant colonel and his wife. James Barrett and the physician he was escorting, John Britton, were both killed. June Barrett suffered a bullet in the arm. In 1995, after two clinic employees were murdered in Brookline, Massachusetts, by yet another anti-choice extremist, the disavowals of any connection between the anti-choice movement and the homicides had lost all credibility.

For at least a decade prior to Dr. Gunn's murder, blockades, vandalism, arson, and bombings were met with a wink and a nod of approval from abortion opponents. Clinic blockades and attacks were tolerated and in some cases encouraged by anti-choice elected officials at the highest levels of government. Following President Ronald Reagan's election in 1980, the number of violent incidents against clinics and clinic personnel, including vandalism, death threats, assault, arson, bombing, and invasion, increased by almost 450 percent.[16] President Reagan's speeches to anti-abortion groups were interpreted by radicals as tacit approval for their vigilantism. Don Anderson, who in 1983 abducted an abortion provider and his wife at gunpoint and held them for more than a week in an abandoned ammunition bunker, stated that he "agreed with pro-choice groups that bombers were encouraged by the absence of direct condemnations of their activities by Reagan. . . . [They feel] they have a green light from the president—that's the impression I got."[17] For his entire first term, President Reagan sat silent in the face of the violence despite repeated requests that he condemn it.

President George Bush more explicitly encouraged the violence by repeatedly intervening on Operation Rescue's behalf in judicial proceedings. In the summer of 1991, Operation Rescue staged a series of massive blockades in Wichita, Kansas, during which two thousand people were arrested. When a federal judge ordered the picketing to stop after three abortion clinics had been shut down, the Bush administration entered the case on the side of lawlessness, contending that the judge had no authority to issue the order.[18] In another case, the Bush Justice Department filed a brief in the U.S. Supreme Court on behalf of Operation Rescue, supporting the group's position that a federal civil rights law did not protect women from the blockades.[19]

Anti-abortion leaders who defended the shootings gained legitimacy as representatives of the "pro-life" movement as more and more supporters expressed their belief that murder was ethically, theologically, and legally justified. The foundation on which the entire movement rested—that a fetus is a person from the moment of conception and that therefore abortion equals murder—had been brought by some to its logical conclusion. Michael Hirsch, a former staff attorney for Pat Robertson's American Center for Law and Justice, wrote a law review article, published and then recalled by the law review at Robertson's Regent University, in which he argued that the murder of abortion providers was a reasonable action necessary to defend "preborn children."[20] After Dr. Gunn was killed, thirty-two activists from nineteen states, including pastors, Catholic priests, and Operation Rescue leaders, asserted that the murder was justified and signed a declaration endorsing the use of violence against doctors.[21]

For many years the tactics of anti-choice activists lobbying for restrictive laws and of radical advocates of "direct action" were mutually reinforcing. Those promoting violence and harassment considered themselves the vanguard of a legitimate political movement. Organizations pursuing legislative goals also derived some benefit from the more extreme actions of their "pro-life" colleagues. The violent wing of the movement made those demanding laws to severely restrict access to safe and legal abortion seem moderate in comparison. In the public mind, however, the "pro-life" position became increasingly associated with brutality. It was not until anti-abortion activists began murdering physicians that less radical leaders, who for years had silently tolerated and subtly encouraged the violence, were forced to finally, reluctantly, speak out against it. Even then, adopting a philosophy of "violence begets violence," many publicly blamed the victims.

Anti-abortion leaders who condemn the murders have continued to imply that violent acts are somewhat justified by the enormity of what they see as the real crime—abortion. Don Treshman of Rescue America asserted that "while Gunn's death is unfortunate, it's also true that quite a number of babies' lives will be saved."[22] After John Salvi stood accused of killing two abortion clinic workers, ultraconservative columnist Cal Thomas disagreed with the "fanatics" who say that homicide is justifiable, but argued strenuously that "the killings of the already born should not be allowed to derail our attention from the killing of the not-yet-born."[23]

Although many anti-choice organizations have explicitly condemned homicide, other violence, including anti-abortion death threats, bombings, arson, acid attacks, and stalking, have gone undenounced. Anti-choice leaders who forcefully declare that shootings have no place in their movement maintain a stunning silence on the almost nineteen hundred reported acts of violence and the eleven thousand acts of disruption committed against abortion providers since 1977.[24] "Wanted" posters picturing clinic doctors are still sanctioned; doctors continue to be branded baby-killers and their children followed to school; and abortion is repeatedly referred to as a Holocaust in anti-abortion literature. No wing of the anti-choice movement has ever devoted energy or committed resources to fighting anti-abortion violence. In fact, virtually every anti-choice organization in the country lobbied forcefully against the Freedom of Access to Clinic Entrances Act (FACE), a federal law that protects abortion clinics against terrorism.

Perhaps the failure of the anti-choice movement to contain its violent wing can be explained, in part, because confrontational, coercive, and violent tactics have reduced the availability of abortion. The climate of fear and terror created among abortion providers has allowed the anti-choice establishment, which has yet to make all abortion illegal, to come closer to making it unavailable. Between 1982 and 1992 the nation experienced an 18 percent decrease in the number of abortion providers.[25] By 1992, in 84 percent of all U.S. counties no physicians were willing to perform the procedure.[26] North and South Dakota have only one abortion provider each, and clinics in many areas are relying more frequently on "circuit riders"—physicians willing to fly or drive hundreds of miles to serve women who live in areas where no local doctors are willing to perform abortions.[27] A recent study by the American Medical Association concluded that the shortage of abortion providers has "the potential to threaten the safety of induced abortion."[28]

Just as the most extreme elements of the anti-choice movement began to make serious inroads into the availability of abortion, anti-choice leaders who had laid their long-term political plans in the early 1980s began to realize successes of their own. After almost a decade of anti-choice appointments to the federal bench, abortion opponents came within one vote of overturning *Roe v. Wade* in the 1989 Supreme Court case *Webster v. Reproductive Health Services*. Four justices voted to overturn *Roe* completely, prompting Justice Harry Blackmun to write: "For today, the women of this Nation still retain the liberty to control their destinies. But the signs are evident and very ominous, and a chill wind blows."[29] Four justices voted to reaffirm the decision, and one sole vote—Justice Sandra O'Connor's—became the controlling opinion. Articulating a new legal standard, O'Connor found that the Missouri law was not an "undue burden" on the right to choose and was therefore constitutionally permissible.

Although O'Connor's new legal test was left largely undefined, it seemed that the right to choose was no longer considered fundamental and worthy of the strictest judicial protection. It appeared, in fact, that before the Court would declare an abortion restriction unconstitutional under the undue burden test, women would have to prove that the law created a substantial obstacle to their ability to obtain an abortion.

The *Webster* decision served as an invitation to state legislators to test just how far the Supreme Court would permit them to go. With enhanced creativity, lawmakers introduced a myriad of restrictive abortion bills, including proposals to make all abortion illegal, prohibitions on abortion "as a means of birth control," bans on abortion for sex selection, husband-consent laws, onerous clinic-licensing laws, and abortion-reporting requirements.[30] Between 1989 and 1992 more than seven hundred anti-choice bills were introduced in state legislatures across the country.[31] Some of the legislators' ideas were new; many had been tried before; and all were designed to push the limits of the Court's most recent abortion ruling.

In 1992 the Pennsylvania Abortion Control Act would shake the foundations of the Court's *Roe v. Wade* decision. In the 1992 decision *Planned Parenthood v. Casey,* while refusing to overturn *Roe* completely, the Court upheld a provision requiring that before obtaining an abortion, a woman must wait at least twenty-four hours after she has received a lengthy and inflexible state-mandated lecture on abortion. In so doing, the Court weakened *Roe* by adopting the less protective standard of judicial review, previously articulated by Justice O'Connor in *Webster,* which permits states to impose restrictions as long as they do not "unduly burden" a woman's right to choose.

Although sweeping criminal bans would still be held unconstitutional, the government was now permitted to impose on women burdensome obstacles such as mandatory waiting periods. Indeed, during the first five months after Mississippi's waiting-period law went into effect in August of 1992, the number of women who left the state to obtain an abortion rose by 17 percent.[32] One twenty-eight-year-old woman who complied with the law hitchhiked 130 miles to a clinic with $265 cash for the procedure and $14 spending money. After an offer to stay at a friend's house fell through, the woman would have been forced to sleep on an outdoor bench had the clinic not paid for her to stay at a nearby motel.[33]

Politically, the *Casey* decision led to a stalemate as both sides immediately declared defeat. NARAL's president Kate Michelman asserted that "George Bush's Court has left *Roe v. Wade* an empty shell that is one Justice Thomas away from being destroyed," and Randall Terry announced that "three Reagan/Bush appointees stabbed the pro-life movement in the back."[34] The fact was that the anti-choice movement had clearly failed to make abortion illegal. Yet, faced with an onslaught of violence and harassment, a shortage of physicians willing to perform abortions, and increasingly burdensome state-imposed restrictions, pro-choice forces had failed to secure for women ongoing access to safe and legal abortion.

Although *Casey* clearly marked the anti-choice movement's failure to gain a majority on the Supreme Court willing to overrule *Roe v. Wade,* abortion opponents may not need criminal bans on abortion in order to make the procedure unobtainable. Mandatory waiting periods, laws prohibiting insurance programs (private and public) from providing coverage for abortion, and parental consent and notice laws are placing onerous and sometimes dangerous restrictions on abortion. In perhaps the most extreme example of the dangers these restrictions pose, Becky Bell, a seventeen-year-old in Indiana, died in 1989 from an illegal abortion because she could not bear to tell her parents, as required by Indiana law, that she was pregnant and needed an abortion.[35] Increasingly burdensome state-imposed restrictions, combined with the climate of terror created by abortion opponents at many health care facilities, seriously threaten the availability of abortion in America.

THE ABORTION DEBATE AND BEYOND: FROM LEGAL RIGHTS TO MORAL RESPONSIBILITIES

Faced with a Court unwilling to fully reaffirm *Roe v. Wade,* state legislatures increasingly hostile to the right to choose, and a public leery of stridency among advocates on both sides of the abortion conflict, pro-choice leaders recognized the need for a change in the terms of the debate. The election of a pro-choice president and the diminished threat that *Roe v. Wade* would be completely overturned provided a welcome opportunity for the pro-choice movement to break out of an antiquated colloquy about the legal status of abortion. In the early 1990s, for the first time in twenty-five years, pro-choice leaders began to state their vision boldly in proactive terms.

As legal scholars continue to debate whether the right to choose abortion is more properly characterized as a "liberty" or an "equality" interest, the pro-choice community has recognized that the right to choose abortion is insufficient to afford women either liberty or equality unless it is accompanied by the ability to make the full range of reproductive choices. As a result, pro-choice advocates have joined other women's rights activists to fight more aggressively for policies that will reduce unintended pregnancy, promote comprehensive sexuality education, encourage contraceptive research and development, and increase the availability of prenatal care and early-childhood health services. The political program of the pro-choice movement is just beginning to reflect a forward-looking vision of a better society where unintended pregnancy is minimized and child rearing is supported as enthusiastically as abortion is discouraged.

The changing perspective of the movement was manifest in 1993, when the National Abortion Rights Action League expanded its mission and, a year later, its name. NARAL president Kate Michelman publicly announced the change, asserting: "we've spent the last 25 years leading the fight for one right—the right to choose abortion. We had to make that fight. It was right to make that fight. Now we've got to begin leading the fight to make abortion less necessary." Renamed the National Abortion and Reproductive Rights Action League (but again retaining the NARAL acronym), the organization pledged "to develop and sustain a constituency that uses the political process to guarantee every woman the right to make personal decisions regarding the full range of reproductive choices, including preventing unintended pregnancy, bearing healthy children, and choosing legal abortion." [36]

The pro-choice drive for policies that will make abortion less necessary is exposing fundamental differences between the pro-choice and anti-choice movements that extend far beyond the abortion debate. The pro-choice vision encompasses the notion that women are moral agents capable of making complex and ethical decisions. The role of government, therefore, should be, not to restrict the capacity of individuals to make responsible and informed decisions, but rather to enhance it. The anti-choice vision promotes quite a different view. The Christian Coalition and other abortion opponents envision a world where government will impose a public morality: laws will outlaw abortion, prohibit schools from offering comprehensive sexuality education, and decrease access to family-planning services.

Sexuality education provides a good example of the difference in approach. Although teens in America are no more sexually active than those in other developed nations, they are less likely to use contraception, more likely to get pregnant, and more likely to contract a sexually transmitted disease.[37] The anti-choice approach to sexuality education is to severely limit the ability of schools to provide comprehensive programs. In 1995, as part of its expanded mission, NARAL published the first national study of sex education laws and legislation. The study found that there is a clear trend toward restrictive and biased programs as a result of the growing influence of right-wing groups over state legislatures and school boards.[38] Right-wing organizations are promoting biased and medically inaccurate curricula that withhold potentially lifesaving information from American youth. Many support a curricula called "Choosing the Best," which advises teens to wash their genitals with Lysol after condom use.[39] Others promote a curriculum commonly referred to as "Teen Aid," which teaches that "several factors have been advanced to explain why subsequent children [of a woman who has an abortion] are battered. Some of the mechanisms are . . . after one has aborted a child, an individual loses instinctual control over rage."[40]

The pro-choice community, on the other hand, has joined child and teen advocates to promote medically accurate programs that emphasize abstinence, pregnancy prevention, prevention of sexually transmitted diseases, life options skills, and access to confidential reproductive health services. A NARAL report in support of President Clinton's nomination of Dr. Henry Foster for surgeon general states:

> Too many adolescents do not know how to prevent pregnancy, and too many girls choose teen motherhood because they believe they have no hope of finding fulfillment elsewhere. Unless teens receive the information, skills and services they need to protect their reproductive health, many of these needless and preventable physical, financial and societal costs will increase. An aggressive national campaign to curb teenage pregnancy . . . is essential to protect our children and promote a healthier society.[41]

Dr. Foster is widely acclaimed for pioneering a program that has become a national model for a comprehensive approach to teen pregnancy prevention. His nomination was derailed by anti-choice senators who claimed he was unfit for office because he had performed legal abortions early in his career as an obstetrician-gynecologist. The nation was thus deprived of a surgeon general uniquely qualified to champion programs that would reduce the need for abortion in America.

Pro-choice advocates want to reduce the need for abortion, not because they believe abortion is wrong, but because they believe abortion represents the failure of society to address critical reproductive health issues. Pro-choice writer Naomi Wolf, in a controversial article published in 1995, accuses the pro-choice movement of relinquishing "the moral frame" around the issue of abortion. Maintaining that pro-choice advocates make a terrible mistake by emptying the act of abortion of moral gravity, she suggests that "it is never right or necessary to minimize the value of the lives involved or the sacrifice incurred in letting them go. Only if we uphold abortion rights within a matrix of individual conscience, atonement and responsibility can we both correct the logical and ethical absurdity in our position—and consolidate the support of the center."[42] Wolf is correct when she asserts that abortion rights must be promoted in a framework of morality and conscience, but she commits a profound error when she suggests that pro-choice advocates have failed to understand and acknowledge the moral significance of the abortion decision.

The pro-choice vision begins with the fundamental truth that women are moral agents whose actions are based on what they believe to be in their own best interests and those of their families. To say that women have the right to make the abortion decision is not to deny the moral significance of the act itself. Legal scholar Robin West argues persuasively that the abortion decision is complex and riddled with moral considerations, and that for precisely that reason, women must be permitted to make the decision for themselves. West maintains:

> Women need the freedom to make reproductive decisions not merely to vindicate a right to be left alone, but often to strengthen their ties to others: to plan responsibly and have a family for which they can provide, to pursue professional or work commitments made to the outside world, or to continue supporting their families or communities. At other times the decision to abort is necessitated, not by a murderous urge to end life, but by the harsh reality of a financially irresponsible partner, a society indifferent to the care of children, and a workplace incapable of accommodating or supporting the needs of working parents. . . . Whatever the reason, the decision to abort is almost invariably made within a web of interlocking, competing, and often irreconcilable responsibilities and commitments.[43]

The pro-choice position does not empty the act of abortion of moral gravity. It is the anti-choice position that drains the abortion decision of its moral complexity by insisting that it is always wrong. In so doing, the anti-choice position denies women the moral capacity to make the decision for themselves.

In the early 1990s anti-choice leaders, faced with the stalemate of *Planned Parenthood v. Casey* and the election of a pro-choice president, were also exploring new approaches to the abortion issue. Disheartened by their failure to overturn *Roe v. Wade* and discredited by the violent confrontational tactics associated with their cause, a faction of the anti-choice movement began suggesting a change in the terms of the debate. Concerned about the deep rifts the abortion issue has caused within the Republican Party, these abortion opponents propose that anti-choice advocates (1) temporarily forgo a constitutional amendment, (2) work vigorously to enact legal restrictions on abortion, and (3) build a foundation for further legal constraints by persuading a majority of Americans that abortion is immoral and both a symptom and a cause of social disorder and cultural decay. Only then, they suggest, will criminalization be politically possible.

These emerging voices urge the anti-choice movement to concentrate more on the immorality of abortion and less on futile political goals that have a track record of failure. In 1995–96, within the space of six months, a flurry of articles appeared in leading opinion journals exhorting this "new" approach to the abortion issue. In an article titled "Abortion and the Republican Party: A New Approach," writer Noemie Emery suggests that anti-choice Republicans frame an attack based on moral dissuasion, stake out a position that abortion is wrong, and demand that it be reduced by aggressive, voluntary, and noncoercive means.[44] William Bennett, moral guru for the nineties, believes that "Emery is surely right in her attempt to move the emphasis from the legal to the moral venue. Why? Because building a moral and political consensus is the necessary precondition for legal reform."[45] In the *Atlantic Monthly*, political science professor George McKenna argues that "the lesson for pro-life advocates is that they need to take the time to lay out their case. They may hope for an immediate end to abortion . . . but their emphasis, I believe, should be on making it clear to others why they have reached the conclusions that they have reached. . . . They need to demand less and explain more."[46]

At first glance, it appears that these advocates are seeking to expand the parameters of the discourse and engage in a more substantive discussion. A closer read reveals that they are not. This purportedly "new" approach does not question the fundamental premise underlying anti-choice ideology—that a fetus is a person and that therefore abortion is murder. Bennett, Emery, and the others begin with the premise that abortion is wrong—period. They never consider that abortion may be bad, but that sometimes it is better than the alternatives. They have not moderated their position by suggesting that abortion should be restricted but not illegal. Rather, they are saying that advocating the least popular remedy to the problem of abortion (i.e., a constitutional amendment) is bad politics and ultimately does more harm than good to the movement's ability to outlaw abortion. Their position derives from and is ultimately indistinguishable from the radical premise at the heart of the anti-choice movement. Theirs is a moral-absolutist philosophy in search of a politically pragmatic agenda.

Perhaps the best evidence that the new voice is no different from the old one is that the campaign of "moral persuasion" looks strikingly similar to the traditional anti-choice campaign of legal coercion. The images remain the same: a babylike fetus, a fetus that sucks its thumb, an aborted fetus, a fetus in a trash can. These images are clearly intended to argue that the fetus is a complete human being, who should be protected by law. "New" legislative proposals promise to be substantially the same, except that there may be a heavier emphasis on the human qualities of the fetus. We can expect more bans on specific abortion procedures, more restrictions on abortions performed late in pregnancy and under the most tragic circumstances, and a call for congressional hearings on prenatal development. And none of these measures will diminish the need for abortion.

Abortion rights advocates have already begun to promote policies that will protect a woman's right to choose and at the same time reduce the incidence of abortion. The challenge for the pro-choice movement today is to reengage the many Americans who are ambivalent about abortion but who firmly believe the procedure should be safe, legal, and available in the United States. Pro-choice leaders must help foster the understanding that in addition to legal rights, the abortion decision involves duties, responsibilities, and complex moral considerations that women, not the government, must weigh for themselves and for their families. Only if women have the right and responsibility to make their own informed decisions about abortion will they have the ability to achieve full equality. An honest accounting of the moral complexities of abortion and what can be done to ensure that fewer women ever have to face the decision is what women need, what Americans want, and what a genuinely pro-choice movement can provide.

NOTES

1. Susan Harlan, Kathryn Kost, and Jacqueline Darroch Forrest, *Preventing Pregnancy, Protecting Health: A New Look at Birth Control Choices in the United States* (New York: Alan Guttmacher Institute, 1991), 21; Stanley K. Henshaw and Jennifer Van Vort, "Abortion Services in the United States, 1991 and 1992," *Family Planning Perspectives* 26, no. 3 (1994): 100; Centers for Disease Control and Prevention, "Teen Pregnancy and Birth Rates—United States, 1990," *Morbidity and Mortality Weekly Report* 42, no. 38 (1993): 733; National Commission to Prevent Infant Mortality, *Troubling Trends Persist: Shortchanging America's Next Generation* (Washington, D.C.: National Commission to Prevent Infant Mortality, 1992), 13; Centers for Disease Control and Prevention and National Center for Health Statistics, "Annual Summary of Birth, Marriages, Divorces, and Deaths: United States, 1992," *Monthly Vital Statistics Report* 41, no. 13 (1993): 7, 28.

2. "Abortion Rights and Real Choice," *Washington Post*, January 13, 1994, A26.

3. David J. Garrow, *Liberty and Sexuality: The Right to Privacy and the Making of Roe v. Wade* (New York: Macmillan, 1994), 271.

4. Laurence H. Tribe, *Abortion: The Clash of Absolutes* (New York: W. W. Norton, 1990), 36.

5. Richard Lamm, "Unwanted Child Births Forced by Law," *Denver Post*, February 2, 1969, G1, G5.

6. Colin Francome, *Abortion Freedom: A Worldwide Movement* (London: George Allen & Unwin, 1984), 108.

7. Garrow, *Liberty and Sexuality*, 603.

8. Ibid., 605.

9. Alice Hartle, "A Human Life Amendment," *National Right to Life News* 1, no.1 (1973): 8.

10. Hearing on S.J. Res. 119 and S.J. Res. 130, Subcommittee on Constitutional Amendments of the Senate Committee on the Judiciary, 93rd Cong., 2nd Sess. (1974), 13 (statement of Mildred Jefferson, chairman of the board of directors, NRLC).

11. Garrow, *Liberty and Sexuality*, 643–44; Tribe, *Abortion*, 164.

12. Victor G. Rosenblum and Thomas J. Marzen, "Strategies for Reversing *Roe v. Wade* through the Courts," in *Abortion and the Constitution: Reversing Roe v. Wade through the Courts*, ed. Dennis J. Horan, Edward R. Grant, and Paige C. Cunningham (Washington, D.C.: Georgetown University Press, 1987).

13. Ibid., 197.

14. Randall A. Terry, *Accessory to Murder: The Enemies, Allies, and Accomplices to the Death of Our Culture* (Brentwood, Tenn.: Wolgemuth & Hyatt, 1990), 224.

15. Stephen J. Hedges, David Bowermaster, and Susan Headden, "Abortion: Who's Behind the Violence?" *U.S. News and World Report*, November 14, 1994, 55.

16. Dallas A. Blanchard and Terry J. Prewitt, *Religious Violence and Abortion: The Gideon Project* (Gainesville: University Press of Florida, 1993), 270–71.

17. Ibid., 270.

18. Michael Kinsley, "TRB from Washington: The Wichita Case," *New Republic*, September 30, 1991, 4.

19. Brief for the United States as Amicus Curiae Supporting Petitioners, *Bray v. Alexandria Women's Health Clinic*, 113 S.Ct. 753 (1993) (No. 90–985); Kinsley, "TRB from Washington," 4.

20. Michael R. Hirsh, "Use of Force in Defense of Another: An Argument for Michael Griffin," 1993 (unpublished); Eric Lipton, "Law Review Cancels Abortion Article," *Washington Post*, August 23, 1994, B2.

21. Defensive Action Declarations (one dated 9/6/94, two undated; on file with NARAL); Fawn Vrazo, "A Small Chorus for Vigilantes," *Detroit Free Press*, January 19, 1995, 1F.

22. Larry Rohter, "Doctor Is Slain during Protest over Abortions," *New York Times*, March 11, 1993, A1, B10.

23. Cal Thomas, "Exploitation of the Clinic Killings: Pro Life Is Not Pro Death," *Washington Times*, January 16, 1995, A16.

24. National Abortion Federation, "Incidents of Violence and Disruption against Abortion Providers, 1995" (Washington, D.C.: National Abortion Federation, 1996).

25. Henshaw and Van Vort, "Abortion Services," 105; Stanley K. Henshaw and Jennifer Van Vort, eds., *Abortion Factbook, 1992 Edition: Readings, Trends, and State and Local Data to 1988* (New York: Alan Guttmacher Institute, 1992), table 11.

26. Henshaw and Van Vort, "Abortion Services," 103.

27. Ibid., 104; Sandra G. Boodman, "The Dearth of Abortion Doctors: Stigma, Low Pay and Lack of Personal Commitment Erode Ranks," *Washington Post*, April 20, 1993, Health sec., 7; Sandra G. Boodman, "A Firm Belief That 'What Goes Around Comes Around,'" *Washington Post*, April 8, 1993, A16.

28. Council on Scientific Affairs, American Medical Association, "Induced Termination of Pregnancy Before and After *Roe v Wade*: Trends in the Mortality and Morbidity of Women," *Journal of the American Medical Association* 268, no. 22 (1992): 3237.

29. *Webster v. Reproductive Health Services*, 109 S.Ct. 3040, 3079 (1989).

30. NARAL and the NARAL Foundation, *Who Decides? A State-by-State Review of Abortion Rights,1991* (Washington, D.C.: NARAL, 1991).

31. NARAL and the NARAL Foundation, *Who Decides? A State-by-State Review of Abortion Rights,1993* (Washington, D.C.: NARAL, 1993), iii.

32. Frances A. Althaus and Stanley K. Henshaw, "The Effects of Mandatory Delay Laws on Abortion Patients and Providers," *Family Planning Perspectives* 26, no. 5 (1994): 231.

33. Fawn Vrazo, "A Preview of Limited Abortion," *Philadelphia Inquirer*, September 14, 1992, A1, A6.

34. Barbara Hinkson Craig and David M. O'Brien, *Abortion and American Politics* (Chatham, N.J.: Chatham House, 1993), 325.

35. Rochelle Sharpe, "Abortion Law: Fatal Effect?" *Gannett News Service,* November 27, 1989.

36. National Abortion and Reproductive Rights Action League, "Leading Pro-Choice Group Adds Sexuality Education, Contraception and Prenatal Care to Its Agenda," January 12, 1994 (news release).

37. Elise F. Jones et al., *Teenage Pregnancy in Industrialized Countries* (New Haven: Yale University Press, 1986), 118–19, 207, 209–15.

38. NARAL and the NARAL Foundation, *Sexuality Education in America: A State-by-State Review, 1995* (Washington, D.C.: NARAL, 1995).

39. Bruce Cook, *Choosing the Best: Student Manual* (Atlanta: Choosing the Best, 1993), 11, 24–27; Bruce Cook, *Choosing the Best: Leaders Guide* (Atlanta: Choosing the Best, 1993), 17.

40. LeAnna Benn and Nancy Roach, *Sexuality, Commitment and Family: Teacher's Manual* (Spokane, Wash.: Teen Aid, 1989), 255.

41. National Abortion and Reproductive Rights Action League, "A Lifetime of Achievement under Assault: Surgeon General Nominee Dr. Henry Foster, Jr.'s Record on Reproductive Health" (Washington, D.C.: NARAL, 1995), 2.

42. Naomi Wolf, "Our Bodies, Our Souls," *New Republic,* October 16, 1995, 26, 33.

43. Robin West, "Taking Freedom Seriously," *Harvard Law Review* 104 (1990): 43, 84–85 (footnotes omitted).

44. Noemie Emery, "Abortion and the Republican Party: A New Approach," *Weekly Standard,* December 25, 1995, 26–27.

45. William J. Bennett, "Abortion and the Republican Party: Three Responses," *Weekly Standard,* January 1 and 8, 1996, 19–20.

46. George McKenna, "On Abortion: A Lincolnian Position," *Atlantic Monthly,* September 1995, 61.

5

Kathryn Kolbert and Andrea Miller

LEGAL STRATEGIES FOR ABORTION RIGHTS
IN THE TWENTY-FIRST CENTURY

Over the last two decades we have witnessed a widespread transformation of women's roles in American society, influenced in large part by
women's greater ability to control their reproductive lives. We have
made much progress in a historically short period of time, moving in a
few decades from the tragic days of back-alley abortions to an era of
safe pregnancy terminations and a related decrease in maternal mortality. Yet our progress has been marred by legislative, judicial, and medical setbacks, which have left some of the most vulnerable women in our
society without access to safe and affordable abortions. For this reason,
we approach the twenty-first century with the understanding that there
is much work to do to secure comprehensive, affordable reproductive
health care for all women. As activists who have dedicated significant
portions of our professional lives to promoting women's equality and
self-determination, we believe we must honestly review our movement's
past achievements and mistakes in order to develop a strategy for a
better future.

In 1973, in *Roe v. Wade*, the United States Supreme Court recognized
that the fundamental constitutional right to privacy encompasses a
woman's right to decide whether to terminate her pregnancy or carry it
to term. In legal terms, *Roe* meant that *women's* reproductive liberties
were judged for the first time under a "strict scrutiny standard"—the
highest level of constitutional protection, akin to that afforded other
fundamental rights, such as freedom of speech and freedom of religion.

Finding a need to balance a woman's right to privacy with the government's interest in protecting potential life, the Supreme Court established a trimester framework for evaluating restrictions on abortion. Under this scheme, federal courts were required to invalidate laws or regulations that interfered with a woman's abortion choice prior to fetal viability—unless a restriction could be shown actually to promote maternal health. After the point of viability, the government was free to ban abortion or take other steps to promote its interest in the protection of fetal life—so long as exceptions were provided to allow abortions when a woman's life or health was at stake.

Although a landmark ruling, *Roe* did not merely spring into existence. The decision was consistent with earlier Supreme Court rulings recognizing a right of privacy that protects intimate and personal decisions—including those affecting childrearing, marriage, procreation, and the use of contraception—from governmental interference.[1] In addition, the decade preceding *Roe* was marked by efforts in both the legislatures and the courts to reverse century-old criminal laws against abortion that resulted in scores of women dying or being maimed from unsafe, illegal, or self-induced pregnancy terminations. During the 1960s and 1970s, a wide range of medical, public health, legal, religious, and women's organizations successfully urged one-third of the state legislatures to liberalize their abortion statutes. At the same time, women's rights litigators challenged onerous abortion bans in a number of states, seeking to establish a constitutional right to choose abortion. Significantly, these attorneys sought to define the right as one belonging *exclusively* to women and one grounded in principles of equality, self-determination, bodily integrity, and privacy.

The Supreme Court's announcement in 1973 that it was striking down criminal abortion statutes from Georgia and Texas was appropriately hailed as a victory for women and a turning point for this nation.[2] Yet *Roe*'s recognition of reproductive decision making *solely* as an aspect of the right of privacy—and a right that is afforded a woman only *"in consultation with her physician"*—marked a diminution of the movement's own articulation of the freedoms at stake in the abortion debate. Rather than confront *Roe*'s limitations head-on in the courts or legislatures, women's rights attorneys pushed for stronger constitutional recognition of equality in other contexts; many activists who had struggled to decriminalize abortion concentrated their energies on the enactment of equal rights amendments at the federal and state levels. Others created health care institutions that could begin providing a full range of reproductive services in woman-centered settings. These feminist health centers joined other women's service organizations—domestic violence centers, rape crisis networks, and women's economic development groups—as a primary focus of the movement's energy.

In contrast, abortion opponents, particularly the Catholic hierarchy, worked with their already sophisticated lobbying arm to limit women's access to this medical care. Setting their sights first on the legislative arena, with an ultimate goal of reversing *Roe* either directly or indirectly, they convinced state and federal lawmakers to enact a wide range of restrictive abortion laws in the decade following the decision. Requirements that married women involve their husbands in their abortion choice, mandates that young women consult their parents in their abortion decisions, restrictions on abortion coverage in state Medicaid programs and state employee health plans, bans on the performance of abortions in public hospitals, mandatory delays or biased counseling requirements, and bans on particular abortion methods were adopted in many states. By 1976 Congress had passed the first Hyde Amendment, which banned the use of federal Medicaid dollars and other Department of Health, Education, and Welfare appropriations for almost all abortions; similar limitations on other federal spending measures— covering federal workers, military personnel, women on reservations, and inmates, among others—were enacted in following years.

Equally problematic, lawsuits challenging the constitutionality of these measures provided the Supreme Court with numerous opportunities to dilute the fundamental right secured by *Roe*. The justices rejected a number of abortion restrictions, particularly those that affected a broad base of women seeking these services: spousal consent, mandatory delays and biased counseling, hospitalization mandates, and restrictions on abortion methods and techniques.[3] Direct attacks on access to abortion for some of the most vulnerable women in our society, however, were more readily accepted by the Supreme Court. A string of cases beginning in the mid-1970s carved a large exception into *Roe*'s guarantees for young women.[4] Despite significant evidence demonstrating that young women are able to make mature and considered judgments about their reproductive health needs—and that parental involvement statutes have harmful effects—the Supreme Court found "that the constitutional rights of children cannot be equated with those of adults [because of] the peculiar vulnerability of children; their inability to make critical decisions in an informed, mature manner; and the importance of the parental role in child rearing."[5]

In another series of decisions early in the same period,[6] the Supreme Court held that the denial of Medicaid funding for abortion does not "interfere" with a low-income woman's right to make reproductive decisions. The reasoning—that an indigent woman "remains free" to exercise her rights with her own funds—turned a blind eye to the realities of poverty and the difficulties of finding physicians willing to make payment arrangements. These rulings effectively denied the protections of *Roe* to those women who cannot afford their own medical care. By 1991 the rationale behind these decisions had been extended to permit tight government control over the performance or advocacy of abortion wherever public funds or facilities are involved, affecting millions of Americans who depend on state governments or the federal government for their health care.[7]

In 1992 the Supreme Court was presented with a new opportunity to overrule or undermine *Roe*'s already limited fundamental rights approach to the abortion choice. Faced with a challenge to several restrictions enacted by the Pennsylvania legislature, the Supreme Court issued an extremely divided opinion that preserved what it deemed to be the central tenet of *Roe:* states are not free to ban pre-viability abortions or even post-viability pregnancy terminations necessary to protect a woman's life or health.[8] A majority also found unconstitutional a mandate that married women notify their husbands of their abortion choice. But most important, the justices used this case—*Planned Parenthood v. Casey*—to reject the strict-scrutiny standard of *Roe* and adopt a new, potentially less protective "undue-burden" standard that allows states to impose limitations on pre-viability abortions, so long as the measures do not have the "purpose or effect of placing a substantial obstacle in the path of a woman seeking an abortion."[9] The Supreme Court applied this two-part analysis to uphold a mandatory delay and biased counseling requirement that had previously been struck down under the *Roe* standard. This ruling marked the first time since *Roe* that the justices allowed infringements on the right to choose that directly affect *all* women seeking abortion services.

In some respects, the erosion of *Roe* was predictable. The well-orchestrated and well-financed political campaign to restrict abortion targeted first those women who are the most politically disenfranchised and thus the least able to protect their rights in the lawmaking process. The early reproductive rights movement was largely unprepared to respond to these threats; many activists believed that the judicial system would protect their newfound rights, and many were unable to relate to the plight of women affected by these measures. As a result, the movement failed to mount the sort of strong and visible political opposition to these retrenchments that has been displayed in more recent years. For example, it was not until 1989, when the Supreme Court in *Webster v. Reproductive Health Services* threatened to overturn *Roe* outright, that the women's movement orchestrated large-scale demonstrations in support of the right to choose abortion.

In addition, because *Roe* formulated the abortion choice as a *negative* right—the right to have the government leave you alone—rather than as an affirmative right—the right to have access to a health care choice central to a woman's equality and autonomy—the decision was vulnerable to attack from the more conservative wing of the Supreme Court and could not protect women from the legislative backlash. Sadly, what some in the movement failed to recognize early enough was that the old adage held true in the context of abortion rights: a threat to one is a threat to all. The legislative and judicial victories of abortion opponents in the 1970s and 1980s set the groundwork for undermining the reproductive rights of every woman in the 1990s. The Supreme Court's reasoning in the context of public funding was that constitutional protections for childbearing choices do not prevent the government from using its financial power to promote childbirth over abortion. It was not a difficult leap from that analysis to the justices' holdings more than a decade later in *Casey* that the right recognized in *Roe* did not keep a state from adopting laws, such as mandatory delays and biased counseling requirements, that express a preference for childbirth over abortion.

It is our hope that, in the future, the pro-choice movement will never forget that small but successive incursions on our liberties can, in the long term, be as damaging as a giant step backwards.[10] We must mobilize for the most disempowered women in society in order to fully guarantee reproductive freedom for all women. Moreover, we hope that in the next phase of the movement for procreative rights we will not limit ourselves simply to winning back what we have lost. Rather, we must commit ourselves to gaining a new "positive rights" articulation of *Roe*, grounded in self-determination and equality, which will not only provide a high level of constitutional protection for reproductive decision making but also enable women to make their choices a reality.

RESPONDING TO THREATS TO CONSTITUTIONAL
PROTECTIONS FOR THE RIGHT TO CHOOSE

In the wake of the Supreme Court's 1992 ruling, reproductive rights litigators are faced with two immediate and interconnected tasks if we are to safeguard women's lives and health and discourage additional limitations on the right to choose. We must urge federal courts to enforce the central tenets of *Roe* that were preserved by the Supreme Court and develop creative strategies to give "teeth" to the undue-burden standard.

Mandatory Delay and Biased Counseling Laws

In August 1992 Mississippi became the first state to enforce a mandatory delay and biased information requirement in the wake of the *Casey* ruling. By January 1996 similar measures were enforced in eleven states.[11] Challenges to these laws, some of which force a woman to schedule two appointments at a health clinic to obtain an abortion, have provided federal courts with the first opportunity to apply the Supreme Court's "undue-burden" test. Litigators have presented extensive evidence that a shortage of physicians forces many women to travel long distances to obtain the procedure and makes it necessary for most clinics to schedule abortion procedures only one or two days each week. Therefore, mandatory delays of only twenty-four hours may routinely result in actual delays of ten days to two weeks. While serving no health purpose, these requirements increase the cost of the procedure and force a woman to take extra time off from work, arrange child care, and remain away from home overnight or pay for another round-trip to the clinic.[12] For young women who must navigate complicated court procedures to avoid parental involvement in their abortion choice and for low-income women who have more difficulty raising money to pay for both the procedure and travel, the delays can be significantly longer. As expected, evidence collected from Mississippi and surrounding states makes clear that the mandatory delay has forced some women to substantially delay or even forgo the abortion procedure.[13] Moreover, Mississippi anti-choice activists have boasted that the two-trip mandate provides them with a chance to track women down and notify their families and neighbors in hopes of preventing them from choosing abortion.

Nonetheless, after several years of litigation, the contours of the undue-burden standard remain largely undefined. A couple of federal courts have blocked enforcement of mandatory delay and biased counseling laws,[14] but more of them have upheld all or part of the measures that they have reviewed.[15] Meanwhile, the Supreme Court has yet to shed further light on its holdings in *Casey* concerning these types of abortion restrictions. (Cases challenging mandatory delay and biased counseling laws in state court, which rely on state constitutional protections and not the federal undue-burden standard, have also met with mixed success.)[16] Because it is difficult to assess whether a challenge to a mandatory delay and biased counseling law will succeed, physicians and attorneys have instead pressed attorney generals and courts in some states to interpret the statutes in a way that alleviates their most onerous aspects—the two-trip requirements and clearly biased data. Not surprisingly, anti-choice legislators have responded by insisting that the laws require two visits with a health care provider and information expressly discouraging abortion. As a result, courts will undoubtedly have to address whether the harsh effects of such statutes constitute an "undue burden." Perhaps the best that litigators can do is develop detailed factual records of the laws' harms in hopes that courts—federal or state—will heed this evidence.

Bans on Methods of Abortion

Since 1992, federal and state courts have repeatedly invalidated statutes and initiatives that sought to criminalize virtually all abortions, and the Supreme Court has refused to review these cases[17]—a signal that the *Casey* plurality remains intact. Determined to find a way to strike at the heart of the right to choose, even if they cannot overrule *Roe* and outlaw abortion, anti-choice legislators are now attempting to ban certain methods of second-trimester and post-viability abortion. Attacks on these procedures, which represent a tiny fraction of pregnancy terminations, take their greatest toll on women with wanted pregnancies who discover very late that their fetus is suffering from severe or fatal anomalies or that their own health is threatened. Recently, statutes have been drafted specifically to restrict these later abortions—without providing exceptions to preserve a woman's life or health. Abortion opponents hope to use such laws to force courts to revisit the Supreme Court's long-standing precedent that physicians, not legislators, must determine when an abortion is necessary. The goal of this new anti-choice strategy

is to get courts to give the government greater latitude to define *health*—
thereby limiting doctors' discretion and restricting women's choices.
Bans on specific methods of abortion and restrictions on later abortions
also allow avowedly anti-choice legislators to focus public attention on
the alleged "cruelty" of the procedure—which is depicted in graphic
and inflammatory detail. Lawmakers who support a limited right to
choose abortion may mistakenly see these legislative battles as cover—
a chance to appease anti-choice constituencies while claiming to pro-
choice voters that they are pro-choice because they do not believe all or
most abortions should be illegal.

In 1995 Ohio became the first state to ban what it deemed dilation
and extraction (D&X) abortions—a modified version of the dilation
and evacuation (D&E) procedure—performed primarily after the twentieth week of pregnancy. The Ohio statute also outlawed post-viability
abortions, without making adequate exceptions when the woman's life
or health is at stake, and placed numerous restrictions on the few procedures that remained legal. As of early 1997, that law had yet to take
effect, thanks to a federal district-court ruling. In a carefully worded
and detailed opinion, which utilizes the "undue-burden" test, the judge
found that a state may not ban a method of abortion that is necessary
to protect women's health. Moreover, the court reaffirmed that doctors
must be free to determine the patient's health needs in light of all factors, including her medical and psychological condition, her life circumstances, and the condition of the fetus.[18]

Unfortunately, the Ohio legislation was only the beginning. By the
end of 1995 both houses of Congress had taken the unprecedented step
of passing—for the first time in our history—a bill that criminalizes the
performance of an abortion method. Although not using a medically
recognized term, the legislation is aimed at the D&X technique but is
so vaguely worded that it could also ban some D&E procedures, the
most common form of second-trimester abortion. (The bill's sponsors
dubbed the procedure "partial-birth" abortion to score political points.)
As expected, President Clinton vetoed the measure in the spring of 1996,
and that fall the 104th Congress failed to override his veto, by a very slim
margin. Far from ending the issue, the veto led to reintroduction of the
bill in the 105th Congress and fueled similar actions in at least half the
state legislatures within the first few months of 1997. Should this type
of legislation gain momentum, anti-choice lawmakers will undoubtedly
move to outlaw additional abortion methods that will affect greater and

greater numbers of women who need this reproductive health care service. This danger is also evident in the strident response of abortion foes to breakthroughs in reproductive health care heralded by the development of nonsurgical abortion methods, which could give women additional choices for how and where to terminate a pregnancy. Future litigation may be necessary to ensure access to these new methods.

REGAINING GROUND LOST IN THE FEDERAL COURTS

Near-Bans on Abortion Coverage for
Low-Income Women

Litigators cannot ignore the damage caused by the U.S. Supreme Court's decisions on public funding for abortions, the devastating effects on both the health and well-being of low-income women and the development of federal and state case law. In theory, with a change in justices, it would seem most efficient to reverse these rulings at their source—the Supreme Court—by filing a new suit against the Hyde Amendment or a similar measure. However, such a strategy seems foolhardy in the wake of the justices' firm adherence in *Casey* to *stare decisis*—sticking to precedent—as one of the principal reasons for maintaining the core holdings in *Roe*. *Stare decisis* would argue against overturning previous decisions that found restrictions on abortion funding constitutional. Future cases may, however, limit the reach of these restrictions or undermine the rationale behind the Court's decision.

To make a difference now, attorneys must choose a more time-intensive route—state-by-state litigation—focusing first where state constitutions have been interpreted to provide strong protections for privacy rights and state courts have proven their independence from federal precedent. This effort, which takes advantage of the way our federalist system allows states to grant greater—but never lesser—rights than the federal government, is already proving successful. As of this writing, seventeen states provide Medicaid funding for low-income women's abortions for health reasons.[19] A dozen of these states are doing so under court rulings, most of which established privacy rights broader than those guaranteed in federal law.[20] And, because more than 45 percent of the Medicaid-eligible women in the nation reside in these seventeen states, successful litigation in just under one-fourth of the states has significantly increased access to abortion services.[21]

Finally, litigators must be on the lookout for creative strategies to nullify funding restrictions even if they do not reverse damaging Supreme Court precedent. For example, in October 1993, advocates for low-income women were given a new opportunity to challenge state Medicaid restrictions in federal court when Congress expanded the list of exceptions to the Hyde Amendment to allow federal funding for abortions in cases of rape and incest as well as cases of life endangerment. Because the federal Medicaid statute and federal case law require states participating in the program to cover all abortions for which federal funds are provided, a dozen states left themselves open to successful court challenges by refusing to cover abortions in cases of rape and incest or imposing onerous reporting requirements. In addition to gaining coverage for rape and incest survivors,[22] these cases had the potential to invalidate state Medicaid restrictions altogether.[23]

Restrictions on Young Women's Access to Abortion

As is true with the Supreme Court rulings on public funding, litigators must counter a Supreme Court precedent that limits the exercise of young women's reproductive rights. In case after case, the justices have given states the go-ahead to enact laws mandating the consent or notification of one or both parents prior to a young woman's abortion.[24] As of January 1997, parental involvement laws were in effect in twenty-eight of the thirty-seven states in which they had been adopted.[25] Again, the principle of *stare decisis* makes it virtually impossible to reverse the ruling that such restrictions do not violate young women's privacy rights under the federal Constitution—unless the membership of the Supreme Court changes significantly. The justices have left some room for federal court challenges to parental involvement laws—but only when legislators fail to fully understand the judicial limits placed on them: the Supreme Court held that states cannot grant parents an *absolute* veto power over their daughter's abortion choice. Parental involvement laws must provide for a confidential and expeditious "alternative"—usually a court hearing—so that a young woman can demonstrate that she is mature enough to choose to terminate her pregnancy without involving her parents or that an abortion is otherwise in her best interests. Thus, challenges to state laws lacking such protections are often successful.[26] They do not, however, recapture federal constitutional protection for young women's reproductive choices.

To secure the rights of young women forsaken by *Roe*'s progeny, it is again necessary to work through state courts. States whose courts have already ruled favorably on public funding may well be the place to begin. For example, courts in both California and Florida have already invalidated parental involvement requirements as violations of state constitutional rights of privacy.[27] If such cases are successfully replicated, young women would again be guaranteed privacy and autonomy and thereby helped to safeguard their lives and health.

Limitations on Who Can Perform Abortion

Roe announced, without explanation, that states may require all abortions to be performed by a licensed physician. Only two years later, the Supreme Court upheld the conviction of a nonphysician, asserting that abortion is only as safe as childbirth if performed by a doctor.[28] Since that time, the availability of physicians performing abortions has dramatically declined, leaving 84 percent of the counties in this nation without an abortion provider. In rural areas, where hospital abortions have declined by 78 percent, physicians performing abortions are even scarcer. Moreover, fewer than 12 percent of medical schools mandate the teaching of abortion as part of gynecological/obstetrical practice at a time when many current abortion providers are reaching retirement age. Late abortions are the least accessible, with only a small number of U.S. physicians performing them. Without doubt, a constitutional right that refers to a woman "in consultation with her physician" will become meaningless if there are no physicians willing and able to provide these critical health services.

In the coming years, litigation must be undertaken to address the physician shortage and ensure that nonphysician medical personnel—such as certified nurse-midwives, physicians' assistants, and nurse-practitioners certified in reproductive health—are able to perform early abortions in freestanding clinics. Data from Vermont have demonstrated that physicians' assistants, for example, perform these procedures as safely as physicians. Recent litigation in Montana shows that some courts may be receptive to challenges to state laws mandating that only physicians may provide this health care.[29] Similarly, attorneys can be instrumental in administrative and legislative reform efforts aimed at permitting nonphysician personnel to perform abortions when they are appropriately qualified.

ADDRESSING THE GROWING CRISIS OF
REPRODUCTIVE HEALTH CARE DELIVERY

Violence and Harassment Aimed at
Women's Health Care Providers

Across the nation, abortion opponents continue to wage a campaign of terror aimed at individuals and facilities that provide abortion services, thereby exacerbating the shortage of physicians performing abortions and the difficulty of obtaining this medical care. Since 1977, there have been more than six thousand clinic blockades and invasions, thousands of acts of violence against abortion providers, more than two hundred attempted or completed acts of arson or firebombings at abortion-related medical facilities, and hundreds of death threats. Physicians and clinic staff have been shot or suffered other serious injuries. From 1993 to 1994, two physicians, two clinic receptionists, and a volunteer security worker were murdered, marking an escalation in both the level of danger facing those who provide abortions and the rhetoric of those committed to ending this health care service.

In response, Congress passed the Freedom of Access to Clinic Entrances Act (FACE) in 1993, making it a federal crime to use force or the threat of force to injure, intimidate, or interfere with reproductive health care providers or women seeking their services.[30] Vigorous enforcement of FACE and defense of the statute's constitutionality are essential to ensure federal assistance against blockades and harassment. The Justice Department has already filed a number of civil and criminal suits for FACE violations, and federal courts have repeatedly found that the law does not infringe on the constitutional rights of abortion opponents.[31] Moreover, in selected circumstances, other legal remedies, such as the federal anti-racketeering law[32] or the federal civil rights statute,[33] may be the best way to stop harassment and intimidation against abortion providers. Cases relying on recently passed state laws barring blockades and creating protective zones around women's health clinics or actions filed under trespass and tort theories can also provide critical injunctive relief and damages to embattled health care providers. Local strategies aimed at specific perpetrators may also need to be further developed, for effective deterrents will vary from opponent to opponent. Most important, if litigation is undertaken, attorneys must be willing to follow through—filing repeated motions for contempt when an injunction is violated and executing financial judgments once courts have ruled. Otherwise, legal remedies are no deterrent to those set on preventing women from obtaining abortions.

Changes in Health Care Delivery

Although health care reform efforts in Congress and most states have collapsed, a revolution is taking place within our nation's health care institutions. Some estimate that the majority of Americans will be covered by managed-care arrangements by the year 2000. A host of reproductive health issues are already being raised as hospitals merge, health care providers form alliances, and managed-care programs expand. Some providers have already forsaken their responsibility to provide the full range of reproductive health care, even though access to such services actually reduces overall medical costs. Particularly as Catholic health institutions merge with non-Catholic hospitals or public facilities are sold, women's services—ranging from abortion and contraception to voluntary sterilization and assisted reproduction—are likely to be abandoned. Creative litigation to address these issues must begin to place an obligation on the government to protect consumers as larger consolidations threaten to leave women without necessary health services. Education about these efforts is also critical. Recently, public outcry has prevented the loss of reproductive health services or forced providers to make arrangements to accommodate women's medical needs. In addition to litigation and public education, new legal protections may also prove an important safeguard against this new threat.

In the long run, any litigation strategy must be combined with strong legislative and political advocacy at the state and federal level. The more we are able to demonstrate the harsh effects of restrictive laws and policies and defeat them in the legislative process, the more energy we'll have to challenge the restrictions already on the books. To achieve our ultimate goals in the courts, we must work now to create the broadest and most protective vision of reproductive rights so that women may make and effectuate these decisions free of governmental interference. Only then, as the Court recognized in *Casey*, will women be able "to participate equally in the economic and social life of this Nation." [34]

NOTES

1. See *Meyer v. Nebraska*, 262 U.S. 390 (1923); *Pierce v. Society of Sisters*, 268 U.S. 510 (1925); *Skinner v. Oklahoma ex rel. Williamson*, 316 U.S. 535 (1942); *Loving v. Virginia*, 388 U.S. 1 (1967); *Eisenstadt v. Baird*, 405 U.S. 438 (1972); *Griswold v. Connecticut*, 381 U.S. 479 (1975).

2. *Roe v. Wade*, 410 U.S. 113 (1973); *Doe v. Bolton*, 410 U.S. 179 (1973).

3. See, for example, *Planned Parenthood v. Danforth*, 428 U.S. 52 (1976); *Colautti v. Franklin*, 439 U.S. 379 (1979); *City of Akron v. Akron Center for Reproductive Health*, 462 U.S. 416 (1983); and *Thornburgh v. American College of Obstetricians and Gynecologists*, 476 U.S. 747 (1986).

4. *Bellotti v. Baird*, 428 U.S. 132 (1976); *Bellotti v. Baird*, 443 U.S. 622 (1979); *H.L. v. Matheson*, 450 U.S. 4398 (1981); *Hodgson v. Minnesota*, 497 U.S. 417 (1990); and *Ohio v. Akron Center for Reproductive Health*, 497 U.S. 502 (1990).

5. *Bellotti v. Baird*, 443 U.S. at 634.

6. *Maher v. Roe*, 432 U.S. 464 (1977); *Beal v. Doe*, 432 U.S. 438 (1977); *Poelker v. Doe*, 432 U.S. 519 (1977); *Harris v. McRae*, 448 U.S. 297 (1980).

7. *Webster v. Reproductive Health Services*, 492 U.S. 490 (1989); *Rust v. Sullivan*, 111 S. Ct. 1759 (1991).

8. *Planned Parenthood v. Casey*, 112 S. Ct. 2791 (1992).

9. Ibid., at 2820.

10. Indeed, some might argue, these small steps back are worse than total losses because it is more difficult to mount political opposition when the loss appears minor or only a small number of women are affected.

11. Idaho, Kansas, Louisiana, Mississippi, Nebraska, North Dakota, Ohio, Pennsylvania, South Carolina, South Dakota, and Utah.

12. The records in these cases also demonstrate that requirements that only a physician may provide specific information to every woman are not as innocuous as they seem. With threats of criminal penalties or license revocation, these laws compel doctors to provide all the information to all women, all the time— even when a physician believes that the particular information will be harmful to a patient or might force the doctor to violate professional ethics. Clearly, there is no health purpose in informing an incest survivor that she can sue her abusive father for child support, or raising an expectation for benefits that a woman may be unable to collect. And the "doctor-only" counseling provisions not only increase the cost of abortion, they prohibit doctors from delegating appropriate tasks to trained health professionals, making it more difficult to provide quality counseling services and reducing the medical services available to women.

13. According to data compiled by the Alan Guttmacher Institute, the number of Mississippi women obtaining abortions was 13 percent lower than expected during the five months following implementation of the law. The mandatory delay also resulted in an 18 percent increase in the proportion of abortions performed in the second trimester of pregnancy.

14. *A Woman's Choice–East Side Women's Clinic v. Newman*, No. IP 95–1148-CH/G (S.D. Ind. November 9, 1995); *Northland Family Planning, Inc. v. Engler*, No. 94-CV-40089 (E.D. Mich. March 22, 1994).

15. *Planned Parenthood, Sioux Falls Clinic v. Miller,* 63 F.3d 1452 (8th Cir. 1995); *Fargo Women's Health Organization v. Schafer,* 18 F.3d 526 (8th Cir. 1994); *Barnes v. Moore,* 970 F.2d 12 (5th Cir. 1992); *Utah Women's Clinic v. Leavitt,* 844 F. Supp. 1482 (D. Utah 1994).

16. State courts in three states have blocked enforcement of such laws—see *Planned Parenthood of Missoula v. Montana,* No. BDV-95-722 (Mont. Dist. Ct. November 28, 1995), *Mahaffey v. Attorney General of Michigan,* No. 94-406793AZ (Mich. Cir. Ct. July 15, 1994), and *Planned Parenthood Association of Nashville v. McWherter,* No. 92C-1672 (Tenn. Cir. Ct. June 24, 1994)— while those in two others have upheld them—see *Preterm Cleveland v. Voinovich,* 89 Ohio App. 3d 684 (Ohio 1993) and *Pro-Choice Mississippi v. Fordice,* No. G-94-374 (Miss. Ch. Ct. August 18, 1994).

17. See, for example, *Sojourner T. v. Edwards,* 974 F.2d 27 (5th Cir. 1992), *cert. denied,* 113 S. Ct. 1414 (1993); *In re Initiative Petition No. 349,* 838 P.2d 1 (Okla. 1992), *cert. denied,* 113 S. Ct. 1028 (1993); *Guam Society of Obstetricians & Gynecologists v. Ada,* 962 F.2d 1366 (9th Cir. 1992), *cert. denied,* 113 S. Ct. 633 (1992); and *Jane L. v. Bangerter,* 61 F.3d 1493 (10th Cir. 1995).

18. *Women's Medical Professional Corporation v. Voinovich,* No. C3-95-414 (S.D. Ohio December 13, 1995).

19. Alaska, California, Connecticut, Hawaii, Idaho, Illinois, Maryland, Massachusetts, Minnesota, Montana, New Jersey, New Mexico, New York, Oregon, Vermont, Washington, and West Virginia.

20. *Women of the State of Minnesota v. Gomez,* CX-94-1442 (Minn. December 15, 1995); *Women's Health Center of West Virginia v. Panepinto,* No. 21924, 21925 (W.V. December 17, 1993); *Planned Parenthood v. Department of Human Resources,* 663 P.2d 1247 (Or. Ct. App. 1983), *aff'd on other grounds,* 687 P.2d 785 (Or. 1984); *Right to Choose v. Byrne,* 450 A.2d 925 (N.J. 1982); *Committee to Defend Reproductive Rights v. Myers,* 625 P.2d 779 (Cal. 1981); *Moe v. Secretary of Administration and Finance,* 417 N.E.2d 384 (Mass. 1981); *New Mexico Right to Choose v. Danfelser,* No. SF-95-867(C) (N.M. Dist. Ct. July 26, 1995); *Jeannette R. v. Ellery,* No. BDV-94-811 (Mont. Dist. Ct. May 1995); *Doe v. Wright,* No. 91 CH 1958 (Ill. December 2, 1994); *Roe v. Harris,* No. 96977 (Idaho Dist. Ct. February 1, 1994); *Doe v. Celani,* No. S81-84CnC (Vt. Super. Ct. May 26, 1986); and *Doe v. Maher,* 515 A.2d 134 (Conn. Super. 1986).

21. As the federal government moves to use block grants for Medicaid dollars, state laws allocating health dollars will need to be revised, giving advocates a new opportunity to ensure access to the full range of health services, including abortion for all women, in both the legislatures and the courts.

22. *Hern v. Beye,* 57 F.3d 906 (10th Cir. 1995), *cert. denied,* 64 U.S.L.W. 3397 (U.S. December 4, 1995); *Hope Medical Group for Women v. Edwards,* 63 F.3d 418 (5th Cir. 1995); *Elizabeth Blackwell Health Center for Women v. Knoll,* 61 F.3d 170 (3d Cir. 1995); *Orr v. Nelson,* No. 4:CV94-3252 (D. Neb. November 4, 1994), *aff'd sub nom. Little Rock Family Planning Services, P.A. v. Dalton,* No. 95-1555 (8th Cir. October 4, 1995); *Utah Women's Clinic, Inc. v. Graham,* 892 F. Supp. 1379 (D. Utah 1995); *Hope v. Childers,* No. 3:95CV-

518-S (W.D. Ky. July 28, 1995); *Fargo Women's Health Organization Inc. v. Wessman,* No. A3–94–36 (D.N.D. March 15, 1995); *Stangler v. Shalala,* No. 94–4221-CV-C-5 (W.D. Mo. December 28, 1994); *Planned Parenthood v. Wright,* No. 94 C 6886 (N.D. Ill. December 6, 1994); *Planned Parenthood Affiliates of Michigan v. Engler,* 860 F. Supp. 406 (W.D. Mich. 1994); and *Planned Parenthood of Missoula Inc. v. Blouke,* 858 F. Supp. 137 (D. Mont. 1994).

23. See, for example, *Little Rock Family Planning Services, P.A. v. Dalton,* 860 F. Supp. 609 (E.D. Ark. 1994), *aff'd,* No. 95–1555 (8th Cir. October 4, 1995).

24. Evidence developed in cases seeking to strike down these laws has shown that, rather than promote family communication, forced parental involvement exposes young women to increased violence and parental rejection and significantly impedes a young woman's ability to obtain abortions. Statistics from states such as Mississippi and Pennsylvania clearly show that the numbers of young women obtaining abortions dropped in the wake of implementation of parental involvement laws. Although many young women obtained abortions in neighboring states, others were unable to obtain these services.

25. Alabama, Arkansas, Delaware, Georgia, Idaho, Indiana, Kansas, Kentucky, Louisiana, Maine, Maryland, Massachusetts, Michigan, Minnesota, Mississippi, Missouri, Nebraska, North Carolina, North Dakota, Ohio, Pennsylvania, Rhode Island, South Carolina, Tennessee, Utah, West Virginia, Wisconsin, and Wyoming.

26. See, for example, *Planned Parenthood, Sioux Falls Clinic v. Miller,* 63 F.3d 1452 (8th Cir. 1995) and *Causeway Medical Suite v. Ieyoub,* No. 95–2164 (E.D. La. October 24, 1995).

27. *American Academy of Pediatrics v. Lungren,* 882 P.2d 247 (Cal. App. 1994) and *In re T.W.,* 551 So. 2d 1186 (Fla. 1989).

28. *Menillo v. Connecticut,* 423 U.S. 8 (1975).

29. *Doe v. Esch,* No. CV-93–060-GF-PGH (D. Mont. November 26, 1995); but see *Armstrong v. Mazurek,* No. CV-95–083-GF (D. Mont. September 29, 1995).

30. 18 U.S.C. § 248.

31. *American Life League, Inc. v. Reno,* 47 F.3d 642 (4th Cir. 1995); *Cheffer v. Reno,* 55 F.3d 1517 (11th Cir. 1995); *United States v. Wilson,* No. 95–1871 (7th Cir. December 29, 1995); *United States v. Dinwiddie,* 885 F. Supp. 1299 (W.D. Mo. 1995); *United States v. Hill,* 893 F. Supp. 1034 (N.D. Fla. 1994); *Reily v. Reno,* 860 F. Supp. 693 (D. Ariz. 1994); *Cook v. Reno,* 859 F. Supp. 1008 (W.D. La. 1994); *Council for Life Coalition v. Reno,* 856 F. Supp. 1422 (S.D. Cal. 1994); *United States v. White,* 893 F. Supp. 1423 (C.D. Cal. 1995); *United States v. Lucero,* 895 F. Supp. 1421 (D. Kan. 1995); *United States v. McMillan,* No. 3:95-CV-633WS (S.D. Miss. November 24, 1995).

32. 18 U.S.C. § 1961.

33. 42 U.S.C. § 1985(3).

34. *Planned Parenthood v. Casey,* 112 S. Ct. 2791, 2809 (1992).

6

■

William Saletan

ELECTORAL POLITICS AND ABORTION

Narrowing the Message

People who care about abortion rights tend to be drawn to the issue's personal dimensions: the predicament of the pregnant woman, the difficulty of finding an abortion facility, the threat of harassment and violence, and the physical and emotional experience of abortion. Media coverage of the debate tends to focus on confrontations between opposing activists at rallies and clinics, since these make exciting television. Perhaps these factors explain why so little attention has been paid to the issue's least personal and perhaps most consequential dimension: mass communication and political persuasion.

Around the time of the 1986 Supreme Court case *Thornburgh v. American College of Obstetricians and Gynecologists,* the nature of the American war over abortion began to change. In *Thornburgh,* the Court came within a single vote of overturning *Roe v. Wade.* The erosion of *Roe* by conservative Supreme Court appointments underscored a more general encroachment of right-to-life politics on judicially protected abortion rights, most notably through statewide ballot measures that sought to change not just abortion policies but state constitutions as well. Pro-choice activists knew that if *Roe* collapsed, this political erosion would have to be stopped. They had to learn to defend the territory of abortion rights, not with the nuances of legal argument, but with the blunt weapons of electoral politics.

Toward that end, in 1986 a circle of pro-choice strategists began to develop what might be called a conservative message strategy. It was a message strategy in that it focused more on conveying a persuasive message through the mass media than on arguing in the courts, confronting right-to-life activists in the streets, or turning out loyal pro-choice voters. It was conservative in that the voters and politicians it aimed to persuade were more conservative than the feminists and civil libertarians on whom the movement usually relied.

In the perilous years between *Webster v. Reproductive Health Services* in 1989 and *Planned Parenthood v. Casey* in 1992, when the right to abortion was most vulnerable to political assault, this strategy played a crucial role in turning the tide of abortion politics. It consolidated public anxiety about banning abortion. It chilled the enthusiasm of politicians who had vowed to outlaw the procedure. It emboldened pro-choice Democratic politicians by showing them how they could use the issue to capture the votes of independents and moderate Republicans. Ultimately, it rescued the legal right to abortion from decimation at the hands of governors and state lawmakers.

But the rescue came at a price. Only the legal right to abortion was saved. Parental involvement laws, prohibitions on public funding, and other abortion restrictions have overrun the nation. The conservative message strategy has failed to stop these restrictions, for the simplest of reasons: its message does not contradict them. In fact, its message can be—and indeed has been—construed to encourage them. If the abortion rights movement intends to move beyond its defense of abortion's legality—if it intends to demand not just privacy but public access and equality—it can no longer rely on the old message.

To understand this period of the abortion war, one must first understand that average people—the people whose voting decisions determine election results—differ in their reasons for favoring or opposing abortion rights, even when they agree on the same conclusion. Some who favor abortion rights care primarily about the autonomy of women. Others care primarily about poverty and the tragedies attending unwanted motherhood. Others care more about curbing the power of the church. Still others care more about restraining the reach of the government. Among those who oppose abortion rights, some are driven by a commitment to protect unborn life. Others see the issue more as a matter of accepting the consequences of sexual intercourse. Still others believe the primary objective is to preserve the traditional family. These motives overlap and coexist in each person. Nevertheless, they are distinct.

For the past decade, the most important battles of the abortion war have been fought among these factions, not with the tools of law, medicine, or terrorism, but with those of political rhetoric. Every day, in Congress, in the courts, and in states and communities, the various factions try to engage each other in political alliances. To succeed, they must grasp how others see the issue and in what ways these other perspectives connect with their own. It is a war of imagination and persuasion, and the stakes are enormous. Since no single perspective commands a majority, the political fate of abortion hangs on this struggle for alliances, this war of ideas.

In the years following *Thornburgh,* a number of pro-choice political strategists, most of them affiliated with the National Abortion Rights Action League (NARAL), forged a decisive alliance in this war. They developed a message persuasive to voters who did not share their deep concerns about women's rights and untimely motherhood. Instead of focusing on women's rights, the strategists learned to criticize abortion restrictions as an encroachment by big government on tradition, family, and property. When the issue was framed this way, many voters with conservative sympathies turned against the right-to-life movement. And with them, the political balance of power turned in favor of abortion rights.

From the beginning, this alliance was unstable. Only on the question of abortion's legality did voters who cared primarily about protecting traditional private institutions from big government agree with activists who cared primarily about women's rights and poverty. When it came to further questions of abortion policy—whether the government should spend tax money on poor women's abortions, or whether teenage girls should have to secure their parents' permission to get abortions—the alliance fell apart. Voters who cared primarily about tradition, family, and property abandoned advocates of poor women and teenage girls, leaving those advocates in the minority.

Many people think that the political struggle over abortion has been resolved and that those who advocate women's rights won. That conclusion is a mistake. The people who hold the balance of power in the abortion debate are those who favor tradition, family, and property. The philosophy that has prevailed—in favor of legal abortion, in favor of parents' authority over their children's abortions, against spending tax money for abortions—is their philosophy. People who believe that teenage girls have a right to abortion without parental consent, or that poor women have a right to abortion at public expense, have largely been defeated. Liberals have not won the struggle for abortion rights. Conservatives have.

Political strategies are born of necessity. The predicament that propelled conservative message politics to the forefront of the abortion war crystallized in Arkansas in 1986, during the tenure of Governor Bill Clinton. Arkansas was then the most vulnerable of several states targeted by right-to-life groups for the abolition of state-funded abortions through referenda. There were not enough liberal and feminist voters in the state to defeat the ballot measure. Clinton, evasive as usual, refused to take a position on it. Pro-choice activists saw that their only hope was to win over moderate and conservative swing voters. They hired a national campaign pollster to figure out how.

Many strategists and politicians have contributed to the conservative message strategy over the years. But there are four in particular without whom that strategy might never have arisen, spread, or changed history as it has. The first is Brownie Ledbetter, the woman who orchestrated the campaign against the 1986 Arkansas ballot measure. The second is Harrison Hickman, the pollster Ledbetter hired to find a way to sell abortion rights to a conservative electorate. The third is Kate Michelman, who as executive director of NARAL gave Hickman the institutional support to refine and nationalize the Arkansas strategy. The fourth is Doug Wilder, the Virginia lieutenant governor who, by wagering his career on that strategy, shattered the conventional wisdom that abortion rights was a losing issue in statewide elections.

The important point is that in 1986 people who understood and appreciated mainstream electoral politics began to take charge of the rhetorical direction of the abortion rights movement. This is not to say that such understanding was utterly lacking prior to 1986. Many pre-*Roe* advocates of legal abortion were meticulously mainstream. But in the 1970s burgeoning feminist and egalitarian movements outstripped the electorate's tolerance for change. To broaden their support, abortion rights advocates had to fall back on more conservative themes.

In the early 1980s, therefore, a few pro-choice strategists began to explore an aggressively anti-government rather than pro-woman message. That exploration finally produced demonstrable success in Arkansas in 1986. In surveys of swing voters in that state, Hickman ascertained that though these voters did not share conventional pro-choice concerns about women's rights and the welfare of teenagers and the poor, they were willing to reject the anti-abortion ballot measure on other grounds. They disliked big government. They treasured the sovereignty of families, as opposed to women or girls. And they saw abortion as a privilege reserved for rape victims, not as a right retained by women who indulged in sex willingly. By appealing to these concerns rather than to liberal or feminist principles, pro-choice activists could attract enough moderate and conservative support to win the election. And they proceeded to do just that.

Eight months after engineering the pro-choice victory in Arkansas, Hickman was hired by Michelman at NARAL to apply his strategic talents to the campaign against Judge Robert Bork's nomination to the U.S. Supreme Court. Hickman's research into the attitudes of Alabama voters confirmed the lesson of Arkansas: abortion rights, presented in the context of a defense of traditional private institutions against big government, could appeal to conservative southerners in the campaign against Bork. This "privacy" issue became, in effect, the right wing of the otherwise liberal anti-Bork coalition. It enabled the coalition to attract supporters who were indifferent or even hostile to the coalition's liberal concerns, such as enforced racial equality.

From 1988 to 1989 NARAL refined the lessons of the Bork campaign and additional public opinion research into a long-term national political strategy. Its object was to fold pro-family, anti-government voters into the pro-choice electoral coalition. In 1988, in the early stages of the development of this strategy, NARAL recommended it to Democratic presidential nominee Michael Dukakis. He adopted the recommended language when forced to discuss abortion, but he declined to use the issue aggressively against his right-to-life opponent, Vice President George Bush.

Immediately after Bush's election, a warning tremor shook the judicial foundations of the abortion conflict. The Supreme Court, egged on by the Reagan Justice Department, announced that it would hear *Webster v. Reproductive Health Services,* an abortion case that presented the best opportunity yet to overturn *Roe.* NARAL not only anticipated defeat in *Webster* but, more important, foresaw that this judicial defeat presented a political opportunity. By overtly stripping abortion rights of judicial protection, the Court would force politicians and voters to confront the issue directly. In that moment, people's basic assumptions on how to think about abortion policy would be open to change. NARAL resolved to seize that opportunity.

With Hickman's guidance, Michelman rounded up a team of

pollsters, wordsmiths, and media consultants to plan and execute a political campaign. Their mission was to frame the issue in such a way
that mainstream America would rally to the defense of abortion rights.
The campaign began with focus groups in which Hickman listened to
mainstream voters, tested various lines of argument, and selected those
lines that proved most persuasive to the participants. Based on his findings, other consultants drew up a thematic communications strategy
and ultimately a series of television commercials. They distilled the pro-
choice message to five words: "Who Decides—You or Them?"

The value of this slogan was that, like the "privacy" slogan used
against Robert Bork in 1987, it could be interpreted in many ways. For
example, voters could agree that "you" should be in charge of abortion
decisions, without agreeing on whether "you" meant women or families, teenagers or parents. In particular, voters with conservative in-
stincts who shied away from the outright prohibition of immoral behavior could embrace NARAL's new message as a rejection of big
government. In the minds of these voters, "them" meant nosy, corrupt
politicians and bureaucrats; "you" meant families and communities.
With the addition of this constituency, NARAL had at last assembled a
plausible majority coalition, a coalition that could control elections.

On July 3, 1989, the subterranean tension that had been building
since *Thornburgh* erupted in a judicial earthquake. In its decision in
Webster, the Supreme Court returned to the states much of their pre-
Roe power to restrict abortions and invited them to demand the rest.
Shock waves rolled across the American political landscape. Thanks to
their preparations over the preceding three years, pro-choice forces
were ready to fight and win in the new environment. In Virginia and
New Jersey, the two states that held gubernatorial elections that fall,
pro-choice candidates defeated right-to-life candidates. And in Florida
the first governor to mount a full-scale legislative assault on abortion
rights was routed and humiliated. The tide of the war had turned.

Looking back in light of the disappointments of 1993 and 1994, it is
easy to forget what a triumphant turnabout the pro-choice movement
scored in the year and a half after *Webster.* Right-to-life activists had
spent sixteen years chipping away at the liberal bloc on the Supreme
Court, confident that if only they could drag the abortion issue back
into the political arena, they would regain control. Right-to-life voters
had intimidated the political establishment by helping to oust promi-

nent liberals from public office. Until 1989 pro-choice leaders hardly ever suggested that candidates could win elections by championing abortion rights. Quite the contrary, they argued that few people voted on the abortion issue. Politicians sympathetic to abortion rights protected their careers either by voting contrary to that sympathy or by avoiding the issue unless forced to address it.

In short, there was every reason to expect that in the wake of *Webster*, pro-choice forces would be steamrollered in elections and legislative debates throughout the country. So why didn't that happen?

Many pro-choice activists may chafe at the idea of crediting the conservative message strategy for the surprising victories of 1989. Pragmatists and idealists have long squabbled with each other over the movement's direction. These days the quarrel often pits groups such as NARAL and Planned Parenthood against groups such as the National Organization for Women, the American Civil Liberties Union, and the Center for Reproductive Law and Policy. Some political operatives consider all of these groups radical in terms of their language and their demands, when contrasted to conciliatory pro-choice politicians such as Clinton. On the other hand, some feminists consider all of these groups too prone to compromise. But everyone can agree that there has always been a spectrum of opinion within the movement on the question of how far it must compromise its language and substantive demands in order to succeed politically.

A careful study of the 1986–96 period suggests a coherent but flexible answer to this question. There is an old maxim in politics that to broaden your base of support, you must narrow your agenda. That is what the conservative message strategy accomplished. It attracted moderate and conservative voters to the abortion rights movement by muting the liberal and feminist elements of the movement's message.

Had the movement failed to marshal this larger audience in 1989, public discomfort about reviving abortion restrictions would not have erupted in the widespread libertarian backlash that halted right-to-life forces in their tracks. Indeed, had the three centrist justices of the Supreme Court not witnessed this backlash from 1989 to 1992, it is doubtful that they would have written, in *Casey*, a decision so explicitly mindful of "pressure to retain" *Roe*, of the "national controversy" over "governmental power to limit personal choice," and of the possibility of "a new social consensus." In short, had abortion rights activists relied on liberal, feminist rhetoric in the battle around *Webster*, they would have faced, at best, a decade-long struggle in numerous states to fend off abortion bans in legislatures and courts. Instead, they crushed that threat in a quick rout.

If it is difficult for critics of the conservative message strategy to concede its success, it is equally difficult for the authors and practitioners of that strategy to concede its cost. They broadened their base at the price of narrowing their agenda. It is important to understand that they never bargained for the latter consequence. They oppose parental involvement laws and restrictions on public funding of abortions just as vehemently today as they did a decade ago. And they did not foresee that by demanding less government and more sovereignty for families, they were thematically sanctioning those restrictions.

This is not to say that the conservative message persuaded swing voters to support such restrictions. They needed no such persuasion. What the conservative message gave these voters was a libertarian rationale that allowed them to identify themselves as pro-choice without renouncing those restrictions. They could embrace parental involvement laws as an extension of their belief in the sovereignty of families. They could spurn public funding of abortions as an affront to their belief in smaller government. A pro-choice message that called for less government and more family sovereignty was music to their ears.

In hindsight, the architects of the conservative message would like to set these voters straight. They would like to explain that being pro-family does not mean favoring parental involvement laws and that being anti-government does not mean opposing public funding of abortions. From the moment they expounded their conservative theme, these architects assumed they were in charge of its interpretation. They failed to anticipate how ideas, once launched into the currents of politics, develop lives of their own. In the wake of *Webster,* the conservative pro-choice message attracted new exponents and new interpreters. Abortion rights activists lost control of it.

Until *Webster,* the conservative message looked like a good strategy on paper, but it remained unproven in the field. It had succeeded in polls and focus groups, in an abortion referendum, and in a Supreme Court nomination fight. But it had yet to be tested in a high-profile campaign for statewide office. Politicians are a cautious lot to begin with, and they were particularly terrified of the abortion issue. They were not about to risk their careers on such a dicey strategy. To change history, one candidate had to step forward and take the chance. That candidate turned out to be Doug Wilder, then lieutenant governor of Virginia.

Wilder, in his bid to be the state's first African-American governor, was not the only gubernatorial candidate to take up the pro-choice banner in 1989. But he stood out from the others in three important ways. First, he was willing to defy strategists who considered the issue too risky to raise in the South. Second, he was willing to bet millions of dollars' worth of television advertising on it, which no prior candidate had done. Third, unlike Jim Florio, the pro-choice gubernatorial candidate in New Jersey, Wilder won his race by a hair's breadth. His abortion message made the difference.

But while vindicating the conservative message strategy, Wilder also usurped it. He refused to challenge Virginia's ban on abortion funding, and he advocated a parental consent law. He thereby affirmed two important conditions that conservative voters attached to freedom of choice: that the government should leave private matters to the heads of families and should not tax them to pay for other people's sexual carelessness. Duplicating a tactic used by pro-choice activists in the 1986 Arkansas referendum, Wilder also distinguished women impregnated through such carelessness from those impregnated by rape. He defended abortion more as a victim's than as a woman's right.

Wilder's campaign, and his victory in November 1989, firmly established this mutant version of abortion rights as a viable alternative to the feminist, egalitarian version originally envisioned by pro-choice activists. And over the next year, as the politics of abortion exploded throughout the country, this mutant strain proved more fit for survival than did the original.

The perilous environment in which these competing versions of abortion rights fought for survival was shaped largely by a disorganized but ideologically coherent counterattack led by right-to-life and Republican strategists. The counterattackers essentially reaffirmed and commandeered the conservative message of less government and more rights for families. In policy terms, this meant that they shifted their focus from banning abortion to banning tax-funded abortion subsidies and giving parents legal control over their daughters' abortion decisions.

These latter restrictions were hardly new ideas. Over the years, they had appeared in waves in numerous states, and the Supreme Court had affirmed their constitutionality on several occasions. But this new wave of restrictions differed from previous waves. Before, such restrictions had been secondary to banning abortion; now, they were primary. Before, they had been at best peripheral to campaigns for statewide office; now, they were often central. Before, they had been justified primarily by rhetoric about human life; now, they were justified primarily by rhetoric about freedom of choice.

What gave the counterattack unprecedented breadth and potency was the attack that had provoked it. First, the abortion rights movement had disseminated a message that focused less on economic equality and women's rights than on protecting tradition, family, and property from big government. Second, Doug Wilder and other candidates had incarnated that message in a mutant pro-choice movement that established parental consent laws and prohibitions on tax-funded abortions as corollaries of freedom of choice. Even as these consecutive innovations galvanized a mainstream, pro-choice backlash against *Webster*, they extended the rationale and political momentum of that backlash to encourage abortion restrictions that could be portrayed as protections of tradition, family, and property.

In short, pro-choice activists gave support and credence to arguments that could be—and soon were—used against them. Republican and right-to-life leaders persuasively accused pro-choice activists of hypocrisy for insisting that the government fund abortions and that parents be denied the legal right to supervise their daughters' abortion decisions. The liberal, feminist strain of abortion rights, already at odds with public opinion, could not withstand this accusation. By contrast, the mutant, conservative strain not only survived but thrived. Driven by polls and libertarian logic, politicians flocked to the political middle. And as this mutant strain proliferated, the feminist strain dwindled.

Several statewide elections in 1990 highlighted this trend. In gubernatorial races in Texas and Michigan, and in the race for the U.S. Senate in North Carolina, Republican candidates blunted attacks on their unpopular right-to-life positions by battering their pro-choice opponents on the issues of parental consent and public funding of abortions. In Oregon and Michigan, parental notification ballot measures gave pro-choice activists fits. The Michigan measure passed easily; the Oregon measure failed only because right-to-life activists unwisely paired it with a ballot measure that would have outlawed abortion altogether.

Many pro-choice activists collaborated in the proliferation of the conservative version of abortion rights and the demise of its liberal alternative. Judith Widdicombe, the president of the clinic that had taken the *Webster* case to the Supreme Court, tried to unite pro-choice voters behind a Missouri ballot measure that, while protecting the legal right to abortion, would have sanctioned state laws requiring parental consent and prohibiting state-financed abortions for poor women. And in the race for governor of Georgia, NARAL and a local pro-choice group refused to endorse former Atlanta mayor Andrew Young, who defended the liberal version of abortion rights, over Zell Miller, the lieutenant governor, who promoted the conservative version.

Between November 1990 and November 1992, the struggle among the three principal camps—those who sought to outlaw abortion, those who deemed it an entitlement even for minors and for women who could not pay for it, and those who deemed it a legal right but not at taxpayers' expense and not without the consent of the head of the family—was essentially resolved in favor of the third faction.

To begin with, the Supreme Court, in a pair of landmark decisions, decisively secured a conservative constitutional theory of abortion rights. In the 1991 case of *Rust v. Sullivan,* the Court upheld a ban on abortion counseling at federally funded clinics. Under this ban, the justices reasoned, "The financial constraints that restrict an indigent woman's ability to enjoy the full range of constitutionally protected freedom of choice are the product not of governmental restrictions on access to abortion, but rather of her indigency." A year later, in *Planned Parenthood v. Casey,* the justices refused to permit abortion's recriminalization but signaled that short of doing so, they would uphold laws that made abortions "more difficult or more expensive to procure" and that denied women the "right to be insulated from all others" in making their decisions.

Meanwhile, the two major presidential tickets converged to galvanize that conservative resolution into a political consensus. The Democratic Party shed the orthodoxy of pro-choice activists by nominating Governor Bill Clinton of Arkansas, who supported parental involvement laws, and Senator Al Gore of Tennessee, who opposed government funding of abortions. Conversely, the Republican nominees, President George Bush and Vice President Dan Quayle, shed the orthodoxy of right-to-life activists. Although these activists did not erupt in full-throated outrage until their putative Republican allies began talking up a pro-choice presidential bid by General Colin Powell in 1995, the GOP's desertion of the right-to-life movement actually began in 1992, when Bush and Quayle gingerly retreated from their previous promises to outlaw abortion.

Of course, significant differences over abortion persisted between the two tickets. But by November 1992 their points of disagreement—and hence the election's outcome—had become less significant than their points of agreement. The old war between left and right, between the right to choose and the right to life, had cooled into a consolidation of the center.

Pro-choice activists wishfully misread Clinton's election as a mandate for their own liberal version of abortion rights. They promptly launched a three-stage campaign against the conservative version. First, they planned to repeal the Hyde Amendment, which banned federal funding of abortions for poor women. Next, they would pass a federal Freedom of Choice Act that would bar states from restricting abortion rights. Finally, they would secure coverage of abortions under Clinton's proposed national health insurance plan.

The next two years dealt these rosy ambitions a series of crushing blows. First, the House renewed the Hyde Amendment by a wide margin, making new exceptions for victims of rape or incest. Even congressmen and congresswomen who had run on pro-choice platforms in 1992 and had taken campaign money from pro-choice activists voted to preserve the ban on abortion funding. Next, the Freedom of Choice Act languished and died when its supporters realized that conservatives had the votes to amend it to allow numerous abortion restrictions short of outright prohibition. Finally, the Clinton health care plan, and with it the last chance to secure federal funding of abortions, was politically destroyed by television ads that derided it as a "government-controlled" assault on "your right to choose doctors." This conservative message, having vanquished right-to-life activists, now dealt pro-choice activists their own coup de grâce.

In November 1994 the largest conservative landslide in U.S. history swept into power a regime of federal lawmakers and governors who stood for the right to choose abortion, the right to choose whether one's daughter could have an abortion, and the right to choose not to pay for anyone else's abortion. By February 1995 every major Republican presidential candidate other than Pat Buchanan had reassured voters that he would not seriously seek a constitutional ban on abortion. By April 1995 Republican House Speaker Newt Gingrich was routinely declaring America "pro-choice but anti-abortion," while the leading Republican presidential candidates focused their abortion comments on the rights of parents and taxpayers.

Over the course of their first year in power, congressional Republicans, often with Clinton's acquiescence, methodically exterminated the last vestiges of pro-choice liberalism. They barred federal employees' health insurance from covering abortions. They outlawed the use of American military hospitals for abortions on U.S. servicewomen and dependents of soldiers stationed abroad. They banned federal funding of abortions for federal prisoners. They abolished federal subsidies to global family-planning agencies that provided abortions or abortion information. And the House of Representatives voted to prohibit abortion subsidies in the District of Columbia and to let states withhold Medicaid coverage of abortions for poor women impregnated by rape or incest. Not only did Clinton fail to make abortion rights a potent issue against Republican presidential nominee Bob Dole in the 1996 presidential election; he spent much of 1996 and 1997 defending himself against a widely supported campaign to restrict late abortions.

America at the close of the twentieth century remains a deeply conservative country. In a June 1995 survey taken by Clinton pollster Stan Greenberg and Republican pollster Fred Steeper, 61 percent of Americans identified themselves as conservative, while just 34 percent classified themselves as liberal, and 5 percent called themselves moderate. A simultaneous poll taken by Epic/MRA-Mitchell found that 79 percent of voters agreed that "government is too big and inefficient and should have less influence in our daily lives." And a July 1995 survey taken by Democratic pollster Celinda Lake and Republican pollster Ed Goeas found that by a margin of 47 to 43 percent, Americans felt that "government is the problem, not the solution to our problems."

The conservative message strategy adopted by the abortion rights movement over the past decade has successfully navigated this hostile environment. It has done little to change it.

7

Dorothy E. Roberts

PUNISHING DRUG ADDICTS
WHO HAVE BABIES

Women of Color, Equality,
and the Right of Privacy

A former slave named Lizzie Williams recounted the beating of pregnant slave women on a Mississippi cotton plantation: "I['']s seen nigger women dat was fixin' to be confined do somethin' de white folks didn't like. Dey [the white folks] would dig a hole in de ground just big 'nuff fo' her stomach, make her lie face down an' whip her on de back to keep from hurtin' de child."[1]

In July 1989 Jennifer Clarise Johnson, a twenty-three-year-old crack addict, became the first woman in the United States to be criminally convicted for exposing her baby to drugs while pregnant.[2] Florida law enforcement officials charged Johnson with two counts of delivering a controlled substance to a minor after her two children tested positive for cocaine at birth. Because the relevant Florida drug law did not apply to fetuses, the prosecution invented a novel interpretation of the statute. The prosecution obtained Johnson's conviction for passing a cocaine metabolite from her body to her newborn infants during the sixty-second period after birth and before the umbilical cord was cut.

A growing number of women across the country have been charged with criminal offenses after giving birth to babies who test positive for drugs.[3] The majority of these women, like Jennifer Johnson, are poor and Black. Most are addicted to crack cocaine. The prosecution of drug-dependent mothers is part of an alarming trend toward greater state intervention in the lives of pregnant women under the rationale of protecting the fetus from harm. This intervention has included compelled medical treatment, greater restrictions on abortion, and increased supervision of pregnant women's conduct.

Such government intrusion is particularly harsh for poor women of color. They are the least likely to obtain adequate prenatal care, the most vulnerable to government monitoring, and the least able to conform to the white, middle-class standard of motherhood. They are therefore the primary targets of government control.

The prosecutions also represent a modern manifestation of racialized population control policies that arose in the United States after World War I, reached their zenith during the eugenics movement, and continued in government-sponsored programs during the 1970s that coerced poor Black, Latina, and Native American women to be sterilized. Eugenic theory was discredited after the Nazi atrocities came to light. Organizations such as the Coalition to End Sterilization Abuse exposed the doctors' violations of Black patients and obtained federal legislation designed to implement informed consent and prevent coercive sterilizations. The 1980s and 1990s, however, witnessed a resurgence of conservative rhetoric blaming poor Black mothers for perpetuating poverty by transmitting a deviant lifestyle to their children.[4] This rhetoric has been accompanied by new reproductive policies that are hostile to poor women but more politically acceptable than those in force earlier in this century. Congress and state legislatures across the country, for example, are debating proposals intended to discourage women on welfare from having children.[5] Although less blatant than the involuntary sterilization laws of the eugenics movement and government-sponsored sterilization abuse, these policies continue to devalue procreation on the basis of race and class.

The debate between those who favor protecting the rights of the fetus and those who favor protecting the rights of the mother has been extensively waged in the literature. This essay does not repeat the theoretical arguments for and against state intervention. Rather, I suggest that both sides of the debate have largely overlooked a critical aspect of government prosecution of drug-addicted mothers. Can we determine the legality of the prosecutions simply by weighing the state's abstract interest in the fetus against the mother's abstract interest in autonomy? Can we determine whether the prosecutions are fair simply by deciding the duties a pregnant woman owes to her fetus and then assessing whether the defendant has met them? Can we determine the constitutionality of the government's actions without considering the race of the women being singled out for prosecution?

Before deciding whether the state's interest in preventing harm to the fetus justifies criminal sanctions against the mother, we must first understand the mother's competing perspective and the reasons for the state's choice of a punitive response. This essay seeks to illuminate the current debate by examining the experiences of the class of women who are primarily affected—poor Black women.

Providing the perspective of poor Black women offers two advantages. First, examining legal issues from the viewpoint of those whom they affect most helps to uncover the real reasons for state action and to explain the real harm that it causes. This approach exposes the way in which the prosecutions deny poor Black women a facet of their humanity by limiting their reproductive choices. The government's choice of a punitive response perpetuates the historical devaluation of Black women as mothers. Viewing the legal issues from the experiential standpoint of the defendants enhances our understanding of the constitutional dimensions of the state's conduct.

Second, examining the constraints on poor Black women's reproductive choices expands our understanding of reproductive freedom in particular and of the right of privacy in general. Much of the literature discussing reproductive freedom has adopted a white middle-class perspective, which focuses narrowly on abortion rights. The feminist critique of privacy doctrine has also neglected many of the concerns of poor women of color.

My analysis presumes that Black women experience various forms of oppression simultaneously as a complex interaction of race, gender, and class that is more than the sum of its parts.[6] It is impossible to isolate any one of the components of this oppression or to separate the experiences that are attributable to one component from experiences attributable to the others. The prosecution of drug-addicted mothers cannot be explained as simply an issue of gender inequality. Poor Black women have been selected for punishment as a result of an inseparable combination of their gender, race, and economic status. Their devaluation as mothers, which underlies the prosecutions, has its roots in the unique experience of slavery and has been perpetuated by complex social forces.

Thus, for example, the focus of mainstream feminist legal thought on gender as the primary locus of oppression often forces women of color to fragment their experience in a way that does not reflect the reality of their lives. Legal scholars Kimberle Crenshaw, Angela Harris, and others have presented a racial critique of this gender essentialism in feminist legal theory.[7] By introducing the voices of Black women, these critics have begun to reconstruct a feminist jurisprudence based on the historical, economic, and social diversity of women's experiences. This new jurisprudence must be used to reconsider the more particular discourse of reproductive rights.

In this essay I present an account of the constitutionality of prosecutions of drug-addicted mothers that explicitly considers the experiences of poor Black women. The constitutional arguments are based on theories of both racial equality and the right of privacy. I argue that punishing drug addicts who choose to carry their pregnancies to term burdens the constitutional right to autonomy over reproductive decisions. Violation of poor Black women's reproductive rights helps to perpetuate a racist hierarchy in our society. The prosecutions thus impose a standard of motherhood that is offensive to principles of both equality and privacy. This essay provides insight into the particular and urgent struggle of women of color for reproductive freedom. Further, I intend my constitutional critique of the prosecutions to demonstrate the advantages of a discourse that combines elements of racial equality and privacy theories in advocating the reproductive rights of women of color.

BACKGROUND: THE STATE'S PUNITIVE RESPONSE
TO DRUG-ADDICTED MOTHERS

The Crack Epidemic

Crack cocaine appeared in America in the early 1980s, and its abuse has grown to epidemic proportions.[8] Crack seems to be especially popular among inner-city women.[9] Indeed, it has been reported that, in several urban areas in the United States, more women than men now smoke crack.[10] Most crack-addicted women are of childbearing age, and many are pregnant. This phenomenon has contributed to an explosion in the number of newborns affected by maternal drug use. In many urban hospitals, the number of these newborns quadrupled between 1985 and 1990. A widely cited 1988 study conducted by the National Association for Perinatal Addiction Research and Education (NAPARE) found that 11 percent of newborns in thirty-six hospitals surveyed were affected by their mothers' illegal drug use during pregnancy.[11] In several hospitals, the proportion of drug-exposed infants was as high as 15 and 25 percent. Extrapolating these statistics to the population at large, NAPARE estimated that as many as 375,000 drug-exposed infants are born every year.[12] This figure covers all drug exposure nationwide, regardless of extent of drug use or its effects on the newborn.

Babies born to drug-using mothers may suffer a variety of medical, developmental, and behavioral problems, depending on the nature of the mother's substance abuse. Research conducted in the late 1980s reported immediate effects of cocaine exposure to include premature birth, low birth weight, and withdrawal symptoms.[13] Cocaine-exposed children have also exhibited neurobehavioral problems, such as mood dysfunction, organizational deficits, poor attention, and impaired human interaction, although it has not been determined whether these conditions are permanent.[14]

Data on the extent and potential severity of the adverse effects of maternal cocaine use are controversial, however. The most recent research can definitively link crack use during pregnancy only to low birth weight.[15] This is because the interpretation of studies of cocaine-exposed infants is often clouded by the presence of other fetal risk factors, such as the mother's socioeconomic status and her use of additional drugs, cigarettes, and alcohol. For example, the health prospects of an infant are significantly threatened because pregnant addicts often receive little or no prenatal care and may be malnourished.[16] Moreover, because the medical community has given more attention to studies showing adverse effects of cocaine exposure than to those that deny these effects, the public has a distorted perception of the risks of maternal cocaine use.[17] Researchers have not yet authoritatively determined the percentage of infants exposed to cocaine who actually experience adverse consequences.[18]

The response of state prosecutors, legislators, and judges to the problem of drug-exposed babies has been punitive. They have punished women who use drugs during pregnancy by depriving these mothers of custody of their children, by jailing them during their pregnancy, and by prosecuting them after their babies are born.

The most common penalty for a mother's prenatal drug use is the permanent or temporary removal of her baby.[19] Hospitals in a number of states now screen newborns for evidence of drugs in their urine and report positive results to child welfare authorities. Several states have enacted statutes that require the reporting of positive newborn toxicologies to state authorities, and many hospitals interpret state child abuse reporting laws to require them to report positive results. Some child protection agencies institute neglect proceedings to obtain custody of babies with positive toxicologies based solely on these tests. More and more government authorities are also removing drug-exposed newborns from their mothers immediately after birth, pending an investigation of parental fitness.[20] In these investigations, positive neonatal toxicologies often raise a strong presumption of parental unfitness, which circumvents the inquiry into the mother's ability to care for her child that is customarily necessary to deprive a parent of custody.

A second form of punishment is the "protective" incarceration of pregnant drug addicts charged with unrelated crimes. In 1988 a Washington, D.C., judge sentenced a thirty-year-old woman named Brenda Vaughn, who pleaded guilty to forging $700 worth of checks, to jail for the duration of her pregnancy.[21] The judge stated at sentencing that he wanted to ensure that the baby would be born in jail to protect it from its mother's drug abuse: "I'm going to keep her locked up until the baby is born because she's tested positive for cocaine when she came before me. . . . She's apparently an addictive personality, and I'll be darned if I'm going to have a baby born that way." Although the *Vaughn* case received the most attention, anecdotal evidence suggests that defendants' drug use during pregnancy often affects judges' sentencing decisions.[22] Finally, women have been prosecuted after the birth of their children for having exposed the fetuses to drugs or alcohol. Creative statutory interpretations that once seemed little more than the outlandish concoctions of conservative scholars are now used to punish women. Mothers of children affected by prenatal substance abuse have been charged with crimes such as distributing drugs to a minor, child abuse and neglect, manslaughter, and assault with a deadly weapon.

This essay considers the constitutional implications of criminal prosecution of drug-addicted mothers because, as I will explain, this penalty most directly punishes poor Black women for having babies. When the government prosecutes, its intervention is not designed to protect babies from the irresponsible actions of their mothers (as is arguably the case when the state takes custody of a pregnant addict or her child). Rather, the government criminalizes the mother as a consequence of her decision to bear a child.

The Disproportionate Impact on Poor Black Women

Poor Black women bear the brunt of prosecutors' punitive approach. These women are the primary targets of prosecutors, not because they are more likely to be guilty of fetal abuse, but because they are Black and poor. Poor women, who are disproportionately Black,[23] are in closer contact with government agencies, and their drug use is therefore more likely to be detected. Black women are also more likely to be reported to government authorities, in part because of the racist attitudes of health care professionals. Finally, their failure to meet society's image of the ideal mother makes their prosecution more acceptable.

To charge drug-addicted mothers with crimes, the state must be able to identify those who use drugs during pregnancy. Because poor women are generally under greater government supervision—through their associations with public hospitals, welfare agencies, and probation officers—their drug use is more likely to be detected and reported.[24] Hospital screening practices result in disproportionate reporting of poor Black women.[25] The government's main source of information about prenatal drug use is hospitals' reporting of positive infant toxicologies to child welfare authorities. This testing is implemented almost exclusively by hospitals serving poor minority communities. Private physicians who serve more affluent women perform less of this screening both because they have a financial stake in retaining their patients' business and securing referrals from them and because they are socially more like their patients.[26]

Hospitals administer drug tests in a manner that further discriminates against poor Black women. One common criterion triggering an infant toxicology screen is the mother's failure to obtain prenatal care, a factor that correlates strongly with race and income.[27] Worse still, many hospitals have no formal screening procedures, relying solely on the suspicions of health care professionals. This discretion allows doctors and hospital staff to perform tests based on their stereotyped assumptions about drug addicts.[28]

Health care professionals are much more likely to report Black women's drug use to government authorities than similar drug use by their wealthy white patients. A study reported in the *New England Journal of Medicine* demonstrated this racial bias in the reporting of maternal drug use.[29] Researchers studied the results of toxicologic tests of pregnant women who received prenatal care in public health clinics and in private obstetrical offices in Pinellas County, Florida. Little difference existed in the prevalence of substance abuse by pregnant women along either racial or economic lines, nor was there any significant difference between public clinics and private offices.[30] Despite similar rates of substance abuse, however, Black women were ten times more likely than whites to be reported to public health authorities for substance abuse during pregnancy. Although several possible explanations can account for this disparate reporting, both public health facilities and private doctors are more inclined to turn in pregnant Black women who use drugs than pregnant white women who use drugs.

It is also significant that, out of the universe of maternal conduct that can injure a fetus, prosecutors have focused on crack use. The selection of crack addiction for punishment can be justified neither by the number of addicts nor the extent of the harm to the fetus. Excessive alcohol consumption during pregnancy, for example, can cause severe fetal injury, and marijuana use may also adversely affect the unborn.[31] The incidence of both these types of substance abuse is high as well.[32] In addition, prosecutors do not always base their claims on actual harm to the child, but on the mere delivery of crack by the mother. Although different forms of substance abuse prevail among pregnant women of various socioeconomic levels and racial and ethnic backgrounds, inner-city Black communities have the highest concentrations of crack addicts.[33] Therefore, selecting crack abuse as the primary fetal harm to be punished has a discriminatory impact that cannot be medically justified.

Focusing on Black crack addicts rather than on other perpetrators of fetal harms serves two broader social purposes. First, prosecution of these pregnant women serves to degrade women whom society believes do not deserve to be mothers and to discourage them from having children. If prosecutors had instead chosen to prosecute affluent women addicted to alcohol or prescription medication, the policy of criminalizing prenatal conduct very likely would have suffered a hasty demise. Society is much more willing to condone the punishment of poor women of color who fail to meet the middle-class ideal of motherhood.

In addition to legitimizing fetal rights enforcement, the prosecution of crack-addicted mothers diverts public attention from social ills such as poverty, racism, and a misguided national health policy and implies instead that shamefully high Black infant death rates are caused by the bad acts of individual mothers. Poor Black mothers thus become the scapegoats for the causes of the Black community's ill health. Punishing them assuages any guilt the nation might feel at the plight of an underclass with infant mortality rates higher than those in some less developed countries. Making criminals of Black mothers apparently helps to relieve the nation of the burden of creating a health care system that ensures healthy babies for all its citizens.

THE DEVALUATION OF
BLACK PROCREATION AND MOTHERHOOD

The systematic, institutionalized denial of reproductive freedom has uniquely marked Black women's history in America. The essence of Black women's experience during slavery was the brutal denial of autonomy over reproduction. Female slaves were commercially valuable to their masters not only for their labor but also for their capacity to produce more slaves.[34] During the twentieth century, Black women have been subjected to policies intended to discourage them from having children. The first publicly funded birth control clinics were established in the South in the 1930s as a way of lowering the Black birthrate.[35] In 1939 the Birth Control Federation of America planned a "Negro Project" designed to limit reproduction by Blacks who "still breed carelessly and disastrously, with the result that the increase among Negroes, even more than among whites, is from that portion of the population least intelligent and fit, and least able to rear children properly." [36]

Coerced sterilization is one of the most extreme forms of control over a woman's reproductive life. By permanently denying her the right to bear children, sterilization enforces society's determination that a woman does not deserve to be a mother. Poor women of color have been subjected to sterilization abuse for decades.[37] The disproportionate sterilization of Black women is yet another manifestation of the dominant society's devaluation of Black women as mothers.

Sterilization abuse has taken the form both of blatant coercion and trickery and of subtle influences on women's decisions to be sterilized.[38] In the 1970s some doctors conditioned delivering babies and performing abortions on Black women's consent to sterilization. In a 1974 case brought by poor teenage Black women in Alabama, a federal district court found that an estimated 100,000 to 150,000 poor women were sterilized annually under federally funded programs.[39] Some of these women were coerced into agreeing to sterilization under the threat that their welfare benefits would be withdrawn unless they submitted to the operation. Despite federal and state regulations intended to prevent involuntary sterilization, physicians and other health care providers continue to urge women of color to consent to sterilization because they view these women's family sizes as excessive and believe these women are incapable of effectively using other methods of birth control.

Current government funding policy perpetuates the encouragement of sterilization of poor, and thus of disproportionately Black, women. The federal government pays for sterilization services under the Medicaid program, while it often does not make available information about and access to other contraceptive techniques and abortion.[40] In effect, sterilization was until recently the only publicly funded birth control method readily available to poor women of color. Every state now makes Norplant, a controversial long-term contraceptive implant, available to poor women through Medicaid.[41]

An important part of this denial of Black women's reproductive autonomy has been the devaluation of Black women as mothers. A popular mythology that degrades Black women and portrays them as less deserving of motherhood reinforces this subordination. Slave owners forced slave women to perform strenuous labor that contradicted the model of female roles then prevalent in the dominant white society.[42] The slave woman was often portrayed as Jezebel, a woman governed by her sexual desires, which legitimated white men's sexual abuse of Black women.[43] The stereotype of Black women as sexually promiscuous has helped to perpetuate their devaluation as mothers.

The disproportionate number of Black mothers who lose custody of their children through the child welfare system is a contemporary manifestation of the devaluation of Black motherhood.[44] This disparate impact of state intervention results in part from Black families' higher rate of reliance on government welfare. Because welfare families are subject to supervision by social workers, instances of perceived neglect are more likely to be reported to governmental authorities for these families than for more affluent families.[45] Black children are also removed from their homes in part because of the child welfare system's cultural bias and application of the nuclear family pattern to Black families.

This devaluation of Black motherhood has been reinforced by stereotypes that blame Black mothers for the problems of the Black family, such as the myth of the Black matriarch—the domineering female head of the Black family. White sociologists have held Black matriarchs responsible for the disintegration of the Black family and the consequent failure of Black people to achieve success in America.[46] Daniel Patrick

Moynihan popularized this theory in his 1965 report, *The Negro Family: The Case for National Action,* which claimed that "at the heart of the deterioration of the fabric of the Negro society is the deterioration of the Negro family."[47]

The myth of the Black Jezebel has been supplemented by the contemporary image of the lazy welfare mother who breeds children at the expense of taxpayers in order to increase the amount of her welfare check.[48] This view of Black motherhood provides the rationale for society's restrictions on Black female fertility. It is this image of the undeserving Black mother that also ultimately underlies the government's choice to punish crack-addicted women.

PROSECUTING DRUG ADDICTS
AS PUNISHMENT FOR HAVING BABIES

Informed by the historical and ongoing devaluation of Black motherhood, we can better understand prosecutors' reasons for punishing drug-addicted mothers. I view such prosecutions as punishing these women, in essence, for having babies; judges such as the one who convicted Jennifer Johnson are pronouncing not so much "I care about your baby" as "You don't deserve to be a mother."

It is important to recognize at the outset that the prosecutions are based in part on a woman's pregnancy and not on her illegal drug use alone. Prosecutors charge these defendants not with drug use but with child abuse or drug distribution—crimes that relate to their pregnancy. Moreover, pregnant women receive harsher sentences than drug-addicted men or women who are not pregnant. The drug user's pregnancy not only greatly increases the likelihood that she will be prosecuted, but also greatly enhances the penalty she faces upon conviction. In most states, drug use is a misdemeanor, while distribution of drugs is a felony.[49]

The unlawful nature of drug use must not be allowed to confuse the basis of the crimes at issue. The legal rationale underlying the prosecutions does not depend on the illegality of drug use. Harm to the fetus is the crux of the government's legal theory. Criminal charges have been brought against women for conduct that is legal but is alleged to have harmed the fetus.

When a drug-addicted woman becomes pregnant, she has only one realistic avenue to escape criminal charges: abortion. Seeking drug treatment is not a viable alternative. First, it is likely that the pregnant addict will be unable to find a drug treatment program that will accept her. Second, even if she successfully completes drug counseling by the end of her pregnancy, she may still be prosecuted for earlier drug use during pregnancy. Thus, she is penalized for choosing to have the baby rather than having an abortion. In this way, the state's punitive action may coerce women to have abortions rather than risk being charged with a crime. Thus, it is the *choice of carrying a pregnancy to term* that is being penalized.

There is also good reason to question the government's justification for the prosecutions—the concern for the welfare of potential children. I have already discussed the selectivity of the prosecutions with respect to poor Black women. This focus on the conduct of one group of women weakens the state's rationale for the prosecutions.

The history of overwhelming state neglect of Black children casts further doubt on its professed concern for the welfare of the fetus. When a society has always closed its eyes to the inadequacy of the prenatal care available to poor Black women, its current expression of interest in the health of unborn Black children must be viewed with suspicion. The most telling evidence of the state's disregard of Black children is the high rate of infant death in the Black community. In 1987 the mortality rate for Black infants in the United States was 17.9 deaths per 1,000 births—more than twice that for white infants (8.6).[50] In New York City, while infant mortality rates in upper- and middle-income areas were generally less than 9 per 1,000 in 1986, the rates exceeded 19 in the poor Black communities of the South Bronx and Bedford-Stuyvesant and reached 27.6 in central Harlem.[51]

The main reasons for these high mortality rates are poverty and inadequate prenatal care.[52] Most poor Black women face financial and other barriers to receiving proper care during pregnancy.[53] In 1986 only half of all pregnant Black women in America received adequate prenatal care.[54] It appears that in the 1980s Black women's access to prenatal care actually declined. The government has chosen to punish poor Black women rather than provide the means for them to have healthy children.

The cruelty of this punitive response is heightened by the lack of available drug treatment services for pregnant drug addicts.[55] Protecting the welfare of drug addicts' children requires, among other things, adequate facilities for the mother's drug treatment. Yet a drug addict's pregnancy serves as an *obstacle* to obtaining this treatment.

Treatment centers either refuse to treat pregnant women or are effectively closed to them because the centers are ill equipped to meet the needs of pregnant addicts. Most hospitals and programs that treat addiction exclude pregnant women on the grounds that their babies are more likely to be born with health problems requiring expensive care. Program directors also feel that treating pregnant addicts is worth neither the increased cost nor the risk of tort liability.[56]

Moreover, there are several barriers to pregnant women who seek to use centers that will accept them.[57] Drug treatment programs are generally based on male-oriented models that are not geared to the needs of women. The lack of accommodations for children is perhaps the most significant obstacle to treatment. Most outpatient clinics do not provide child care, and many residential treatment programs do not admit children. Furthermore, treatment programs have traditionally failed to provide the comprehensive services that women need, including prenatal and gynecologic care, contraceptive counseling, appropriate job training, and counseling for sexual and physical abuse. Predominantly male staffs and clients are often hostile to female clients and employ a confrontational style of therapy that makes many women uncomfortable. Moreover, long waiting lists often make it impossible for women to get help before their due date.

Finally, and perhaps most important, ample evidence reveals that prosecuting addicted mothers may not achieve the government's asserted goal of healthier pregnancies; indeed, such prosecutions probably have the opposite result. Pregnant addicts who seek help from public hospitals and clinics are the ones most often reported to government authorities. The threat of prosecution based on this reporting may force women to remain anonymous and thus may have the perverse effect of deterring pregnant drug addicts from seeking treatment.[58] For this reason, the government's decision to punish drug-addicted mothers is irreconcilable with the goal of helping them.

Pregnancy may be a time when women are most motivated to seek treatment for drug addiction and make positive lifestyle changes. The government should capitalize on this opportunity by encouraging substance-abusing women to seek help and providing them with comprehensive treatment. Punishing pregnant women who use drugs only makes their children worse off. It deprives infants of their mothers' care, while creating an adversarial health care system that threatens the welfare of countless babies in the future.

CLAIMING THE RIGHT OF PRIVACY FOR WOMEN OF COLOR

Identifying the Constitutional Issue

In deciding which of the competing interests involved in the prosecution of drug-addicted mothers prevails—the state's interest in protecting the health of the fetus or the woman's interest in preventing state intervention—it is essential as a matter of constitutional law to identify the precise nature of the woman's right at stake. In the *Johnson* case, the prosecutor framed the constitutional issue as follows: "What constitutionally protected freedom did Jennifer engage in when she smoked cocaine?" [59] That was the wrong question. Johnson was not convicted of using drugs. Her "constitutional right" to smoke cocaine was never at issue. Johnson was prosecuted because she chose to carry her pregnancy to term while she was addicted to crack. Had she smoked cocaine during her pregnancy and then had an abortion, she would not have been charged with such a serious crime. The proper question, then, is "What constitutionally protected freedom did Jennifer engage in when she decided to have a baby, even though she was a drug addict?"

Understanding the prosecution of drug-addicted mothers as punishment for having babies clarifies the constitutional right at stake. The woman's right at issue is not the right to abuse drugs or to cause the fetus to be born with defects. It is the right to choose to be a mother that is burdened by the criminalization of conduct during pregnancy. This view of the constitutional issue reveals the relevance of race to the resolution of the competing interests. Race has historically determined the value society places on an individual's right to choose motherhood. Because of the devaluation of Black motherhood, protecting the right of Black women to choose to bear children has unique significance. I contend that the prosecutions of addicted mothers violate traditional liberal notions of privacy, and, in light of how the issue of race informs the traditional analysis, I call for a reassessment of the use of privacy doctrine in the struggle to eliminate gender and racial subordination.

Overview of Privacy Arguments

Prosecutions of drug-addicted mothers infringe on two aspects of the right to individual choice in reproductive decision making. First, they infringe on the freedom to continue a pregnancy that is essential to an individual's personhood and autonomy. This freedom implies that state control of the decision to carry a pregnancy to term can be as pernicious as state control of the decision to terminate a pregnancy. Second, the prosecutions infringe on choice by imposing an invidious government standard for the entitlement to procreate. Such imposition of a government standard for childbearing is one way that society denies the humanity of members of subordinated groups. The first approach emphasizes a woman's right to autonomy over her reproductive life; the second highlights a woman's right to be valued equally as a human being. In other words, the prosecution of crack-addicted mothers infringes upon both a mother's right to make decisions that determine her individual identity and her right to be respected equally as a human being by recognizing the value of *her* motherhood.

Inherent in the thesis of this essay is a tension between reliance on the liberal rhetoric of choice and acknowledgment of the fallacy of choice for poor women of color. This essay also seeks to incorporate liberal notions of individual autonomy while acknowledging the collective injury perpetrated by racism. This tension may be an example of what critical race theorist Mari Matsuda calls "multiple consciousness." [60] Matsuda observes that "outsider" lawyers and scholars must often adopt a "dualist approach" that incorporates an elitist legal system and the concept of legal rights while seeing the world from the standpoint of the oppressed. "Unlike the post-modern critics of the left . . . outsiders, including feminists and people of color, have embraced legalism as a tool of necessity, making legal consciousness their own in order to attack injustice." [61]

This internal struggle between the embrace of legalism and the recognition of oppression characterizes a process of enlightenment. Working through the privacy analysis from the perspective of poor Black women uncovers unexplored benefits to be gained from liberal doctrine while revealing liberalism's inadequacies. This process of putting forth new propositions for challenge and subversion will produce a better understanding of the law and the ways in which it can be used to pursue social justice.

The Right to Choose Procreation

Punishing drug-addicted mothers unconstitutionally burdens the right to choose to bear a child. Certain interests of the individual—generally called "rights"—are entitled to heightened protection against government interference under the due-process clause of the Fourteenth Amendment. The right of privacy is recognized as one cluster of such interests, implicit in the "liberty" that the Fourteenth Amendment protects.[62] The right of privacy has been interpreted to include the "interest in independence in making certain kinds of important decisions."[63] This concept of decisional privacy seeks to protect intimate or personal affairs that are fundamental to an individual's identity and moral personhood from unjustified government intrusion. At the forefront of the development of the right of privacy has been the freedom of personal choice in matters of marriage and family life.[64] Once an interest has been deemed part of the right of privacy, the government needs a compelling reason to intervene to survive constitutional scrutiny.

Considerable support exists for the conclusion that the decision to procreate is part of the right of privacy. The decision to bear children is universally acknowledged in the privacy cases as being "at the very heart" of these constitutionally protected choices.[65] In *Eisenstadt v. Baird,* for example, the Supreme Court struck down a Massachusetts statute that prohibited the distribution of contraceptives to unmarried persons.[66] Although the case was decided on equal protection grounds, the Court recognized the vital nature of the freedom to choose whether to give birth to a child: "If the right of privacy means anything, it is the right of the individual, married or single, to be free from unwarranted governmental intrusion into matters so fundamentally affecting a person as the decision whether to bear or beget a child."[67]

The right of privacy protects equally the choice to bear children and the choice to refrain from bearing them. The historical experiences of Black women illustrate the evil of government control over procreative decisions. Their experiences demonstrate that the dual nature of the decisional right recognized in the privacy cases goes beyond the logical implications of making a choice. The exploitation of Black women's foremothers during slavery to breed more slaves and the sterilization abuse that Black women have suffered reveal society's pervasive devaluation of Black women as mothers.

Burdening both the right to terminate a pregnancy and the right to give birth to a child violates a woman's personhood by denying her autonomy over the self-defining decision of whether she will bring another being into the world. Furthermore, criminalizing the choice to give birth imposes tangible burdens on women, as well as an intangible infringement on personhood. Punishing women for having babies is in this sense at least as pernicious as forced maternity at the behest of the state.

If a woman's decision to bear a child is entitled to constitutional protection, it follows that the government may not unduly burden that choice. Even under the Court's current analysis, which distinguishes between direct and indirect governmental interference in reproductive decision making, government intrusion as extreme as criminal prosecution would unduly infringe on protected autonomy. The Court has expressly distinguished, for example, the government's refusal to subsidize the exercise of the abortion right from the infliction of criminal penalties on the exercise of that right.[68] Criminal prosecutions of drug-addicted mothers do more than discourage a choice; they exact a severe penalty on the drug user for choosing to complete her pregnancy.

These privacy concepts have two benefits for advocating the reproductive rights of women of color in particular: the right of privacy stresses the value of personhood, and it protects against the totalitarian abuse of government power. First, affirming Black women's constitutional claim to personhood is particularly important because these women historically have been denied the dignity of their full humanity and identity. The principle of self-definition has special significance for Black women. Angela Harris recognizes in the writings of Zora Neale Hurston an insistence on a "conception of identity as a construction, not an essence. . . . [B]lack women have had to learn to construct themselves in a society that denied them full selves." [69] Black women's willful self-definition is an adaptation to a history of social denigration. Excluded from the dominant society's norm of womanhood, Black women have been forced to resort to their own internal resources. Harris contrasts this process of affirmative self-definition with the feminist paradigm of women as passive victims. Black women willfully create their own identities out of "fragments of experience, not discovered in one's body or unveiled after male domination is eliminated." [70]

The concept of personhood embodied in the right of privacy can be used to affirm the role of will and creativity in Black women's construction of their own identities. Relying on the concept of self-definition celebrates the legacy of Black women who have survived and transcended conditions of oppression. The process of defining one's self and declaring one's personhood defies the denial of self-ownership inherent in slavery. Thus, the right of privacy, with its affirmation of personhood, is especially suited for challenging the devaluation of Black motherhood underlying the prosecutions of drug-addicted women.

Another important element of the right of privacy is its delineation of the limits of governmental power. The protection from government abuse also makes the right of privacy a useful legal tool for protecting the reproductive rights of women of color. Poor women of color are especially vulnerable to government control over their decisions. The government's pervasive involvement in Black women's lives illustrates the inadequacy of the privacy critique presented by some white feminist scholars. Catharine MacKinnon, for example, argues that privacy doctrine is based on the false liberal assumption that government nonintervention into the private sphere promotes women's autonomy.[71] The individual woman's legal right of privacy, according to MacKinnon, functions instead as "a means of subordinating women's collective needs to the imperatives of male supremacy."[72]

This rejection of privacy doctrine does not take into account the contradictory meaning of the private sphere for women of color. Feminist legal theory focuses on the private realm of the family as an institution of violence and subordination. Women of color, however, often experience the family as the site of solace and resistance against racial oppression.[73] For many women of color, the immediate concern in the area of reproductive rights is not abuse in the private sphere but abuse of government power. The prosecution of crack-addicted mothers and coerced sterilization are examples of state intervention that pose a much greater threat for women of color than for white women.

Another telling example is the issue of child custody. The primary concern for white middle-class women with regard to child custody is private custody battles with their husbands following the termination of a marriage.[74] But for women of color, the dominant threat is termination of parental rights by the state. Again, the imminent danger faced by poor women of color comes from the public sphere, not the private. Thus, the protection from government interference that privacy doctrine affords may have a different significance for women of color.

A Critique of the Focus on Abortion

Another aspect of the reproductive rights literature that limits our understanding of reproductive freedom is its focus on abortion rights. One problem is that this focus provides an inadequate response to a central argument in support of the regulation of pregnancy. Procreative rights scholar John Robertson, for example, has contended that if a woman forgoes her right to an abortion, she forfeits her right to autonomy and choice.[75] If abortion is at the heart of women's reproductive rights, then state policies that do not interfere with that right are acceptable. Similarly, if the full extent of reproductive freedom is the right to have an abortion, then a policy that encourages abortion—such as the prosecution of crack-addicted mothers—does not interfere with that freedom.

The emphasis on abortion also fails to incorporate the needs of poor women of color. White, middle-class women are primarily concerned about laws that restrict choices otherwise available to them, such as statutes that make it more difficult to obtain an abortion. Poor women of color, however, are mainly concerned about the material conditions of poverty and oppression that restrict their choices. If the facilities necessary to effectuate a reproductive decision cost money, poor women may not be able to afford to take advantage of them. Prenatal care, abortion services, new reproductive technologies, fetal surgery, contraceptives, and family-planning counseling are some examples of the means to realize a reproductive choice that may be financially inaccessible to low-income women.[76] The reproductive freedom of poor women of color, for example, is limited significantly not only by the denial of access to safe abortions, but also by the lack of resources necessary for a healthy pregnancy and parenting relationship. Their choices are limited not only by direct government interference with their decisions, but also by the failure of the government, as well as the private sector, to facilitate them. The focus of reproductive rights discourse on abortion neglects this broader range of reproductive health issues that affect poor women of color. Addressing the concerns of women of color will expand our vision of reproductive freedom to include the full scope of what it means to have control over one's reproductive life.

The Intersection of Privacy and Equality

The equal protection clause and the right of privacy provide the basis for two separate constitutional challenges to the prosecution of drug-addicted mothers. The singling out of Black mothers for punishment combines in one government action several wrongs prohibited by both constitutional doctrines. Black mothers are denied autonomy over procreative decisions because of their race. The government's denial of Black women's fundamental right to choose to bear children serves to perpetuate the legacy of racial discrimination embodied in the devaluation of Black motherhood. These two constitutional challenges appeal to different but related values. They are related in the sense that underlying the protection of the individual's autonomy is the principle that all individuals are entitled to equal dignity. A basic premise of equality doctrine is that certain fundamental aspects of the human personality, including decisional autonomy, must be respected in all persons.

Theories of racial equality and privacy can be used as related means to eliminate the legacy of racial discrimination that has devalued Black motherhood. Both aim to create a society in which Black women's reproductive choices, including the decision to bear children, are given full respect and protection. The full scope of the government's violation can better be understood, then, by a constitutional theory that acknowledges the complementary and overlapping qualities of the Constitution's guarantees of equality and privacy. From this perspective, the prosecutions of pregnant crack addicts can be viewed as imposing a racist government standard for procreation.

Poor crack addicts are punished for having babies because they fail to measure up to the state's ideal of motherhood. Prosecutors have brought charges against women who use drugs during pregnancy without demonstrating any harm to the fetus. Moreover, a government policy that has the effect of punishing primarily poor Black women for having babies evokes the specter of racial eugenics, especially in light of the history of sterilization abuse of women of color. These women are not being punished simply because they may harm their unborn children. They are being punished because the combination of their poverty, race, and drug addiction is seen as making them unworthy of procreating.

This aspect of the prosecutions implicates both equality and privacy interests. The right to have children goes to the heart of what it means to be human. The value we place on individuals determines whether we see them as entitled to perpetuate themselves in their children. Denying someone the right to bear children—or punishing her for exercising that right—deprives her of a basic part of her humanity. When this denial is based on race, it also functions to preserve a racial hierarchy that essentially disregards Black humanity.

The abuse of sterilization laws to effect eugenic policy demonstrates the potential danger of governmental standards for procreation. During the first half of the twentieth century, the eugenics movement embraced the theory that intelligence and other personality traits are genetically determined and therefore inherited.[77] This belief in heredity, coupled with the reform approach of the Progressive Era, fueled a campaign to remedy America's social problems by stemming biological degeneracy. Eugenicists advocated compulsory sterilization to prevent reproduction by people who were likely to produce allegedly defective offspring. Eugenic sterilization was thought to improve society by eliminating its "socially inadequate" members. Many states around the turn of the century enacted involuntary sterilization laws directed at those deemed burdens on society, including the mentally retarded, mentally ill, epileptics, and criminals.[78]

In a 1927 decision, *Buck v. Bell,* the United States Supreme Court upheld the constitutionality of a Virginia involuntary sterilization law.[79] The plaintiff, Carrie Buck, was described in the opinion as "a feeble minded white woman" committed to a state mental institution who was "the daughter of a feeble minded mother in the same institution, and the mother of an illegitimate feeble minded child." The Court approved an order of the mental institution that Buck undergo sterilization. Justice Oliver Wendell Holmes, himself an ardent eugenicist, gave eugenic theory the imprimatur of constitutional law in his infamous declaration: "Three generations of imbeciles are enough."[80]

The salient feature of the eugenic sterilization laws is their brutal imposition of society's restrictive norms of motherhood. Governmental control of reproduction in the name of science masks racist and classist judgments about who deserves to bear children. It is grounded on the premise that people who depart from social norms do not deserve to procreate. Carrie Buck, for example, was punished by sterilization, not because of her mental disability, but because of her deviance from society's social and sexual norms.[81]

Explanations of the eugenic rationale reveal this underlying moral standard for procreation. One eugenicist, for example, justified his extreme approach of putting the socially inadequate to death as "'the surest, the simplest, the kindest, and most humane means for preventing reproduction among those *whom we deem unworthy of the high privilege.*'"[82] Dr. Albert Priddy, the superintendent of the Virginia State Epileptic Colony, similarly explained the necessity of eugenic sterilization in one of his annual reports: the "'sexual immorality' of 'antisocial' 'morons' rendered the inmates 'wholly unfit for exercising the *right of motherhood.*'"[83]

Fourteen years after *Buck v. Bell,* the Court acknowledged the danger of the eugenic rationale. Justice William O. Douglas recognized both the fundamental quality of the right to procreate and its connection to equality in a later sterilization decision, *Skinner v. Oklahoma*.[84] *Skinner* considered the constitutionality of the Oklahoma Habitual Criminal Sterilization Act, authorizing the sterilization of persons convicted two or more times for "felonies involving moral turpitude." An Oklahoma court had ordered Skinner to undergo a vasectomy after he was convicted once of stealing chickens and twice of robbery with firearms. The statute, the Supreme Court found, treated unequally criminals who had committed intrinsically the same quality of offense. For example, men who had committed grand larceny three times were sterilized, but embezzlers were not. The Court struck down the statute as a violation of the equal protection clause. Declaring the right to procreate to be "one of the basic civil rights of man," the Court applied strict scrutiny to the classification and held that the government failed to demonstrate that the statute's classifications were justified by eugenics or the inheritability of criminal traits.[85]

Skinner rested on grounds that linked equal protection doctrine and the right to procreate. Justice Douglas framed the legal question as "a sensitive and important area of *human rights*."[86] The reason for the Court's elevation of the right to procreate was the Court's recognition of the significant risk of discriminatory selection inherent in state intervention in reproduction. The Court also understood the genocidal implications of a government standard for procreation: "In evil or reckless hands [the government's power to sterilize] can cause races or types which are inimical to the dominant group to wither and disappear."[87] The critical role of procreation to human survival and the invidious potential for government discrimination against disfavored groups make heightened protection crucial. The Court understood that use of governmental power to sterilize in a manner that discriminated against certain types of criminals was as invidious as if the government "had selected a particular race or nationality for oppressive treatment."[88]

Although the reasons advanced for the sterilization of chicken thieves and the prosecution of drug-addicted mothers are different, both practices are dangerous for similar reasons. Both effectuate judgments by the government that certain members of society do not deserve to have children. As the Court recognized in *Skinner,* the enforcement of a government standard for procreation denies the disfavored group a critical aspect of human dignity.

The history of compulsory sterilization demonstrates that society deems women who deviate from its norms of motherhood—in 1941 delinquent teenage girls like Carrie Buck who bore illegitimate children, and today poor Black crack addicts who use drugs during pregnancy— "unworthy of the high privilege" of procreation. The government therefore refuses to affirm their human dignity by helping them overcome obstacles to good mothering. Rather, it punishes them by sterilization or criminal prosecution and thereby denies them a basic part of their humanity. When this denial is based on race, the violation is especially serious. Governmental policies that perpetuate racial subordination through the denial of procreative rights, which threaten both racial equality and privacy at once, should be subject to the highest scrutiny.

Toward a New Privacy Jurisprudence

Imagine that courts and legislatures had accepted the argument that the prosecution of crack-addicted mothers violates their right of privacy. All pending indictments for drug use during pregnancy were dismissed, and bills proposing fetal abuse laws were discarded. Would there be any perceptible change in the inferior status of Black women? Pregnant crack addicts would still be denied treatment, and most poor Black women would continue to receive inadequate prenatal care. The infant mortality rate for Blacks would remain deplorably high. In spite of the benefits of privacy doctrine for women of color, liberal notions of privacy are inadequate to eliminate the subordination of Black women. There are two approaches that I believe are necessary for privacy theory to contribute to the eradication of racial hierarchy. First, we need to develop a positive view of the right of privacy. Second, the law must recognize the connection between the right of privacy and racial equality.

The most compelling argument against privacy rhetoric, from the perspective of women of color, is the connection that feminist scholars have drawn between privacy and the abortion-funding decisions. Critics of the concept of privacy note that framing the abortion right as a right merely to be shielded from state intrusion into private choices provides no basis for a constitutional claim to public support for abortions. As the Court explained in *Harris v. McRae,* "although government may not place obstacles in the path of a woman's exercise of her freedom of choice, it need not remove those not of its own creation." [89] MacKinnon concludes that abortion as a private privilege rather than a public right only serves to perpetuate inequality:

Privacy conceived as a right from public intervention and disclosure is the opposite of the relief that *Harris* sought for welfare women. State intervention would have provided a choice women did *not* have in [the] private [realm]. The women in *Harris,* women whose sexual refusal has counted for particularly little, needed something to make their privacy effective. The logic of the Court's response resembles the logic by which women are supposed to consent to sex. Preclude the alternatives, then call the sole remaining option "her choice." The point is that the alternatives are precluded *prior* to the reach of the chosen legal doctrine. They are precluded by conditions of sex, race, and class—the very conditions the privacy frame not only leaves tacit but exists to *guarantee.*[90]

This critique is correct in its observation that the power of privacy doctrine in poor women's lives is constrained by liberal notions of freedom. First, the abstract freedom to choose is of meager value without meaningful options from which to choose and the ability to effectuate one's choice. The traditional concept of privacy makes the false presumption that the right to choose is contained entirely within the individual and not circumscribed by the material conditions of the individual's life. Second, the abstract freedom of self-definition is of little help to someone who lacks the resources to realize the personality she envisions or whose emergent self is continually beaten down by social forces. Defining the guarantee of personhood as no more than shielding a sphere of personal decisions from the reach of government—merely ensuring the individual's "right to be let alone"—may be inadequate to protect the dignity and autonomy of the poor and oppressed.

The definition of privacy as a purely negative right serves to exempt the state from any obligation to ensure the social conditions and resources necessary for self-determination and autonomous decision making. Based on this narrow view of liberty, the Supreme Court has denied a variety of claims to government aid.[91] MacKinnon notes that "it is apparently a very short step from that which the government has a duty *not* to intervene in to that which it has no duty to intervene in."[92] An evolving privacy doctrine need not make the step between these two propositions. Constitutional law professor Laurence Tribe, for example, has suggested an alternative view of the relationship between the government's negative and affirmative responsibilities in guaranteeing the rights of personhood: "Ultimately, the affirmative duties of government cannot be severed from its obligations to refrain from certain forms of control; both must respond to a substantive vision of the needs of human personality."[93]

This concept of privacy includes not only the negative proscription against government coercion, but also the affirmative duty of government to protect the individual's personhood from degradation and to facilitate the processes of choice and self-determination. This approach shifts the focus of privacy theory from state nonintervention to an affirmative guarantee of personhood and autonomy. Under this postliberal doctrine, the government is not only prohibited from punishing crack-addicted women for choosing to bear children; it is also required to provide drug treatment and prenatal care. Legal scholar Robin West has eloquently captured this progressive understanding of the due-process clause in which privacy doctrine is grounded: "The ideal of due process, then, is an individual life free of illegitimate social coercion facilitated by hierarchies of class, gender, or race. The goal is an affirmatively autonomous existence: a meaningfully flourishing, independent, enriched individual life." [94]

This affirmative view of privacy is enhanced by recognizing the connection between privacy and racial equality. The government's duty to guarantee personhood and autonomy stems from the needs not only of the individual but also of the entire community. The harm caused by the prosecution of crack-addicted mothers is not simply the incursion on each individual crack addict's decision making; it is the perpetuation of a degraded image that affects the status of an entire race. The devaluation of a poor Black addict's decision to bear a child is tied to the dominant society's disregard for the motherhood of all Black women. The diminished value placed on Black motherhood, in turn, is a badge of racial inferiority worn by all Black people. The affirmative view of privacy recognizes the connection between the dehumanization of the individual and the subordination of the group.

Thus, the reason that legislatures should reject laws that punish Black women's reproductive choices is not an absolute and isolated notion of individual autonomy. Rather, legislatures should reject these laws as a critical step toward eradicating a racial hierarchy that has historically demeaned Black motherhood. Respecting Black women's decision to bear children is a necessary ingredient of a community that affirms the personhood of all of its members. The right to reproductive autonomy is in this way linked to the goal of racial equality and the broader pursuit of a just society. This broader dimension of privacy's guarantees provides a stronger claim to government's affirmative responsibilities.

Feminist legal theory, with its emphasis on the law's concrete effect on the condition of women, calls for a reassessment of traditional privacy law. It may be possible, however, to reconstruct a privacy jurisprudence that retains the focus on autonomy and personhood while making privacy doctrine effective. Before dismissing the right of privacy altogether, we should explore ways to give the concepts of choice and personhood more substance. The word *privacy* may be too imbued with limiting liberal interpretation to be a useful descriptive term. *Privacy* connotes shielding from intrusion and thus may be suitable to describe solely the negative proscription against government action. Moreover, the word conjures up the public-private dichotomy. *Liberty,* on the other hand, has more potential to include the affirmative duty of government to ensure the conditions necessary for autonomy and self-definition. In reconstructing the constitutional guarantees I have been discussing, it may be more appropriate to rely on the broader concept of liberty. In this way, the continuing process of challenge and subversion—the feminist critique of liberal privacy doctrine, followed by the racial critique of the feminist analysis—will forge a finer legal tool for dismantling institutions of domination.

CONCLUSION

Our understanding of the prosecutions of drug-addicted mothers must include the perspective of the women whom they most directly affect. The prosecutions arise in a particular historical and political context that has constrained reproductive choice for poor women of color. The state's decision to punish drug-addicted mothers does not help them but rather stems from the poverty and race of the defendants and from society's denial of their full dignity as human beings. Viewing the issue from their vantage point reveals that the women prosecutions punish for having babies are women whose motherhood has historically been devalued.

A policy that attempts to protect fetuses by denying the humanity of their mothers will inevitably fail. I hear this false dichotomy in the words of Muskegon, Michigan, narcotics officer Al Van Hemert: "If the mother wants to smoke crack and kill herself, I don't care. Let her die, but don't take that poor baby with her." [95] We must question such a policy's true concern for the dignity of the fetus, just as we question the motives of the slave owner who protected the unborn slave child while whipping his pregnant mother. Although the master attempted to separate the mother and fetus for his commercial ends, their fates were inextricably intertwined. The tragedy of crack babies is initially a tragedy of crack-addicted mothers. Both are part of a larger tragedy of a community that is suffering a host of indignities, including, significantly, the denial of equal respect for its women's reproductive decisions.

It is only by affirming the personhood and equality of poor women of color that the survival of their future generation will be ensured. The first principle of the government's response to the crisis of drug-exposed babies should be the recognition of their mothers' worth and entitlement to autonomy over their reproductive lives. A commitment to guaranteeing these fundamental rights of poor women of color, rather than punishing them, is the true solution to the problem of unhealthy babies.

NOTES

A longer version of this essay was published in *Harvard Law Review* 104 (1991): 1419–82 (copyright © 1991 by the Harvard Law Review Association). I would like to thank my colleagues Howard Latin, James Pope, and Nadine Taub for their careful comments on an earlier draft of the article. Anita Allen, Regina Austin, and Dwight Greene also gave me helpful suggestions. I am also grateful to Anita Brown, Nina Loewenstein, Elizabeth Marshall, Eric Pennington, Claudia Wernick, and Andrea Williams for their research assistance.

1. Michael P. Johnson, "Smothered Slave Infants: Were Slave Mothers at Fault?" *Journal of Southern History* 47 (1981): 493–520, 513.

2. See *State v. Johnson,* No. E89–890-CFA, slip op. at 1 (Fla. Cir. Ct. July 13, 1989), aff'd, No. 89–1765, 1991 Fla. App. LEXIS 3583 (Fla. Dist. Ct. App. April 18, 1991).

3. Lynn M. Paltrow, *Criminal Prosecutions Against Pregnant Women* (New York: Reproductive Freedom Project, American Civil Liberties Union Foundation, 1992).

4. See Martha A. Fineman, *The Neutered Mother, the Sexual Family, and Other Twentieth-Century Tragedies* (New York: Routledge, 1995), 101–18.

5. Dorothy E. Roberts, "The Only Good Poor Woman: Unconstitutional Conditions and Welfare," *Denver University Law Review* 72 (1995): 931–48; Lucy A. Williams, "The Ideology of Division: Behavior Modification Welfare Reform Proposals," *Yale Law Journal* 102 (1992): 719–46.

6. See Angela P. Harris, "Race and Essentialism in Feminist Legal Theory," *Stanford Law Review* 42 (1990): 581–616, 604; Marlee Kline, "Race, Racism, and Feminist Legal Theory," *Harvard Women's Law Journal* 12 (1989): 115, 121; Judith Scales-Trent, "Black Women and the Constitution: Finding Our Place, Asserting Our Rights," *Harvard Civil Rights–Civil Liberties Law Review* 24 (1989): 9.

7. See Harris, "Race and Essentialism"; Kimberle Crenshaw, "Demarginalizing the Intersection of Race and Sex: A Black Feminist Critique of Antidiscrimination Doctrine, Feminist Theory, and Racist Politics," *1989 University of Chicago Legal Forum* (1989): 139–67. See also Elizabeth V. Spelman, *Inessential Woman: Problems of Exclusion in Feminist Thought* (Boston: Beacon Press, 1988).

8. See "Crack: A Disaster of Historic Dimension, Still Growing," *New York Times,* May 28, 1989, sec. 4: 14.

9. See Diane Alters, "Women and Crack: Equal Addiction, Unequal Care," *Boston Globe,* November 1, 1989, 1.

10. See Gina Kolata, "On Streets Ruled by Crack, Families Die," *New York Times,* August 11, 1989, A13.

11. See Jean Davidson, "Drug Babies Push Issue of Fetal Rights," *Los Angeles Times,* April 25, 1989, pt. 1: 3.

12. See Douglas Besharov, "Crack Babies: The Worst Threat Is Mom Herself," *Washington Post,* August 6, 1989, B1.

13. Ira J. Chasnoff et al., "Temporal Patterns of Cocaine Use in Pregnancy: Perinatal Outcome," *Journal of the American Medical Association* 261 (1989): 1741; M. G. Neerhof et al., "Cocaine Abuse During Pregnancy: Peripartum Prevalence and Perinatal Outcome," *American Journal of Obstetrics and Gynecology* 161 (1989): 633; D. B. Petitti and C. Coleman, "Cocaine and the Risk of Low Birth Weight," *American Journal of Public Health* 80 (1990): 25.

14. Ira J. Chasnoff, "Cocaine, Pregnancy, and the Neonate," *Women and Health* 15 (1989): 23, 32–33; Ira J. Chasnoff et al., "Cocaine Use in Pregnancy," *New England Journal of Medicine* 313 (1985): 666.

15. Linda Mayes, "The Problem of Prenatal Cocaine Exposure: A Rush to Judgment," *Journal of the American Medical Association* 267 (1992): 406; Barry Zuckerman and Deborah A. Frank, "Crack Kids: Not Broken," *Pediatrics* 89 (1992): 337.

16. Marilyn Poland, Joel Ager, and Jane Olson, "Barriers to Receiving Adequate Prenatal Care," *American Journal of Obstetrics and Gynecology* 157 (1987): 297–303; L. Ryan, S. Ehrlich, and L. Finnegan, "Cocaine Abuse in Pregnancy: Effects on the Fetus and Newborn," *Neurotoxicology and Teratology* 9 (1987): 295; S. N. MacGregor et al., "Cocaine Abuse during Pregnancy: Correlation between Prenatal Care and Perinatal Outcome," *Obstetrics and Gynecology* 74 (1989): 882.

17. G. Koren et al., "Bias against the Null Hypothesis: The Reproductive Hazards of Cocaine," *Lancet,* December 16, 1989, 1440.

18. Kathleen Nolan, "Protecting Fetuses from Prenatal Hazards: Whose Crimes? What Punishment?" *Criminal Justice Ethics* 9 (1990): 13, 14.

19. Rorie Sherman, "Keeping Babies Free of Drugs," *National Law Journal,* October 16, 1989, 1.

20. Bonnie Vergeer, "Note, the Problem of the Drug-Exposed Newborn: A Return to Principled Intervention," *Stanford Law Review* 42 (1990): 745, 749, 752, n.25.

21. *United States v. Vaughn,* Crim. No. F 2172–88 B (D.C. Super. Ct. August 23, 1988); Kary L. Moss, "Pregnant? Go Directly to Jail," *American Bar*

Association Journal, November 1, 1988, 20; Richard Cohen, "When a Fetus Has More Rights Than the Mother," *Washington Post,* July 28, 1988, A21.

22. Davidson, "Fetal Rights," 19.

23. Black women are five times more likely to live in poverty, five times more likely to be on welfare, and three times more likely to be unemployed than are white women. See United States Commission on Civil Rights, *The Economic Status of Black Women* (Washington, D.C.: Government Printing Office, 1990), 1.

24. Molly McNulty, "Pregnancy Police: The Health Policy and Legal Implications of Punishing Pregnant Women for Harm to Their Fetuses," *New York University Review of Law and Social Change* 16 (1988): 277–319, 319.

25. Vergeer, "Drug-Exposed Newborn," 753, 782 n.157; Kolata, "Streets Ruled by Crack," A13.

26. Ira J. Chasnoff, Harvey J. Landress, and Mark E. Barrett, "The Prevalence of Illicit-Drug or Alcohol Use during Pregnancy and Discrepancies in Mandatory Reporting in Pinellas County, Florida," *New England Journal of Medicine* 322 (1990): 1202–6; Carol Angel, "Addicted Babies: Legal System's Response Unclear," *Los Angeles Daily Journal,* February 29, 1988, 1.

27. Vergeer, "Drug-Exposed Newborn," 753, 798–99.

28. Ibid., 754, n. 36; Chasnoff, Landress, and Barrett, "Illicit-Drug or Alcohol Use," 1206.

29. Chasnoff, Landress, and Barrett, "Illicit-Drug or Alcohol Use."

30. Ibid., 1204.

31. S. K. Clarren and D. W. Smith, "The Fetal Alcohol Syndrome," *New England Journal of Medicine* 298 (1978): 1063; Elizabeth Rosenthal, "When a Pregnant Woman Drinks," *New York Times Magazine,* February 4, 1990, 30; Barry Zuckerman et al., "Effects of Maternal Marijuana and Cocaine Use on Fetal Growth," *New England Journal of Medicine* 320 (1989): 762.

32. Nolan, "Protecting Fetuses from Prenatal Hazards," 15; "Doctors Criticized on Fetal Problem," *New York Times,* December 11, 1990, B10; Sandra Blakeslee, "Parents Fight for a Future for Infants Born to Drugs," *New York Times,* May 19, 1990, A1; Rosenthal, "When Pregnant Woman Drinks," 49.

33. James A. Inciardi, Dorothy Lockwood, and Anne E. Pottieger, *Women and Crack-Cocaine* (New York: Macmillan, 1993), 1–13.

34. Angela Davis, *Women, Race, and Class* (New York: Vintage Books, 1981), 7; Jacqueline Jones, *Labor of Love, Labor of Sorrow: Black Women, Work, and the Family from Slavery to the Present* (New York: Vintage Books, 1986), 12.

35. Linda Gordon, *Woman's Body, Woman's Right: A Social History of Birth Control in America* (New York: Grossman, 1976), 329–40.

36. Ibid., 332.

37. Davis, *Women, Race, and Class,* 220.

38. Rosalind Petchesky, "Reproduction, Ethics, and Public Policy: The Federal Sterilization Regulations," *Hastings Center Report* 9 (1979): 29; "Note, Sterilization Abuse: Current State of the Law and Remedies for Abuse," *Golden Gate University Law Review* 10 (1980): 1147, 1152–53.

39. See *Relf v. Weinberger,* 372 F. Supp. 1196, 1199 (D.D.C. 1974), on remand sub nom. *Relf v. Mathews,* 403 F. Supp. 1235 (D.D.C. 1975), vacated sub nom. *Relf v. Weinberger,* 565 F.2d 722 (D.C. Cir. 1977).

40. Petchesky, "Reproduction, Ethics, and Public Policy," 39; "Note, Sterilization Abuse," 1154.

41. Tom Bethell, "Norplant Is Welfare State's New Opiate: Contraceptive Doesn't Address Causes of Illegitimate Births, *Los Angeles Times,* January 24, 1993, M5.

42. Davis, *Women, Race, and Class,* 5; Deborah White, *Ar'n't I a Woman? Female Slaves in the Plantation South* (New York: Norton, 1985), 16, 27–29.

43. White, *Ar'n't I a Woman?* 28–29, 61.

44. Silvia A. Gray and Lynn M. Nybell, "Issues in African-American Family Preservation," *Child Welfare* 69 (1990): 513.

45. Peggy Cooper Davis and Guatam Barua, "Custodial Choices for Children at Risk: Bias, Sequentiality, and the Law," *University of Chicago Law School Roundtable* 2 (1995): 139; Michael Wald, "State Intervention on Behalf of 'Neglected' Children: Standards for Removal of Children from Their Homes, Monitoring the Status of Children in Foster Care, and Termination of Parental Rights," *Stanford Law Review* 28 (1976): 629 n.21.

46. Paula Giddings, *When and Where I Enter: The Impact of Black Women on Race and Sex in America* (New York: Bantam Books, 1984), 325–35; bell hooks, *Ain't I a Woman: Black Women and Feminism* (Boston: South End Press, 1981), 70–83.

47. Office of Planning and Policy Research, U.S. Department of Labor, *The Negro Family: The Case for National Action* (Washington, D.C.: Government Printing Office, 1965), 5.

48. See Wahneema Lubiano, "Black Ladies, Welfare Queens, and State Minstrels: Ideological War by Narrative Means," in Toni Morrison, ed., *Race-ing Justice, En-Gendering Power: Essays on Anita Hill, Clarence Thomas, and the Construction of Social Reality* (New York: Pantheon, 1992), 323, 332.

49. Jan Hoffman, "Pregnant, Addicted—and Guilty?" *New York Times Magazine,* August 19, 1990, 44.

50. U.S. Department of Commerce, Bureau of the Census, *Statistical Abstract of the United States* (Washington, D.C.: Government Printing Office, 1990), 77 (table 110).

51. Francis G. Caro, Debra Kalmuss, and Iris Lopez, *Barriers to Prenatal Care* (New York: Community Service Society, 1988), 1.

52. D. B. Binsacca et al., "Factors Associated with Low Birthweight in an Inner-City Population: The Role of Financial Problems," *American Journal of Public Health* 77 (1987): 505; K. J. Leveno et al., "Prenatal Care and the Low Birth Weight Infant," *Obstetrics and Gynecology* 66 (1985): 599.

53. Caro, Kalmuss, and Lopez, *Barriers to Prenatal Care*; M. A. Curry, "Nonfinancial Barriers to Prenatal Care," *Women and Health* 15 (1989): 85–87; Ruth Zambrana, "A Research Agenda on Issues Affecting Poor and Minority Women: A Model for Understanding Their Health Needs," *Women and Health* 14 (1988): 137, 148–50.

54. Dana Huges et al., *The Health of America's Children* (Washington, D.C.: Children's Defense Fund, 1989), 4 (table 1.1).

55. Wendy Chavkin, "Drug Addiction and Pregnancy: Policy Crossroads," *American Journal of Public Health* 80 (1990): 483; McNulty, "Pregnancy Police," 301–2.

56. Chavkin, "Drug Addiction and Pregnancy," 485; Molly McNulty, "Combatting Pregnancy Discrimination in Access to Substance Abuse Treatment for Low-Income Women," *Clearinghouse Review* 23 (1989): 21.

57. Dorothy E. Roberts, *Women, Pregnancy, and Substance Abuse* (Washington, D.C.: Center for Women Policy Studies, 1991); Chavkin, "Drug Addiction and Pregnancy," 485.

58. American Medical Association, "Report of the Board of Trustees on Legal Interventions during Pregnancy: Court Ordered Medical Treatments and Legal Penalties for Potentially Harmful Behavior by Pregnant Women," *Journal of the American Medical Association* 264 (1990): 2663–70.

59. Trial transcript, *State v. Johnson*, 364.

60. Mari J. Matsuda, "When the First Quail Calls: Multiple Consciousness as Jurisprudential Method," *Women's Rights Law Reporter* (1989): 7, 8.

61. Ibid.

62. *Roe v. Wade*, 410 U.S. 113, 152–56 (1973); Jed Rubenfeld, "The Right of Privacy," *Harvard Law Review* 102 (1989): 737.

63. *Whalen v. Roe*, 429 U.S. 589, 599–600 (1977).

64. See, for example, *Roe v. Wade*, 410 U.S. 113 (1973) (right to choose whether to terminate a pregnancy); *Loving v. Virginia*, 388 U.S. 1 (1967) (right to choose one's spouse); *Griswold v. Connecticut*, 381 U.S. 479, 485 (1965) (right to decide whether to use contraceptives); *Skinner v. Oklahoma*, 316 U.S. 535 (1942) (right to procreate).

65. *Carey v. Population Services International*, 431 U.S. 678, 685 (1977).

66. 405 U.S. 438 (1972).

67. Ibid., 453 (emphasis omitted).

68. *Colautti v. Franklin*, 439 U.S. 379, 386 n.7 (1979); *Maher v. Roe*, 432 U.S. 464, 474 n.8 (1977).

69. Harris, "Race and Essentialism," 613.

70. Ibid.

71. Catharine MacKinnon, "Roe v. Wade: A Study in Male Ideology," in *Abortion: Moral and Legal Perspectives*, ed. Jay L. Garfield and Patricia Hennessey (Amherst: University of Massachusetts Press, 1984), 51–53.

72. Ibid., 49.

73. Jacqueline Jones, " 'My Mother Was Much of a Woman': Black Women, Work, and the Family under Slavery," *Feminist Studies* 8 (1982): 235–69; Kline, "Race, Racism, and Feminist Legal Theory," 122–23.

74. Kline, "Race, Racism, and Feminist Legal Theory," 129.

75. John Robertson, "Procreative Liberty and the Control of Conception, Pregnancy, and Childbirth," *Virginia Law Review* 69 (1983): 405, 437–38, 445–47.

76. Dorothy E. Roberts, "The Future of Reproductive Choice for Poor Women and Women of Color," *Women's Rights Law Reporter* 12 (1990): 59.

77. Mark H. Haller, *Eugenics: Hereditarian Attitudes in American Thought* (New Brunswick, N.J.: Rutgers University Press, 1984).

78. Phillip Reilly, *The Surgical Solution: A History of Involuntary Sterilization in the United States* (Baltimore: Johns Hopkins University Press, 1991).

79. 274 U.S. 200 (1927).

80. Ibid., 207.

81. Apparently, Carrie was sterilized because she was poor and had been pregnant out of wedlock. Paul A. Lombardo, "Three Generations, No Imbeciles: New Light on *Buck v. Bell*," *New York University Law Review* 60 (1985): 30, 51.

82. Haller, *Eugenics*, 42 (quoting eugenicist W. Duncan McKim); emphasis added.

83. Lombardo, "Three Generations, No Imbeciles," 46 (quoting Report of the Virginia State Epileptic Colony [1922–23], 27); emphasis added.

84. 316 U.S. 535 (1942).

85. Ibid., 541.

86. Ibid., 536 (emphasis added).

87. Ibid., 541.

88. Ibid.

89. 448 U.S. 297, 316 (1980).

90. Catharine MacKinnon, *Feminism Unmodified* (Cambridge, Mass.: Harvard University Press, 1987), 101.

91. See, for example, *DeShaney v. Winnebago County Department of Social Services*, 489 U.S. 189, 196 (1989): "our cases have recognized that the Due Process Clauses generally confer no affirmative right to governmental aid, even where such aid may be necessary to secure life, liberty, or property interests of which the government itself may not deprive the individual."

92. MacKinnon, *Feminism Unmodified*, 96.

93. Laurence H. Tribe, *American Constitutional Law* (Mineola, N.Y.: Foundation Press, 1988), 1305.

94. Robin West, "Progressive and Conservative Constitutionalism," *Michigan Law Review* 88 (1990): 641, 707.

95. Hoffman, "Pregnant, Addicted—and Guilty?" 34.

PART THREE

ACTIVISM

Several decades of fierce public struggle over abortion rights push us to rethink what we know about activism and activists in this arena. The four essays in this section look at different activist sectors to define the principles of abortion activism or, in the case of Faye Ginsburg's essay, to illuminate contemporary anti-secular, anti-abortion political activism.

Loretta Ross captures the little-known history of African-American women's activist determination to control their own fertility. She locates the roots of this activism in the nineteenth and early twentieth centuries, in individual efforts as well as in the African-American women's movement and women's organizations. Ross demonstrates a recurrent, if not continuous, connection between the civil rights and reproductive rights struggles of African Americans. Most fundamentally, she refutes the claim that abortion is not an African-American women's issue and challenges reproductive rights activists and organizations today to set goals and practice an activism that includes all women.

Marlene Fried is also deeply concerned with how an inclusive activist community and politics can be created and sustained. In response to anti-rights successes during the 1980s and 1990s, Fried puts forth an energizing mission statement that defines an expanded pro-rights activism and expanded notions of abortion rights. In part she draws on recent insights and activities of organizations of women of color in the United

States and on an internationalist perspective fed by her participation in the 1995 women's conference in Beijing.

Faye Ginsburg explores the personnel and the context that gave rise to the direct-action anti-rights group Operation Rescue. She finds the agenda and ideology of this radical activist organization consistent with those of groups throughout U.S. history that have been unwilling to acknowledge the legitimacy of secular law and secular society.

Finally, Marie Bass reports from the front lines of coalition-building among diverse pro-rights constituencies. As a founder of the Reproductive Health Technologies Project, Bass recounts her own experience with the complexities of building coalitions. She underscores the profound necessity to do so at this point in the abortion rights struggle, an imperative recognized by Ross and Fried as well.

8

Loretta J. Ross

AFRICAN-AMERICAN WOMEN
AND ABORTION

Only justice can stop a curse.

Alice Walker

This essay reviews the activism of African-American women in the abortion rights movement, highlighting the past fifty years.[1] Many observers mistakenly view African-American women's struggle for abortion rights and reproductive freedom in the 1990s as reflecting a relatively recent commitment. More accurately, this activism should be placed in the context of our historical struggle against racism, sexism, and poverty.

The fact is, when methods of fertility control have been available and accessible, African-American women have advocated for and used these strategies even more frequently than their white counterparts.[2] For example, when family planning was first institutionalized in Louisiana in 1965, Black women were six times more likely than white women to sign up for contraception.[3]

But when contraceptives were unavailable and abortion was illegal, septic abortions were a primary killer of African-American women. One study estimated that 80 percent of deaths caused by illegal abortions in New York in the 1960s involved Black and Puerto Rican women.[4] In Georgia between 1965 and 1967 the Black maternal death rate due to illegal abortion was fourteen times that of white women.[5]

Central to my argument is the fact that African-American women have never been "one-dimensional victims of patriarchy."[6] Nor have we been one-dimensional activists. African-American women have made consistent and critical activist contributions to the evolution of the reproductive rights movement in the United States. Already in the early 1920s the Black women's club movement joined forces with early proponents of birth control and called for the placement of family-planning clinics in Black neighborhoods while criticizing eugenics or population control forces.

Black women in the 1920s and 1930s wanted individual control over fertility, while at the same time they resisted government and privately funded anti-natalist population control campaigns.[7] This dual-value system seeded an expanded vision of reproductive freedom that guides our work today.

The early African-American activists understood the complex nature of Black womanhood and believed that fertility control was an essential part of the movement to rise from the brutal legacy of slavery. In the words of Brenda Joyner, reproductive rights activism by Black women has been and is "a feminism which realizes that the issues of reproductive control are broader than just the fight for gender equality. It is a feminism which understands the world simultaneously from race and class as well as gender perspectives."[8] This essay does not attempt to identify an essential Black women's viewpoint regarding these issues but seeks to provide "critical self-consciousness about our positionality, defined as it is by race, gender, class and ideology."[9] The time has come for us to understand both our powerlessness in society and our influence on the reproductive rights movement.

Despite the fact that much of the decline in the fertility rates of African Americans since the Civil War resulted from the activism and determined choices of African-American women, our contributions to the birth control and abortion movements in the United States have been obscured by racist and sexist assumptions about us, our sexuality, and our fertility. Distilling fact from myth is difficult because so many accounts of African-American and women's history are written from perspectives that fail to acknowledge our impact. This omission distorts the contemporary views of African-American women about the reproductive freedom movement and our ownership of it.

The Black feminist commitment to reproductive rights has remained buried for at least three important reasons. First, the movement for abortion rights is erroneously seen as belonging to the predominantly white women's movement. Feminist literature often (but not always) reflects a popularized perception that African-American women's awareness regarding gender equality and abortion rights is underdeveloped. Brenda Joyner, who has been an abortion provider for the past fifteen years, believes that white mainstream women's groups have undervalued the participation and concerns of women of color in the reproductive rights movement: "Perhaps the question is not really where are women of color in the abortion rights and reproductive rights movement. Rather, where is the primarily white middle-class movement in our struggles for freedom? Where was a white middle-class movement when the [1977] Hyde Amendment took away Medicaid funding of abortions for poor women?"[10]

Second, the struggle for reproductive rights is not commonly perceived as a part of the civil rights movement, although in fact it was part of that movement until after World War II. In the early twentieth century Black organizations were often visible supporters of fertility control for Black women, linking reproductive rights to racial advancement. For example, from the mid–nineteenth century to the present, the growth rate of the African-American population has been more than halved.[11] Historians and demographers typically attribute this and other declines in African-American birthrates to poverty, disease, coercive family planning, or other external factors. These assumptions ignore the possibility that African Americans were in any way consciously responsible for the change by choosing to use birth control and abortion. In the 1930s African-American women were never *passive* victims of eugenics (the "improvement" of humankind through selective breeding), forced sterilization, and other medical, commercial, and state policies or reproductive control. Current debates over the genetic causes of criminality, the validity of IQ tests, inherited intelligence, welfare reform, quotas, and affirmative action all suggest the extent to which the eugenics movement still affects public policy. But for the past sixty years, African-American women have been at the forefront of challenging the relationship between racist science and public policy in our society.

Thus, a third reason that the Black feminist tradition has been obfuscated is that racist and sexist assumptions held by population experts, feminists, or the African-American community itself ignore our power as African-American women to make responsible reproductive and political decisions for ourselves. A historical perspective is necessary to understand and place in context the contemporary views of African-American women on abortion and birth control.

I have been a reproductive rights activist for the past twenty-three years, beginning with work in the early 1970s on sterilization abuse. Because I have organized Black women around reproductive rights, I have witnessed the development of a strong reproductive freedom movement among Black women during this period. In doing research to support my activism, I discovered a long tradition of reproductive rights advocacy by Black women that was either undocumented or not widely understood. Despite the lack of a full or easily accessible historical record, I became determined to reconnect the work of Black activists at the beginning of the twentieth century to the work and ideology of those at the end.

Many African-American women are alienated from the abortion issue. Our slave history makes many of us determined never again to relinquish control over our reproduction to anyone. As a 1989 brochure published by African American Women for Reproductive Freedom put it, "Somebody owned our flesh, and decided if and when and with whom and how our bodies were to be used. Somebody said that Black women could be raped, held in concubinage, forced to bear children year in and year out, but often not raise them." [12] This haunting specter of slavery is real and moving. This is the collective nightmare that haunts our vision of a racist system controlling our bodies.

However, this rationale for abortion—that because as slaves we were valued for our procreative capacity, we should never be a slave to pregnancy again—is somewhat short of the Black feminist analysis necessary to understand the complexities of abortion and its impact on the lives of African-American women. Every Black woman must believe she has a right to control her body simply because she is human. This belief does not deny her femaleness or her Blackness but rests upon a fundamentally solid acceptance of her own uniqueness and sense of self-esteem—a belief in her *human rights* and right to bodily self-determination. [13]

When we demand control over our own bodies, we must not depend solely on our history of slavery, our African traditions, or even on a colorized white feminist analysis. We need to support abortion rights from an analysis that is built from a strong and shared understanding of how the forces of racism, sexism, homophobia, and economic oppression affect our lives. Equating the denial of abortion rights to slavery is convenient intellectual shorthand, but it leaves Black women vulnerable to manipulation by sexists who believe that our role is either to have babies for the long-awaited Black revolution or to cease reproducing altogether, to comply with racist assumptions about our "overpopulation."

It is equally futile to romanticize our claim to "traditional" African society, even though abortion and birth control were seen as the province of women, not the decisions of men, in most African societies. Traditional knowledge and skills are almost totally inaccessible to African-American women today. Sadly, they are even inaccessible to many African women because of the profuse marketing of contraceptives and other devices that has eroded the chain of knowledge that made women self-reliant in the past.

What we need is a new feminist theory of reproductive freedom for Black women. We have a strong understanding of the role that race, class, and gender have played in our lives—our triple-oppression theories. But despite our history of activism, many Black women still do not see abortion rights as a stepping-stone to freedom because abortion rights do not automatically end the oppression of Black women. On the other hand, these rights do allow some control over our biology, freeing us from unwanted pregnancies, and they are fundamental to bodily and political self-determination. To ask whether African-American women favor or oppose abortion may currently be fashionable and an opportunity for manipulative politicians. But the answer is obviously yes: we obtain 24 percent of the abortions in the United States, more than 500,000 annually.[14] The question is not *if* we support abortion, but how, and when, and why. Our circumstances have dictated our choices. Neither persuasive analysis nor ideology influenced African-American women to support abortion and birth control. We did so because we needed to. Necessity was the midwife to our politics.

Regrettably, African-American women have been reluctant to analyze our history regarding abortion and to speak out collectively and publicly in support of abortion rights. To do so in the 1960s and 1970s seemed to support arguments of Black genocide, a charge that was not unreasonable in view of a multitude of attacks on African Americans. To speak out also risked highlighting abortion over other aspects of our struggle to achieve reproductive freedom. These struggles involve our experiences of pregnancy, infant mortality, sterilization abuse, welfare abuse, and sexuality in general. Even since legalization, the word *abortion* has remained one of the most emotionally charged words within the African-American community, bringing forth twin fears of genocide and suicide. In some circles, we still refer to it as the "A" word!

To compound the problem, Black women are ambivalent about the mainstream pro-choice movement. While a 1991 poll by the National Council of Negro Women and the Communications Consortium revealed that 83 percent of African Americans support abortion and birth control, little of that support translates into membership in predominantly white pro-choice organizations.[15] The pro-choice movement, as a subset of the larger women's movement, has not been able to attract significant numbers of Black women into its ranks, even though many special projects targeting women of color proliferated in the 1980s.[16]

At the same time, the anti-abortion movement became adept at manipulating Black fears about genocide to silence the voices of Black women who believe in reproductive freedom. Anti-abortion proponents have made frightening inroads into Black churches, which often find it difficult to openly discuss issues of Black sexuality including abortion, AIDS, homosexuality, premarital sex, and teen sexuality. A generation ago, Black ministers were in the forefront of the struggle for reproductive freedom. Today, the silence of our churches—the moral cornerstones of our community—is a reflection of the church's disconnection from the real history of African-American women.

It is up to Black women living in these difficult times to define abortion rights for ourselves. By exploring the nature of our silence, we can connect ourselves to our foremothers who were activists for reproductive freedom. As Black feminist bell hooks says, "Moving from silence into speech is a revolutionary gesture."[17] Our "revolutionary gesture" means finding our voices and rediscovering our history. We must document our own stories and give ourselves permission to speak proudly about the experiences of "ordinary" Black women whose "unexceptional" actions enabled us and the race to survive. We must dispel the myths surrounding our fertility and activism by developing our own critical analysis of abortion and birth control that does more than simply appropriate someone else's dogma. To extend bell hooks's observation, our struggle is not simply to move from silence into speech, but to change the nature and direction of our speech, to make a speech that is heard. We must make a speech that deliberately combines the personal stories and the objective reality that create the authority, authenticity, and uniqueness of the African-American female experiences. As an expression of my commitment to this credo, in this essay I draw, wherever possible, on the experiences of today's activists.

HISTORICAL CONTEXT: SLAVERY, EARLY BLACK FEMINISM, AND FERTILITY CONTROL ACTIVISM

Before the Civil War, almost 20 percent of the total United States population consisted of African-American slaves.[18] Plantation owners tried to keep knowledge of birth control and abortion away from both slaves and white women to maintain the system of white supremacy used to justify slavery and to increase their investments in human chattel.[19] In addition to the rape of slave women by slave masters to increase the number of children, breeding techniques included giving pregnant slave women lighter workloads and more rations to increase their willingness to have children. Punitive measures were also used: infertile women were treated "like barren sows and . . . passed from one unsuspecting buyer to the next."[20]

African Americans covertly used contraceptives and abortions to resist slavery. Often they employed African folk knowledge to do so. In the context of slavery, abortion and infanticide expressed a woman's desperate determination to resist the oppressive conditions of slavery.[21] As Angela Davis points out, when Black women resorted to abortion, the stories they told were not so much about the desire to be free of pregnancy, but rather about the miserable social conditions that dissuaded them from bringing new lives into the world.[22]

Throughout the nineteenth century, white southerners repeatedly expressed their racist nightmares about a huge Black population increase. In fact, the Black population of the South was growing much more slowly than the white population. In 1870 there were 5 million Blacks in the South, and in 1910 there were 8.7 million, whereas there were 8.6 million whites in 1870 and 20.5 million in 1910.[23]

By the early 1900s Black women were making significant gains in controlling their fertility by marrying late and having few children.[24] In this era the Black women's club movement, the organized voice of African-American women during the late nineteenth and early twentieth centuries, directly addressed issues of Black women's sexuality[25] and sought to "confront and redefine morality and assess its relationship to "true womanhood."[26] Stereotypes about Black women's sexuality and alleged immorality prompted many African-American women to "make the virtues as well as the wants of the colored women known to the American people . . . to put a new social value on themselves."[27] The main organization for Black women's clubs, the National Association of Colored Women, had between 150,000 and 200,000 members, mainly middle-class women, in forty-one states in the mid-1920s.[28] The club movement was integral to the networks that shared contraceptive information and supported "voluntary motherhood."[29]

In 1894 *The Women's Era,* an African-American women's journal edited by Josephine St. Pierre Ruffin, declared that "not all women are intended for mothers. Some of us have not the temperament for family life."[30] Club members and others supported this perspective, and many responded to advertisements in Black newspapers in the early twentieth century for a medicated douche product called Puf, which was reported to "end your calendar worries."

THE BIRTH CONTROL CAMPAIGN, 1915–1950

Today it is commonplace to link the emergence of the birth control movement in the early twentieth century to the coercion of African-American women by a population control establishment anxious to limit Black fertility. While the population control establishment may have had its agenda, African Americans were willingly involved in the national birth control debate for their own reasons. African-American women were sensitive to the intersection of race, gender, and class issues that affected their drive for equality in early-twentieth-century American society. According to historian Jessie Rodrique, grassroots African Americans were "active and effective participants in the establishment of local [family-planning] clinics . . . and despite cooperation with white birth control groups, Blacks maintained a degree of independence" that allowed the development of an African-American analysis of family planning and the role it played in racial progress.[31]

African-American women saw themselves not as breeders or matriarchs but as builders and nurturers of a race, a nation. Sojourner Truth's statement, "I feel as if the power of a nation is within me!"[32] affirmed the role of African-American women as "seminal forces of the endurance and creativity needed by future generations of Blacks not merely to survive, but to thrive, produce, and progress."[33]

In this spirit, the Black women's club movement supported the establishment of family-planning clinics in Black communities. In 1918 the Women's Political Association of Harlem became the first Black organization to schedule lectures on birth control. They were soon joined by dozens of other clubwomen seeking information about birth control in their communities. The National Urban League requested that the Birth Control Federation of America (the forerunner to Planned Parenthood) open a clinic in the Columbus Hill section of the Bronx in 1925. Several ministers held discussions about birth control at their churches, and in 1932 the Reverend Adam Clayton Powell of the Abyssinian Baptist Church spoke at public meetings in support of family planning.[34]

African-American organizations, including the National Association for the Advancement of Colored People (NAACP), the National Urban League, and leading Black newspapers like the *San Francisco Spokesman* (1932) and the *Pittsburgh Courier* (1936) promoted family planning. The Black press espoused this strategy as a means for uplifting the race, perhaps partially in response to the economic ravages of the Depression. The African-American newspapers of the period also reported the mortality rate of women who had septic abortions and championed the causes of Black doctors who were arrested for performing illegal abortions.[35]

The *Baltimore Afro-American* wrote that pencils, nails, and hat pins were instruments commonly used for self-induced abortions, and that abortions among Black women were deliberate, not the spontaneous result of poor health or sexually transmitted diseases. Statistics on abortions among African-American women are scarce, but 28 percent of Black women surveyed by an African-American doctor in Nashville in 1940 said they had had at least one abortion.[36]

REACTION

The opposition to fertility control for women in the 1920s came primarily from the Catholic Church, from white conservatives who feared the availability of birth control for white women, and from Black nationalist leaders like Marcus Garvey, who believed in increasing the African population in response to racial oppression. President Theodore Roosevelt condemned the tendency toward smaller family sizes among white women as race suicide. He denounced family planning as "criminal against the race."[37]

As racism, lynchings, and poverty took their heavy toll on African Americans in the early twentieth century, fears of depopulation arose within a rising Black nationalist movement. These fears produced a pronatalist shift in the views of African Americans. The change from relative indifference about population size to using population growth as a form of political currency presaged the inevitable conflict between those who believed in the right of Black women to exercise bodily self-determination and those who stressed the African-American community's need to foster political and economic self-determination.

In the United States, eugenics proponents believed that the future of native-born whites in America was threatened by the increasing population of people of color and whites who were not of Nordic-Teutonic descent. The eugenics movement not only affected the thinking in social Darwinist scientific circles, but it also grew to affect public policy, receiving the endorsement of President Calvin Coolidge, who said in 1924, "America must be kept American. Biological laws show . . . that Nordics deteriorate when mixed with other races."[38]

Unlike Malthus, the neo-Malthusians of the eugenics movement believed in contraception, at least for those they deemed inferior. To promote the reproduction of self-defined "racially superior" people, eugenics proponents argued for both "positive" methods, such as tax incentives and education for the desirable types, and "negative" methods, such as sterilization, involuntary confinement, and immigration restrictions for the undesirables.[39] The United States became the first nation in the world to permit mass sterilization as part of an effort to "purify the race." By the mid-1930s about 20,000 Americans had been sterilized against their will, and twenty-one states had passed eugenics laws.

Among supporters of eugenics were not only the rabid haters in the Ku Klux Klan but also respectable mainstream white Americans who were troubled by the effects of urbanization, industrialization, and immigration. During this same period, thousands of Blacks fled the Jim Crow South and migrated to the North. These fast-paced demographic changes alarmed many nativist whites, who questioned birth control for themselves but approved it as a way to contain people of color and immigrants.

When the movement for birth control began, organizers like Margaret Sanger believed that fertility control was linked to upward social mobility for all women, regardless of race or immigrant status. Because the medical establishment largely opposed birth control, Sanger initially emphasized woman-controlled methods that did not depend on medical assistance. Her arguments persuaded middle-class women, both Black and white, to use birth control when available.[40]

Sanger's immediate effect on African-American women was to help transform their covert support for and use of family planning into the visible public support of activists in the club movement. But African-American women envisioned an even more pointed concept of reproductive justice: the freedom to have, or not to have, children.

The early feminism of the birth control movement, which promoted equality and reproductive rights for all women regardless of race or economic status, collapsed under the weight of support offered by the growing number of nativist whites. Under the influence of eugenicists, Sanger changed her approach, as did other feminists. In 1919 her Amer-

ican Birth Control League began to rely heavily for legitimacy on medical doctors and the growing eugenics movement.[41] The eugenics movement provided scientific and authoritative language that legitimated
women's right to contraception.[42] This co-optation of the birth control
movement produced racist depopulation policies and doctor-controlled
birth control technology.[43]

The resulting racist and anti-immigrant public policies assumed
Black and immigrant women had a moral obligation to restrict the size
of their families. While birth control was demanded as a right and an
option for privileged women, it became an obligation for the poor.[44] In
1934 Guy Irving Burch, founder of the Population Reference Bureau,
said, "I think there is good reason to be optimistic about the future of
the native [white] American stock if birth control is made available to
the millions of aliens in our cities and the millions of colored people in
this country."[45]

African Americans protested these policies. The *Pittsburgh Courier*, a
Black newspaper with an editorial policy that favored family planning,
advocated in 1936 that African Americans should oppose depopulation
programs proposed by eugenicists because the burden would "fall upon
colored people and it behooves us to watch the law and stop the
spread" of eugenic sterilization.[46]

One such program was the Negro Project, designed by Sanger's Birth
Control Federation in 1939. It hired several African-American ministers
to travel through the South to recruit African-American doctors. The
project proposal included a quote by W. E. B. DuBois, saying that "the
mass of ignorant Negroes still breed carelessly and disastrously, so that
the increase among Negroes, even more than the increase among
Whites, is from that part of the population least intelligent and fit, and
least able to rear their children properly."[47] This quote, often mistakenly attributed to Sanger, reflected the shared race and class biases of
the project's founders.

The Negro Project relied on Black ministers because of its white
sponsors' belief that "the most successful educational approach to the
Negro is through a religious appeal."[48] Sanger wrote, "We do not want
word to go out that we want to exterminate the Negro population and
the minister is the man who can straighten out that idea if it ever occurs
to any of their more rebellious members."[49] The doctors recruited by
the ministers were supposed to work for the project for free or, at best,
demand payment from their patients. In contrast, the Birth Control Federation at the time paid most of the white doctors who worked on its
behalf.

According to historian Linda Gordon, the project was the product of elitist birth control programs, whose design eliminated the possibility of popular, grassroots involvement in promoting birth control as a cause.[50] Notions of civil rights, women's rights, or combating southern poverty were missing from this program. Politicians in southern states at this time were particularly interested in spreading birth control among African Americans to limit Black population growth, which could threaten their political and economic hegemony.[51]

It is extremely likely that the racism of the birth control organizers, coupled with the genocidal assumptions of eugenics supporters, increased Black distrust of the public health system and has fueled Black opposition to family planning up to the present time. By 1949 approximately 2.5 million African-American women were organized in social and political clubs and organizations.[52] Many of them supported birth control and abortion, but at the same time they offered a strong critique of the eugenicists. A clear sense of dual or "paired" values emerged among African-American women: they wanted individual control over their bodies, but at the same time they resisted government and private depopulation policies that blurred the distinction between incentives and coercion.

POST-WORLD WAR II ACCESS

The birth control clinics established by Sanger and others met only a fraction of the demand for contraceptive services. The methods of birth control most commonly available to Black women in the 1950s included abstinence or infrequency of coitus, the withdrawal method, spermicidal douching, condoms, diaphragms, and the rhythm method. Of course when these methods failed (and they frequently did), Black women relied on underground abortion.

The majority of abortions available to African-American women in the 1950s and early 1960s were provided by doctors, midwives, and quacks operating illegally. Little information is available regarding the Black midwives who provided abortions, except for arrest records and court transcripts. Information on physicians is slightly more accessible. For example, Dr. Edward Keemer, a Black physician in Detroit, practiced outside the law for more than thirty years until his arrest in 1956. He was sent to prison for fourteen months and afterward sold vacuum cleaners in New Jersey until he was able to win reinstatement of his medical license in the early 1960s. His assistant, LaBrentha Hurley, was jailed for sixty days and had to fight to get her children back after she was released. When Keemer resumed his practice, he continued openly to defy the law. By this time, he had become militant in the fight for reproductive rights. At a 1971 press conference held by the National Association for the Repeal of Abortion Laws, Keemer described an illegal abortion he had performed the previous day and pledged he would continue to save women's lives, whatever the consequences. He and his assistant were rearrested several days later and again faced prosecution.[53]

Ebony magazine published an editorial in 1951 that stereotyped illegal abortionists, ignoring highly skilled practitioners like Keemer and others. The article warned readers that "each year nearly 700,000 abortions are performed on unfortunate, desperate women [by abortionists] whose criminal and unethical methods annually claim the lives of about 8,000 victims." According to Rickie Solinger, *Ebony*'s readers had reason to be concerned because a disproportionate number of Black women died abortion-related deaths, many caused by self-induced abortions. A study of such deaths in Detroit, for example, from 1950 to 1965, revealed that of the 138 fatalities from septic abortions, all involved poor women, most of them Black.[54]

Long after the majority of "granny" midwives in other ethnic groups had been replaced by medically based hospital practices, there were still hundreds of Black lay midwives practicing in the Deep South, who provided most of the abortion and contraceptive services for southern Black women.[55] According to Linda Janet Holmes, some of these women had midwifery lineages that extended as far back as slavery. Although these services were technically illegal, the women developed informal networks of communication that furtively shared contraceptive and abortion information.

Abortion was every bit as illegal in the 1950s as it had been in the 1920s, but until the years after World War II the crime of abortion had a protected status because law enforcement authorities often tolerated the practice as long as no women died.[56] After World War II, however, the medical profession and the legal authorities stepped up their campaign to eliminate underground practitioners who provided illegal abortions. Black women who provided underground abortions were harassed and prosecuted more frequently than their white counterparts, especially white men.[57]

Lay midwives were especially easy targets, in part because independent midwifery associations did not exist. In reviewing the behavior of law enforcement in the 1950s, Solinger observed that the police were especially eager to arrest women who performed abortions, regardless of their safety records.[58] Technically untrained and unprotected women were easier to convict than doctors. By the middle of the 1960s, most lay midwives had been forced out of business, except in those places where racism, isolation, and poverty prevented ready access to both medical care and law enforcement.

Middle-class women could sometimes persuade doctors to arrange for a clandestine abortion or to provide a referral. Poor women either had the unplanned children or went to "the lady down the street"—either a midwife or partially trained medical personnel. Abortions from these illegal providers cost between fifty and seventy-five dollars, which was expensive considering that a pregnant woman might earn ten dollars a day.[59] Many white women came to Black neighborhoods to obtain abortions, from doctors who were often also involved in the civil rights movement.[60] White women were frequently charged more than Black women in order to subsidize the cost of poor women's procedures.

If complications developed from illegal abortions, women visited physicians who operated in the poorer sections of the city. Only as a last resort did they go to hospitals, fearing the legal consequences of having obtained an illegal abortion. This pattern artificially lowered the number of septic abortions reported to hospitals and understated the incidence of abortions among Black women.

Dr. Joe Beasley, who helped establish one of the country's first statewide family-planning programs in Louisiana in the 1960s, observed that the leading causes of maternal mortality were the medical complications of criminal or medically unsupervised abortions:

> The other thing we saw was tremendous problems of induced abortion, with the highest predominance in the lower socio-economic group, and the middle and the upper getting more expensive abortions. So we see women very carved up—very crude abortions—knitting needles, cloth packing. And we see them coming in highly febrile, puerperal discharge in the vagina, germs in their blood, blood poisoning, septicemia, and those who survive have a very high probability of being reproductive cripples . . . then when we looked at it, there was a very low pattern of contraception in the lower socio-economic group, in spite of what seemed to be a very strong desire not to have unwanted children . . . I mean, if a woman will risk her very life with a criminal abortion, that's pretty damn strong motivation.[61]

Dangerous, self-administered procedures probably killed many women. Nurses reported that "sticks, rocks, chopsticks, rubber or plastic tubes,

gauze or cotton packing, ballpoint pens, coat hangers, or knitting needles" were frequently used by desperate women. Or they chose to use
"douches believed effective in inducing abortions made from deter-
gents, orange juice, vinegar, bleach, disinfectant, lye, potassium per-
manganate, or colas. The gaseous explosions of soft drinks [were] said
to cause a miscarriage; some teenagers consider[ed] them spermicidal."[62] Clearly Black women needed and wanted abortion and contraception services. But few had access to safe and affordable treatment.

POPULATION POLICIES FOR THE
AFRICAN-AMERICAN COMMUNITY

In the mid-1950s population "time-bomb" theories offered an updated
approach to eugenics. These still-fashionable theories suggested that
population growth in the Third World threatened the ability of the
United States to govern world affairs. Brochures published by groups
like the Draper Fund and the Population Council showed "hordes of
Black and brown faces spilling over a tiny earth."[63] By the early 1960s
the United States government began supporting population control policies overseas, and linked foreign aid to anti-natalist depopulation programs. Many U.S. politicians argued by analogy that urban whites in
America needed to be protected from the "explosiveness" of overpopulated Black ghettos.

The expression of these fears coincided with the growth of the civil
rights movement, in response to the militancy of the movement and
its potential for sweeping social change. The political instability of the
African-American population convinced many members of the white
elite and middle class that Black population growth should be curbed
through government intervention. White Americans feared, out of proportion to reality, that a growing welfare class of African Americans
concentrated in the inner cities would not only cause rampant crime but
would also balloon the national debt and eventually produce a political
threat from majority-Black voting blocs in urban areas.

The new politics of population of the late 1950s was implemented
domestically in the 1960s, with the establishment of family-planning
programs in the South in predominantly Black urban areas. This occurred at the same time that African-American leaders were expressing
interest in "taking over" the big cities and "holding them as enclaves
against increasing repression."[64] Federal and private campaigns to

make family planning available and accessible to Black women, particularly in the South, split white conservative opinion on the issue. Some conservatives wanted a eugenically minded set of programs for African Americans that would reduce the Black birthrate. For example, Leander Perez of Louisiana, who supported birth control, was quoted as remarking, "The best way to hate a nigger is to hate him before he is born." [65]

But many conservatives, already threatened by racial integration, strongly doubted the wisdom of letting women of any race have control over their fertility.[66] In addition to opposition from the Catholic Church, Protestant fundamentalists believed that family planning was a Communist plot imposed by northern "carpetbaggers." [67] In fact, they persuaded many white women not to go to newly established family-planning clinics. One center in Louisiana reported that in its first year of operation, 96 percent of its clients were Black. The proportion of white clients never rose above 15 percent.[68]

Generally speaking, family planning associated with racism was most frequently supported; associated with sexism, this support evaporated. This fissure among white conservatives about women's reproductive rights is still apparent today.

The 1960s launched a "boom period" for federally supported family planning to "eliminate poverty." President Lyndon Johnson, in his 1965 State of the Union message, singled out family planning as one of the four most critical problems in the nation. Even many Republicans jumped on the bandwagon. By 1970 President Richard Nixon claimed, "It is my view that no American woman should be denied access to family planning assistance because of her economic condition." [69]

The year after passage of the 1964 Voting Rights Act, the U.S. Congress pressured the newly created Office of Economic Opportunity (OEO) to wage a war on poverty by emphasizing family-planning programs for African Americans. Among politicians, one of the most persuasive arguments for family planning linked these programs with the reduction in health and welfare costs. Family planning, which offered a wide range of maternal and child-care services to poor women, was included in Medicaid coverage after a series of fights with Catholics and conservatives at the state level.

Despite this political agenda, with its racist undertones, some medical experts opposed family planning for African Americans, convinced that Black women "wanted to be pregnant and have all those children and that even if they did not want repeated pregnancies, they could not possibly understand the principles of birth control because they were not bright enough and lack behavioral control."[70]

The opposition from such odious sources did not confuse African-American supporters of family planning. By the late 1960s family planning became once again "synonymous with the civil rights of poor women to medical care."[71] Dr. Martin Luther King, Jr., writing in 1966 in a Planned Parenthood publication, echoed this sentiment: voluntary family planning is "a special and urgent concern" for African Americans and "a profoundly important ingredient in [our] quest for security and a decent life."[72] After the 1965 Supreme Court decision legalizing birth control for married couples, the NAACP reaffirmed its earlier commitment to family planning by adopting a 1966 policy statement that read in part, "Mindful of problems of family health and of economic stability, we support the dissemination of information and materials concerning family health and family planning to all those who desire it."[73]

During this period African-American women were not blind to the irony of a government plan to make contraceptives free and extremely accessible to Black communities that lacked basic health care. They criticized linking the alleged population problem with women's personal decisions to control their fertility. The only population problem, according to many African-American women, was that some people had problems with some segments of the population. There was much in the debate on population pressures that was reminiscent of the eugenicists. Those who blamed every social issue—riots, pollution, hunger, high taxes, ghettos, crime, and poor health—directly on the population growth of people of color ignored the maldistribution of land and wealth and racist and sexist discrimination in the job market.[74]

Because of the unavailability of contraceptives and abortions, many desperate African-American women chose sterilization as their only hope for avoiding unwanted pregnancies. Birth control by hysterectomy was widely available, and some Black women adapted themselves to the limited choices that existed. Yet African-American women warily watched state legislative proposals to sterilize poor women who had too many "illegitimate" children. None of these proposals succeeded, largely because of the militancy of women activists like Fannie Lou Hamer, who said that "six out of every ten Negro women were . . . sterilized for no reason at all. Often the women were not told that they had been sterilized until they were released from the hospital."[75] A national fertility study conducted by Princeton University found that 20 percent of all married African-American women had been sterilized by 1970.[76]

Despite the ways that racist politics cut across the bodily integrity of African-American women in the 1960s and 1970s, many women continued to sustain informal networks that spread the news about the availability of services. They became activists in support of birth control, for better health care, for abortion rights, and against sterilization abuse and population control, linking these issues to the project of improving the overall health status of the African-American community.

THE FEMINIST UNDERGROUND RAILROAD

Before abortion was legalized nationally in 1973, countless women perilously attempted self-abortion, and dangerous practitioners flourished because there were no safety standards without legalization. Despite the dangers, it is estimated that 200,000 to 1,000,000 illegal abortions occurred annually in the late 1960s.[77]

During the last decade of the illegal era, a few organizations operated an "underground railroad," referring women to illegal practitioners.[78] Underground abortions were facilitated by church and community-based referral services and cooperative doctors' networks in the 1960s. In 1967 the Clergy Consultation Service on Abortion began operating out of a New York City Baptist church, even before New York State legalized abortion in 1970. A similar service was started in Chicago in 1969. The clergy groups usually referred women to practitioners in Puerto Rico, Mexico City, and England, and helped thousands of women obtain abortions.[79] Often women from the South traveled north to obtain abortions, sometimes paid for by untraceable discretionary funds from family-planning clinics.[80]

To address the problems associated with the lack of safe and affordable abortions, a group of women in Chicago began to provide abortions in 1969 through an illegal, floating underground network called Jane, officially known as the Abortion Counseling Service of Women's Liberation. Deliberately patterned after the Underground Railroad that freed slaves, the group provided over 11,000 safe abortions between 1969 and 1973.[81] While abortions from other illegal practitioners cost between $600 and $1,000, the women in Jane learned how to do abortions themselves and lowered the cost to an average of

$40.[82] During its last year of operation, more than half of the collective's clients were women of color, most of whom were poor and Black.[83]

Although the members of the collective were predominantly white, there were a few Black women who provided services, according to Jane member Laura Kaplan. Because the group's clients were increasingly African American, the collective felt an urgency to seek out Black women to join the collective. They did not feel that turning to the militant Black organizations was an option, since most radical Black groups believed that abortion was genocide. Black male spokespersons viewed women's liberation as a threat to Black solidarity and claimed that abortion was a weapon against their community.[84]

One of the earliest African-American members of Jane was Lois Smith,[85] who has described her experiences as an abortion provider:

I discovered Jane when I escorted a girlfriend to get an abortion. You have to understand that the main problem was the secrecy; you couldn't tell people what you were doing. When I arrived at the facility, I saw that the clients were predominantly Black, but all the workers were white. Even while I waited for my friend, I began counseling the women, telling them they would be all right.

When I joined the collective, our primary problem was the illegality of what we were doing. This produced extreme secrecy and paranoia, but in a sense, it helped us bond as a group. It wasn't a Black or a white thing, but a women's need. The only alienation I experienced was caused by the secrecy, but our family and friends supported us. Sometimes we even used their houses, but we couldn't tell anyone outside of our circle. The Black women were most supportive by keeping silent and taking risks. Fears of police arrests were real. Women had to endure many risks to give our number to a friend, but the networking was steady in the Black women's community.

But abortion was not openly discussed in the Black community because other survival issues were key. Women had been surviving for years using abortion as necessary. But the illegality of the procedure made women feel marginalized and terrified. They had heard so many horror stories about back-alley abortionists that they were often afraid when they came to us. They couldn't tell their doctors or nurses or their husbands. They got support from each other. It was very consistent how sisters supported each other.

The Black women who worked at Jane didn't come in as a group. Mostly we were involved one at a time, so we could never develop a critical mass, or even three to four of us, to get together to talk about what we were doing. But we didn't look on it as a Black or white women's issue; women needed termination of pregnancies, and there was unity created by women who were desperate.[86]

BLACK OPPOSITION TO REPRODUCTIVE RIGHTS

In the 1960s and 1970s, visible Black male political support for abortion rights was limited. As Angela Davis concluded, this was "a period in which one of the unfortunate hallmarks of some nationalist groups was their determination to push women into the background. The brothers opposing us leaned heavily on the male supremacist trends which were winding their way through the movement."[87] Some Black male scholars of the period echoed the genocidal arguments previously used, but infused their analyses with new elements of sexism and anti-Semitism. Dick Gregory, a popular political activist, expressed his opposition to abortion rights this way: "My answer to genocide, quite simply, is eight Black kids and another on the way."[88]

Whitney Young, leader of the Urban League, reversed his organization's earlier support for family planning in 1962. Marvin Davies, head of the Florida NAACP, said, "Our women need to produce more babies, not less . . . and until we comprise 30 to 35 percent of the population, we won't really be able to affect the power structure in this country."[89] This was a major ideological shift away from the early positions of the NAACP and the Urban League, when both organizations had supported women's reproductive rights as a means of racial progress. The NAACP of the 1920s would have been horrified in the 1960s to find itself sounding more like Marcus Garvey and less like W. E. B. Du Bois.

On the other hand, Black nationalist groups that traced their ideological roots back to Garvey were entirely consistent when they opposed family planning. In the late 1960s several birth control clinics were invaded by Black Muslims associated with the Nation of Islam, which published cartoons in *Muhammed Speaks* that depicted bottles of birth control pills marked with a skull and crossbones or graves of unborn Black infants. The Pittsburgh branch of the NAACP declared that the local family-planning clinic was an instrument of genocide. William "Bouie" Haden, leader of the militant United Movement for Progress, went one step further and threatened to firebomb the Pittsburgh clinic, and a clinic in Cleveland was burned.[90]

The Black Power conference held in Newark in 1967, organized by Amiri Baraka (LeRoi Jones), passed an anti–birth control resolution. Two years later, the May 1969 issue of *The Liberator* warned, "For us to speak in favor of birth control for Afro-Americans would be comparable to speaking in favor of genocide."[91] Four years later, Congress appeared to confirm their suspicions: testimony before the U.S. Senate revealed that at least two thousand involuntary sterilizations had been performed with OEO funds during the 1972–73 fiscal year.[92]

The Black Panther Party was the only nationalist group to support free abortions and contraceptives on demand, although not without considerable controversy within its ranks.[93] "Half of the women in the Party used birth control, and we supported it because of our free health care program. We understood the conditions of the Black community," remembers Nkenge Toure, a former member. He also recalls that although there were no formal political education discussions around the issue, there was support from many party women.[94] Interestingly, not one female party member joined the mostly young, male militants who denounced family planning and attempted to shut down family-planning clinics in New Orleans and Pittsburgh.[95] However, many of the Black churches that had supported family planning in the 1940s and 1950s did not join the opponents of family planning in the late 1960s because many Black ministers held the line. As one woman reported, "We converted a lot of brothers."[96]

BLACK WOMEN RESPOND

The assault on birth control and abortion came from both the left and the right. White conservatives saw family planning as an assault on traditional values of motherhood, while some Blacks saw it as a race- and class-directed eugenics program. That such disparate forces aligned themselves against African-American women demonstrated that both white bigots and Black sexists could find common cause in the assertion of male authority over women's decisions regarding reproduction.

In contrast, many African-American women exerted a dynamic and aggressive influence on the family-planning movement. These activists were articulate and well organized and constituted the largest single bloc of support for family planning. They were so visible that politicians in some states began to see them as a potential political threat. In Louisiana it was estimated that family planners could mobilize as many as 70,000 women if they wanted to. This palpable power increased the determination of white conservatives, particularly in the South, to undermine public and private funding of family planning, as an effort of the "New Right" revolution that was beginning in the mid-1970s. In the last days of the Nixon administration, government agencies were dismantling many anti-poverty programs, which included family planning.

Public policy initiatives shifted from helping poor women control the size of their families to punishing them when they failed to do so.

African-American women noticed that "most of the commotion about the clinics . . . seemed to be coming from men—men who do not have to bear children." [97] Even when Black men successfully shut down clinics, as in Cleveland and Pittsburgh, women organized to reopen them because they "did not appreciate being thought of as random reproduction machines that could be put to political use." [98] African-American women fully understood the racist impulse that located Planned Parenthood clinics in poor Black neighborhoods but not in poor white neighborhoods. Still, they perceived the free services to be in their own best interests. Quoting from Du Bois, they declared, "We're not interested in the quantity of our race. We're interested in the quality of it." [99]

In Pittsburgh about seventy women members of the National Welfare Rights Organization rebuffed attempts by African-American men to close family-planning clinics. They rejected the leadership of William "Bouie" Haden, who, it was discovered, was on the payroll of the Catholic Church. "Who appointed him our leader anyhow?" asked Georgiana Henderson. "He is only one person—and a man at that. He can't speak for the women of Homewood. . . . Why should I let one loud-mouth tell me about having children?" [100] The women organized to remove Haden as a delegate from the Homewood-Brushton Citizens Renewal Council in a demonstration of political strength that frightened both Black and white men. Other African-American women around the country declared they would not tolerate male expressions of territorial rights over women's bodies.

Anti-feminism was not only a male prerogative. One noted Black critic of feminism was Linda LaRue, who wrote in 1970, "Black adoption of the white values of women . . . has created a politicized, unliberated copy of white womanhood." LaRue asked in the same article, however, "How many potential revolutionary warriors stand abandoned in orphanages while Blacks rhetorize disdain for birth control as a 'trick of The Man' to halt the growth of Black population? . . . Would it not be more revolutionary for Blacks to advocate a five-year moratorium on Black births until every Black baby in an American orphanage was adopted by one or more Black parents?" [101]

In this period, in diverse places and in different ways, African-American women took leadership roles in promoting African-American women's rights to control their own bodies. Dr. Dorothy Brown, one of the first Black female general surgeons in the South, graduated from Meharry Medical College in 1948 and, while in the Tennessee state legislature, became one of the first state legislators to introduce a bill to legalize abortion in 1967.[102] Her bill, which would have legalized abortion for victims of rape and incest, fell only two votes short of passing. Marion Sanders, in a 1970 issue of *Harper's Magazine*, published "The Right Not to Be Born," in which she described the experiences of a Black woman who was denied an abortion after being exposed to German measles. She subsequently gave birth to a severely retarded daughter.[103] This mainstream article supporting abortion rights for Black women in a sense foretold the current controversy about the conflicting rights of women to control their fertility and the rights of disabled people to be born.

A distinct Black feminist consciousness began consistently to counter the reactionary opponents to family planning. Shirley Chisholm, the first Black woman in Congress, dismissed the genocide argument when asked to discuss her views on abortion and birth control:

> To label family planning and legal abortion programs "genocide" is male rhetoric, for male ears. It falls flat to female listeners and to thoughtful male ones. Women know, and so do many men, that two or three children who are wanted, prepared for, reared amid love and stability, and educated to the limit of their ability will mean more for the future of the Black and brown races from which they come than any number of neglected, hungry, ill-housed and ill-clothed youngsters.[104]

In 1969 Frances Beal, then head of the Black Women's Liberation Committee of the Student Nonviolent Coordinating Committee (SNCC), wrote, "Black women have the right and responsibility to determine when it is in *the interest of the struggle to have children or not to have them and this right must not be relinquished.*"[105]

This sentiment was echoed by writer Toni Cade Bambara in 1970: "I've been made aware of the national call to Sisters to abandon birth control . . . to picket family planning centers and abortion referral groups and to raise revolutionaries. What plans do you have for the care of me and the child?"[106] Black feminists argued that birth control and abortion are, in themselves, revolutionary—and that African-American liberation in any sense cannot be won without women controlling their lives. The birth control pill, in and of itself, cannot liberate African-American women, but it "gives her the time for liberation in those other areas."[107] As the Black Women's Liberation Group of Mt.

Vernon, New York, wrote in 1970, "Birth control [and abortion] is the *freedom* to *fight* genocide of Black women and children."[108]

In the early 1970s African-American women believed it was absurd to coerce Black women to be sterilized in order to limit their family size, when these women were willing to have fewer children voluntarily, if safe (and less permanent) methods were accessible. This combined support for fertility control and opposition to population control, a unique voice within the women's movement at the time, did much to inform both the feminist and the civil rights movements in later decades. African-American women rejected the single-issue focus of the women's movement on abortion, which excluded other issues of reproductive freedom. They also opposed the myopic focus on race of the male-dominated civil rights movement, which ignored concerns of gender justice. Activist women also learned a valuable lesson about sexist backlash that equated Black male domination with African-American progress.

REPRODUCTIVE RIGHTS LEADERSHIP
AFTER *ROE V. WADE*

The demand by Black women for reproductive freedom in the early 1970s was crystallized and refined by the development of Black feminist leadership in the second wave of the American women's movement in the late 1960s.[109] African-American women were involved in the movement from its beginning, but both "outside reactionary forces and racism and elitism within the movement itself have served to obscure our participation."[110] The fact is, Black women have made significant contributions to the reproductive freedom movement since the Supreme Court legalized abortion in 1973.

In the spring of 1973 Doris Wright, a Black feminist writer, called a meeting to discuss "Black Women and Their Relationship to the Women's Movement." The result was that Black feminists, primarily located in New York, formed the National Black Feminist Organization (NBFO) in November 1973, under the leadership of Margaret Sloan and Flo Kennedy.[111] Among those present were Shirley Chisholm, Alice Walker, and Eleanor Holmes Norton.[112] NBFO activists organized (among other things) against sterilization abuse and for abortion rights. They organized support activities for Dr. Kenneth Edelin, a Black physician on trial in 1975 for performing an illegal abortion, who went on to become the chairman of the board of directors of Planned Parenthood. NBFO also worked to end violence against women by advocating justice for Joann Little and Inez Garcia, women of color who were imprisoned for defending themselves against rapists.

It is important to highlight the connection between the anti-violence and the reproductive rights movements because many of the newer activists in the abortion rights movement in the mid-1970s actually came from the movement to end violence against women. They, like myself, worked at rape crisis centers or battered women's shelters. Significantly, few of the early activists came directly out of the civil rights movement without passing through some feminist crucible that heightened their awareness of gender inequalities.

Unfortunately, the early feminists in NBFO report that frictions within the group split them apart. Fortunately, the ideas they promoted remain our legacy.

Some Boston-based activists in NBFO, including noted author Barbara Smith, formed the Combahee River Collective in 1975, named after a Harriet Tubman guerrilla action in 1863 that freed more than 750 slaves and is the only military campaign in American history planned and led by a woman.[113] This collective issued a Black feminist manifesto in 1976 that became a rallying cry for Black feminists, combining for the first time a comprehensive critique of racism, sexism, poverty, and heterosexism for Black women activists seeking ideological cohesion. Collective members worked for abortion rights and against sterilization abuse and presented many workshops in communities and on college campuses on Black feminism, reaching hundreds of young Black women.

In addition to the African-American women in Jane, others worked with early feminist women's health centers, learning not only how to advocate for abortions but, most important, how to *perform* them. Family-planning programs in the 1970s reduced the medical mystique and rigid hierarchies by hiring nonmedical outreach workers from the communities being served.[114] Pioneers like Annie Joseph, Gloria Favorite, and Jacqueline Harvey from Louisiana proved that women formerly on welfare could become effective advocates for family planning.[115] This limited democratization had an impact on the belief among women that we can or, more important, *should* learn more about our bodies to control our fertility.

In the early 1970s Byllye Avery (later founder of the National Black Women's Health Project) was part of a referral network for women who wanted to travel to New York to obtain abortions because they were illegal in Florida. Because flying to New York was not an affordable option for many poor women, she and several white women opened the Gainesville Women's Health Center in 1974 and learned how to perform abortions.[116] Avery defined her clients' predicament this way: "For poor women abortion is a matter of survival: if I have this one more child, it etches away my margin of survival."[117] Brenda Joyner of the Tallahassee Feminist Women's Health Center and Byllye Avery pioneered a new wave of Black feminists in the feminist women's health center movement that reached from Florida to California.

The SNCC Black Women's Liberation Committee changed its name in the 1970s to the Third World Women's Alliance and then, in the 1980s, to the Alliance Against Women's Oppression. According to Toni Cade Bambara, "We heard each other in Fran Beal's Third World Women's Alliance Newspaper."[118] Beal wrote: "The lack of the availability of safe birth control methods, the forced sterilization practices, and the inability to obtain legal abortions are all symptoms of a sick society that jeopardizes the health of Black women (and thereby the entire Black race) in its attempt to control the very life processes of human beings."[119]

When the Hyde Amendment, which eliminated subsidies for poor women's abortions, was upheld by the Supreme Court, a number of Black women joined or started reproductive rights organizations, such as the multiracial Committee for Abortion Rights and Against Sterilization Abuse (CARASA). Brenda Joyner assessed the post-Hyde situation this way: "The government will not pay for a $200 or $300 abortion procedure for a poor woman on Medicaid. But it will pay for a $2,000 to $3,000 sterilization procedure for that same poor woman."[120]

In the years immediately following *Roe v. Wade*, other pro-choice organizations had African-American women leaders. Former congresswoman Shirley Chisholm (who had supported abortion reform while a New York assemblywoman) was invited to be the first national president of the National Association for the Repeal of Abortion Laws, or NARAL (now the National Abortion and Reproductive Rights Action League). She was reluctant at first to accept the invitation, but became NARAL's first honorary chairwoman because, as she put it:

> It had begun to seem to me that the question was not whether the law should allow abortions. Experience shows that pregnant women who feel they have compelling reasons for not having a baby, or another baby, will break the law and, even worse, risk injury and death if they must get one. Abortions

will not be stopped. . . . The question becomes simply that of what kind of abortions society wants women to have—clean, competent ones performed by licensed physicians or septic, dangerous ones done by incompetent practitioners.[121]

Most prominently, Faye Wattleton, a former nurse-midwife at Harlem Hospital, became the first African-American president of Planned Parenthood Federation of America in 1978. Wattleton was motivated, she said, because of her memories of the "desperation and suffering that resulted from unintended pregnancy and illegal, unsafe abortions."[122] Between 1978 and 1992, Wattleton made a tremendous impact on the visibility of African-American women in the reproductive freedom movement.

Other Black women, such as Joan Smith in Louisiana and Joycelyn Elders in Arkansas, managed statewide family-planning programs. Smith, speaking in 1981 about the family-planning boom of the 1970s, said, "What caught my fancy was the idea of offering services to indigent women the same as private doctors were giving. Nobody, and I mean nobody, was talking then about treating poor women with dignity. We said we'd do it and we did."[123]

These and other women were determined to forge ahead with new ideas about the empowerment of African-American women, built upon the gains of the civil rights and women's movements; however, they were visionaries who lacked a strong base among African-American women. They were often leaders without a constituency. Writer Michele Wallace has reflected on this predicament: "We exist as women who are Black who are feminist, each stranded for the moment, working independently because there is not yet an environment in this society remotely congenial to our struggle—because, being on the bottom, we would have to do what no one else has done: we would have to fight the world."[124]

The fact is, many African-American women did not join mainstream pro-choice organizations, despite the visible Black leadership. In 1981 Gloria Joseph and Jill Lewis wrote, "The negative feelings expressed by Black women in 1969 about the women's movement are virtually unchanged today. Most Black women still feel a sense of distrust: they believe that the White women in the movement are largely middle-class and exhibit racist mentalities, and they are convinced that the concerns of the movement are not relevant to their material conditions."[125]

At this time abortion rights was not on the agenda of many of the major Black women's organizations, although many, like the sororities and women's professional associations, worked against teen pregnancy and infant mortality as part of the larger reproductive freedom movement. Black women instinctively understood what later research would prove: no country or population within a country has ever achieved a low birthrate as long as it has a high infant mortality rate.[126]

A larger base of support for Black feminism and reproductive rights did not emerge until the 1980s. In her groundbreaking 1981 book, *Ain't I a Woman,* bell hooks laid out the ideological framework for this embryonic movement. She wrote, "Only a few Black women have rekindled the spirit of feminist struggle that stirred the hearts and minds of our nineteenth-century sisters. We, Black women who advocate feminist ideology, are pioneers. We are clearing a path for ourselves and our sisters."[127] Alice Walker, writing a few years earlier, had called on Black women to reevaluate their relationship to the women's movement: "To the extent that Black women disassociate themselves from the women's movement, they abandon their responsibilities to women throughout the world. This is a serious abdication from and misuse of radical Black herstorical tradition: Harriet Tubman, Sojourner Truth, Ida B. Wells, and Fannie Lou Hamer would not have liked it."[128]

AFRICAN-AMERICAN WOMEN MOBILIZE

Several key events increased African-American women's visibility in the abortion rights movement in the late 1970s and 1980s. Among these were the United Nations' Decade for Women, the formation of several new Black women's organizations, the fight for the Civil Rights Restoration Act of 1988, and the *Webster* Supreme Court decision in 1989.

The Decade for Women

The World Decade for Women was declared by the United Nations in 1975 to highlight the status and progress of women in their quest for equality around the world. During the decade, three World Conferences for Women were held: in Mexico City (1975), in Copenhagen (1980), and in Nairobi (1985). The United States held a National Conference for Women in Houston in 1977. These mega-events were extremely influential in spurring our activism.

The goal of the first world conference was to develop a global "plan of action" to improve the status of women; the mid-decade conference assessed progress on the plan; and the end-decade conference in Nairobi presented a plan of action for women to be implemented until the year 2000. The goal of the Houston conference was to create a United States version of the world plan for American women.

The decade was particularly significant for African-American women because it sparked many opportunities for organizing locally, nationally, and internationally. Many impressive advances were made during the decade, not the least of which was the tripling of the actual number of organizations of women of color in the United States, from approximately 300 to nearly 1,000.[129]

The 1985 Nairobi conference was the watershed event of the decade for African-American women. Because the conference was in Africa, over 1,100 African-American women were among the nearly 20,000 women attending. This was the largest number of women ever to come together at a global women's rights conference and certainly the largest number of Black women ever to attend an international conference.

The Nairobi conference signaled the massive entry of African-American women into the international women's movement and into the debates on reproductive freedom, both locally and globally. Strategies challenging population control policies by agencies such as the U.S. Agency for International Development, the World Bank, and the International Monetary Fund coincided with our growing influence on the reproductive rights movement in the United States. Melanie Tervalon, speaking at a workshop in Nairobi, said:

> There are three key and interconnected aspects of reproductive rights—access to abortion, [prevention of] infant mortality and [prevention of] forced sterilization. . . . As Black women and women of color from the U.S., we have learned . . . that we share many of the same conditions as our sisters around the world—high infant mortality rates, forced sterilization, poor quality or nonexistent prenatal care, inadequate sex education, high under- and unemployment and the attendant disproportionate poverty for our families and children. . . . As Black women in the U.S., reproductive rights issues are central to our political work.[130]

For many African-American women, this speech symbolized how reproductive rights activism had moved from the margins to the center of our feminist work. After Nairobi, organizing by Black women for reproductive freedom exploded. Some of it was in response to the increasing repression promoted by the Reagan administration, but mostly it occurred because Black feminism was an idea embraced by activist women. Although many Black women still rejected the word *feminism* for themselves, they strongly identified with feminist causes, particularly the movements to support reproductive freedom and to end violence against women.

New Black Women's Groups

National Black Women's Health Project The National Black Women's Health Project (NBWHP) was founded in 1983 by Byllye Avery, who at the time was a board member of the National Women's Health Network. The network, a national advocacy group for women's health rights, sought to encourage the participation of African-American women in the health activist movement. In 1981 planning began for the First National Conference on Black Women's Health sponsored by the National Women's Health Network, which was held in June 1983 at Spelman College in Atlanta.

Originally, the planners expected about 500 women, but excellent organizing and outreach produced nearly 2,000 attendees. The Black women at the conference demanded the creation of an independent grassroots organization devoted to Black women's health. NBWHP was born.

Abortion and reproductive rights were key issues at the founding conference, and in the words of Dr. Dorothy Brown, who addressed the conference: "We should dispense quickly with the notion that abortion is genocide because genocide in this country dates back to 1619 [when the first Africans arrived in the English colonies] and continues today." [131]

The Project (as it was fondly called) sponsored conferences on reproductive health in 1987 and 1990, and pioneered the practice of forming hundreds of small self-help groups among women to enable them to discuss, often for the first time, their reproductive health experiences. An *Essence* article written by Bebe Moore Campbell in 1981 discussed the "shame" and "silence" that cloaked abortion practices of generations of African-American women. [132] The Project determined to break through this conspiracy of silence. By the end of 1989, NBWHP had chapters in twenty-two states and was the fastest-growing Black women's organization in the country.

In its reproductive rights organizing, the Project identified a curious tendency among African-American women. Approximately one-half of the Project members were personally opposed to abortion, but all identified as "pro-choice." The Project thus modeled how women who both favored and opposed abortion could collaborate to protect the rights of all women to reproductive freedom. This was particularly significant because no other sector of the pro-choice movement was as divided about whether they would personally choose to have an abortion. Yet the Black women in the Project were entirely united when it came to preventing the government from recriminalizing abortion.

National Political Congress of Black Women In 1984, during Jesse Jackson's first campaign for president, the National Political Congress of Black Women was formed by Shirley Chisholm, Maxine Waters, C. Delores Tucker, Eleanor Holmes Norton, and the Reverend Willie Barrow, among others, because of the racist and insensitive politics of the mainstream women's movement.[133] African-American women were particularly incensed at the 1984 Democratic National Convention, where the National Organization for Women and other mainstream women's organizations, in closed-door sessions, chose to endorse the Walter Mondale/Geraldine Ferraro ticket instead of supporting Jackson. Feeling betrayed, they formed the congress to help Black women campaign for political offices in the two major political parties.

The racial insensitivity white women displayed in the 1980s as they pursued influence within the Democratic Party was extremely unfortunate, as it coincided with Black women's public visibility within the feminist movement. Black women felt the same sense of betrayal that club women of the 1890s did when they were refused membership in white women's organizations, and that anti-lynching crusaders like Ida B. Wells felt when they looked in vain for support from white feminists of that era.

The National Political Congress of Black Women, with Donna Brazile as its first executive director, brought grassroots women into contact with elected officials from both the Republican and Democratic parties and issued one of the first statements by African-American women in support of abortion rights in 1986. The statement was supported by hundreds of women through local and national political activities and was key to the development of the African American Women for Reproductive Freedom coalition in 1989.

NOW's Women of Color Program The National Organization for Women created a Women of Color Program in 1985 to mobilize support for its planned "March for Women's Lives" in April 1986. I was the first director of this program, from 1985 to 1989. My daunting task was to attract the endorsement of organizations of women of color for the first national march dedicated to abortion rights.

NOW did not enjoy a good reputation among most women of color, despite the fact that a Black woman, Pauli Murray, a lawyer and later an Episcopalian priest, had co-authored NOW's first statement of purpose in 1966 and had articulated a vision for African-American women that included working for reproductive freedom. Aileen Hernandez, a commissioner for the Equal Employment Opportunity Commission and a union organizer with the International Ladies' Garment Workers' Union, became NOW's second national (and first Black) president in 1971. Along with other early Black NOW activists, such as Addie Wyatt and Flo Kennedy, she insisted that NOW add other issues affecting African-American women to its agenda.[134] NOW, Hernandez asserted, "cannot afford the luxury of a single-issue focus—even when that issue was as important as the ERA."[135] Hernandez resigned from NOW in 1979 after sponsoring a resolution saying that Black women should not join the organization until it had confronted its own racism. California state senator Diane Watson concurred: "If they [NOW] don't really go after a mixed group of women, we should not support such an organization, and we should dramatize our non-support."[136]

NOW's negligence regarding racism dissuaded many Black women from affiliating. Only seven organizations of women of color had endorsed NOW's Equal Rights Amendment (ERA) march in 1978, and little changed over time. In some cases, relations got much worse between Black women and NOW, over such issues as which candidate to support at the 1984 Democratic National Convention.

In 1986 Black women were skeptical about joining a march for abortion rights sponsored by what was perceived as a white women's organization. For one thing, though abortion had shaped the personal experiences of many of these women, it was not part of their lives as political activists. Although all the leaders of Black women's organizations I contacted privately supported abortion rights, many perceived the issue as marginal, too controversial, or too "white" for their ready endorsement. Only a few, like Byllye Avery, Shirley Chisholm, and Dorothy Height, spoke out publicly in support of the march. Many of the others, as Angela Davis has observed, were uncomfortable about subtleties that seemed to escape popular discussion of abortion among white women—for example, "the distinction between *abortion rights* and the general advocacy of *abortions*. The [abortion rights] campaign often failed to provide a voice for women who wanted the right to legal abortions while deploring the social conditions that prohibited them from bearing more children."[137] Because the abortion rights movement focused on legality and public advocacy, it failed to touch the lives of many women for whom access—simply having a clinic to go to and the means to pay for service—was the only understanding of abortion they felt they needed. The same class and race issues that segregated the women's movement in the 1890s hampered our collaboration in the 1980s.

By 1987 NOW was responding more clearly to the voices of women of color; it sponsored the First National Conference on Women of Color and Reproductive Rights in Washington, D.C., which attracted over 400 women of color, two-thirds of whom were African Americans. No national organization of women of color working on reproductive rights existed at the time, and this conference was significant because it was the first conference in history that brought women from the feminist, civil rights, and Black nationalist movements together to promote reproductive freedom.

Although the April 1986 abortion rights march was endorsed by 107 organizations of women of color, three years later, when NOW held its second abortion rights march, more than 2,000 women came together, to form the largest delegation ever of women of color marching to support abortion rights. The National Black Women's Health Project sent thirteen busloads of people to the 1989 march, becoming the largest single delegation of African-American women.[138]

This time, prominent civil rights leaders also affirmed their support for abortion rights. In January 1989 a statement denouncing Operation Rescue's attempts to shut down abortion clinics was signed by thirty-four leaders, including Maxine Waters, Andrew Young, Rosa Parks, John Lewis, Barbara Jordan, William Gray, Cardiss Collins, Leah Wise, Julian Bond, Louis Stokes, John Jacob, and Roger Wilkins.[139] Jesse Jackson, who spoke at the abortion marches in 1986 and 1989, recruited other Black male leaders to the cause. Joseph Lowery, head of the Southern Christian Leadership Conference, made his first appearance at an abortion rights demonstration in 1989.[140]

Teen Pregnancy and Other Programs During the 1980s, many black feminists were involved in activities related to reproductive health, particularly teen pregnancy programs, which received significant funding in the Reagan/Bush years, and which sometimes demanded silence on the abortion issue in exchange for federal funding.

The National Council of Negro Women, Delta Sigma Theta, the Urban Coalition, and the Coalition of 100 Black Women all mounted teen pregnancy projects, as did civil rights organizations such as the National Urban League, the Southern Christian Leadership Conference, and the NAACP. All attempted to respond to charges in the media that Black teen pregnancy rates were out of control. A 1986 CBS Special Report, for example, on the "vanishing" Black family attributed teen pregnancy to the so-called moral degeneracy of the Black family. In a report that refuted this racist and sexist premise, the Alan Guttmacher Institute examined interstate and racial differences in teen pregnancy rates. Research sponsored by the institute found that although one of every four Black children is born to a teenage mother, states with higher percentages of poor people and people living in urban areas—whatever their race —have significantly higher teen pregnancy and birthrates.[141] Poverty, not race, the institute explained, was the major factor in teen pregnancy.

Black women involved in social work founded programs to combat infant mortality, a problem closely associated with poverty and teen pregnancy. As an indicator of Black progress, or lack thereof, infant mortality and teen pregnancy programs received relatively strong support from the government, particularly when compared with the attack on abortion and contraceptive programs for African Americans, manifested by the passage of the 1977 Hyde Amendment, the 1980 Mexico City policy (which prohibited funding for abortions overseas), and the 1989 "gag rule."[142]

By the mid-1980s, in response to the Reagan administration's various attacks on reproductive rights, and as an outgrowth of increased organizing by women of color after the Decade for Women, African-American and other women of color were beginning to voice strong support for reproductive rights. At this time, Eleanor Holmes Norton declared, "We ought to be out there explaining that we stand at the head of the line on the issue of reproductive rights. We are, after all, the first and foremost affected."[143]

African American Women for Reproductive Freedom In the late 1980s many Black women determined to focus on mainstream civil rights organizations. A series of legislative fights pitted abortion rights against civil rights when opponents of both tried to divide and weaken the civil rights coalitions. The effort to pass the Civil Rights Restoration Act of 1988—a bill intended to close several loopholes in the law regarding civil rights coverage—was a case in point. Opponents added several anti-abortion amendments to the bill. In a compromise (mostly between Black and white men), the bill was passed with the anti-abortion amendments, weakening the alliance between the women's and the civil rights movements. This divide-and-conquer strategy would likely have failed if Black feminists had had a role in the debate, because we bridge both worlds. Our absence allowed men to trade away abortion rights and offered an alarming glimpse into the future—if we are silent.

At the time, most civil rights groups believed they had other priorities: AIDS, drug wars, teen pregnancy, attacks on affirmative action, crime—and simply did not recognize the accumulating threats on *Roe v. Wade* that alarmed Black women. But the Supreme Court's *Webster* decision changed all that. "Now we have to mobilize," declared Faye Wattleton.[144]

Following the *Webster* decision, which opened the door for more restrictive state regulation of abortion, African-American women responded with furious organizing. In fact, the *Webster* decision created its own form of political backlash as the "carts full of mail" and "streets full of demonstrators" that Supreme Court justice Antonin Scalia predicted indeed materialized.

In August 1989 Donna Brazile and I organized a telephone conference among twelve leaders of Black women's organizations to discuss creating a national response to the *Webster* decision. This group became the coalition of African American Women for Reproductive Freedom (also called African American Women for Reproductive Choice in some newspaper accounts).

These powerful and highly visible women decided to issue a statement that would "give permission" for African-American women to talk publicly about abortion. This was a critical decision because most of the leaders of major Black women's organizations had not yet publicly affirmed their support for abortion, although several had endorsed marches and other campaigns by mainstream pro-choice organizations—a situation that underwrote the silence of Black women around the country.

The public statement affirming abortion rights, written by Marcia Gillespie of *Ms.* magazine, became a brochure titled "We Remember: African American Women for Reproductive Freedom." Emily Tynes, former press secretary at NARAL and a sophisticated media consultant, organized a press conference the day before the opening of the 1989 Congressional Black Caucus national conference at which Faye Wattleton became the first reproductive rights activist to receive the CBC's national leadership award. Featured at the press conference were Dorothy Height (National Council of Negro Women), Faye Wattleton (Planned Parenthood), Congresswoman Cardiss Collins, Byllye Avery (National Black Women's Health Project), Beverly Smith (Delta Sigma Theta), Janet Ballard (Alpha Kappa Alpha), Jewell McCabe (Coalition of 100 Black Women), Pat Tyson (Religious Coalition for Abortion Rights), and Shirley Chisholm (National Political Congress of Black Women). These women spoke forcefully about the need to maintain and expand women's access to reproductive services. Willie Barrow of Operation Push and Jacqui Gates of the National Association of Negro Business and Professional Women's Clubs sent messages as well. Such broad support from Black women's organizations, church groups, sororities, and political leaders was unprecedented in the history of our movement.

Two thousand copies of the brochure were initially printed, but we underestimated the huge demand. The strategy awoke what one reporter called "the sleeping giant of the pro-choice movement."[145] By the end of an eighteen-month campaign, over 250,000 copies of the brochure had been distributed in response to requests from African-American women from around the country.

The brochure campaign was extremely effective because it linked the collective powerlessness Black people felt about the slavery experience to the callous assault on abortion rights in the 1980s. The public statement did, in fact, give everyday Black women "permission" to bring abortion out of the closets of our lives. The brochure read in part:

> Choice is the essence of freedom . . . we have known how painful it is to be without choice in this land. . . . Now once again somebody is trying to say that we can't handle the freedom of choice . . . [that] African American women can't think for themselves . . . that we must have babies whether we choose to or not. . . . We understand why African Americans seek safe legal abortion now. It's . . . a matter of survival.[146]

A year later, in June 1990, African American Women for Reproductive Freedom joined the National Black Women's Health Project in sponsoring the first-ever national conference on Black Women and Reproductive Rights at Spelman College, which was also supported by the National Council of Negro Women, the Coalition of 100 Black Women,

Delta Sigma Theta, Operation Push, the National Urban Coalition, and the National Association of Negro Business and Professional Women's Clubs. The strategy of the conference was to mobilize Black women in as many ways and organizations as possible. Over the next two years, most of these groups sponsored their first-ever conferences on reproductive rights for Black women. "We Remember!" became a rallying cry for our movement as Black women demanded the right to speak for themselves in the abortion debate.

Additional Actions for Reproductive Freedom In 1988 the Center for Women's Development at Medgar Evers College in New York sponsored its first conference on Black women and reproductive rights. The center's work to date had focused on the rights of single Black mothers, and the expansion into reproductive rights activism was a significant shift—the result of the center's Black "nationalist feminist" politics and its leadership role in the Black nationalist movement.

Black students on college campuses also became involved in the movement; for example, students at Spelman published a statement in defense of abortion rights in the student newspaper late in 1989. Black students at Yale and Howard also organized reproductive rights events in the late 1980s. This infusion of young people into the reproductive rights movement is perhaps the best achievement of our activism—the true legacy for the future.

Black women who worked within the pro-choice mainstream created partnerships with Black women's organizations, bringing financial resources together with the militancy of the African-American women. For example, NOW, NARAL, and Planned Parenthood funded the "We Remember" brochures while agreeing to respect the organizational autonomy of African-American women.

In 1988 the Reagan administration began to push regulations limiting the right of women to receive information about abortion from federally funded family-planning clinics. The proposed "gag rule" deeply offended African-American women, who viewed the regulations as encroachments on free speech and on the patient-doctor relationship. Most seriously, the proposal threatened the health needs of poor women, for whom abortion can be a necessity. In response, Sherrilyn Ifill and Charlotte Rutherford of the American Civil Liberties Union (ACLU) and the NAACP Legal Defense and Education Fund, respectively, organized an amicus brief that was submitted to the Supreme Court on behalf of women of color. More than one hundred organizations of women of color became signatories to the first abortion rights brief in history submitted by African-American and other women of color to the Supreme Court.[147]

Earlier, the Women of Color Partnership Program of the Religious Coalition for Abortion Rights, established in the mid-1980s, had begun organizing pro-choice women of color in churches. Its first director was an African-American woman, Judy Logan-White. Working with NOW's Women of Color Program, regional conferences were organized in Washington, D.C., Oakland, Philadelphia, and Atlanta between 1986 and 1992. Other conferences sponsored by RCAR were held in Hartford, Connecticut; Sioux Falls, South Dakota; and Raleigh, North Carolina. In collaboration with the ACLU Reproductive Freedom Project under Lynn Paltrow and the NOW Women of Color Program, in 1989 the Partnership Program sponsored "In Defense of *Roe*," a national conference in Washington, D.C., for women of color.

In July 1994 Black women attending a national pro-choice conference in Chicago decided to launch another highly visible campaign for abortion rights because the Clinton administration was in the process of designing a health care reform proposal that many Black women feared would deemphasize abortion rights. Under the leadership of "Able" Mable Thomas, the group called itself Women of African Descent for Reproductive Justice (the Reproductive Justice Coalition, for short). Fast-paced organizing brought together more than 800 Black abortion rights supporters, who raised more than $21,000 in two weeks to purchase a full-page signature ad in the *Washington Post* on August 16, 1994. The ad sent a clear message to members of Congress that the various health care reform proposals must address concerns of Black women, including abortion, universal coverage, equal access to health care services, and protection from discrimination.

This remarkable series of events, compressed into a relatively brief period, marked the first time many African-American activists had ever publicly defended abortion rights and demonstrated a new awareness among African-American women who mobilized support for an expanded reproductive freedom agenda. They had an impact on both the Black community and the women's movement. By now, prominent Black male writers, such as Manning Marable, openly challenged sexist views on reproductive rights. Marable insisted: "We must fight for women's rights to control their own bodies and not submit to the demagogues of the rabid right who would return us to back alley abortionists, to those who would destroy young women's lives. Those who oppose the woman's right to choose express so much love for the rights of the fetus, yet too frequently express contempt for child nutrition programs, child care, and education after the child has come into the world."[148]

Despite the difficulties in Black male-female dialogue about such issues as the Anita Hill / Clarence Thomas sexual harassment charges, it appears that African-American men and women are entering into a new (and yet old) consensus about the importance of reproductive rights for racial progress.

By the mid-1990s African-American and other women of color have forced the abortion rights movement to become a broader struggle for reproductive freedom. I do not believe it is an overstatement to say that the activism of Black women and other women of color expanded the focus of the abortion rights movement in the 1990s. This activism influenced several pro-choice organizations to change their names and priorities: the National Abortion Rights Action League was renamed the National Abortion and Reproductive Rights Action League in 1994; the Religious Coalition for Abortion Rights became the Religious Coalition for Reproductive Choice that same year. NOW added welfare rights as one of its top priorities in 1993. This broadening of the agenda of organizations that were primarily seen as narrowly focused was due, in large part, to the demands of women of color for a more inclusive and relevant reproductive rights movement.

This transformation in the politics of the pro-choice movement required an assessment of the interrelatedness of race, gender, and class issues and how they affected different groups of women. Despite our biological similarities, different groups of women cope with vastly different social realities. Black women have placed reproductive health issues in a historical context that makes the reproductive freedom movement relevant to the ongoing struggle against racism and poverty. Today, more Black women publicly support abortion and birth control than ever before; more are working with predominantly white women's organizations than before; and, in many ways, the ideological gaps between Black and white feminists have diminished as the reproductive freedom movement seeks to make services available and accessible to all women.

Abortion rights has moved from the margin to the center of the dialogue about Black feminist activism. The leadership of the 1960s was finally matched by a constituency in the 1990s that supported full reproductive rights for Black women. In a sense, the deferred dreams of our foremothers of the 1920s were finally affirmed when Black women declared, "We Remember!"

CONCLUSION: IN PURSUIT OF PERFECT CHOICE

As we plan our activist future, we must clearly envision what we want to create for ourselves, so that we end up where we want to be. We must wrestle with concepts like "perfect choice," the opposite of the very imperfect choices we presently have. (I first heard this sentiment expressed by Naima Major at the National Black Women's Health Project in 1989, when I was its program director; it seemed to capture our aspirations so accurately.) We demand perfect choice: the right to have the resources to make the reproductive choices that make sense.

Perfect choice must involve access not only to abortion services but also to prenatal care, quality sex education, contraceptives, maternal infant and child health services, housing, and reform of the health care delivery system. As Gloria Joseph has said, "Given these realities of health care seen by Black people, White women must understand why Black women do not devote their full energies to the abortion issue. The emphasis has to be on total health care."[149]

For example, the scientific community must provide us with safe contraceptive and abortion choices. At the same time, we will not allow those who pursue pharmaceutical profits and political objectives to use us as human guinea pigs in experimental reproductive technologies.

We oppose all bad reproductive technology, just as we oppose the abusive use of promising technology. For example, the contraceptive implant Norplant was the first new birth control offered to American women in twenty-five years and as such was a welcome development because we have so few contraceptive choices. However, within a year of its introduction, an African-American woman in California was ordered by a judge to accept temporary sterilization with Norplant as a condition of her parole.[150] Only the fierce vigilance of the ACLU Reproductive Freedom Project stopped the judge's dangerous order. This type of abuse is what happens when a racist and insensitive system devises politicized applications of technology, to our detriment.

We demand to be in control of our own bodies and to have access to the best available technology, without limits because of income, race, or sexual preference. We, not doctors or courts or even the men in our lives, should decide if and when we have children.

When perfect choices do not exist, women adapt themselves, using whatever is available. Women often beg for sterilization when that is the only way (short of abstinence) to control their fertility. If abortion is recriminalized, then women will again resort to self-induced abortions, some using life-threatening methods.

The practical imperatives of this work are apparent: We must sponsor more conferences, retreats, think tanks, and we must produce more documentation and research in order to advance our movement and our struggle for freedom, and offer younger women a vision for the future. Poet and writer Audre Lorde expressed our project best: "For Black women, learning to consciously extend ourselves to each other and to call upon each other's strengths is a life-saving strategy. In the best of circumstances surrounding our lives, it requires an enormous amount of mutual, consistent support for us to be emotionally able to look straight into the face of the powers aligned against us and still do our work with joy. It takes determination and practice." [151]

The history of African-American women's activism in the reproductive freedom movement is just now being researched, more than one hundred years after it began. This work is urgent because unless we define for ourselves our own history and our impact, others' descriptions of our contributions will never be accurate or authentic. Today, more African-American women than ever before are active in the struggle to maintain legal and accessible abortion services. This militancy may once again produce tension for African-American men regarding the relationship of race and sex, a reaction I call "blacklash." However, our new militancy will also produce definitions of power, activism, and resistance that will frame the way our activism is recorded as history.

NOTES

1. Linda Gordon, in her critically acclaimed book *Woman's Body, Woman's Right* (New York: Penguin, rev. ed., 1990), separates the reproductive freedom movement into distinct historical phases, evolving from "voluntary motherhood" to "birth control" to "family planning" to "reproductive freedom." Each of these phrases has historical antecedents and associations, but for the purpose of this essay I will use them rather interchangeably.

2. Martha C. Ward, *Poor Women, Powerful Men: America's Great Experiment in Family Planning* (Boulder: Westview Press, 1986), 18.

3. Ibid., 55.

4. Robert Staples, *The Black Women in America* (Chicago: Nelson Hall, 1974), 146.

5. Melanie Tervalon, "Black Women's Reproductive Rights," in *Women's Health: Readings on Social, Economic and Political Issues,* ed. Nancy Worcester and Marianne H. Whatley (Dubuque, Iowa: Kendall/Hunt, 1988), 136.

6. E. Frances White, "Africa on My Mind: Gender, Counterdiscourse, and African-American Nationalism," in *Words of Fire: An Anthology of African-American Feminist Thought,* ed. Beverly Guy-Sheftall (New York: New Press, 1995), 519.

7. Rosalind Pollack Petchesky, *Abortion and Woman's Choice: The State, Sexuality, and Reproductive Freedom* (Boston: Northeastern University Press, rev. ed., 1990), 130.

8. Brenda Joyner, "Fighting Back to Save Women's Lives," in *From Abortion to Reproductive Freedom: Transforming a Movement,* ed. Marlene Gerber Fried (Boston: South End Press, 1990), 208.

9. Guy-Sheftall, *Words of Fire,* xiv.

10. Fried, *From Abortion,* x.

11. Gordon, *Woman's Body,* 48.

12. Brochure published by African American Women for Reproductive Freedom, Washington, D.C., September 1989.

13. The Combahee River Collective, "A Black Feminist Statement," in *All the Women Are White, All the Blacks Are Males, But Some of Us Are Brave: Black Women's Studies,* ed. Gloria T. Hull, Patricia Bell Scott, and Barbara Smith (Old Westbury, N.Y.: Feminist Press, 1982), 15–16.

14. Stanley K. Henshaw, Lisa M. Koonin, and Jack S. Smith, "Characteristics of U.S. Women Having Abortions," *Family Planning Perspectives* 23 (March/April 1991): 75–81.

15. National Council of Negro Women and Communications Consortium Media Center, "Women of Color Reproductive Health Poll," August 30, 1991.

16. Hull et al., *But Some of Us Are Brave,* xx.

17. bell hooks, *Talking Back* (Boston: South End Press, 1989), 6.

18. Thomas B. Littlewood, *The Politics of Population Control* (Notre Dame, Ind.: University of Notre Dame Press, 1977), 18.

19. Patricia Hill Collins, *Black Feminist Thought: Knowledge, Consciousness and the Politics of Empowerment* (New York: Routledge, 1991), 50; Deborah Gray White, *"Ar'n't I a Woman?": Female Slaves in the Plantation South* (New York: Norton, 1985), 98.

20. D. White, *"Ar'n't I a Woman?"* 101.

21. Elizabeth Fox-Genovese, *Within the Plantation Household: Black and White Women in the Old South* (Chapel Hill: University of North Carolina Press, 1988), 324.

22. Angela Davis, "Racism, Birth Control, and Reproductive Rights," in Fried, ed., *From Abortion,* 17.

23. Gordon, *Woman's Body,* 151.

24. Paula Giddings, *When and Where I Enter: The Impact of Black Women on Race and Sex in America* (New York: William Morrow, 1984), 137.

25. Guy-Sheftall, *Words of Fire,* 6.

26. Giddings, *When and Where I Enter,* 85.

27. Gerda Lerner, ed., *Black Women in White America* (New York: Vintage, 1972), 576.

28. Nancy F. Cott, *The Grounding of Modern Feminism* (New Haven: Yale University Press, 1987), 92–93.

29. Gordon, *Woman's Body*, xix.

30. Giddings, *When and Where I Enter*, 108.

31. Many thanks are due Jessie Rodrique, the first scholar I encountered who was doing serious research on the birth control activism of Black women. It was her work that encouraged me to investigate and expand on this history to include abortion rights history and to connect it with modern-day activism. As a measure of the sensitivity of her work, most of the Black women who read her research did not realize she was white until she confessed it on the last page. The familiar racial biases and assumptions that frequently mar white women's writings on Black women were totally absent from her work, a tribute to her feminist consciousness and feminist ethics. See Jessie M. Rodrique, "The Black Community and the Birth Control Movement," in *Unequal Sisters: A Multicultural Reader in U.S. Women's History*, ed. Ellen Carol Dubois and Vicki L. Ruiz (New York: Routledge, 1990), 335, 333.

32. Roseann P. Bell, Bettye J. Parker, and Beverly Guy-Sheftall, eds., *Sturdy Black Bridges: Visions of Black Women in Literature* (New York: Anchor, 1979), 117.

33. Ibid.

34. Rodrique, "The Black Community," 338.

35. Ibid., 335.

36. Ibid.

37. Gordon, *Woman's Body*, 133.

38. Alan L. Stoskopf, "Confronting the Forgotten History of the American Eugenics Movement," *Facing History and Ourselves News*, 1995, 7.

39. Petchesky, *Abortion and Woman's Choice*, 86.

40. Ward, *Poor Women*, 8.

41. Cott, *Grounding of Modern Feminism*, 91.

42. Carole R. McCann, *Birth Control Politics in the United States, 1916–1945* (Ithaca, N.Y.: Cornell University Press, 1994), 100.

43. Betsy Hartmann, *Reproductive Rights and Wrongs: The Global Politics of Population Control and Contraceptive Choice* (New York: Harper & Row, 1987), 97.

44. Davis, "Racism, Birth Control," 20.

45. Gena Corea, *The Hidden Malpractice: How American Medicine Mistreats Women* (New York: Harper & Row, 1985), 138, 141.

46. Rodrique, "The Black Community," 338.

47. W. E. B. DuBois, "Black Folk and Birth Control," *Birth Control Review*, June 1932, 166.

48. Gordon, *Woman's Body*, 328.

49. Ibid.

50. Ibid.

51. Eugenics and birth control policies targeting African Americans were not the only reasons African Americans were concerned about American public health policies. In 1931 a pilot project to study syphilis was launched in

Tuskegee, Alabama, funded by the Rosenwald Fund. The Tuskegee program ran from 1932 to 1972, until it was exposed as an unethical research project that left syphilis untreated in poor, uneducated Black farmers so that public health officials could trace the unmedicated development of syphilis in humans. This program fed a strong distrust among African Americans of public health policies and the role of private philanthropy in supplementing the role and funding of the state. See James H. Jones, *Bad Blood: The Tuskegee Syphilis Experiment* (New York: Free Press, 1981), 86–87.

52. Claudia Jones, "An End to the Neglect of the Problems of the Negro Woman!" in Guy-Sheftall, *Words of Fire*, 113.

53. Daniel Friedman and Sharon Grimberg, *Back-Alley Detroit: Abortion before Roe v. Wade: A Video Documentary,* Filmmakers Library, New York, 1992.

54. Rickie Solinger, *The Abortionist: A Woman Against the Law* (New York: Free Press, 1994), 36.

55. Linda Janet Holmes, "Thank You Jesus to Myself: The Life of a Traditional Black Midwife," in *The Black Women's Health Book: Speaking for Ourselves,* ed. Evelyn C. White (Seattle: Seal Press, 1990), 98.

56. Solinger, *The Abortionist,* 5.

57. Ibid., 15.

58. Ibid., 14.

59. Ward, *Poor Women,* 15.

60. Laura Kaplan, *The Story of Jane: The Legendary Underground Feminist Abortion Service* (New York: Pantheon, 1995), 7.

61. Ward, *Poor Women,* 22–23.

62. Ibid., 14.

63. Petchesky, *Abortion and Woman's Choice,* 118.

64. Littlewood, *Population Control,* 9.

65. Ward, *Poor Women,* 31.

66. Ibid., 27.

67. Ibid., 62.

68. Ibid., 59.

69. Ibid., 68.

70. Ibid., 17.

71. Ibid., xiii.

72. Martin Luther King, Jr., "Family Planning—A Special and Urgent Concern" (New York: Planned Parenthood–World Population, 1966), 4.

73. NAACP Policy Statement on Family Planning, adopted July 1966, 57th Convention, Los Angeles.

74. Corea, *Hidden Malpractice,* 144.

75. Littlewood, *Population Control,* 80.

76. Davis, "Racism, Birth Control," 23.

77. Ibid., 12.

78. Ward, *Poor Women,* 58.

79. Kaplan, *Story of Jane,* 61–64.

80. Ward, *Poor Women,* 58.

81. Jane, "Just Call Jane," in Fried, *From Abortion,* 93.

82. Ibid., 95.

83. Kaplan, *Story of Jane,* 267.

84. Ibid., 175.

85. Not her real name. Ms. Smith requested anonymity.

86. Author's interview, January 17, 1996.

87. Giddings, *When and Where I Enter,* 317.

88. Littlewood, *Population Control,* 75.

89. Ibid.

90. Ibid., 69.

91. Giddings, *When and Where I Enter,* 318.

92. Ward, *Poor Women,* 95.

93. Ibid., 92.

94. Author's interview with Nkenge Toure, March 5, 1993.

95. Littlewood, *Population Control,* 97.

96. Ward, *Poor Women,* 93.

97. Littlewood, *Population Control,* 72.

98. Ibid., 79.

99. Ward, *Poor Women,* 93.

100. Littlewood, *Population Control,* 72.

101. Linda LaRue, "The Black Movement and Women's Liberation," in Guy-Sheftall, *Words of Fire,* 171–72.

102. Author's interview with Dr. Brown, January 12, 1992.

103. Beverly Smith, "Black Women's Health: Notes for a Course," in Hull et al., *But Some of Us Are Brave,* 107.

104. Shirley Chisholm, *Unbought and Unbossed* (New York: Hodge Taylor, 1970), 114–15.

105. Frances M. Beal, "Double Jeopardy: To Be Black and Female," in *Sisterhood Is Powerful,* ed. Robin Morgan (New York: Random House, 1970), 393.

106. Toni Cade Bambara, "The Pill, Genocide or Liberation," in *The Black Woman,* ed. Toni Cade Bambara (New York: Penguin, 1970), 163–64.

107. Ibid., 166.

108. Beal, "Double Jeopardy," 393.

109. Space does not permit me to name all of the African-American women who were influential in the reproductive freedom movement during the 1970s and 1980s. It would be remiss of me, however, to neglect to mention the important activists (and sometimes writers) who contributed to the development of a Black feminist reproductive freedom analysis: Audre Lorde, Angela Davis, bell hooks, Paula Giddings, Safiya Bandele, Gloria Joseph, Nkenge Toure, Dazon Dixon, Vickie Alexander, Barbara Smith, Donna Brazile, Eleanor Holmes Norton, Stanlie James, Vanessa Northington-Gamble, Sakinah Ahad, Melanie Tervalon, June Dobbs Butts, Brenda Joyner, Faye Williams, Mary Lisbon, Linda Leaks, Flo Kennedy, Sherrilyn Ifill, Charlotte Rutherford, Virginia Floyd, Sharon Parker, Pam Freeman, Jamala Rogers, Eleanor Hinton-Hoytt, Julia Scott, Byllye Avery, and Bernice Reagon. These women, along with many other women of color and white women, directly and indirectly encouraged many African-American women to become involved in the women's movement. It is

my hope that future books will affirm the innovative contributions of each of these heterosexual and lesbian women.

110. "The Combahee River Collective," in Hull et al., *But Some of Us Are Brave*, 14.

111. Ibid., 11–14.

112. Guy-Sheftall, *Words of Fire*, 15.

113. Combahee River Collective, "A Black Feminist Statement," in *This Bridge Called My Back: Writings by Radical Women of Color*, ed. Cherrie Moraga and Gloria Anzaldua (Watertown, Mass.: Persephone Press, 1981), 211.

114. Ward, *Poor Women*, 51.

115. Ibid., 52–53.

116. Byllye Y. Avery, "Breathing Life into Ourselves: The Evolution of the National Black Women's Health Project," in Evelyn C. White, *Black Women's Health Book*, 5.

117. Byllye Y. Avery, "A Question of Survival / A Conspiracy of Silence: Abortion and Black Women's Health," in Fried, *From Abortion*, 76.

118. Moraga and Anzaldua, *This Bridge*, viii.

119. Beal, "Double Jeopardy," 393.

120. Ninia Baehr, *Abortion without Apology: A Radical History for the 1990s* (Boston: South End Press, 1990), 56.

121. Chisholm, *Unbought and Unbossed*, 113–22.

122. Planned Parenthood Federation of America, biographical sketch of Faye Wattleton, president, March 1989.

123. Ward, *Powerful Men*, 64.

124. Michele Wallace, "A Black Feminist's Search for Sisterhood," in Hull et al., *But Some of Us Are Brave*, 12.

125. Gloria I. Joseph and Jill Lewis, *Common Differences: Conflicts in Black and White Feminist Perspectives* (New York: Anchor Books, 1981), 276.

126. Hartmann, *Reproductive Rights and Wrongs*, 9.

127. bell hooks, *Ain't I a Woman? Black Women and Feminism* (Boston: South End Press, 1981), 196.

128. Alice Walker, "One Child of One's Own: A Meaningful Digression within the Work(s)—An Excerpt," in Hull et al., *But Some of Us Are Brave*, 42.

129. National Women's Conference Committee, *A Decade of Achievement, 1977–1987: A Report on a Survey Based on the National Plan of Action for Women* (Beaver Dam, Wis.: National Women's Conference Center, May 1988), 54.

130. Tervalon, "Black Women's Reproductive Rights," 136–37.

131. Edith Butler, "The First National Conference on Black Women's Health Issues," in Worcester and Whatley, *Women's Health*, 39.

132. Petchesky, *Abortion and Woman's Choice*, 155.

133. Author's interview with Donna Brazile, March 19, 1989.

134. Giddings, *When and Where I Enter*, 300–311.

135. Ibid., 346.

136. Ibid., 347.

137. Davis, "Racism, Birth Control," 205–206.

138. Judy D. Simmons, "Abortion: A Matter of Choice," in Evelyn C. White, *Black Women's Health Book,* 120.

139. Statement on "Operation Rescue" by National Civil Rights Leaders, January 22, 1989.

140. Sam Fulwood III, "Black Women Reluctant to Join Pro-Choice Forces," *Los Angeles Times,* November 27, 1989, 18.

141. Faye Wattleton, "Teenage Pregnancy: A Case for National Action," in Evelyn C. White, *Black Women's Health Book,* 108–9.

142. Infant mortality programs received special attention because Black infants in America die at twice the rate of white infants in the first year of life. This Black/white infant mortality gap has always existed, and since the 1920s, has actually widened. While the African-American infant mortality rate declined throughout the 1970s, the rate subsequently leveled off and then rose in the 1980s, a trend that can be attributed in part to cuts in federal programs. See Virginia David Floyd, "Too Soon, Too Small, Too Sick: Black Infant Mortality," in *Health Issues in the Black Community,* ed. Ronald L. Braithwaite and Sandra E. Taylor (San Francisco: Jossey-Bass, 1992), 165.

143. Chiquita G. Smith, "A Congresswoman's Call to Action," in *Common Ground, Different Planes,* ed. Religious Coalition for Abortion Rights (Washington, D.C., 1992), 1.

144. Paul Ruffins, "Blacks Backing Pro-Choice Add a Compelling Voice," *Los Angeles Times,* September 17, 1989, 2.

145. Ibid., 1.

146. African American Women for Reproductive Freedom, brochure, September 1989.

147. Loretta Ross, Sherrilyn Ifill, and Sabrae Jenkins, "Emergency Memorandum to Women of Color, " in Fried, *From Abortion,* 147.

148. Manning Marable, "Black America: Multicultural Democracy in the Age of Clarence Thomas and David Duke, and the Los Angeles Uprisings," in *Open Fire,* ed. Greg Ruggiero and Stuart Ashulka (New York: New Press, 1993), 256.

149. Joseph and Lewis, *Common Differences,* 40.

150. Barbara Mintzes, Anita Hardon, and Jannemieke Hanhart, *Norplant: Under Her Skin* (Amsterdam: Women's Health Action Foundation, 1993), 115.

151. Audre Lorde, *A Burst of Light* (Ithaca, N.Y.: Firebrand Books, 1988), 123.

9

Marlene Gerber Fried

ABORTION IN THE UNITED STATES—
LEGAL BUT INACCESSIBLE

"Mary" calls me from South Dakota, asking if we can help. "Susan," her seventeen-year-old daughter, is pregnant. The man involved is the father of Susan's two-year-old child, but Susan has a restraining order against him. She is in her second trimester, and the only clinic in their state doesn't do abortions past fourteen weeks, so she will have to go to Kansas to have the abortion. Susan and her mother have tried, but they can't raise all the money needed for the trip and the procedure. The man's mother could contribute, but she is pressuring Susan to have the baby and give it to her to raise. Mary is worried and scared. She is also angry, after calling all the pro-choice groups she knows and finding no resources for women in her daughter's situation.

As the contact person for the National Network of Abortion Funds, I get many calls like this from women all over the country—women in prison, young women, women who have been raped, "undocumented" women, women without resources, desperate women. We repeatedly hear desperate stories from girls and women. A seventeen-year-old with one child, for example, drank a bottle of rubbing alcohol to cause a miscarriage; a fourteen-year-old asked her boyfriend to kick her in the stomach and push her down the stairs.

Although legal abortion is one of the safest surgical procedures in the United States—comparable to a tonsillectomy—these calls from low-income women are a constant reminder that safety itself is a privilege. Today, because of the inaccessibility of safe, legal abortion, some women are again resorting to illegal abortions and self-abortions. And there are new risks, as forces within the anti-abortion movement pursue strategies of harassment, terrorism, violence, and murder. Recently our local abortion rights fund received a piece of hate mail enjoining "pro-lifers" to "attack" abortion providers and other "peddlers of death. . . . When we shoot, we should aim for the lower spine and the buttocks. At this time we probably don't need to kill to discourage some pro-deathers from implementing their agenda." [1]

A "Defensive Action Pledge," written in support of Michael Griffin, the accused (and subsequently convicted) murderer of Dr. David Gunn, actually asserts "the justice of taking all Godly action necessary to defend innocent human life including the use of force." [2] Abortion rights activists know that this threat is aimed right at us.

For years anti-abortion activists called us murderers in their "peaceful" demonstrations. When asked to publicly condemn the violence aimed at abortion providers, leaders of the anti-abortion movement and the Catholic Church chose instead to talk about the "violence of abortion." This prevails at the highest levels. Consider the March 1995 encyclical, in which Pope John Paul II condemns abortion in the strongest possible terms as "a crime against humanity." He goes on, "I declare that direct abortion . . . always constitutes a grave moral disorder, since it is the deliberate killing of an innocent human being." He describes laws permitting abortion as "unjust, invalid and devoid of moral authority." [3]

Although we have always seen this language as inflammatory, we have typically ignored it; we tossed out hate letters or read them for comic relief. The murders of doctors and clinic workers in Florida and Massachusetts changed that.[4] The link between rhetoric and action seems more direct. So now we seal such communications in plastic bags and turn them over to the FBI, which finally has a clinic violence task force.

At the same time, we do not feel we can depend on law enforcement to protect us. After all, while two hundred clinics were bombed in the 1980s, the attention of federal law enforcement officials was captured only after the murders. As a pro-choice supporter asked, "Can you imagine the response of law enforcement if it had been two hundred banks?" We also harbor no illusions about local police. Repeated tussles at the clinics have made clear that many police are not on our side.

Since the murders, hate letters and "Wanted" posters underscore our vulnerability. We have to acknowledge the threat and struggle not to let it paralyze us. Now that the circle of terror has been widened, we understand more clearly what every abortion provider has faced for years. Anti-abortionists have personalized and broadened their targets to include anyone who has *anything* to do with abortion, anyone at an abortion clinic. In Brookline, Massachusetts, it was the receptionists who were killed.

Yes, we are frightened. It seems that there is no limit to what anti-abortion zealots will do to stop us. I know there are more like John Salvi and Paul Hill—others who will proclaim their right to murder us. The Justice Department may have had to convene a grand jury (early in 1995) to decide whether there is a national conspiracy, but the activist community knows what we are dealing with—as one pro-choice attorney in Florida grimly quipped, "It's an army of lone gunmen."

This fear has become the setting for women's abortion experiences. We do not yet know the emotional consequences for women who, in order to get their abortions, must walk through metal detectors, go through back doors, leave all bags at the door, worry that someone with a gun will shoot them. Women still come for abortions. One and a half million U.S. women a year (about 55 million women worldwide) are still determined to end unwanted pregnancies. They will come as they always have. But under what conditions? At what personal cost?

In the late 1990s the life of a woman who needs an abortion is most visibly endangered by the threat of personal violence. But even before she goes to a clinic, she may be endangered because she cannot find either a provider or the funds required. For women like Mary's daughter, it is as if *Roe* never happened. And there are so many women like her, whose youth, race, and economic circumstances, together with the lack of accessible services—especially for later abortions—translate into daunting barriers. Before legalization, access to abortion was dependent on one's economic resources. Activists in the 1970s and 1980s who focused on the plight of low-income women saw that although legalization had tremendously increased accessibility, access was still dependent on ability to pay. In 1995 obstacles *define* abortion rights. The ability of a woman today to obtain an abortion is as dependent as ever on her economic status, age, race, and where she lives.

Since legalization of abortion in 1973, the anti-abortion movement has been pursuing a dual strategy, aiming at recriminalization of abortion in the long run while working to decrease access immediately. They have been successful. The abortion rights of uncountable women have effectively been taken away through the lack of federal and state funding, through decreases in available services and providers, by ongoing violence and harassment of clinics and clinic personnel, and by state legislative restrictions, such as parental consent laws and mandatory waiting periods. It is conservatively estimated that one in five Medicaid-eligible women wanting an abortion is unable to obtain it.[5] This proportion will increase as women's economic situation worsens, as welfare is cut, as Medicaid is restricted (in 1995 Congress yielded to the religious right and permitted states to deny Medicaid funding for rape and incest), and as the anti-abortion movement moves on to new ground, as in the effort to outlaw certain late-term abortions.[6]

Although these erosions have shaped women's abortion experiences, many people, even those who favor abortion rights, are unaware of the realities of diminishing access. There is a widespread perception that the abortion battle is essentially over for now, with only the zealots on both sides still having the energy to fight. Articulating this view, a progressive woman columnist recently asked: Why the fuss about Charles Fried's nomination to the state supreme court in Massachusetts? Pro-choice activists found the question outrageous, given the candidate's background. When Fried served as solicitor general under Ronald Reagan, he aggressively worked against abortion rights. He argued to overturn *Roe v. Wade,* and after his government tenure he supported the "gag rule" preventing federally funded clinics from giving information about abortion. The columnist apparently thought this was irrelevant since, as she pointed out, the battle over abortion is over and the pro-choice side won. But has it?

The pro-choice movement itself has not adequately attended to access issues. Its focus has too often been on maintaining the legal right to abortion, while the unequal ability of different groups of women to exercise that right is slighted. The mainstream and predominantly white middle-class pro-choice movement has always responded weakly, if at all, to restrictions on low-income women's abortion rights. It was only in the 1980s, when *all* women's rights were threatened, that hundreds of thousands of women leaped to defend abortion clinics and *Roe v. Wade.* There have been no comparable large-scale mobilizations to protect the rights of low-income women. The challenge to the movement has been clearly stated by Joan Coombs, director of Planned Parenthood, Philadelphia: "Will women of means fight and be activists with and on behalf of poor women and teens just as if their own rights were under attack?"

Thus far, the answer has been no. The fight has been left to organizations of women of color, which clearly see the importance of such battles. In 1993 the National Black Women's Health Project took the lead in fighting to repeal the Hyde Amendment. It understood that the consequence of separating rights from access is that low-income women have no rights. But it has had to push hard to bring the mainstream movement to this perspective.

Abortion rights organizations will have to develop strategies and analyses that not only reflect an understanding of the connection between access and rights in the context of abortion, but also ground abortion rights in other aspects of reproductive freedom.

The right *not* to have children must be part of a vision that allows women to determine their own sexual and reproductive lives. We need a vision based on the understanding that the denial of control takes different forms. Activists must as strenuously oppose coercive contraception and the denial of the social services needed to support childbearing as they do policies that restrict abortion. Only then will we be able to create a movement capable of fighting for and winning reproductive freedom for all women.

When I think about Mary, when I read threatening letters aimed at intimidating providers and activists, I am furious and moved to action. While I will be more mindful of who is around me, and I will give the hate mail to the FBI, I will also personally resist: I refuse to have an unlisted phone number. I refuse to take the "Abortion—Every Woman's Right" bumper sticker off my car. I refuse to stop being a spokesperson to the media.

CONSTRAINING ACCESS

The impact of eroding access to abortion has been felt most severely by low-income women, young women, and women of color, who comprise a disproportionate number of the poor. Access has been undermined primarily through denial of public funding for abortion, parental involvement laws, and the loss of abortion services.

Public funding, an absolute necessity if all women are to have access to abortion rights, was lost in 1976, just three years after *Roe v. Wade.* The Hyde Amendment, which prohibits federal Medicaid funding except in cases of life endangerment, has been renewed by Congress every year since. Most states have followed the federal precedent and prohibit the use of state funds for abortions. As of September 1995, only 13 percent of abortions were paid for with public funds, almost all state funds;[7] and as of January 1996, only seventeen states covered abortions for health reasons.[8]

Exceptions for rape and incest were added to Hyde in 1993, only after a long battle. Even this minimal "liberalization" was resisted, and several states refused to comply. In August 1995 Congress rescinded the exceptions and returned to life endangerment as the only grounds for funding.[9]

Between 1973 and 1977 the federal government paid for about one-third of all abortions: 294,600 in 1977. After Hyde the decline was dramatic, and it continued over the following decade. In 1978 fewer than 2,500 abortions were covered by federal Medicaid funds (down 99 percent from 1977). By 1992 Medicaid paid for only 267 abortions.[10] A few examples illustrate how the rigid federal standard has disqualified virtually all women from federal support.

- A twenty-three-year-old woman with cervical cancer was told that Medicaid would pay for a hysterectomy but not for an abortion, which was a prerequisite to appropriate treatment of the disease.
- A woman who had tried to self-abort with a coat hanger was hospitalized with an infection. Medicaid paid for treating the infection but would not pay for an abortion because her pregnancy was not seen as life-threatening.
- A woman carrying a twenty-two-week fetus with a fatal heart defect was denied funding for an abortion.

The Hyde Amendment primarily affects low-income women, but it also applies to federal workers, military personnel and their dependents, women living on Native American reservations, and women in federal prisons. Its impact has been devastating. The average cost of a first-trimester abortion is $296, nearly two-thirds the amount of the average maximum monthly payment under Aid to Families with Dependent Children (AFDC) for a family of three.[11] Clearly, some welfare recipients cannot afford abortions at all. Others are forced to divert money from other essentials, such as food, rent, and utilities. Even when women are able to raise the money, the time it takes to search for funding makes it more likely they will need a more costly and more difficult second-trimester procedure. It is estimated that one in five Medicaid-eligible women who had second-trimester abortions would have had a first-trimester abortion if the lack of public funds had not resulted in delays while the woman was trying to raise funds.[12]

The lack of funding contributes to other aspects of diminished access, including the unavailability of abortion services and the decrease in the number of abortion providers. Significantly fewer hospitals, clinics, and private physicians' offices provide abortions in states with funding restrictions.

Publicity surrounding the murders of doctors and clinic workers has made the public at large sharply aware of the extreme vulnerability of abortion providers. In fact, clinics and providers have been targets of violence since the early 1980s. In 1993 alone, half of all clinics responding to a survey about clinic violence reported severe anti-abortion attacks. These acts included death threats, stalking, attacks with chemicals such as butyric acid, arson, bomb threats, invasions, and blockades. While federal legislation such as the Freedom of Access to Clinic Entrances (FACE) Act will certainly help, anti-abortionists are increasingly turning to harassment of individual doctors and their families, picketing their homes, following them, circulating "Wanted" posters.

The provider shortage has only recently come to public attention, although it represents a major threat to abortion rights. The number of abortion providers (including hospitals, clinics, and physicians' offices) dropped 18 percent between 1982 and 1992, with the greatest loss occurring between 1988 and 1992.[13]

While the overall numbers themselves are very disturbing, of even greater concern is the very uneven distribution of services. Nine of ten abortion providers are now located in metropolitan areas; about one-third fewer counties have an abortion provider now than did in the late 1970s. Ninety-four percent of nonmetropolitan counties have no services (85 percent of rural women live in these underserved counties). One-quarter of women having abortions travel more than fifty miles from home to obtain their abortions.[14]

Anti-abortion activists aim also to cut off the supply of potential future providers. They have targeted medical students, generating understandable concerns about taking up practice in such a dangerous and marginalized field. A group called Life Dynamics promoted its agenda with "Bottom Feeder," a fourteen-page "joke" book sent to 35,000 medical students. One of the jokes: "What do you do if you find yourself in a room with Hitler, Mussolini and an abortionist, and you have only two bullets? *Answer:* Shoot the abortionist twice." Each person receiving the mailing is also told: "The anti-abortion movement knows where to find you."

Few medical students are being trained in abortion techniques, despite the fact that abortion is the most common obstetrics surgical procedure. Almost half of graduating obstetrics and gynecology residents have never performed a first-trimester abortion. Many hospitals do so few abortions they cannot even be appropriate training sites. In February 1995 the American Council for Graduate Medical Education issued guidelines mandating abortion training. Anti-abortion challenges were immediately set in motion, and by August 1995 Congress had voted to protect federal funds for medical schools that refuse to teach abortion techniques.

Another area in which the anti-abortion movement has had considerable legislative and ideological success is the restriction of abortion for young women. Parental involvement laws requiring either parental consent or notification before minors can obtain abortions affect millions of young women. About 40 percent of the one million teens who become pregnant annually choose abortion.

Thirty-five states have these laws, and they are enforced in twenty-three states. In some states a physician is required to notify at least one parent either in person, by phone, or in writing. Health care providers face losing their licenses and sometimes criminal penalties for failure to comply.

Parental notification or permission laws, with their judicial bypass provisions, often require travel, extra time, and money. Although most teens who must request a judicial bypass are ultimately given permission, the whole process is typically humiliating and traumatizing. Judges have a great deal of leeway in these cases. Just after Pennsylvania's Abortion Control Act went into effect, a teenager seeking the court's permission to have a confidential abortion had to threaten legal action to prevent the judge from bringing her parents into the proceedings.

Although defenders of such laws argue for the importance of parental rights and the need to foster better parent-daughter communication, the evidence from young women, social workers, and health care providers gives a different picture. Their experiences demonstrate that these laws mainly create barriers for young women seeking abortions. Further, the laws are dangerous, exposing young women to physical and emotional abuse. A majority of teens do tell at least one parent. Those who don't fear physical abuse, violence between their parents, or exacerbating a parent's drug or alcohol abuse problem.[15]

All of these infringements on abortion access have curtailed the abortion rights of millions of women. In addition, the anti-abortion movement has used access issues to further its long-term political objective of criminalizing abortion. Anti-abortion activists have been able to use battles over funding, training of doctors, and parental consent as opportunities for consolidating their movement, drawing in new supporters, and building support for other restrictions on abortion. These fights also play a significant ideological and symbolic role.

STIGMATIZING ABORTION AND WOMEN: SOCIAL SCORN AS SOCIAL POLICY

Generating moral disapproval of abortion has been high on the anti-abortion movement's agenda. Adherents have seen it as key to their efforts to recriminalize abortion. Thus, while legalizing abortion did transform it from a dangerous, often life-threatening experience into a safe one, it has not removed the stigma.

Anti-abortion campaigns to restrict abortion have been turned into referenda on morality. They are vehicles through which the anti-abortion movement asserts a kind of conscience clause for the general public. We see an example of this in the area of public funding with appeals such as "Abortion may be legal, but why should we be forced to pay for something that is morally repugnant (to us)?" Anti-abortionists have been increasingly successful in suppressing the parentheses, portraying the matter as if there were a universal consensus that abortion is morally illegitimate.

As we have seen, anti-abortion extremists have taken up this moral mandate in their campaigns against abortion providers. They use the moral "illegitimacy" of abortion to legitimize their claim that anyone participating in abortion delivery is morally tainted and must be stopped. It has not been difficult for anti-abortion extremists to seize this as justification for their acts of violence. Despite recent efforts by the mainstream anti-abortion movement to distance itself from the perpetrators of anti-abortion violence, the only substantive difference I can see is over the means, not the moral zeal or the goals.

Anti-abortion activists understand that restricting access for young women and denying public funding are strategic ways to isolate and stigmatize the doctors who perform abortions, the hospitals and clinics that provide abortion services, abortion itself, and ultimately, the women who have abortions. Indeed, women bear the brunt of the social disapproval. Anti-abortionists have been able to portray women having abortions as selfish, sexually irresponsible, unfeeling, and morally blind individuals who kill their own children for "convenience." Only the women who are true victims—whose pregnancies result from rape or incest—are above contempt, though even in those cases, anti-abortionists argue, the victims should be provided with sympathy, not abortions. In short, women simply cannot be trusted to make major moral decisions. They must be controlled.

Contempt for women, especially those who have the fewest resources, pervades other aspects of the conservative political program. Central to that agenda are attacks on welfare and illegitimacy that make young, low-income, unwed women of color the scapegoats for poverty, child abuse, drug addiction, violence, and general societal deterioration.

Conservatives have proposed solutions in the form of a series of callous, punitive, and coercive measures designed to control the lives and reproductive capacity of poor women. These include Learnfare (reducing parents' benefits if their kids skip school), Workfare (tying benefits to jobs), Bridefare (requiring minors to get married as a condition of receiving benefits), Contraceptive Fare (requiring women to consent to the long-term contraceptive Norplant), and Minorfare (terminating welfare benefits absolutely for unmarried minors). "Reforms" also include family caps, child exclusion policies, and time-limited benefits.

These proposals are derived from an analysis that sees poverty as caused by poor women having too many children, not by racism, sexism, or lack of jobs that pay a living wage, and certainly not by lack of government supports for low-income families. These "welfare reforms" have been designed with the overt goal of deterring unwed motherhood by making it more difficult for single, teenage mothers and their children to survive economically.

Under the "reforms," receiving benefits is conditional on "good" behavior. Such efforts to control young women's reproduction through punishment substitute social disapproval for meaningful social policy. Little attention and less money are directed toward supporting young motherhood or enhancing educational and job opportunities for young low-income women. Instead, the punitive ideological and legislative policies championed by conservatives call for the restoration of the stigma of illegitimacy and a renewed emphasis on the connection between illegitimacy, poverty, and social decay.[16] Defining women's sexuality and reproduction as the source of social problems has taken many different forms in the United States—coercing sterilization of Latina, African-American, and Native American women, imposing long-term contraceptives (Norplant and Depo Provera) on low-income women of color, making welfare benefits conditional on having abortions, making abortion unobtainable.[17] Behind these efforts to control reproduction is a misogynist contempt for women's sexuality, intertwined with racism. As a result, social scorn and punitive policies such as "welfare reforms" are directed most sharply against young low-income women of color.

There is a thread linking these policies to those aimed at controlling *all* women. Welfare restrictions limiting the possibilities for low-income women to have children are really just the other side of the abortion restriction coin. Both deny a woman the right to control her childbearing, as is made painfully clear in proposed legislation that ties the restoration of Medicaid funding for abortion to a "family cap" (women who have additional children while on welfare receive no additional benefits). Here, poor women's right to have children is pitted against the right not to.

While conservatives may have taken the lead in attempts to institutionalize a mandate against unwed pregnancy and childbearing, they have been joined by many liberals anxious to show their own traditional-family-values credentials. The effort to stop young low-income women from having children resonates even in pro-choice circles. Historically, reproductive choice in the United States has not encompassed childbearing. The abortion rights movement has focused on women's efforts not to have children; it has not adequately supported the right to have them.

CONSTRAINING OUR VISION

Surveying the most onerous restrictions on abortion reminds us of how much ground has been lost since legalization. Feminists saw *Roe v. Wade* as the first step in expanding women's reproductive rights. While millions of women have obtained safe, legal abortions since 1973, abortion rights advocates are now fighting to hold on even to the legal right.

Since many supporters define abortion today as a necessary evil and fail entirely to connect abortion to a broader conception of women's rights, it is no wonder opponents are having a public relations field day. Over the past two decades anti-abortion activists have claimed the moral high ground. The abortion rights movement is once again struggling to convince judges, legislators, politicians, and the general public that a woman's ability to control her body and her life are fundamental human rights.

Throughout much of the 1970s and 1980s, the post-legalization period, a politics of defensiveness shaped the strategies and goals of the most visible pro-choice organizations. The visible movement that emerged in the 1980s was formed in reaction to an all-out anti-choice offensive, which included initiatives in legislatures, courts, abortion clinics, and the media. In the effort to hold onto past gains and to avoid alienating possible supporters, this new abortion rights movement avoided talk about women's rights and even abortion. The focus was on the intolerance and extremism of the other side.

The language of abortion rights proponents changed. In the pre-legalization period, when the women's liberation movement took up the fight for abortion rights, it called for sexual freedom and abortion on demand. During the Reagan-Bush era, in the face of the fierce attack by an aggressive anti-abortion movement, efforts were made to sanitize pro-choice demands so they would be more palatable. The word *abortion* itself was too controversial. The movement favored the more euphemistic notions of *choice, personal freedom,* and *privacy,* in hopes that even conservatives wouldn't find this discourse objectionable.

Along with these changes, the movement developed a narrow agenda calling for safe, legal abortion rather than reproductive and sexual freedom for all women. In the conservative climate of the 1980s, the movement came to believe that it would have to settle for less, that compromises would have to be made, that it couldn't protect every woman's rights.

The shift in approach had enormous consequences for the development of the movement. Fighting for choice rather than justice appeals to those who already have choices, not to those who don't—low-income women, women of color, young women. As we have seen, these women have borne the brunt of the attacks on abortion. Until very recently, however, fighting for access has been the weakest part of the pro-choice strategy. It has taken very dire circumstances to change this.

For example, the movement has been wary of directly challenging parental involvement laws. Even among supporters of abortion rights, young women's rights remain an "unpopular" cause. The conservative pitch that parents have a right to control their daughters' behavior clearly resonates. Because of this, pro-choice activists at first preferred to create mechanisms such as free lawyers that would enable young women to have access in spite of the laws, rather than attempting repeal campaigns. The death of Becky Bell in 1989, however, and her family's crusade against parental consent laws, helped make this issue a visible part of the pro-choice agenda.

WHERE DO WE GO FROM HERE?

In the midst of the conservative "revolution" in Congress, and as a longtime abortion rights activist, I believe that it is urgent that we resist all intrusions on reproductive freedom (restrictions on abortion rights, "welfare reform," attacks on sex education and contraception, anti-gay initiatives). I also believe that a politics based on fear is less compelling and enduring than a politics based on hope. To combat the serious erosions in access to abortion and to make future gains, we must shift the movement's message and adopt a new approach. The abortion rights movement must emphasize women's right to make their own decisions while advocating public policies that expand opportunities for all women. It must affirm the human right to be sexual and at the same time resist the negative characterizations of abortion and women's sexuality. It must, as I have already suggested, defend a woman's right to have a child with as much fervor as it defends her right not to.

Several organizations and models already hold the potential to meet the challenges we face. In the 1980s and 1990s a number of reproductive rights groups were formed by women of color. Groups such as the National Black Women's Health Project, Women of Color Partnership Program (of the Religious Coalition for Reproductive Choice), National Latina Health Organization, National Asian Women's Health Organization, and Native American Women's Health and Education Resource Center have a more inclusive vision and agenda based on the needs of women in their communities. All of these groups locate abortion within a broader agenda of women's health and reproductive choices. They also see the opportunities for building a more inclusive movement.

The National Black Women's Health Project (founded in 1981)

states: "The purpose of NBWHP is the definition, promotion, and maintenance of health for Black women, including full reproductive rights and the essential authority of every woman to choose when, whether, and under what conditions she will bear children."[18] This vision is echoed in the statement of the National Latina Health Organization (founded in 1986): "[Our] definition of good health is holistic and includes not only freedom from disease but a wellness approach that encompasses access to quality education, the right to jobs that are environmentally safe and afford us the economic means to good, safe housing; the fundamental right to accessible quality health care and service that are culturally sensitive and language appropriate; and physical and spiritual well-being."[19]

The National Asian Women's Health Organization (created in 1993) articulates its vision as a community-based health advocacy organization: "NAWHO develops and implements a broad agenda for Asian women's and girls' health issues and addresses the varied and complex factors that impact the physical, emotional, mental, social and spiritual well-being of Asian women and girls."[20]

These groups also provide us with an expanded notion of activism that includes new models of self-help, combining mutual support and political advocacy with an emphasis on grassroots advocacy and organizing. Their organizational agendas include "hands-on" strategies that complement advocacy. The NBWHP talks about enabling African-American women to take control and become active participants in their own health: "empowerment through self-determination is the foundation for taking greater control of our health practices and lifestyles."[21] And they don't just talk. They organize self-help groups in African-American communities and have exported their model to Africa through their Sistereach Project.

Inspired by these groups, I joined with several women in 1992 to create the National Network of Abortion Funds. Our goal was to strengthen grassroots efforts to give direct assistance to women seeking abortions, to advocate for public funding for abortion and women's health care, and to provide visibility and a voice for women currently being denied their right to a safe, legal abortion. Those of us involved in this organization are concerned that the pro-choice movement has paid little attention to securing abortion services, to women's experiences of abortion, and to quality-of-care issues.

All of these groups bring into the movement the voices of women who have been excluded. They emphasize the importance of listening to young women, to low-income women, to women of color. The National Network of Abortion Funds, for example, has collected the stories of twenty-six women around the country.[22] In the introduction to a 1995 report, "Perceptions of Risk," the founding executive director of the National Asian Women's Health Organization, Mary Chung, writes, "In order to advocate for the improvement of the health status of Asian American women and girls, it is necessary to first educate ourselves and our communities about what the most important needs and problems are; and to learn this from Asian American women and girls themselves."[23] Some of the most widely publicized and useful information about the health status of women of color in the United States is coming from these groups.

Other groups have felt marginalized by the mainstream movement. Younger activists, who swelled the ranks of the abortion rights movement in the late 1980s, have been frustrated by the lack of interest in their leadership or input into agenda setting. Having to negotiate their sexual and reproductive lives through the terrain of AIDS and other sexually transmitted diseases, sexual abuse, violence against women, attacks on abortion rights, and demonization of young women, gay men, and lesbians gives them a broader understanding of the feminist project. Some of these issues are addressed in the publication "Young Women's Voices."[24]

Several new programs emphasize and encourage the leadership of young women and grassroots participation. The Clothesline Project, where women make T-shirts commemorating victims of domestic violence in their communities, is making its way around the country. The Civil Liberties and Public Policy Program based at Hampshire College sponsors the National Young Women's Day of Action, a day of nationally coordinated local actions connecting a range of issues, including abortion, contraception, violence, health care, gay and lesbian liberation, jobs, education, and child care. The program also organizes an annual conference featuring activists involved in a broad range of reproductive rights and women's issues, and it publishes a newsletter for campus activists.

Broad vision and grassroots organizing have been given a real boost in the international arena. A series of United Nations conferences, including the Earth Summit in Rio de Janeiro in 1992, the International Conference on Population and Development in Cairo in 1994, the Economic Summit in Copenhagen in 1995, and the Fourth World Conference on Women in Beijing in 1995, have given women's activists and organizations throughout the world unprecedented opportunities for interaction.

Internationally, especially in the developing world, the women's agenda integrates a wide range of issues. Advocates for women's rights and health place abortion in a broad human rights framework, which includes concerns about maternal and infant mortality, population control, economic justice, violence against women, and environmental destruction, just to name a few.

I believe that the vision of activists and the mainstream movement in the United States will be dramatically changed and strengthened by participation in the global women's movement. A global perspective broadens our understanding of women's oppression by attending to the rights of the least privileged women in the world and encouraging resistance to fundamentalism, militarism, and the drain of economic resources from the underdeveloped world.

Strategically, the global movement's emphasis on grassroots organizing is significant. Within the United States advocacy has become increasingly defined in terms of the ability to influence elected officials. The international gatherings have drawn attention to new strategies for increasing participation in social change activities. The extent to which women worldwide, in the most dangerous and personally threatening situations, have formed groups to resist oppression and to create new modes of living is truly inspirational.

In Beijing I was impressed with how much we can really teach and learn from each other across our geographical and cultural differences. I believe our movement can be reinvigorated by learning about other women's struggles. We can gain new perspectives to help with the difficult questions facing the abortion rights movement in the United States: Why have we tolerated an escalation of rhetoric that has legitimized the erosions of rights and led to the violent actions by the anti-abortion movement? How have opponents of abortion managed to seize the moral high ground and, incredibly, to hold onto it even when those on their side are committing murder? Why did we sacrifice the rights of some women in order to hold onto rights for others? How can we secure reproductive rights for all women?

It is time to soundly and publicly reject the premises of the anti-abortion movement. We must reclaim the debate. We cannot allow terror and harassment at clinics to be acceptable, or for Operation Rescue and the Catholic Church hierarchy to be positioned as *moderates*. And we must not let *abortion* remain a dirty word.

We must reject pro-choice sentiments like President Clinton's that take the form of saying that abortion should be legal but rare. We should challenge the increasing calls for compromise in the wake of the clinic murders. We must protest legislatures that are trading away the rights of young and low-income women in order to preserve the rights of the more privileged.

The abortion rights movement has little ground to yield as it is. After all, *Roe v. Wade* was already a significant compromise between every woman's right to self-determination sought by women's advocates and the more limited right to privacy acknowledged by the Supreme Court. As one longtime activist put it: "We have to disagree when our erstwhile allies call abortion a 'necessary tragedy.' Abortion is no tragedy. No moral slip for which we forgive hapless, weak women. Abortion is one of the concrete, fundamental ways we assert women's right to design our own lives. It is one of the ways we claim ourselves—for ourselves. As such, it is as profoundly ethical an act as any of us will ever see."[25]

Abortion is also a profoundly radical act. No wonder the religious right cannot let it go. Abortion rights—as a necessary ingredient of reproductive rights—assert women's power, at least the power to say no. The fight for abortion funding, like the battles over other restrictions, is also a symbolic fight about who gets to make reproductive decisions for women.

In the mid-1990s the mainstream movement was finally moved, taking up welfare reform, affirmative action, and attacks on immigrants, and making links with communities of color around violence. These efforts must be carefully nurtured. There is a long and difficult history and little shared work on which to base these crucial alliances.

It is my hope that the contemporary abortion rights movement will take the opportunity to expand people's understanding of what reproductive freedom means without sacrificing any of us. The leadership of women of color and young women should be models for the movement. The abortion rights movement must strongly claim the value, integrity, and reality of all women's lives. Our struggle and our future hang in the balance.

NOTES

1. "Cassandra" letter, no signature, no return address.
2. Apparently, several versions of this petition were circulated at the time of the Michael Griffin trial. I think there is some variation in the signatories. I

quote from a petition with the following names on it: Mike Bray, C. Roy McMillan, Andrew Burnett, Cathy Ramev, Matt Trewhella, Paul Hill, Paul de-Parrie, Regina Dinwiddie, Michael Dodds, Henry Felisone, Tony Piso, Jacob Miller, Dan Bray, David Crane, Donald Spitz, Michael Jarecki, Bill Koehler, Kenneth Arndt, Dave Leach, Mike Walker, Thomas Carleton, Valerie Ayskowski, Joseph F. O'Hare, David Graham, David Trosch.

3. "Evangelium Vitae" (The Gospel of Life), encyclical issued March 30, 1995. Quotations from *Boston Globe*, March 30, 1995, and *Wall Street Journal*, April 3, 1995.

4. In March 1993 Dr. David Gunn was killed outside a clinic in Pensacola, Florida. Michael Griffin was convicted of the murder and sentenced to life in prison.

In July 1994 Dr. John Britton and clinic escort James Barrett were murdered at the Ladies' Center in Pensacola, and Barrett's wife, June, was wounded. Paul Hill was convicted of the murders and sentenced to death. Hill was also the first person convicted under FACE.

In December 1994 in Brookline, Massachusetts, Shanon Lowney, a receptionist at a Planned Parenthood clinic, and Leanne Nichols, a receptionist at Preterm Health Services, were murdered (five others were wounded in these attacks). John Salvi III was tried and convicted of the murders in February 1996 and later committed suicide.

5. Pat Donovan, *The Politics of Blame: Family Planning, Abortion and the Poor* (New York: Alan Guttmacher Institute, 1995), 23.

6. In 1995 legislation was proposed in Congress that would criminalize a particular method for completing a midtrimester abortion, dilation and extraction (D&X). Those advocating the ban are calling these procedures "partial birth" abortions. Because very few late abortions are performed—fewer than 1 percent past the twentieth week; fewer than 0.1 percent after twenty-four weeks (National Abortion Federation, "Midtrimester Abortion," June 1995)—it seems that the effort to ban these procedures is part of the right wing's campaign to ban abortion altogether, step by step if need be.

7. Fact sheet prepared by Alan Guttmacher Institute for September 1995 press briefing for journalists.

8. "Portrait of Injustice: Abortion Coverage under the Medicaid Program" (New York: Center for Reproductive Law and Policy, January 2, 1996).

9. This provision was attached to the major appropriations bill for family planning. In a familiar scenario, funds for family planning were secured at the expense of abortion rights. The right wing opposes both, but it takes what it can get while continuing to push for its full agenda.

10. Donovan, *Politics of Blame*, 34. Donovan also points out that even before Hyde, not all women in need of subsidized abortion services were able to obtain them. An estimated 133,000 Medicaid-eligible women were unable to obtain a publicly funded abortion because the services were not available or accessible to them or because the states had policies prohibiting coverage.

11. Donovan, ibid., 25–26.

12. Fact sheet by Alan Guttmacher Institute.

13. Ibid.

14. Ibid.

15. The information on parental involvement laws comes from ACLU Reproductive Freedom Project, "Parental Involvement Laws" (New York: Center for Reproductive Law and Policy, July 1994), and "Mandatory Parental Consent and Notification Laws" (New York: Center for Reproductive Law and Policy, July 1994).

16. Charles Murray described illegitimacy as "the single most important social problem of our time—more important than crime, drugs, poverty, illiteracy, welfare or homelessness because it drives everything else" ("The Coming White Underclass," *Wall Street Journal,* October 29, 1993). Despite the fact that young African-American women bear the brunt of the demonization in the furor surrounding illegitimacy, Murray's focus is on white teenagers. Some critics argue that his real concern is the breakdown of white families and white male authority.

17. In the United States, coercive contraception has historically been an issue for women in third world communities. For example, Native American and Puerto Rican women have sterilization rates that are among the highest in the world, in both cases over one-third of the female population.

Norplant, a new long-acting contraceptive, has raised many concerns. Judges have imposed sentences on women that give a "choice" between jail or Norplant insertion.

18. Position paper on reproductive rights, in Marlene Gerber Fried, ed., *From Abortion to Reproductive Freedom* (Boston: South End Press, 1990), 291.

19. National Latina Health Organization, "Essential Principles for Responsible Health Care Reform" (Oakland, Cal.: NLHO, n.d.).

20. From brochure advertising "Coming Together/Moving Strong: Mobilizing an Asian Women's Health Movement," the first national Asian women's health conference sponsored by the National Asian Women's Health Organization, November 1995.

21. *Vital Signs* (publication of National Black Women's Health Network), no. 1 (January–March 1993).

22. "Legal But Out of Reach: Experiences from the National Network of Abortion Funds," May 1995. Available by writing to NNAF c/o CLPP, Hampshire College, Amherst, MA 01002.

23. National Asian Women's Health Organization, "Perceptions of Risk: An Assessment of the Factors Influencing Use of Reproductive and Sexual Health Services by Asian American Women," NAWHO, Fall 1995.

24. "Young Women's Voices," published in 1993 by the Civil Liberties and Public Policy Program at Hampshire College, available for a fee from Young Women's Voices, c/o CLPP, Hampshire College, Amherst, MA 01002.

25. Stephanie Poggi, "Abortion in the Media," *Resist Newsletter,* February 1995.

10

Faye Ginsburg

RESCUING THE NATION

Operation Rescue and the Rise of
Anti-Abortion Militance

If you were to track the whole abortion controversy, you'd find that in
1984 it almost went away. It was the
rescues that brought it back, that rede-
fined the extremes of pro-life activity.
And if the Right to Life Committee
thinks otherwise, they're fooling themselves.

Randall Terry[1]

When the Lord put the vision in my
heart, it was not just to rescue babies
and mothers but to rescue the country.
This is the first domino to fall.

Randall Terry[2]

At six o'clock in the morning on November 28, 1987, Randall Terry, a
lanky, twenty-seven-year-old born-again Christian from upstate New
York, led his first official "rescue," a blockade of an abortion clinic in
Cherry Hill, New Jersey. As Terry described it, nearly 300 rescuers had
sealed off access to the building: "We sang, prayed, read psalms, and
basically had a church service on the doorstep of hell for nearly eleven
hours! No babies died. It was glorious, peaceful, and prayerful." By the
end of the day, 211 "mothers, fathers, grandmothers, grandfathers, and
singles"[3] were arrested, charged with trespassing, and released. The
event served as a trial demonstration of the militant anti-abortion organization Operation Rescue (OR). The group was formally established
in the spring of 1988 by Terry, and it quickly escalated its activities,
gaining a prominent, if notorious, reputation even among fellow travel-
ers in the "pro-life" movement.

According to Operation Rescue's figures, by 1990 over 35,000 people had been jailed and 16,000 had risked arrest in "rescues."[4] In the summer of 1991 this momentum climaxed in a stunning forty-six-day showdown at abortion clinics in Wichita, resulting in 2,600 arrests—a demonstration that put Operation Rescue on the front page of every major American newspaper.[5] Yet Operation Rescue was in decline by 1993; Terry had stepped down as head, and the organization had decentralized into approximately 100 loosely connected "rescue" groups throughout the country.[6] "Operation Rescue is virtually dead," a *New York Times* reporter commented in 1995. "What is left of the group is a handful of new regional leaders with headquarters in Dallas, who have recently been able to muster only a few dozen people for clinic protests."[7]

What caused the precipitous rise and fall of this group, the best known in the direct-action wing of the pro-life movement? In the mid- to late 1980s Operation Rescue (and other groups) offered a new vision and strategy to a battle-worn pro-life movement that had achieved few of its specific goals through more moderate methods. Operation Rescue had a catalytic effect on a new generation of activists, part of a rising tide of conservative Christian activism; its tactics and ideology also provoked serious reactions. As early as 1990, court rulings and large fines resulting from lawsuits brought by pro-choice organizations against Operation Rescue and its leaders started to take their toll. Bill Clinton's election in 1992 brought even more stringent prosecution of individuals and organizations harassing clinics in rescues. Fewer and fewer people were willing to support protests that would result in lengthy jail terms and large fines. Additionally, as clinic defense groups mobilized across the country, rescues were increasingly met with effective counteroffensives organized by pro-choice activists and local law enforcement officials. While Operation Rescue felt its actions curtailed, violence against abortion clinics and their staff escalated; in response, Congress passed the Freedom of Access to Clinic Entrances (FACE) Act in May 1994, making it a federal crime to block access to clinics.

The actions of more extreme activists created a new kind of crisis for Operation Rescue in the early 1990s. The murders of two doctors and three abortion clinic workers between March 1993 and December 1994 not only inspired terror among clinic clients and staff but also created a severe credibility problem for Operation Rescue.[8] It did not matter that Operation Rescue issued a public disavowal of violence, or that no direct link could be traced between the murderers and OR. The group—

with its slogan "If you think that abortion is murder, act like it"—was seen as creating an environment in which the murder of abortion doctors came to be seen by some as "justifiable homicide in defense of life." The legitimacy of harassment and rescues based on a higher-laws ideology—that God's law takes precedence over civil law—was seriously undermined, and moderates in the movement sought to distance themselves from these positions. At a 1994 meeting of pro-life activists, Operation Rescue officially parted company with more radical pro-lifers, declaring its disapproval of those who would justify murder in the name of God.[9] In turn, leaders of direct-action groups who condoned the violence formed a new national organization called the American Coalition of Life Activists (ACLA).[10]

Currently, Randall Terry has no formal connection to Operation Rescue (although the group continues to be identified with him); he has expanded his scope from abortion to a broad concern with bringing conservative Christian values into the public sphere and has become involved in the United States Taxpayers Party (USTP), a far-right group with operations in forty states. He also has been organizing Christian leadership institutes "to train militant and unmerciful activists for a new era," has a nationally syndicated radio show, continues to write,[11] and ran, unsuccessfully, as a USTP candidate in the state of New York in 1996.[12]

None of this is surprising if one tracks the key influences on Operation Rescue. Terry was inspired initially by the teachings of the evangelical Protestant author Francis Schaeffer, who viewed legal abortion as the epitome of twentieth-century decadence.[13] In his 1981 book, *A Christian Manifesto,* Schaeffer recommended the use of civil disobedience to oppose abortion as a way for evangelicals to "challenge the entire legitimacy of the secular modern state, withholding allegiance until the nation returns to its religious roots in matters like public prayer and religious education."[14] Here, opposition to abortion is not the end so much as the means to a larger goal of returning America to "traditional Christian values."

THE ROOTS OF DIRECT ACTION

The raison d'être of the right-to-life movement since its inception in the early 1970s has been to overturn the 1973 Supreme Court ruling in *Roe v. Wade,* which legalized abortion. Although the movement was well organized, with a large membership, and quite sophisticated regarding political action, by the mid-1980s it had gained only modest political victories through legislative or judicial channels, signaled by the defeat of two congressional initiatives in 1983 that attempted to legislate either that life begins at conception or that abortion legislation should be returned to the control of the states. The mainstream right-to-life leadership, which had managed to prevail over the more radical elements by arguing that direct action would undercut public sympathy for pro-life efforts,[15] could no longer contain a diverse movement by working within the political system.

For those who had long scorned the civil tactics that had dominated the pro-life movement's political style, the disarray became an opportunity; radical elements became increasingly active and more visible.[16] By the mid-1980s groups that advocated "direct action"—harassing patients, holding sit-ins, intimidating abortion providers—emerged with new confidence, straining alliances among right-to-lifers. Two groups in particular gained strength: the Pro-Life Action League, established in Chicago in 1980 by ex–Benedictine monk Joe Scheidler, and Operation Rescue, founded in 1988 by Randall Terry with considerable help from Scheidler. To justify actions such as illegally entering clinic operating rooms and disrupting abortions in progress, Scheidler and Terry cited the "doctrine of necessity"—a belief that violence is permissible as a last resort to stop or prevent greater violence (i.e., in their view, abortion). Terry's philosophy also involves the strictly fundamentalist idea of "biblical obedience": scriptural passages are understood as mandates to action.[17]

Randall Terry's divine inspiration and born-again history seem fitting for someone born, raised, and residing in upstate New York's "burned-over district," so named because so many American social movements smoldered and caught fire there in the nineteenth century, notably evangelical revivals and the first wave of feminism.[18] Like many of the young men caught up in the religious enthusiasms of the past, Terry grew up in a middle-class, liberal, churchgoing family (which includes some strong feminists) but found himself attracted—as he came of age in the 1970s—to the social turbulence of the 1960s.[19] An honor student and talented musician, Terry left high school early and hitchhiked to the South, getting involved with drugs as he unsuccessfully sought his fortune in rock and roll. Shortly after he returned home, at age seventeen, he was "saved," joined a charismatic independent church, and began preaching first to his family, then on the street and in malls. Two years later he entered the "transdenominational" Elim Bible Institute, with plans to become a missionary in Central America. After graduating in 1981, he married a fellow student, Cindy Dean, and worked in a variety of jobs, from fast food to auto sales, eventually moving to Binghamton, New York, where the couple was "called to the mission field of abortion clinics."[20]

In January 1986 Terry met with Joe Scheidler to discuss plans to blockade clinics across the country, incite mass arrests, and thus disrupt the business of abortion and gain mass media coverage.[21] The next week, Terry organized his first "rescue mission" at the Binghamton clinic. He and seven others gained access to one of the inner rooms of the clinic.[22] All were arrested for criminal trespass and resisting arrest. Only Terry refused to pay his fine and went to jail. This experience led to further development of his tactics: "By the end of my jail term in the summer of 1986, I had a more definite idea of what it was going to take to secure justice again for the children. . . . I also realized that the pro-life movement was not creating the tension and upheaval necessary to produce political and social change. We were being too nice."[23]

Terry continued to meet with Scheidler and other pro-life advocates of direct-action protest.[24] Disturbed by the escalation of arson and bombings at abortion clinics, they called meetings in order "to coordinate their activities and adopt standards of behavior."[25] At a 1987 meeting Terry reportedly presented a plan to expand the movement's reach by organizing nationwide "rescues," with demonstrations planned for the 1988 Democratic National Convention.[26] Terry's strategy of blockades (rather than invasions) at clinics, arrests, and noncooperation with police in the name of "the doctrine of necessity" and "higher law" showed the influence of Scheidler's philosophy and tactics; it was generally well received.[27]

THE GROWTH OF OPERATION RESCUE

Operation Rescue was officially established in April 1988 as a for-profit business, because of the group's avowed commitment to breaking the law, and also in hopes of avoiding financial disclosure.[28] Operation Rescue became national news (as was intended) when it descended on Atlanta abortion clinics during the 1988 Democratic National Convention, beginning five months of protests called "The Siege of Atlanta." Over 1,300 demonstrators, including Terry, were jailed for trespassing between July and October. To replace those arrested, hundreds of people poured in on buses, summoned via the Christian broadcasting networks. Many followed instructions not to give their names, identifying themselves as "Baby Doe" (in solidarity with the unborn); the intention (and result) was to clog the jails and courts, since the arrested demonstrators could not be released without identification.[29] Despite much negative response from other pro-life groups and prominent Christians, the publicity attracted a flood of financial contributions, including support from Jerry Falwell.[30] The movement was mushrooming. It seemed, indeed, that Randall Terry's claim of success at the time was an accurate reflection of the moment:

> We have been completely successful. We have shut down abortion facilities, we have rescued babies, we have maintained a peaceful, prayerful atmosphere. We have injected new vision and hope into the pro-life movement. This was a week of on-the-job training for future leaders. Now we will see a major turn in the battle toward more peaceful blockades. Every major political change in this country has been preceded by social upheaval and that has been the missing element of the pro-life movement.[31]

Pro-choice sources estimate that over the next year there was at least one local Operation Rescue blockade every weekend.[32] Operation Rescue managed to magnify the impact of its demonstrations through unusually savvy management of image and performance and a relatively sophisticated understanding of the media.[33]

By the end of the 1980s, OR had become the umbrella sheltering extremists who shared a commitment to uncompromising interventionist tactics and absolutist Christian ideology. For this new style of right-to-lifer, the preoccupation of moderates with building or maintaining a public image as reasonable, good citizens was simply beside the point. They were succeeding by immediately disrupting abortion services and gaining media attention for their cause, amplifying their small numbers through dramatic tactics that attracted television cameras and news reporters.

Dramatic demonstrations have brought Operation Rescue's views on abortion to the public. But perhaps the "rescues" are most significant for those who participate. Political performances reinforce for activists the righteousness of their own cause. As one reporter of Operation Rescue's tactics observed, "Carrying a picket or blockading a doorway is a radicalizing event for the thousands of conservative Christians who follow Terry's lead. Being dragged by the neck to a paddy wagon is an epiphany."[34] For most rank-and-file members, sporadic participation in rallies and "rescues" constitutes the central activity.[35] Unlike those allied with other more moderate anti-abortion groups, who hold regular meetings, call upon political representatives, and in other ways operate within ongoing arenas of action, the Operation Rescue leadership has relied on the existing infrastructure of independent fundamentalist churches and local Christian activist groups as its base.

Some have identified Operation Rescue's style of protest as a "male" tendency, in terms of both the gender of participants and the aggressive and militant style of their actions. For example, Terry's methodical "rescues" were built on the stealthy maneuver of "troops" and a "chain of command" of "warriors organizing for war."[36] Reliance on pastors leads to male bias as well as adherence to traditional roles. "Most people, men and women included, are more comfortable following men into a highly volatile situation," Terry explained. "It's just human nature. It's history."[37]

Although the "direct-action" groups have distinguished their activities from bombings and arson, it is not altogether clear where or whether the line between violence and rescue tactics should be drawn. Direct action has a variety of manifestations, which typically include accosting women and clinic staff entering abortion clinics and blocking their access to abortion facilities, confronting them verbally and bodily, following them, or even tracing license plate numbers and calling them at home. Physicians and clinic personnel have had their homes picketed and received threatening letters and phone calls. In addition to the personal toll exacted by such working conditions, as security grows more precarious at clinics, leases are lost and insurance costs escalate. Private guards, bomb checks, and escorts for patients are now considered essential for most facilities.[38]

On July 3, 1989, the U.S. Supreme Court upheld lower-court rulings in a Missouri case, *Webster v. Reproductive Health Services,* thereby allowing states to impose restrictions on abortion.[39] Randall Terry, along with many other Christian activists, took *Webster* as a sign of the success of grassroots direct action and began to expand his work toward his larger agenda. "We are launching a two-pronged offensive," he announced. "Thousands will surround abortion mills to rescue children and mothers, and we will impact state legislatures with equal force."[40] Operation Rescue began holding political training camps for hundreds of would-be rescuers, who learned how to resist arrest and elect conservative politicians, while absorbing lectures on the evils of feminism and liberal government.[41] Through these actions, the implicit differences between Operation Rescue and other pro-life groups became more explicit. Mobilizing against abortion is seen only as a means to an end; the ultimate goal is to refashion a godless society according to the beliefs and values of Christian fundamentalism.[42]

AS YOU SOW . . .

In two ways, Operation Rescue's political tactics marked a radical break with prior anti-abortion organizing: (1) by endorsing and mobilizing confrontational direct action against clinics as a regular strategy, and (2) by drawing large numbers of conservative Protestants into ongoing, organized, militant anti-abortion demonstrations. Building on the cresting fundamentalist and evangelical participation in political action that began in America in the mid-1970s, OR brought thousands of conservative Christians into the anti-abortion movement, transforming them in the process. The blockades carried out by Operation Rescue have been described by observers with different points of view as anything from "biblical obedience" to civil disobedience to harassment, violence, terrorism, or even a form of racketeering. The distinct positions represented by these terms index the complex and often ironic impact of this group. In addition to expanding the revival of fundamentalist political action and pushing right-to-life activism in a more confrontational direction, Operation Rescue helped reinvigorate the organization and focus of its opponents in the pro-choice movement, especially after the *Webster* decision. "I always figured someone else would fight the battle," one abortion rights activist in her twenties explained in 1991. "But the *Webster* decision was such an affront. Before, I didn't pay much attention to Randy Terry. He was just some jerk chaining himself to things."[43]

Local and national pro-choice leaders brought a range of lawsuits against Operation Rescue and other groups, while at the grassroots level, action focused on clinic defense. Indeed, by 1989 more than a dozen lawsuits were pending around the country. Based on his actions during the Democratic National Convention in 1988, an Atlanta jury found Terry guilty of trespassing and illegal assembly and charged him $1,000. After refusing to pay the fine, Terry was jailed on October 5, 1989.[44] Around the same time, a federal appeals court levied penalties of $50,000 against the group for violating court orders that barred protesters from blocking access to abortion clinics in the New York area.

Operation Rescue's appeal on the basis of First Amendment rights was denied; the court ruled that while protesters may make speeches, counsel women, and hand out pamphlets, "blocking access to public and private buildings had never been upheld as a proper method of communication in an orderly society."[45] In December 1989 the U.S. attorney's office in New York seized Operation Rescue's payroll accounts and financial information in an effort to collect the unpaid fines. By January 1990, when Terry was released from jail in Atlanta (after an anonymous donor paid his fine), he announced that because of escalating fines, legal fees, and a $70,000 debt, he would be stepping down as head of Operation Rescue and closing its Binghamton headquarters. Both pro-choice and anti-abortion activists considered the decision a tactical strategy to avoid having money seized by the government.[46] Refusing to admit defeat, Terry announced, "The rescue is not through. There are more than 100 [legally autonomous] rescue groups around the country. They will continue doing what they have been doing."[47] However, less than a month later, the actions of Judge Robert Ward of New York's federal district court undermined Terry's strategy; Judge Ward took the unusual step of imposing additional fines of $400,000 on ten *individuals* as well as the expected organizations, thus warning potential rescuers that they could be *personally* liable.[48] Commenting on his unusual decision, Judge Ward explained that prior rulings "were ignored and did not stop the protests. It was necessary to take coercive action."[49]

Operation Rescue's appeal to a conservative U.S. Supreme Court failed. In May 1990 the Court let stand decisions in Atlanta and New York that prohibited protesters from blockading abortion facilities or abusing or harassing people entering or leaving clinics. "We're following God's law, and that's more important than man's law," Terry responded in an interview shortly after the Supreme Court rulings, a chilling foreshadowing of more violent activity to come.[50] Unlike less radical fundamentalist activists, such as Falwell, who operate successfully within the political system, Terry seemed genuinely shocked that the American judicial system was unmoved by his appeal to "higher laws," calling it anti-Christian bigotry. He began organizing a Christian Defense Council to educate Christians about "police oppression, judicial tyranny and political harassment."[51]

At the end of 1990 Operation Rescue sponsored its first national event in over a year, a three-day conference and rescue in Washington, D.C., at which Operation Goliath was introduced as "an all-out holy war on the child-killing industry, one mill at a time."[52] On July 15,

1991, hundreds of demonstrators began a siege of three abortion clinics in Wichita, Kansas, and actually succeeded in closing them for the first week. Operation Rescue leaders had chosen their site carefully: Wichita's mayor, police chief, and city manager, as well as the governor of Kansas, were staunchly pro-life. The behavior of local police did little to quell the clinic blockades.[53] The majority of the protesters in Wichita and virtually all of the leadership were from out of town. Most were housewives, schoolteachers, service workers, and technicians—or retired and unemployed people. One-third were over sixty years of age.[54] Some of the protesters called themselves "Lambs of Christ,"[55] part of a hard core of approximately two hundred devoted "rescuers" who have given up jobs and other commitments to travel around the country, blockade clinics, and risk arrest multiple times.[56]

In response, the pro-choice movement escalated its activities, sponsoring a huge abortion rights march in Washington in April 1992, the first such event since 1989.[57] Locally, clinic defense groups began to organize effectively against rescues in their vicinity.[58] Injunctions began to hamper demonstrations, and holding people personally liable for court fines has tested even the most dedicated right-to-lifers.[59] Operation Rescue's "Spring of Life" demonstrations in 1992 showed a clear decline in support.[60] Following Clinton's election in 1992 and his clear demonstration of support of abortion rights, violence against clinics doubled.[61]

In early 1993 right-to-life direct action took a new and extreme turn with the killing of Dr. David Gunn by Michael Griffin in March, followed by the attempted murder of Dr. George Tiller in Wichita by Rachelle Shannon. Operation Rescue members were divided in their view of the murders, a split that became clear at a May 1994 meeting in Chicago; the debate focused on a petition circulated by Paul Hill, who argued that shooting doctors who performed abortions is a defensive action because of the potential lives that will be saved. Four months later, Hill shot and killed Dr. John Britton and his escort, Lt. Col. James H. Barrett.[62] While many portrayed Hill as a lone extremist, with no following, it had been apparent even before the Chicago meeting that the idea of executing abortion doctors had significant support; it had been discussed in publications such as the *Prayer and Action Weekly News* and the monthly *Life Advocate* magazine, and it was the focus of Hill's Defensive Action statement, which supported Griffin's murder of Dr. Gunn and was signed by a loose network of activists from around the country.[63] According to some analysts, elements of the far-right wing of the movement overlap with the militia movement.[64]

In December 1994 John Salvi III shot and killed Shannon Lowey and Leanne Nichols, workers at two different abortion clinics in Brookline, Massachusetts. In addition, there were nine attempted murders and a sharp rise in arson attacks on clinics.[65] All of these provoked considerable public attention and alarm, as attested in the political arena by passage of the 1994 FACE legislation and assignment of federal marshals to clinics. However one assesses the effectiveness of such measures,[66] they register a bipartisan acknowledgment at the national level of the extreme situation now faced by abortion clinics and their staff. Beyond the nightmarish stress of working under the threat of such violence, it is getting increasingly difficult to find doctors willing to work at abortion clinics, and fewer and fewer medical students are learning to perform abortions, especially as medical schools have cut back on that training.[67]

Operation Rescue has attempted to disassociate itself from the murders; nonetheless, it is seen by many both in and outside the movement as on a continuum with such violence. Those who condone violent action (many of them former members of OR) organized the American Coalition of Life Activists in 1994 to "reconcile newly formed factions, and eliminate the autocratic organization that Operation Rescue had established";[68] the ACLA leaders also issued a list of twelve doctors targeted for harassment, called the Deadly Dozen. It seems paradoxical that many of these direct-action right-to-life militants, who hope to overturn much of the social change of the 1960s, originally took the civil rights movement as a model.[69] The shift to militant action is part of a consistent pattern in the style of American social movements. When they feel themselves stymied, regardless of their position on the ideological spectrum, violence comes to be seen as a political resource in the interest of hastening a purportedly utopian vision of society.[70] In an editorial written shortly after the killings in Brookline, historian David Garrow underscored this point, interpreting the violence as the death throes of an anti-abortion movement. "Court rulings, energetic civil litigation and Congressional approval of FACE have put OR and its progeny on the defensive," wrote Garrow. "Indeed the denouement of America's abortion struggle . . . strikingly resembles the one by which the segregationist South, after considerable violence, finally accommodated the racial revolutions of 1964 and 1965. . . . The tragedy of the slaying should not confuse us as to what we are witnessing here: people who kill for life represent the last throes of a struggle in which armed terrorism represents the final fringe."[71]

While extremists may indeed be provoked by frustration, many are not convinced that the murders are carried out by isolated fanatics. In January 1994 the Supreme Court ruled that the National Organization for Women (NOW) could use the Racketeer Influenced and Corrupt Organizations (RICO) Act (passed in 1970 to prosecute profit-making enterprises like the Mafia) against Joe Scheidler on the grounds that his Pro-Life Action League constituted a criminal conspiracy to close abortion clinics.[72] The conspiracy framework has been used in civil cases as well; Planned Parenthood of Texas, for example, won a case against OR and Rescue America for conspiring to shut down their abortion clinics during the Republican National Convention in 1992; the jury awarded Planned Parenthood more than $1 million, although the money has been almost impossible to collect.[73] In late 1994 Attorney General Janet Reno organized a federal task force and two grand juries to investigate whether groups like Operation Rescue and ACLA, as well as individual activists, form a criminal conspiracy to close abortion clinics and destroy doctors.[74] Sociologist and journalist Sarah Diamond assessed the moment as a positive one for reproductive rights. "Years' worth of clinic harassment," she wrote, "had finally yielded restrictive decisions by the Supreme Court, and the executive branches. In effect, state agencies moved to repress the militant wing of the anti-abortion movement, to the advantage of women in need of abortions and political supporters of reproductive choice."[75]

For most pro-life moderates, direct action and especially violence undercut one of the larger objectives of the right-to-life movement: to gain credibility for their position with the American people in order to gain support for a constitutional amendment banning abortion.[76] For example, the influential National Right to Life Committee has maintained its policy of silence on Operation Rescue's activities but makes clear its differences with the group by underscoring the motives for its own commitment to legal and nonviolent action. "We will want people to obey the new abortion law we are working for, so it is important we let the nation know we are responsible people ourselves. We will not win with violence," explained its president in 1988. "That is the tactic of the abortionist."[77] However, television and the secular press in general give disproportionate attention to dramatic political confrontation, with little concern for distinctions between groups. News stories tend to conflate those who carry out controversial activities with the movement as a whole. Not surprisingly, the more extreme and reprehensible pro-life activities receive the most coverage. Sociologist James Davison Hunter has summarized the situation succinctly: "When Operation Rescue emerged in the late 1980s, with dramatic blockades of clinics and colorful leaders like Terry, it and all its direct action derivatives quickly became the face of the anti-abortion movement. Mr. Terry was the movement's Abby Hoffman, staging press conferences with dead fetuses. . . . Reporters could hardly resist him. He confirmed, after all, an anti-abortion stereotype that studies had shown many journalists already entertained."[78]

While the media attention has made people aware of Operation Rescue and other more extreme direct-action groups, evidence suggests that, increasingly, the publicity has mobilized the opposition.[79] Following the murders in 1994, support for the pro-choice position shifted for the first time in years from 29 percent to 38 percent.[80] In the newly charged atmosphere of the 1990s, tactics like rescues and sieges and the invocation of higher laws have raised serious questions that have alienated some pro-life supporters and aggravated differences with many Catholic pro-lifers. A police lieutenant—Catholic and pro-life—described this shift eloquently, when he was interviewed after the shootings in the two Brookline clinics in December 1994: "Operation Rescue had one great effect. . . . Before them, a lot of cops were anti-abortion. . . . They'd say, 'I ain't working the baby killer detail.' Then it became all anti-rescue. It opened some people's eyes. It was more like 'make your statement but don't break the law.' I'm pro-law. Those two clinics are not abortion mills. They're women's health care centers."[81]

SAVING AMERICA'S SOUL

Some commentators have explained the appeal of Operation Rescue from the perspective of gender, generation, and class. Noting that 56 percent of arrested activists are men, and half of Operation Rescue's active participants were born in the late 1950s and early 1960s, author Susan Faludi sketches a profile of these fundamentalist men of "the late baby-boom generation" as sociological mirrors of Randall Terry, with an economic grudge against "careerist" women. They are, in her words, "downwardly mobile sons, condemned by the eighties economy to earning less than their fathers, unable to buy homes or support families.

These are men who are losing ground and at the same time see women gaining it."[82] While undoubtedly there is some truth in this framework, it does not encompass the majority of those attracted to this movement and tends to dismiss the power and appeal of this most recent version of American muscular Christianity.

Whatever face Operation Rescue presents to the outside, it is clear from the writings and speeches of its founder and leader, Randall Terry, that he and those inspired by him see it as a vehicle for a much broader agenda for Christian social action. It is mobilizing people not just to stop abortion but to impose a conservative Christian culture on American society at large. Terry has succeeded in catalyzing the direct participation in anti-abortion politics of thousands of evangelicals and fundamentalists who had never before been involved in political action. Charging Christians with apathy and their need to repent for the neglect of the abortion issue, he compares them to Christians who did not resist the Nazis in Germany during the Holocaust. "A single speaking engagement before an Evangelical congregation, with the endorsement of the pastor, can reap a busload of volunteers," noted one observer.[83] Some estimate that because of Operation Rescue, the pro-life movement, once dominated by Catholics, is now almost two-thirds evangelical Protestant.[84] Terry has never put exclusive labels on Operation Rescue. His home church is an independent ministry; his training was nondenominational; he seems uninterested in discussing his theological position on the millennium. These characteristics, coupled with his embrace of Catholics and non-Christians in the movement and his emphasis on political involvement (including law-breaking), are a break with the long-standing emphasis on separatism that has characterized American fundamentalism for nearly half a century, part of a general resurgence of activism among contemporary American evangelicals. Operation Rescue did not *create* this interest so much as catch "the wave of evangelical involvement just as it began to crest."[85]

Gary Wills, in a provocative essay on Operation Rescue, suggests that these newly mobilized Christians represent a distinct group on America's religious and political landscape. They are not interested in the eschatological disputes that dominated fundamentalism in the previous generation but in issues that seem to shape their immediate world. They came of age during the mobilization of the Christian Right in the 1970s and accept that movement as a model of political action. As Wills notes:

If these thirty-year-old demonstrators did not exemplify a new kind of evangelical movement when they went into such activities, they are emerging from them with drastically new attitudes. While paying their respect to elders who helped evangelicals get engaged in politics—to Jerry Falwell or Pat Robertson—the Operation Rescue leaders are also gently dismissive of them as armchair warriors, people resting on their laurels and not taking the heat of today's battle. Terry's people talk of the televangelists as tied down to their assets, like bishops in their dioceses. They see themselves as roving carriers of a burning message . . . and the ties they form with other opponents of abortion speed the process, already noticed by sociologists, whereby evangelism has been losing its hostility to Jews, Catholics, blacks and Hispanics.[86]

If one looks at Operation Rescue historically, one sees parallels with the situation of seventy years ago, when fundamentalism first emerged as a powerful presence on the American landscape.[87] Contemporary struggles over abortion, school prayer, and pornography draw fundamentalists (and others) into what James Davison Hunter calls "culture wars,"[88] in much the same way that opposition to the teaching of evolution in the schools mobilized fundamentalist reformers in the early part of the century. The militantly anti-modernist evangelicals of the 1920s had multiple cultural, theological, and organizational roots, but they shared a developing premillennial theology that recommended separation from the world.[89] When they failed to halt the "modernizing" of American Protestantism, they retreated from active engagement in both secular arenas and mainline religion, in order to develop their own parallel network of exclusive institutions.[90] Although there were some calls to activism in the 1940s and 1950s from both the right and the left, the central activity and strategy of fundamentalism for five decades was personal witnessing.[91]

By the 1970s the expanding organizational structures and increasing numbers of mainstream, middle-class Americans attracted to evangelical Christianity gave fundamentalist activists the infrastructure, intellectual framework, social base, and membership to carry out successful political action. For some, this crossing of the boundary into the corrupt world undermined the legitimacy of people like Falwell and his organization, the Moral Majority.[92] Yet Operation Rescue went much further in breaking the boundary of separation between Christian activists and the world. Indeed, recriminalizing abortion is only the first "domino" to fall in their hoped-for campaign to reverse the effects of liberal hegemony of the 1960s and 1970s through Christian social action. In Terry's plan, "Child killing will fall, child pornography and pornography will follow, euthanasia, infanticide—we'll totally reform the public education system . . . we'll take back the culture."[93]

Whether Operation Rescue manages to surmount the legal obstacles imposed on it and disassociate itself from groups like ACLA in order to continue its blockades; or whether it transforms itself into a wing of Randall Terry's Christian Defense Council, there is no question that the movement has had an irreversible impact. Through an organization committed to direct action, Terry revived long-term right-to-life loyalists, who had become discouraged at the minimal gains of fifteen years of legislative efforts, and delivered thousands of new activists to the cause. Operation Rescue's law-breaking tactics and controversial media coverage altered the public image of right-to-lifers in the late 1980s from that of people motivated by civil morality to one of radical Christians, unwilling to accept the framework of secular law. In so doing, it also divided the movement, especially with the escalation of violence in the 1990s. But taking action into the "real world" has its real-world consequences. In the pluralist setting of America, displaying contempt for the rights of others and the legal system—even in the name of God— was bound to bring stiff penalties. However, for a movement that takes as a primary image a martyred and militant Christ, suffering at the hands of the Romans, the punitive actions of the state are only confirmation of the activists' righteousness.

Fundamentalist militance in America has never confined itself to a single issue, and Operation Rescue is one of the latest incarnations of the evangelical impulse to impose fundamentalist views on others. Operation Rescue has offered an ever-increasing number of conservative Christians in America an incontrovertible experience of militant fundamentalist social action. For "rescuers," fighting abortion is simply a first step in reversing America's "moral decline." Armed to enter the public sphere, these new Christian soldiers are not concerned with the boundaries of separation that restrained fundamentalist activism for half a century. The future envisioned by these warriors is nothing short of the "rescue" of a nation on fundamentalist Christian terms.

NOTES

I want to thank Rickie Solinger for her interest, collegiality, patience, and inspiring scholarship, and Sue Heinemann for her excellent copyediting. For support and insightful comments on early versions of this essay, I would like to thank Fred Myers, along with Scott Appleby and Dick Norton of the Fundamentalism Project, who originally encouraged me to write on this topic. Portions of this essay appeared in "Saving America's Souls: Operation Rescue's Crusade Against Abortion," in *Fundamentalisms and the State: Remaking Politics, Economies, and Militance,* ed. Martin Marty and R. Scott Appleby (Chicago: University of Chicago Press, 1993), 567–88. I am grateful to a number of journalists, particularly Susan Church and Barbara Brotman, who sent me their articles and discussed ideas with me. I also thank documentary maker Julie Gustafson for sharing her ideas and letting me look at many hours of her videotapes for a work in progress on the abortion controversy, particularly her interviews with Randall Terry and her documentation of the October 1988 rescue in Vestal, New York. Meg McLagan and Ruth Von Goeler, my research assistants during 1989–90 and the summer of 1995, did excellent work. Some of the material on the background of the right-to-life movement is drawn from my book *Contested Lives: The Abortion Debate in an American Community* (Berkeley: University of California Press, 1989).

1. Quoted in Tamar Lewin, "With Thin Staff and Thick Debt, Anti-Abortion Group Faces Struggle," *New York Times,* June 11, 1990.

2. This quote is from an interview with Randall Terry videotaped by Julie Gustafson in Operation Rescue's Binghamton offices, October 27, 1988.

3. Randall Terry, *Operation Rescue* (Springdale, Pa.: Whitaker House, 1988), 25.

4. Randy Frame, "Rescue Theology," *Christianity Today,* November 17, 1989, 46–48. Many activists have been arrested multiple times, so arrest numbers are greater than the number of protesters.

5. Isabel Wilkerson, "Drive Against Abortion Finds a Symbol: Wichita," *New York Times,* August 4, 1991.

6. In December 1990 Terry declared Operation Rescue an "underground" organization and named Keith Tucci as head of an unincorporated aboveground organization called Operation Rescue National, originally located in South Carolina. Tucci's successor was the Reverend Flip Benham, who moved the offices to Dallas, Texas. Tucci now heads Life Coalitions International, in Melbourne, Florida. See Sarah Diamond, *The Road to Dominion: Right Wing Movements and Political Power in the United States* (New York: Guilford Press, 1995), 252.

7. Timothy Egan, "Conspiracy Is an Elusive Target in Prosecuting Foes of Abortion: Abortion Violence, a Special Report," *New York Times,* June 18, 1995, A18.

8. Ibid. Details on these murders are given later in this essay.

9. Ibid.

10. The American Coalition of Life Activists is made up of many former OR activists and members of other militant groups, such as Missionaries to the Preborn. The coalition is led by Andrew Burnett, Joe Foreman (a former Presbyterian minister), and Donald Treshman, one of the most militant abortion opponents. The goal, as stated in Burnett's *Life Advocate* magazine, "is to

find those abortionists who are hiding out from public scrutiny and expose them." These leaders have been targeted by federal investigators and have been questioned before one of the two grand juries looking into anti-abortion violence. See ibid.

11. In addition to frequent columns and pamphlets, his books include *Operation Rescue: Why Does a Nice Guy Like Me Keep Getting Thrown in Jail?* (Binghamton, N.Y.: Huntington House Press); and a work in progress, *The Sword: The Blessing of Righteous Government and the Overthrow of Tyrants.*

12. John Goetz, "Randall Terry and the U.S. Taxpayers Party," *Front Lines Research* 1, no. 2 (August 1994): 1 ff.

13. In an interview with Gary Wills ("Evangels of Abortion," *New York Review of Books,* June 15, 1989), Randall Terry said, "You have to read Schaeffer's *Christian Manifesto* if you want to understand Operation Rescue" (15), and indicated that he considers Schaeffer "the greatest modern Christian philosopher" (18).

14. Wills, "Evangels of Abortion," 15.

15. See Ginsburg, *Contested Lives,* 46–54.

16. In 1983 President Ronald Reagan published an influential book-length anti-abortion essay, "Abortion and the Conscience of the Nation," claiming that the alarming increase in attacks on abortion clinics did not constitute terrorism because the attacks were not carried out by an "organized group," a position that some interpreted as a sign of Reagan's support for individual acts of violence. (Cited in Dallas A. Blanchard and Terry J. Prewitt, *The Gideon Project: Religious Violence and Abortion in America Today* [Gainesville: University of Florida Press, 1993].)

17. R. Terry, *Operation Rescue,* 35. Scheidler, following Catholic exegetical practice, is less concerned with literal readings of the Bible. He claims a philosophy of nonviolence and blames the media for linking his actions with those of violent extremists. He nonetheless makes public his sympathy and identification with those more radical than he. Until the mid-1980s the zealotry and controversial actions he advocates had consigned him to the fringe of the pro-life movement. He was seen as disruptive of efforts to gain the moral and political high ground through legislative actions. However, as the pro-life movement attempted to regroup after its 1983 defeats, people like Scheidler gained at least some temporary legitimacy with the mainstream. He was invited to speak at the annual convention of the National Right to Life Committee in 1984 and was among a handful of national pro-life leaders who met with President Reagan in 1984 during the annual January 22 "March for Life" in Washington, D.C. (After Scheidler asked the president to meet with clinic bombers, he was not invited back to the White House.)

18. See Susan Faludi, "Where Did Randy Go Wrong?" *Mother Jones,* November 1989.

19. See R. Terry, *Operation Rescue.* My description and analysis of Randall Terry and Operation Rescue draw on a number of interviews and investigative pieces done on the movement since 1988. Much of the material is redundant. I used the following pieces for this section: Susan Church, "Abortion: A Community Speaks," "Abortion Battle Comes Home," and "Terry's Absence Raises

Questions about Operation Rescue," *Binghamton Press and Sun Bulletin*, November 19 and 20, 1989: Jeff Davis, "Randall Terry's Crusade," and "Terry's Fight Creates Family Feud," *Binghamton Press and Sun Bulletin*, January 20 and 24, 1989; Faludi, "Where Did Randy Go Wrong?" 23 ff.; Mary Suh and Lydia Denworth, "The Gathering Storm: Operation Rescue," *Ms.*, April 1989, 92–94; R. Terry, *Operation Rescue*; Francis Wilkinson, "The Gospel According to Randall Terry," *Rolling Stone*, October 5, 1989, 85–92; Wills, "Evangels of Abortion," 15–21; "Save the Babies," *Time*, May 1, 1989, 26–28.

20. In 1984 the Terrys started what they called Project Life, demonstrating in front of Southern Tier Women's Services, a Binghamton abortion clinic. When the clinic responded by providing client escorts, Terry mobilized thirty people from his home church, the Church at Pierce Creek, for a protest. Although by the summer of 1984 he had also opened the Crisis Pregnancy Center "to offer women free pregnancy tests, confidential counseling, baby clothes, baby furniture, and other services," that nurturant part of the vision never went much further as he concentrated on "the war" (R. Terry, *Operation Rescue*, 17).

21. Faludi, "Where Did Randy Go Wrong?" 61–62.

22. In the words of an unsympathetic reporter, "they locked themselves in the counseling room, ripping out the phone system, smashing furniture, wedging the door so tight the police had to break it down with a crowbar" (ibid., 61).

23. R. Terry, *Operation Rescue*, 22

24. These included leftist "seamless garment" Catholics such as John Cavanaugh-O'Keefe, who extend the pro-life position on abortion to include opposition to capital punishment, nuclear weapons, and child abuse. For a discussion of this, see Wills, "Evangels of Abortion," 19.

25. Ibid.

26. In February 1988 a team of organizers ran a series of trial actions in New York City, blockading three abortion facilities, preventing each from conducting any business for one day. The goal was to gain publicity and support and to familiarize "rescuers" with Terry's distinct direct-action approach, which borrowed from both Scheidler and Cavanaugh-O'Keefe. Over 1,600 of these mostly white, middle-aged evangelicals, who came from thirty-five states, were arrested. By the end of the week a federal judge, Robert Ward, issued a temporary restraining order banning them from blocking entrances to medical services, and he threatened a $25,000 a day fine for violations. When the order became a permanent injunction early in 1989, Operation Rescue immediately incurred a $50,000 fine for two days of protests at New York's Margaret Sanger Clinic in January 1989 (Nadine Brozan, "Effectiveness of Abortion Protests Is Debated," *New York Times*, May 8, 1989, 28).

27. In most public venues, Scheidler remains largely unacknowledged by Terry as an influence. Suh and Denworth interpret that fact as an indication that Terry became Scheidler's "front man" when negative media coverage and a 1986 lawsuit brought by the National Organization for Women (NOW) forced Scheidler to scale down his presence. As evidence, they cite Terry's involvements with Scheidler's protests in Pensacola in 1986. By contrast, Susan Faludi

suggests that Terry usurped Scheidler and implies that once Terry got the spotlight, he was unwilling to share it.

28. Wilkinson, "Gospel According to Terry," 86.

29. "Days of Abortion Protest End with 40 More Atlanta Arrests," *New York Times*, October 9, 1988.

30. Wilkinson, "Gospel According to Terry," 86. Before the "siege," Operation Rescue had about $5,000 coming in each month; by December 1988 the monthly income had jumped to $60,000 (Wills, "Evangels of Abortion," 21). Most of the information on Operation Rescue's finances and relations with other political organizations is drawn from depositions made by Lynn Schopf, the group's accountant, on January 5, 1989, and by Terry on July 7, 1989, for legal suits brought by NOW and other complainants.

31. Brozan, "Effectiveness of Abortion Protests," 28

32. Suh and Denworth, "The Gathering Storm," 92.

33. As Terry noted during an interview in 1988, "If we can get the press there, we don't need to send out a press release" (interview with Julie Gustafson).

34. Wilkinson, "Gospel According to Terry," 92.

35. For a useful journalistic portrait of Operation Rescue's membership, see Alissa Rubin, "In God They Trespass," *Washington Post*, May 16, 1993.

36. Wilkinson, "Gospel According to Terry," 91; R. Terry, *Operation Rescue*—for example, chapters 11 and 12 are titled, respectively, "There's a War Going On" and "Called to the Front Lines."

37. Quoted in Wilkinson, "Gospel According to Terry," 86.

38. Tamar Lewin, "Abortion Providers Attempt to Handle Growing Threat," *New York Times*, December 31, 1994.

39. In July 1989 the Supreme Court upheld a Missouri law banning the use of public funds, facilities, and employees in counseling or performing abortion, effectively granting state legislatures considerable power over abortion procedures. Sarah Diamond writes, "From the perspective of the Christian Right, the *Webster* decision underscored the value of grassroots, state-based anti-abortion activism, as opposed to earlier attempts to overturn *Roe* in one fell swoop" (*Road to Dominion*, 249).

40. Quoted in Ronald Smothers, "Organizer of Abortion Protests Is Jailed in Atlanta," *New York Times*, July 12, 1989, A10.

41. Susan Church, "Tactics Change as Time Passes," *Binghamton Press and Sun Bulletin*, November 20, 1989, 5A.

42. His language makes clear his agenda: "What we *can* work for is a nation where once again the Judeo-Christian ethic is the foundation for our politics, our judicial system, and our public morality; a nation not floating in the uncertain sea of humanism, but a country whose unmoving bedrock is Higher Laws" (R. Terry, *Operation Rescue*, 175).

43. Quote from Susan Church, "Poll Shows Terry's Tactics Disliked," *Binghamton Press and Sun Bulletin*, November 20, 1989, 1.

44. Jerry Schwartz, "Abortion Protester Jailed after Objecting to Fine," *New York Times*, October 6, 1989.

45. Constance Hays, "Abortion Foes Lose Appeal on Protests," *New York Times*, September 21, 1989, A1.

46. "Rescue Bails Out," *Time*, February 12, 1990, 29

47. Quoted in Kim Lawton, "Operation Rescue HQ Closed," *Christianity Today*, March 5, 1990.

48. The fines were for breaking injunctions preventing people from blocking women's access to abortion clinics.

49. Craig Wolff, "Judge Fines 10 for Protests over Abortions" *New York Times*, February 28, 1990.

50. Quoted in Lewin, "With Thin Staff and Thick Debt," A16.

51. Ibid.

52. Operation Rescue's D.C. Project II brochure (Greenport, Md., n.d.).

53. Associated Press, "Judge Orders U.S. Marshals to Prevent Closing of Abortion Clinics," *New York Times*, July 30, 1991.

54. There were nearly 3,000 arrests of approximately 1,500 individuals, costing Wichita $400,000. See Wilkerson, "Drive Against Abortion."

55. In early 1989 Father Norman Weslin, a former lieutenant colonel in the U.S. army paratroopers, joined with activists Joan Andrew and Randall Terry to form what he describes as a "rapid deployment force, a special group of 50–200 dedicated persons who will fly to any part of the nation on short notice to assist any rescue operations with needed reinforcements" (Stanley Interrante, *Wanderer*, February 16, 1989). Originally, he called this group the Victim Souls of the Unborn Christ Child, and later, Lambs of Christ.

According to Ann Baker, who runs a pro-choice watchdog organization called the 80% Majority, Weslin's group chooses its own targets and hopes there will be local support. "Lambs" are supposed to identify with the fetus, calling themselves either Baby John or Baby Jane Doe. They refuse to give their names or walk anywhere from the time they are arrested until they are sentenced. The period of incarceration accomplishes several goals: it ties up local law enforcement systems, provides a focus for fund-raising, and allows the core group members—who have no jobs—free room and board. It appears that there are between fifty and one hundred dedicated itinerant militants who follow Weslin's leadership directly, although there are others who behave similarly but are not as extreme. Three other organizations—Victim Souls (an offshoot of Weslin's original group), Pro-Life Police, and Rescue Outreach—offer support and probably fund-raising. In 1990–91, the Lambs blockaded clinics in Burlington, Vermont; Pittsburgh, Pennsylvania; Toledo and Youngstown, Ohio; Appleton, Wisconsin; Lufkin, Texas; South Bend, Indiana; Dobbs Ferry, New York; Asheville, North Carolina; and Fargo, North Dakota. See Ann Baker, "A Report on the Direct Action Militants," *Campaign Report* 4, no. 9: 5–8.

56. Don Terry, "Face of Protests in Wichita Is Religious and Undoubting," *New York Times*, August 12, 1991.

57. Karen De Witt, "Huge Crowd Backs Right to Abortion in Capital March: At Least 500,000 Gather," *New York Times*, April 6, 1992.

58. See, for example, Catherine Manegold, "Abortion Foes See Tactics Backfire in New York," *New York Times*, July 19, 1992, A8; Catherine

Manegold, "Abortion Protesters Gather as a Fight Builds in Buffalo," *New York Times*, April 20, 1992.

59. Barbara Brotman, "Abortion Opponents Regroup," *Chicago Tribune*, May 20, 1990, 9.

60. Manegold, "Abortion Foes See Tactics Backfire," A10; Alisa Solomon, "Holding the Line: Operation Rescue Loses the Battle of Washington," *Village Voice*, February 4, 1992.

61. Diamond, *Road to Dominion*, 302; Associated Press, "Abortion Foes Plan to Challenge New Law Banning Blockades," *New York Times*, May 26, 1994, A17.

62. Egan, "Special Report," A18.

63. Tamar Lewin "A Cause Worth Killing For? Debate Splits Abortion Foes," *New York Times*, July 30, 1994, A18; Diamond, *Road to Dominion*, 302.

64. This point was made by Chip Berlet, an analyst with Political Research Associates, Cambridge, Massachusetts, in Egan, "Special Report," A18.

65. Lewin, "Cause Worth Killing For?" 1.

66. Robert Pear, "Abortion Clinic Workers Say Law Is Being Ignored," *New York Times*, September 23, 1994. At a September 1994 hearing of the House Judiciary Subcommittee on Crime, people who worked at abortion clinics testified that they and their patients were still being subjected to violence and harassment because neither federal nor state officials had done much to enforce the new law.

67. According to the *Wall Street Journal*, in 1985 nearly 25 percent of residency programs offered training in abortion procedures for first and second trimesters. By 1992 only 12 percent offered first-trimester training, and 7 percent trained residents in second-trimester procedures (Helen Cooper, "Medical Schools, Students Shun Abortion Study," *Wall Street Journal*, March 12, 1993, B1).

68. Carla Maxwell, "Introduction: Beyond Polemics and Toward Healing," in *Perspectives on the Politics of Abortion*, ed. Ted Jelen (Westport, Conn.: Praeger, 1995), 11.

69. "The prolife movement has failed to learn the lessons of history, which show how the labor movement, the civil rights movement, Vietnam protest, and gay liberation all occurred because a group of people created social tension" (R. Terry, quoted in Lyn Cryderman, "A Movement Divided," *Christianity Today*, August 12, 1988, 48).

70. Commenting on the conditions under which extremism has emerged in American social life, historian Thomas Rose writes: "Violence is a political resource when the bargaining process provides no other alternatives, or at least when some groups perceive no other alternatives. Political violence is an intelligible pattern of interaction that exists in America, but we refuse to understand and confront it as integral to our life" ("How Violence Occurs: A Theory and Review of the Literature," in *Violence in America*, ed. T. Rose [New York: Vintage Books, 1969], 30).

71. David Garrow, "A Deadly, Dying Fringe," *New York Times*, January 6, 1995, A28.

72. Diamond, *Road to Dominion*, 302. Diamond also points out that this ruling could have "perilous consequences" for any dissident demonstrators.

73. Tamar Lewin, "Abortion Foes' Court Losses Are Frustrating the Victors," *New York Times*, June 11, 1994.

74. Egan, "Special Report," A18.

75. Diamond, *Road to Dominion*, 305

76. Former NRLC president Jack Willke argues that Operation Rescue's publicity has had a negative impact because OR is equated with the whole pro-life movement. "Generally," he says, "the kind of publicity [Operation Rescue] receives when they demonstrate is bad for the movement. In the sixties, the media were behind the civil rights movement. They are not behind the prolife movement. They portray those demonstrators as a bunch of kooks, religious fanatics. [A sit-in may stop a few abortions] but if it postpones the reversal of *Roe v. Wade* for just one day by turning people off to the cause, that's 4,000 babies" (quoted in Cryderman, "A Movement Divided").

77. Willke, quoted in ibid., 49.

78. James Davison Hunter, quoted in Peter Steinfels, "The Moral Emotion of the Abortion Debate Finds a Parallel in the Domestic Conflict over Vietnam," *New York Times*, July 6, 1994, A22.

79. As another example, in a 1991 poll by Terry's hometown newspaper, the *Binghamton Press and Sun Bulletin*, 70 percent of county residents said they disapproved of Operation Rescue demonstrating near abortion clinics, and 90 percent disapproved of the organization's blocking or entering the clinics illegally. Of those polled, 63 percent had a positive impression of the pro-choice movement, while only 37 percent were favorably impressed with the pro-life movement. However, while the Southern Tier Clinic of Binghamton is still in business after enduring multiple rescues, local doctors no longer provide abortions (Church, "Poll Shows Terry's Tactics Disliked," 1).

80. On the bases of analyses by the National Opinion Research Center (NORC) and Gallup Polls between 1973 and 1985, it appears that the level of approval for legalized abortion remained stable during this time. Approximately 23 percent believed that abortion should be legal in all cases, while 19 to 22 percent believed it should be illegal. The remainder believed it should be legal for some cases, such as rape, incest, or endangerment to a woman's life. For further analyses of these data, see Daniel Granberg, "The Abortion Issue in the 1984 Elections," *Family Planning Perspectives* 19, no. 2 (1987): 59–62. In 1994, according to the General Social Survey Data of NORC, the numbers shifted dramatically toward pro-choice positions, from 29 percent to 38 percent ("Pro-Choice? Pro-Life? No, Pro-Middle," *General Social Survey News*, 1994, 2).

81. Sara Rimer, "Brookline Shows Fervor in Keeping Clinics Open," *New York Times*, January 3, 1995, A12.

82. Faludi, "Where Did Randy Go Wrong?" 25.

83. Wilkinson, "Gospel According to Terry," 86.

84. Jack Willke (a Catholic) described it as "an awakening from its slumber of literally millions of deeply committed Protestant folk. This is no longer a Catholic movement. This is very much ecumenical [almost] to the point of being

a Protestant Christian Movement" (Kim Lawton, "Can the Prolife Movement Succeed?" *Christianity Today,* January 15, 1988, 36).

85. Wills, "Evangels of Abortion," 21.

86. Ibid.

87. Many scholars use broad understandings of American fundamentalism, as opposed to narrower readings based on such definitive characteristics as separatism and the theology of dispensational premillennialism. Among those who use the broader reading are Nancy Ammerman, *Bible Believers: Fundamentalists in the Modern World* (New Brunswick, N.J.: Rutgers University Press, 1987); Steve Bruce, *The Rise and Fall of the New Christian Right* (New York: Oxford University Press, 1988); Susan Harding, "Casting Out the Fundamentalist Other: The Problem of the Repugnant Cultural Other," *Social Research* 58, no. 2 (Summer 1991): 373–93; George M. Marsden, *Fundamentalism and American Culture* (New York: Oxford University Press, 1980); Martin Marty, "Fundamentalism as a Social Phenomenon," *Bulletin of the American Academy of Arts and Sciences* 42, no. 2 (November 1988): 15–29.

Ernest Sandeen, in *The Roots of Fundamentalism* (Chicago: University of Chicago Press, 1970), espouses the more specific definition of fundamentalism, based on the above-mentioned doctrinal differences.

88. James Davison Hunter, *Culture Wars: The Struggle to Define America* (New York: Basic Books, 1991).

89. Marsden, *Fundamentalism and American Culture,* 5.

90. Ibid., 186; Nancy Ammerman, "North American Protestant Fundamentalism," in *Fundamentalism Observed* (Chicago: Fundamentalism Project, 1990), 28–55.

91. According to Ammerman, in her essay "North American Protestant Fundamentalism," by the 1950s the "choice facing the movement was between cultural relevance and cultural separation"(58). On one side was the evangelical leader Carl Henry, who argued in his influential 1948 book, *Remaking the Modern Mind,* that Christians should be socially and politically active in an effort to reestablish claims in a civilization dominated by secular humanism; the quintessential separatist was the anti-communist right-wing crusader Carl McIntire. Ammerman notes: "A few fundamentalists had joined the anti-communist crusades of the fifties, but most had remained relatively inactive in politics, preferring instead to put energy into the churches and institutions that made their view of the world possible. Evangelism and missions far outweighed social reform on their agendas" (61).

92. Ibid., 74.

93. Randall Terry quoted in Wilkinson, "Gospel According to Terry," 92.

11

▬

Marie Bass

TOWARD COALITION

The Reproductive Health Technologies Project

The Reproductive Health Technologies Project began in the late 1980s as an ambitious citizens' campaign with a single purpose: to see a product like the French abortion pill RU 486 brought to market in the United States. It turned into something broader, subtler, more diverse and diffused, yet potentially far more significant. In the 1990s the project has matured into an eclectic collection of individuals from various disciplines who collaborate on issues of reproductive technology where science, politics, and the reproductive needs of women converge—and often clash.

The project's twenty-five-member board reflects a broad and rich landscape of individuals and organizations, including senior persons from mainstream national and international organizations like Planned Parenthood and the Population Council as well as leaders from U.S. women's health advocacy groups, such as the National Women's Health Network, the National Latina Health Organization, the National Black Women's Health Project, and the National Asian Women's Health Organization. The board also includes local community advocates, such as a Latina from San Diego who conducts health education programs for sex workers in Tijuana, a Sioux woman from North Dakota who trains hospital workers to understand and observe the reproductive health concerns of Native American women, and an organizer for the

National Welfare Rights Union who is herself a former homeless single mother.

This diverse group has learned how to talk about, educate itself about, and build consensus on complex and controversial issues of reproductive technology. The group's view of technology is neither positive nor negative. Rather, the group believes that it should serve women and men in their efforts to control their fertility. Project members acknowledge the limits of technology: there is unlikely ever to be a perfect method of contraception or a perfect technological fix for unintended pregnancy. No technology works if people are afraid or unwilling to use it, or do not use it correctly.

The project's members have learned from each other, the scientist teaching the nonscientist and the nonscientist teaching the scientist. White women learn from Black and Latina women, who explain why they recoil almost instinctively from the introduction of any new, highly touted birth control technology; why they may view it as an attempt to coerce and control rather than to liberate them. Middle-class participants learn from poor women about the harsh realities of these women's lives, which overrule the moral or ideological soapboxes that others are privileged enough to speak from.

As with any political or coalition endeavor, the Reproductive Health Technologies Project is the collective product of the contributions of many individuals working at different levels and in different ways. What follows is my own perspective drawn from working on the project since its inception. By relating the story in this manner, I believe readers may appreciate how the personal is still political.

In the early 1980s, after Ronald Reagan had been elected president with strong support from anti-abortion groups, and the United States Senate and House of Representatives appeared perilously close to overturning or at least diminishing *Roe v. Wade*, I served as the political action director of the National Abortion Rights Action League (NARAL) in Washington, D.C. It was not a satisfying professional experience for me—but not because I did not believe in the cause or enjoy the people I worked with. It was because I felt continually offended by the way in which this most personal, private, often agonizing matter—a woman's decision to have an abortion—had been appropriated by shallow, insensitive, and opportunistic politicians.

Candidates for Congress (usually male, but not always) typically chose their position on the issue of abortion by determining how the political winds in their state or district were blowing—or how they perceived them to be blowing. Often their stance was the result of who among their voters made the most fuss, and most often, they were the anti-abortion zealots.

Public opinion polls demonstrated, then and now, that Americans believe that abortion, especially early abortion, should be legal and that the basic decision should be a woman's. However, most people with this attitude are neither "single-issue" voters nor likely to engage in public political activities to support their views on abortion.

As the political action director at NARAL, I discovered that politicians who claimed to be pro-choice were often the most frustrating. For example, when asked at a community forum or issues panel, "What is your position on the issue of abortion?" a candidate (again, usually male, but not always) would begin, "Well, I am personally opposed to abortion, but . . . " We'd then have to endure a laborious recitation about his deeply felt reverence for human life, how his parents reared him in a religious environment, how precious his wife and children are to him, how our country has a long tradition of separation of church and state, and so forth. This kind of tortured non-answer was guaranteed to please no one, but it gave the politician the opportunity to come back to us at NARAL and say, "You see, I try to be on your side, but it gets me nowhere." It is notable that over the past fifteen years, many pro-choice politicians have finally learned to say simply, "I'm pro-choice" or "It's a woman's decision" and let it go at that.

Back in the early 1980s I doubted whether many politicians on either side gave much thought to what abortion was really about. Perhaps they were as offended as I was that it was an issue they had to address at all. Candidates for office did what they needed to do in order to win office or to stay in office. In this way, the abortion issue was no different from many other issues in politics, just more politically acrimonious— and more reflective of the status of women in our society.

After the 1984 elections I left NARAL, tired and dispirited. Ronald Reagan and Jesse Helms had been reelected. Their "pro-choice" opponents had failed to use the issue of reproductive choice in a way that might have helped them, that is, by declaring their positions in a strong and straightforward manner and thus energizing and mobilizing a genuine "woman's vote." Their campaign consultants (again, usually male) had advised them to steer clear of this and other social or women's issues, and therefore it was not hard to understand why many women were less than enthusiastic about supporting them.

Even more disturbing was what happened to former congresswoman Geraldine Ferraro in her historic vice presidential campaign in 1984. Throughout the general election, she was brutally assaulted for her audacity, as a Catholic woman, to espouse a position on abortion that contradicted the Church's. Cardinal John O'Connor (later archbishop) relentlessly denounced her and instructed other clergy to do the same. Curiously, O'Connor had found it possible to countenance prominent male Catholics with the same position, notably Mario Cuomo, then governor of New York, and Senator Ted Kennedy of Massachusetts. Evidently, men could be indulged in a little waywardness, but a Catholic woman—never!

During the 1980s there were also sporadic incidents of clinic terrorism—nowhere near what we have witnessed in the 1990s but still very frightening. There seemed to be no limit to what fanatic people, acting in the name of their own strange moral callings, would do to punish women for their choices. Not surprisingly, fewer and fewer doctors were willing to perform abortions, and the abortion procedure was rarely taught in medical schools. The burden for poor women, as always, was even greater; most state Medicaid programs would no longer pay for poor women's abortions. The "right" to an abortion was becoming a hollow legal shell having nothing to do with the ability to obtain one.

When I first heard about the drug called RU 486 in the mid-1980s, it was well on its way to market in France. My first thought was that maybe—just maybe—this was a way out of the quagmire of the abortion issue. If such a product were safe and effective and women accepted it, perhaps it could take the abortion issue out of the political arena and put the decision back in the hands of women and medical practitioners, where it belonged.

I was not alone in this hope. By early 1987 Joanne Howes and I had founded our political consulting firm in Washington, D.C., which specializes in women's issues and public policy. As former senior lobbyist in Planned Parenthood's national office, Joanne had been as closely involved with abortion politics and policy as I had been at NARAL. Knowing very little about the drug approval process, we wondered what it would take to get a product like RU 486 onto the market in the United States. Our friend Nanette Falkenberg, who had been executive director and my boss at NARAL, was equally interested and committed. Together, the three of us decided to "do something."

We turned to another friend and colleague in Missouri, Judith Widdicombe, who helped us obtain a grant from the Sunnen Foundation in St. Louis to survey attitudes about RU 486 among doctors, research scientists, pharmaceutical company representatives, drug regulatory experts, pro-choice and family-planning leaders, women's health activists, politicians, and others. Our goal was to learn how much people already knew about RU 486, what they thought of it, and what they felt were its prospects for entering the U.S. market.

To the extent people had heard about the drug, they were enthusiastic. This was encouraging to hear, especially from the physicians and scientists who had studied the research findings from Europe and elsewhere. Already, one small trial among U.S. women had been conducted by Dr. David Grimes at the University of Southern California, sponsored by the Population Council. Of one hundred women who had been given RU 486 to terminate an early pregnancy, eighty-five had had a complete abortion.

We learned about other research being conducted under the umbrella of the National Institutes of Health. Some of this research was exciting and dramatically promising, concerning the possible use of the drug for contraception, endometriosis, labor induction, and treatment of several conditions unrelated to the reproductive system. Dr. Gary Hodgen at the Jones Institute for Reproductive Research in Virginia, who was an especially avid proponent of the new compound, was conducting research on monkeys.

While doctors and scientists spoke highly about the promise of RU 486, they were virtually unanimous in saying that the product was unlikely to come to the United States because anti-abortion forces would frighten decision makers at the relevant pharmaceutical houses. Even the research depended on the willingness of the French manufacturer, Roussel Uclaf, to make supplies of the drug available. Several researchers reported difficulty in obtaining the drug, and they were convinced that the company was wary about sending the product to the United States. At least two other European companies were working on similar compounds, but theirs were far behind RU 486 in development.

U.S. pharmaceutical companies were nowhere in the picture. The giants in birth control—Johnson and Johnson, Searle, Upjohn, among others—who had developed the birth control pill and other products into a multibillion-dollar market, made it clear they would take a pass on this product. They cited lack of profit potential (unlike the Pill, a woman would use RU 486 only sporadically), fear of litigation and product liability,[1] and of course, anti-abortion political activism.

Pharmaceutical companies abhor controversy unless they stand to make a great deal of money for their trouble. The profit potential for RU 486 was nowhere near enough to make up for the headache a company would face. For all these reasons, the major American companies wanted nothing to do with it.

By late 1987, when Joanne, Nanette, and I wrote the report of our three-month survey, titled "RU 486: The Prospects for Use in the United States," we were in a high state of moral indignation. Clearly, RU 486 was a good product. It was already well documented as an early form of nonsurgical or noninvasive abortion—a long-sought-after "missing link" in fertility control. Professor Carl Djerassi, the renowned Stanford chemist who synthesized the first oral contraceptive in the 1950s, had called RU 486 the *only* new discovery in fertility research since the Pill. Beyond that, RU 486 was the prototype of an entire new class of drugs known as progesterone antagonists, or antiprogestins, which held promise for diseases like breast cancer and AIDS. Yet not one major company in the United States would go near the drug.

Our report concluded that a large, dedicated public education campaign was needed in this country, beginning with the pro-choice and family-planning activist community, then widening to the medical and scientific community, health groups, legal and consumer groups, policy makers, and the media. A significant new medical breakthrough was off-limits in the United States, not for medical or scientific reasons, but because the anti-choice movement was intimidating the scientific community and the pharmaceutical industry. Surely the great pro-choice (but nonactivist) majority of citizens would object to this injustice, if only they knew about it.

Throughout our work on the project, we had consulted with our colleagues in the leading pro-choice and family-planning groups, including Planned Parenthood, NARAL, the Alan Guttmacher Institute, the National Abortion Federation, and Catholics for a Free Choice. Leaders of these groups were interested in RU 486 and concerned that anti-abortion groups were already putting out scurrilous materials about "the death pill" and "chemical warfare on the unborn." As always, the opposition seemed to have its sound bites and graphic messages down pat before our side was ready to say anything at all.

But at the end of 1987 and during 1988, pro-choice and women's rights groups were consumed by their efforts to defeat the nomination of Robert Bork to the Supreme Court and, following that victory, by the coming November elections. Their agenda was overcrowded as it was, and their resources were limited. RU 486 was not a priority.

Joanne, Nanette, and I had long since used up the modest grant we had received to do our survey and report, so our resources were negligible. We had sent the report to several hundred opinion leaders in the women's rights, family-planning, pro-choice, and medical communities. We had received considerable positive feedback, but no one had offered us a means to pursue our work, nor were we sure at the time how to ask. Moreover, there was no institutional affiliation or "home" for our work. We were three unconnected, free-floating individuals, still with a burning desire to "do something."

Throughout 1988 we followed the progress of RU 486 in France. In September the drug was formally approved there, as expected, for use in combination with a small dose of a prostaglandin that caused uterine contraction and the expulsion of the embryo. One regimen had to be administered by a physician in a strict four-step protocol in a licensed abortion clinic. It could be used only through the first forty-nine days of pregnancy, dating from the beginning of the last menstrual period. Despite the complicated procedure and the brief window of time in which the method could be used, everything seemed to be going well and the drug's approval was greeted with enthusiasm.

In October there was stunning news. Roussel Uclaf announced in Paris that it was suspending the sale of RU 486, only one month after the drug had gone on the market. The company's president, Edouard Sakiz, said that, after enduring repeated protests from the French Catholic Church and anti-abortion groups, Roussel Uclaf had reluctantly concluded that "the public is not ready for RU 486."

The day after the announcement, Joanne and I had lunch with our friend Sharon Camp at a favorite Indian restaurant in downtown Washington. Sharon and her colleague Joseph Speidel were at the helm of the Population Crisis Committee (now renamed Population Action International) and had been enormously helpful throughout our project. Working with them, we had learned a great deal about the shocking extent of maternal mortality in developing countries that is associated with unsafe abortion, usually botched attempts to self-abort. This was a primary motivation for their interest in RU 486.

Over lunch, Sharon commiserated with Joanne and me about the distressing news from Paris. Coincidentally, the biennial international meeting of obstetricians and gynecologists was convening the following day in Rio de Janeiro. This topic was certain to loom large. In her charismatic and very direct manner, Sharon challenged us to get ourselves there: "If the two of you really want to be involved, you've simply got to get into the game. A big campaign needs to happen, and the two of you could make it happen." Joanne and I mumbled about our lack of resources and institutional connections. Sharon replied, "No one will join up or give you money if you're not doing anything. Start making things happen, and the support will come."

Before the end of lunch, we had decided that Joanne would go to Rio, as I had no time to make child care arrangements. She excused herself to telephone our office and speak with the lone full-time assistant we employed at the time. "I know this sounds crazy," Joanne told her, "but call the Brazilian embassy and find out if I can get a visa this afternoon. Then see if I can get onto a flight to Rio de Janeiro this evening." By the time we got back to the office, our very resourceful staffer had all the answers, and at 7 P.M. Joanne was bound for Rio.

The topic of RU 486 did indeed loom large at the Rio meeting. Thanks to the quick organizing efforts of Rebecca Cook, a prominent professor and outstanding attorney for women's rights on the international level, a petition objecting to Roussel's actions was circulated and signed by more than a thousand doctors. There were impromptu news conferences and late-night strategy sessions to assess how to keep the drug afloat.

In Paris two days later, the drama continued. The French minister of health made a simple, elegant statement ordering the drug back onto the market on the grounds that he could not allow the abortion debate to deprive women of a product that represented medical progress. From the moment the government approved the product, he said, it had become "the moral property of women."

And so, the company was under court order, in effect, to resume selling its product in France. No one has ever conclusively proved whether Roussel Uclaf's managers staged the entire episode in order to be "forced" to market their brand-new product and in addition enjoy free front-page press in major newspapers throughout the world for several days running. In any case, this episode proved that the corporate managers of Roussel were highly susceptible to pressure from outside parties.

Our small cabal of collaborators decided to call a meeting in Washington for late November to strategize about how to convince the company to expand its marketing to the United States and elsewhere. We invited top persons from women's health, family-planning, pro-choice, and international population organizations. Some we knew, but many we did not. To our amazement, virtually everyone we invited accepted.

By the time of the meeting, the 1988 November elections had taken place, and the results were not good from a pro-choice point of view. George Bush, who had long since abandoned his moderate stance on reproductive issues in order to join Ronald Reagan's ticket in 1980, had been elected president. In Dan Quayle, Bush had chosen a vice president whose simplistic rhetoric and Senate voting record were strongly anti-abortion. Throughout the election campaign, Democratic opponent Michael Dukakis had tried to articulate a clear pro-choice position, but there was little evidence that it gained him any votes. Ballot measures on state funding for abortion went down to defeat in three states. Longtime Senate abortion rights leader Lowell Weicker of Connecticut lost his reelection bid.

Apart from losing ground in the elections, there was the chilling matter of the Supreme Court. Three aging liberal justices were likely to be replaced during the Bush years with conservative justices. And the Reagan administration's intervention in *Webster v. Reproductive Health Services* seemed to have set the stage for the overthrow of *Roe v. Wade.*

The troubling political atmospherics served to heighten the drama on the day of our first meeting in late November 1988. With about forty persons seated around a large, hollow-square table, Joanne and I made brief statements to open the meeting. What we all had in common, we said, was that we were strongly pro-choice and believed in the right of women to have access to the safest, most humane methods of birth control. With this in mind, the purpose of the meeting was to develop a successful strategy for bringing RU 486 to the United States.

When I look back on that day, I marvel that something so enduring and significant and, in my opinion, productive as the Reproductive Health Technologies Project could have been born out of such a gathering. It is amazing that the meeting ended in anything other than a complete discordance of words meaning different things to different people. True, everyone at the table was pro-choice, but there the similarities ended. Joanne and I had been unaware how widespread the differences were—differences in ideology and philosophy, in levels of information, or both.

A few participants knew enough about RU 486 to have well-formed opinions, and they wanted to jump ahead to discuss what the Food and

Drug Administration (FDA) and Congress were likely to do. A surprising number knew very little about the drug and wanted a baseline review of the science behind it and how it worked. The most experienced women's health consumer advocates, such as Judy Norsigian of the Boston Women's Health Book Collective, introduced concerns about whether the drug affected white women and women of color differently and about access to hospital care in the event of emergencies such as prolonged bleeding.

Further divisions soon became apparent between those who were inclined to favor new technologies in general and those who believed that technologies have too often been used coercively to promote population control policies at the expense of women's autonomy and health. Several people were quick to recall how drugs or devices that were once highly touted had turned into disasters for women—diethylstilbestrol (DES), thalidomide, the Dalkon Shield, to name three.[2]

While working at NARAL, I had been introduced to a basic dynamic of group process by a wise woman named Mary Parish. With a simple exercise called "Who Am I?" she had taught us that a group of persons meeting together, whether two or sixty in number, must pass through four stages to be able to work together successfully. In the first stage each participant must establish and validate herself or himself to the group—must, in effect, answer the question "Who am I?" In the second phase, the question becomes "Who am I with you?" The participants must now define themselves as a group, determine how they relate to one another, and find a common thread in their reasons for assembling. Reaching consensus at this level enables the group to proceed to the third stage, which addresses the question "What are we going to do?" Only after these three stages have been satisfactorily completed, in the proper order, can the group proceed to the fourth and essential stage: "How are we going to do it?" Failing to pass through any one of the stages, or taking the stages out of order, leads to a breakdown of the group at some point. It will then have to backtrack and reconstruct itself, or, as often occurs, it will simply flounder and disintegrate.

Our meeting that first day was a classic example of sloppy group process. Clearly I hadn't remembered a thing that Mary Parish had taught. By starting with the question "How are we going to bring RU 486 to this country?" we committed exactly the mistake that she had warned against—skipping over the first three essential stages.

For all its shortcomings, the daylong meeting concluded with all but a few of the participants committing themselves to a special project on RU 486 that Joanne and I would manage. The precise goals of the project were still vague, but there was enough energy to propel us forward until we could spell out a mission and a set of objectives. The strongest consensus point was simply that the anti-choice groups were mounting a campaign against RU 486, thereby compelling pro-choice groups to do something.

Over the next two years, the Reproductive Health Technologies Project convened periodic meetings to bring together the same kinds of leaders, to keep them informed of the progress of RU 486 in Europe and elsewhere, and to develop common messages and themes. We brought in experts from the scientific and medical community to brief us; we invited colleagues from family-planning and women's groups in Europe with whom we could collaborate on political strategies.

In turn, many groups began to launch their own efforts. Planned Parenthood undertook negotiations with the French company to serve as a partner in bringing the product to the United States. Its president, Faye Wattleton, traveled to Paris several times to try to convince the company, a campaign that seemed hopeful for a time but ultimately proved fruitless. The Feminist Majority Foundation, under Eleanor Smeal's direction, organized a prestigious delegation of U.S. doctors and scientists who called on Roussel Uclaf in Paris and its parent company, Hoechst AG in Frankfurt, to try to convince them to introduce the drug into the United States. The Population Council continued its research on RU 486, including initiating important studies of the attitudes of women who had used the drug. NARAL undertook a series of benchmark public opinion polls and focus groups to measure the understanding of the general public about RU 486 and to learn which messages would best advance that understanding. Many other groups and individuals joined the campaign and made their voices heard.

By 1990 the Reproductive Health Technologies Project had become a clearinghouse for information, distributing thousands of information kits to organizations, public officials, and the media. We fielded press calls and put journalists in touch with doctors and researchers who could speak authoritatively about the drug. We assisted organizations that were writing resolutions of support, legislators who wanted to introduce resolutions or hold hearings, and academics who were putting together conferences. Sharon Camp had been right in her "build it and they will come" advice to Joanne and me. It took a while, but once we could demonstrate tangible results for our efforts, we were able to raise funds from foundations.

Beyond the campaign-like activities and all the hustle and bustle, a subtle but very interesting phenomenon had begun to come into focus. The project's meetings had become a forum for listening and learning, for establishing consensus, painstakingly but genuinely. Participants were building new respect for each other, exploring possible interests, and testing new forms of collaboration. People who agreed on almost nothing else had reached a consensus that RU 486 was an important new technology that should be available to women. They could agree on that and agree to disagree on other matters, such as the safety of DepoProvera or the relative risks and benefits of the oral contraceptive.

In 1991 RU 486 was approved for use in Great Britain, a step perceived as a signal that the company was finally ready to expand its marketing beyond France. There were indications that other western European companies were in line for marketing, and the United States and Canada should not be far behind.

Sensing that we were making progress on RU 486, and that the group was becoming a cohesive unit, several of us who had been among the earliest participants in the project began to discuss the possibility of using the same process of dialogue and consensus building to address other topics related to reproductive technologies. It was clear that where consensus could develop, the group was a powerful force for advocacy, outreach, and public education. Already it was impressively diverse and multidisciplinary, but we felt that it was important to go even further. We needed to seek out individuals who could speak from the perspective of poor women, women of color, women who were not part of the established health care system.

At the original meeting in November 1988, only one woman of color had been in the room—Emily Tynes, a former NARAL colleague who became a full partner in the project, working on media strategies. Plenty of people spoke with genuine concern about the interests of black women, Latinas, Asian women, Native American women, and women in poverty. But no matter how well-meaning we may have been, as white middle-class women, we simply could not represent the interests of women from other groups.

In early 1992 we recruited some outstanding women of color to the project's board. Among those who accepted were Julia Scott of the National Black Women's Health Project, Luz Alvarez Martinez of the National Latina Health Organization, and Helen Rodriguez-Trias, a physician and health care consultant of Puerto Rican heritage who was the incoming president of the American Public Health Association. They and others joined with full knowledge that they would be serving with persons from the world of "population control," which they viewed at best with suspicion and distrust.

The first meeting of the newly constituted board occurred in July 1992, and Sharon Camp of Population Action International was elected chair. At the outset, several in the group nervously joked that, except for RU 486 for early abortion, there might be no other issue on which the members could agree. We reiterated our commitment to the process of dialogue and consensus building, however, and during a daylong discussion we found three additional areas where consensus was also strong.

The first was the desperate need for woman-controlled products to protect us from sexually transmitted diseases, including the AIDS virus. More than a decade into the AIDS epidemic, the single public health message for the prevention of the disease is "Use condoms." This directive ignores the reality that many women lack the power within relationships to insist on condom use, and lack the power outside relationships to abandon partners who put them at risk. Even the female condom, while an important new option, is strictly speaking not a woman-controlled method, since a woman can use it only with her partner's consent. The group agreed that what is needed is a vaginal "microbicide"—a topical substance formulated into a foam, cream, jelly, or suppository that women can use each time they have sex. Such a product would need to be cheap, easy to use, and something that women would simply make a part of their lives, like toothpaste or deodorant.

The second area of consensus that the board reached easily was the need for greater awareness and use of emergency or "postcoital" contraception. Here the technology is not a new one, but one that already exists and is readily available. Sometimes called "the best kept contraceptive secret in the United States," an elevated dose of standard oral contraceptives, taken up to three days after unprotected intercourse, will prevent a pregnancy from developing. The insertion of a copper IUD up to seven days after unprotected sex will do the same. While the medical community is aware of postcoital contraception and some college health services and Planned Parenthood clinics prescribe it, many women still do not know that this option exists. The project decided to approach the issue from a woman's right-to-know standpoint. It was time to let women in on the secret!

The third area of consensus concerned the Pill, although in this case, the group recognized a special set of complexities. In the thirty-five-year history of oral contraceptives, it has been accepted practice in the United States that a woman must visit a health care professional, undergo a physical examination, and receive a prescription to obtain her pills. With the Pill's record of safety and success, it is reasonable to consider making it available over the counter in pharmacies and grocery stores, as many other medications now are. This would demedicalize the Pill and allow easier access for many women, and it would probably reduce the cost for those who now pay full price for a monthly supply. Proponents of the switch argue that women are capable of reading and following instructions for using the Pill correctly, just as we are able to follow instructions for using tampons or taking cold medication.

For many women, however, their visit to a clinic to obtain pills may be the only time they see a health care provider and their only real contact, as tenuous it may be, with the health care system. It is the one time when some women have their blood pressure checked, have a breast examination, and get checked for vaginal or genital infection. It may be the only time when a health care professional looks into a woman's eyes and inquires, "How are you?" For the woman who lacks adequate insurance coverage, the pills prescribed by a doctor or nurse at a community clinic will be free or cost far less than if a private physician had written the prescription. Moreover, the Pill is not as simple to use as cold medications or other over-the-counter products. If a woman misses a day or several days on the Pill, she may not know what to do. She could make the wrong judgment and inadvertently expose herself to unprotected sex.

The project's board members have not yet reached a consensus on whether the Pill should go over the counter; in fact, there is deep division. Everyone agrees, however, that this is an important topic to address and analyze. This issue has generated some of the tensest moments for the project's participants. The conflicts have less to do with the Pill in its current form than with the history of the Pill, how it was developed, and earlier versions of the Pill that contained much higher doses of hormones and thus carried greater health risks. The conflict also centers on whether one is inclined to view the Pill as a step toward women's sexual liberation or as an attempt to coerce poor women and women of color to limit their childbearing and family size, and thus to limit their communities.

As a white, middle-class woman brought up in middle America with middle-of-the-road values, I have had to strive to put myself into the shoes of those born in very different circumstances. I am sure I can never fully empathize, but with respect to birth control issues, I can understand the perspective of many women of color and poor women. The United States has a very troubling history of coercive birth control practices, from forced sterilization to more recent examples of women "sentenced" to Norplant. In the 1950s the Pill was tested not among women who reflect the racial and socioeconomic variety of this country, but among poor Puerto Rican women, who were subjected to high levels of hormones that caused them to suffer significant side effects.

A dialogue about the Pill, therefore, between white women and African-American and Latina women must begin with an understanding and acknowledgment of these opposing historical viewpoints. When the participants in the project began discussing the Pill, it was important to the black women in particular to establish this context. One woman vehemently stated, "You may not understand my perspective, or you may choose not to agree with it. But it is mine, and you must listen to it."

In the late 1990s RU 486 (or mifepristone, as it is now called) is still not available in the United States or in most of the world. Despite high hopes after its approval in Great Britain in 1991, the drug has not been particularly well received in that country and has not become available in other countries, with the exception of Sweden and China.[3] Roussel Uclaf, because of multiple mergers and acquisitions involving its German parent company, Hoechst, is no longer a company in its own right, and the new company has a hands-off policy toward the drug, apart from manufacturing it for the French market. Many of the French scientists and physicians who helped develop and test the product have become frustrated and embittered that despite the pressures from all over the world, RU 486 has barely begun to be used.

It is tempting, therefore, to conclude that all the good efforts of so many people have been a failure, but here again, the oral contraceptive and its history may be instructive. What began as a highly speculative venture against enormous odds in the late 1940s and early 1950s is today an enormously profitable product whose availability is taken for granted in almost every country. The story of the Pill includes a roster of dramatis personae not unlike that of RU 486—determined activists, such as the radical and controversial birth control pioneer Margaret Sanger, brilliant chemists and doctors, reluctant and risk-averse pharmaceutical executives, and not least, the Catholic Church hierarchy, whose opposition was absolute. Skepticism about the Pill ran a lengthy gamut: health and safety concerns, legal obstacles (many states still had laws limiting the sale, distribution, or advertising of contraceptives), speculation that it would be too expensive for women to afford on a mass basis, concern that the FDA would never approve such a product, lack of interest and support on the part of the mainstream medical community, and on and on. One after another, the major drug companies declined to be involved. When the first product became available, it was approved by the FDA not for pregnancy prevention but for the treatment of "menstrual irregularities."

Whatever the fate of RU 486, or mifepristone, clearly the several years of intense public education and activism by the Reproductive Health Technologies Project and many other groups have paid off in motivating the political establishment, the medical community, and even industry to take this matter very seriously.

In May 1994 Donna Shalala, secretary of health and human services, announced that after prolonged negotiations an agreement had been reached with Roussel Uclaf under which the company would donate rights to RU 486 to the nonprofit Population Council in New York. According to the agreement, the council would be free to pursue on its own getting the drug onto the market in this country, including identifying another commercial manufacturer for the product and a distributor. Roussel agreed to make available a quantity of the drug sufficient for a clinical trial of two thousand women in the United States and turn over the technology in due course. In a crowded press conference on Capitol Hill, Shalala stood among members of Congress and the administration, leaders of women's organizations, and executives from the Population Council and Roussel Uclaf. Under the bright lights of the television cameras, there was an air of victory and celebration. The following day, front-page stories ran in the major newspapers across the country.

Throughout 1995 and 1996 the saga of mifepristone continued, as the Population Council tried to find investors and negotiate agreements with potential manufacturers and distributors. The process was not a smooth one, and the politics surrounding abortion produced an atmosphere of excessive caution and fear that hindered progress. Still, there were important steps forward.

In July 1996 the reproductive health advisory committee of the Food and Drug Administration voted to recommend mifepristone as safe and effective. More than thirty groups testified in the public portion of the hearings, and two-thirds of these strongly favored making mifepristone available in the United States.

In September the FDA responded to the advisory committee's recommendation by issuing an "approvable letter," affirming the safety and efficacy of the drug for early abortion. Although this is not full approval, it is a strong statement of confidence in the method, and it essentially means that when the manufacturing and distribution details are finalized, approval will be granted.

In addition, during 1996 there was important progress in expanding our concept of early nonsurgical or "medical" abortion to include other products besides mifepristone. There may be dozens of already available drugs that will induce an early, safe abortion. Planned Parenthood Federation of America has made one such drug, methotrexate, available at clinic sites throughout the country, and more and more private physicians are also recommending these drugs. Thus, the eventual availability of nonsurgical medical abortion in the United States is not in question. With research and increasing knowledge about other compounds, more than one product should be available in the future.

I submit that the story of the Reproductive Health Technologies Project illustrates the benefits of successful group process, relationship building, and diverse coalitions. As a result of taking on the issue of postcoital contraception and enlisting many groups to become involved, the project's work has led to the use of the term *emergency contraception* on a widespread basis. In February 1997 the Food and Drug Administration declared standard oral contraceptives safe and effective for emergency contraception, a highly unusual move, since no pharmaceutical company had yet applied for approval to market their products in this way. Doctors are now talking more openly and telling their patients how to use the conventional Pill for emergency contraception when they need to. This progress is in part due to the efforts of the Reproductive Health Technologies Project and its participants.

The desperate need for the development of topical vaginal microbicides for women is another issue that has created a worldwide call to action. It is tragic that it has taken more than a decade of women dying of AIDS throughout the world and suffering incalculably from sexually transmitted diseases to get to this point. Our project is by no means a pioneer in this work, but we have been able to devote resources toward producing much-needed informational packets for the media and policy makers, and getting the call to action through to the many networks and constituencies of the project's participants. We have helped convene meetings bringing leading researchers in the field together with women's and AIDS advocates for joint strategizing to speed the development of such products. We have lobbied the federal research establishment to make this a higher biomedical research priority. We have, once again, as with RU 486 and emergency contraception, worked hard to turn a new term—*microbicide*—into a household word.

The lesson in group process that Mary Parish taught holds true. If a group fails to invest the time to understand one another as individuals first, to address "Who am I?" and then "Who am I with you?" it will sooner or later break down and be forced to revert to these basic questions. The project has matured into a model for building strong and effective coalitions because it brings to the table as equal partners persons with dramatically different cultural, ethnic, economic, and professional experience and perspective. They do not simply sit at the table together but learn together and, ultimately, act together.

It is through the existence of this kind of coalition that we can withstand the inevitable upsets of the electoral process. When Bill Clinton, who campaigned on a strong pro-choice plank, was initially elected in 1992, it seemed that the abortion issue might finally be settled. Yet we have since seen the ascendancy of the anti-abortion lobby and the religious right in unprecedented and frightening ways. There is no choice but to press forward and take a long view. I remind myself that it took women more than a hundred years to get the right to vote in this country—one freedom mercifully no longer in question.

NOTES

1. Not only has the Dalkon Shield intrauterine device caused severe health problems for many women, rendering some infertile, but the resulting lawsuits cast a pall over the entire contraceptive industry, a tragedy upon a tragedy that is still felt today.

2. Several people in the room had been on opposite sides during a bitter battle just a few years earlier over the injectable contraceptive DepoProvera. After a tortuous process, the FDA had failed to approve it in the 1980s because of questions about its safety, and there was still plenty of anger as a result of this fight. In 1992 the FDA approved DepoProvera.

3. China manufactures its own version of the product.

PART FOUR

PHYSICIANS AND THE
POLITICS OF PROVISION

This section includes three essays written by physicians—all abortion providers—and an essay written jointly by a sociologist, an activist medical student, and the director of a new organization called Medical Students for Choice. Given the sacrifices incurred by abortion practitioners in the United States today and the dangers they confront, the three physicians' essays express a remarkable commitment to their work. Each doctor evidences both an impulse to trace the roots of her or his commitment and a fierce determination to pursue the work, including public advocacy of abortion rights, even in the face of unprecedented, almost unbelievable obstacles. All three physicians have written quite personal essays, in which they explore the gratification they have derived from serving as abortion providers and, in the case of the two providers currently in practice, the deep personal frustration and anger that they must cope with in the face of anti-abortion forces. Elizabeth Karlin lays out, in remarkably calm and loving terms, her prescription for the feminist practice of abortion. Jane Hodgson, a pioneering abortion rights practitioner, has created an autobiography of her feminist consciousness. And Warren Hern has prepared a calendar of terrorism in order to consider the consequences of violence.

Carole Joffe, Patricia Anderson, and Jody Steinauer review the medical context in which these and other practitioners have worked and continue to work today. They chart and analyze the medical profession's changing stances toward abortion and examine the promise of the contemporary surge of abortion rights activism within the profession.

12

Elizabeth Karlin

"WE CALLED IT KINDNESS"

Establishing a Feminist Abortion Practice

I am an unapologetic feminist physician. I perform unapologetic, feminist abortions. Medical school did not teach me that I need not apologize, nor that women have abortions, nor the feminist view, nor how to do abortions. But I know that millions of thoughtful and compassionate women have had abortions throughout history. Some of the most insightful made their decisions before they ever got pregnant. Others came to their decision slowly, painfully, and with disbelief at finding themselves in that situation. Many women and girls made these decisions at great personal peril.

I have discussed these decisions and the lives that led to them with almost nine thousand women who have come to me for abortions. My experience has confirmed my trust in the thoughtfulness of my patients. I know that none of them had sex with the intention of having an abortion. I know that women have abortions because they have a sense of what it is to be a good mother. Many of them deserve medals. Their primary doctors were sometimes ignorant and sometimes evil in their inability to help them with contraception. These women have made deliberate, caring decisions to have abortions. But their decisions to have unprotected or poorly protected intercourse, to be in bed with the wrong man, or to ignore the possibility of pregnancy and emerge full of shame, these decisions have not been healthy.

And so, in the name of feminism and good medicine, I have chosen not to judge patients but to support them in their difficult decision, and then to help them change behaviors that are not working for them. I cannot both judge and practice good medicine. Many people use abortion to judge women, invoking good and evil, life and murder. Whether these judgments spring from the medical establishment, the anti- or pro-choice community, or the pope, they remain irrelevant to the abortion decision. Nobody has avoided an abortion by saying, "I don't believe in abortion." Knowing what does cause abortion helps. Sperm cause abortion. Women's self-perceived weakness and related unhealthy behaviors cause abortion. My job as a doctor is to help my patients change unhealthy behaviors.

As a feminist physician, therefore, I can think of no greater, more interesting, or more challenging work than providing and preventing abortions. I get to live my ideals daily. I get to treat women well, even those who expect to be despised, and I am constantly reminded through emotional and sometimes physical violence against me and my patients what important work we do. I get to do what every anti-abortion protester wishes (s)he could do: I get to decrease abortions. I feel blessed.

At this time when physicians are as unhappy as they have ever been—and survey after survey shows doctors exhorting their children not to enter medicine—I have found the elusive job satisfaction they seek. I am happy to go to work in the morning. Medical offices and hospitals around the country are overpopulated not with patients or physicians, but with administrators constrained to enforce a business agenda. In my office we work together, strengthened, not beaten down, by our enemies' intervention.

My practice has taught me that there are levels of feminist medicine. To begin with, all abortion providers are, by definition, feminist, because they provide safe abortions for women who request them. At the second level, some practitioners—and I include myself—encourage patients to feel positive and actively proud of their decision. There are certainly a few women who choose to leave our office flagellating themselves, saying things like "I should have been able to do it," as though motherhood were as simple as multiplication tables. Occasionally a patient may leave the office muttering that she will never recover. A few are anti-abortion protesters between their abortions, as a way of proving they are good women.

Speaking against abortion and then having one, as many of our patients have done, is distressing and unhealthy. Helping suffering and conflicted patients is our daily fare. Women don't have abortions because things are going well. We try to support the best and healthiest forces in our patients.

We believe our patients capable of learning about their bodies and their sexuality, of thinking about how the violence in their lives has hurt them, how birth control can help. We hope that they will be more likely to avoid this difficult decision in the future. Respect for our patients means we understand that their behavior during the procedure depends on who they were before, on what they expect from us, on what we have taught, and on how kind we can be at a time when we are invading a woman's vagina.

At the third level of our feminist practice, we must be vocal and public about what we do in order to assume our leadership role in women's health. (I would like to add I don't think men get such a fair shake in the doctor's office either. But here I am considering the abortion procedure, therefore women.) And last, in our feminist practice, we encourage our patients to be as outspoken as possible in support of all women's right to as safe an abortion as they themselves have had.

ABORTION—FEMALE TROUBLES

"Listen," she said, leaning over to hiss at me, the hugest black cross swinging from her neck, "I am not *like the other bimbos in here!"*

Abortion is an integral part of the woman's condition, and the woman's condition only. Men don't have them. Many women who have had sperm ejaculated into their vaginas have had abortions—natural (idiopathic: we don't know why they happened), self-induced, or medically induced. Between 30 and 50 percent of pregnancies naturally end in abortion, most before the woman is even aware it. We have all, even the atheists among us, prayed for a natural abortion when our periods were late: "Please, God, make my period come, and I'll never yell at the kids again!" For most of our lives, it is natural *not* to want to be pregnant. I do not judge how a woman feels about no longer being pregnant. She is not a better woman if she cries, just sadder.

Many of our patients despise themselves. This is in part because abortion is so often cast as a more offensive sexual act than the intercourse that led to it. And unfortunately, women's sexuality is fair game for degradation and derision. Where abortion is considered a medical, social, or public health necessity—as in Holland, for example—a woman who gets an abortion isn't criticized, and there are few abortions. When observers focus on the evil of abortion (or on the status of unwed motherhood), the shared sex act is eclipsed by the abortion, which is purely the woman's. Denial of sexuality is an all too common cause for abortion:

She was only sixteen and came to the office with her father and her twenty-three-year-old boyfriend. Her abortion went easily and she was in the recovery room, lying on the couch with her boyfriend engaged in some hot and heavy petting. He was stroking her buttocks and hips. I asked her to sit up and tell me what she knew about taking her pill. "She won't be needing those," her father said. "She isn't having sex until she's married."

When we accept the abortion, then can we decrease its incidence, since we are able to talk about its origin—the sex. Much has been written about the sexualization of abortion, about how public and church concentration on the abortion underwrites inattention to unhealthy, frequently violent sexuality.[1] When we concentrate on what caused the abortion, what kind of sex, when, and with whom, then we can prevent unhealthy sexual sequelae. Medically, sex is either healthy or unhealthy, and as a physician I am determined to make it healthier.

At the present time, when our society is meaner than it has been in many years, fundamentalist and reactionary factions are making it increasingly easy to disparage women. We hear talk about the wonderful 1950s and that *Ozzie and Harriet* housewife. (Before she died, Harriet Nelson had to remind people that she sometimes spent twelve hours working on the set to create the illusion of that life.) Surely in the fabulous fifties and arguably more frighteningly today, the religious radicals have pressured the dominant culture to enforce a series of assumptions about abortion that degrade women. Women have to agree, or be silent in their disagreement, for these assumptions to work:

- Women must be stupid and naive in need of help. (*A woman phoned our office, about five days after unprotected mid-cycle intercourse. "I can't be pregnant," she said. "He said he would protect me."*)
- Women seeking abortion are slutty.
- Abortionists are creepy.
- Women performing abortions are the most depraved of practitioners, sexually invasive and demented. (I received only one phone call from the press in 1995. I am usually only contacted when there has been

a murder, and there wasn't one in 1995. The reporter who called me put the question this way: "A nurse who is well acquainted with the abortion situation says that the women doctors who do abortions in Wisconsin are well known for putting their patients to sleep and performing lesbian sex acts on them. ['*What is a lesbian sex act on an anesthetized woman?*' *I thought. The mind boggles.*] Would you care to comment?")

- Government and media have to respect, tolerate, or ignore anti-abortion groups.

- Doctors must ignore or degrade patients who seek abortions and their colleagues who do them.

No wonder our patients are frightened. And they *are* frightened.

Patients still call and say in a low voice to the receptionist or assistant, "I have to speak to the doctor." "I can help you," she responds. "No! I have to speak to the doctor!" "Do you need to make an appointment for an abortion," the receptionist asks? The patient is stunned to hear the word spoken publicly. She did not believe the staff knew what I did. She was sure I would drag her into some filthy basement to do the procedure—or worse.

When I started doing abortions in 1990, anti-choice demonstrations were escalating. Violence against women at the clinics was escalating. Clearly, it would continue. At that time there had been no abortion-related murders. By 1996 two physicians had been killed; two young women working in abortion offices had been killed. One retired army officer had been killed for supporting a physician. His wife was injured. Four physicians (two in the United States and two in Canada) were wounded, two severely enough not to work. Another death of an abortion provider was suspicious.

Anti-choice factions have been successful in establishing twenty-four-hour waiting periods in many states, giving them time to stalk and harass abortion seekers. President Bill Clinton, elected on a pro-choice ticket, and Hillary Clinton publicly called abortion bad or wrong, giving ammunition to the violent Christian fundamentalists who publicly and unimpeded plan violence and killings. I hear on the news that the FBI, instead of dismantling these violent cults, allocates resources to the investigation of a Massachusetts abortion-providing physician who may have overcharged his patients. It is in this climate that I revel in defining the feminism of abortion.

A FEMINIST ABORTION PRACTICE

One of the medical assistants in our office, from whom I learned the abortion practice as I now know it, was asked what it was like when I took over and formed a feminist practice. "This office always had a feminist practice," I interjected. "We never called it feminist," she said. "We called it kind."

The core attributes of a feminist practice are respect and kindness. If these are present, then it is feminist. If not, it is not. That the woman's abortion, decided for the best motives, became a symbol of woman's depravity and weakness is enough of an intellectual reason for me to do abortions. The medical reason is that women enter the office afraid and suffering. They leave stronger, healthier, frequently happier, and better educated. Sometimes the visit can improve their entire lives. They can have healthier, happier children, and they can like themselves better. Nevertheless, women are despised and frequently despise themselves for this decision. (They aren't treated too well if they have the child, either. Clearly, abortion is not the problem. Too many people still despise women.)

Once a woman is pregnant, she must decide whether to carry the pregnancy to term or to have an abortion. If she carries the pregnancy to term she may choose to be the mother of the child or give it up for adoption. Her decision that she cannot carry the pregnancy to term, as she cannot see herself as the mother her child deserves—this is a decision of insight, intelligence, compassion, and respect for motherhood. The decision to let a naked penis in her unprotected vagina is not.

As a feminist abortion provider I have a set of principles that guide my work:

1. My office provides safe abortions for women who request them.
2. We do it with professionalism, kindness, and nurturing.
3. We teach our patients while they are with us about birth control in particular and health in general.
4. We pay attention to the devastating background some women come from and practice methods of kindness during pelvic exams and procedures.
5. We are committed both to our position in the forefront of women's medicine and to understanding and speaking out against the evil forces in our society. We know the relationship between clinic bombers, the Klan, and other white supremacist groups. We spread

awareness about the violence committed against all disenfranchised factions in our society, including women.

6. We take roles as political and emotional leaders because of our intimate knowledge of women's worst problems.

7. We participate in the process of organizing the forty million or so women in this country who have had abortions to be feminist leaders. We must convince these women to strip away the guilt and shame that keeps them shackled and silenced. If and when we get to the point where women are not embarrassed by their brave decision, steps 1 through 6 will follow easily.

ALL ABORTION PROVIDERS ARE FEMINISTS

By definition, all abortion provision is a feminist endeavor. In a simple interaction, a woman defines her own problem and comes to a doctor or physician's assistant to ask for a specific procedure. She says, "May I please have an abortion?" and the practitioner replies, "Yes you may." The physician, generally accustomed to controlling the interaction, providing nomenclature, diagnosis, and treatment, listens to the woman and does what she asks. Where else in medicine do we consistently find this happening?

The fact is, physicians don't have a history of feminism.[2] The original intention of nineteenth-century physicians who wrested control of abortion from the midwives, herbalists, other female practitioners, and pharmacists, was to establish medical control of women's pregnancies in the name of morality or health.[3] In the mid-twentieth century, women forced to appeal to committees for permission to obtain an abortion and those who had to look for providers out of the country were not the beneficiaries of woman-centered medicine. Even physicians committed to legalizing abortion in the early 1970s, before *Roe v. Wade*, had reservations about relinquishing their power. At the American Medical Association convention in 1970 one physician complained, "Legal abortion makes the patient truly the physician: she makes the diagnosis and establishes the therapy."[4] Even Alan Guttmacher, a strong advocate of legal abortion, expressed his concern about being a "rubber stamp."[5]

Nevertheless, all physicians who have chosen to devote themselves to doing abortions have been motivated by a clear understanding of the cruelties affecting women's lives and by a commitment to help women without resources escape from these cruelties. They have also been determined to save women from unsafe abortions. In the past some physicians saw women maimed from unsafe abortions and said, "I can do better; I can save these young women. This is the kind of medicine I want to do."

Now, there is again violence against both patient and doctor. But had there not been protests and fear of violence, I, like many of the new generation of providers, never would have started doing abortions. Today the cruelties are committed by Christian fundamentalist cults out to harass and kill abortion providers and to frighten women asking for abortions. By inaction, our government concurs. The health care establishment, in its own arrogance and ignorance about abortion, hurts women by doing an inadequate job of offering birth control, by claiming women have been irrevocably damaged by their abortions, by adding thousands of dollars to medical bills by treating nonexistent abortion-related complications, and by participating in unfounded and malicious lawsuits. Many women feel constrained to withhold the information that they have had an abortion from their primary-care doctors, and because most abortion practitioners are highly skilled, there are no traces to alert the physicians.

Abortion provision is also a feminist exercise because the physician and patient are both willing to risk societal or church censure for what they believe is healthy, moral conduct. There will always be people ready to punish both groups for going ahead with an abortion because a segment of the population is unwilling to accept abortion as a normal part of women's health. Sadly, demeaning women is a common and accepted part of medical practice. For example, some women seek abortions because when they asked an obstetrician for a tubal ligation after the previous pregnancy (or the one before that), the obstetrician belittled their ability to make such a decision and denied them the procedure. They were told that with only one, or two, or four children, they might want more. These women know exactly what they are asking for—good birth control—but are offered inferior contraception and become pregnant. Abortion practitioners risk everything to help women break that cycle.

Not all abortion providers define their feminist commitment in the same way. Some are feminists as they help women exert control over their own lives. Others extend the meaning of their feminism by constructing woman-centered practices and by becoming politically active spokespersons for reproductive rights. The community of abortion providers in the United States, already besieged by medical marginalization and anti-abortion violence, is further challenged by lack of a shared vision of the relationship between abortion provision and feminism.

HOW I CAME TO START MY PRACTICE

I became an abortion provider, not because I realized how many more providers were needed, but because I was asked. Of course, I was pro-choice and a feminist, and I was known for delivering eloquent, moving, and completely ineffectual testimony before an increasingly anti-choice Wisconsin legislature.[6] Yet when I finished my residency in 1983, I entered a traditional medical practice doing internal medicine.

Even at that time, however, I knew I wanted to open a real women's clinic, and I began to investigate what that might mean. I visited the Women's Health Resource Center in Chicago and took a trip studying feminist health centers on the West Coast. I found that health facilities that had started as authentic feminist health care centers in the 1970s frequently had a core of abortion provision, and if they were really advanced, like the Oakland Feminist Health Center, offered some of the most loving infertility treatment in the nation as well. When I talked to my colleagues about opening such a facility in Madison, Wisconsin, the response was not welcoming. Several local hospitals then created "women's centers" to encourage middle-aged, insured women—a population without an overriding need for contraceptive care and abortion—to enter their health care network. By the 1980s hospital-based women's health centers no longer mentioned the word *abortion*.

Despite my interest in women's health care, it would not have occurred to me to do abortions if violent demonstrations had not been increasing. In 1990 Maggie Cage, then administrator of the Fox Valley Reproductive Center in Appleton, Wisconsin (now a Planned Parenthood facility), called to say that their physician needed time off for surgery—could I learn to do abortions and help temporarily? Had there been no violence and turmoil around the procedure, Maggie could probably have found someone else to fill in. But the few trained abortion specialists were already overcommitted. In a context of increasing violence nobody else would come, and so I learned. Had there been no violence and turmoil, I would not have said yes.

In many ways I was an unlikely candidate. I had been trained as an internist. I *had* spent a year in East Africa doing the most harrowing and complicated obstetrics and pediatrics. For example, I sewed up a ruptured uterus in a hospital where no blood was available, and I did curettage on women who were hemorrhaging and who had friable and disfigured genitalia from gonorrhea and female circumcision. I was, however, naively unable to translate my work in East Africa into a response to similar need in the United States.

Nevertheless, I agreed to learn. I asked Dr. Dennis Christensen to teach me to do abortions. He agreed and, when I confessed that I was an internist, did not hold it against me. (I subsequently learned that many incoming abortion providers are not gynecologists, and that the incidence of abortion-related complications is decreasing. This is an association. Despite the temptation, I make no claims to cause and effect.) I trained to our mutual satisfaction, and then went to Appleton—the hometown of the infamous Senator Joe McCarthy. The idea of doing abortions in the hometown of this evil man gave me the push I needed to overcome my fears. (That Appleton is also the hometown of one Erik Weisz, a.k.a. Houdini, did not enter into my decision.)

In 1990 I thought of myself as an aware feminist. But when I arrived at the clinic in Appleton that first day, I realized how ignorant and naive I was. The anti-abortion forces had bought the house next door, and out-of-tune hymns blasted me as I was buzzed through the locked clinic door. I entered a waiting room full of silent, despairing women. They looked poor. They looked young. They looked at the end of their tether. It hit me suddenly that in my internal medicine practice in Madison, my client population was the middle-aged insured, with access to health care. In abortion practice I saw those outside the American medical system but at the beginning of their adult lives. After one day of working in Appleton, I knew that this was my work. I wanted to do abortions, and I wanted to make the practice of abortion a model of women's health care—an art form.

After finishing my stint in Appleton, I decided to leave my practice of internal medicine to specialize in abortion. It was my good luck that at the same time a Madison physician who had been providing abortions for fifteen years decided to retire because of his own declining health and in response to increasing protests. This physician did not identify himself as an abortion provider in the phone book; although he was known among a few physicians as a provider, I did not know that he was. When I realized that my patients did not feel free to tell me about their abortions, I was hurt and began to understand the great secret that abortion remains.

When this physician learned about my desire to enter abortion practice, he invited me to visit his office. The basement office (handy for its inaccessible street-side windows) was a shock. Half the waiting room was carpeted in green plaid, the other half red plaid. The burgundy couch and purple and orange chairs hugged the walls. Calendar kittens were hung high on the walls. Through the doors to the examination and procedure rooms, the green carpet matched the olive, gold, and orange cabinets pretty well. The decor couldn't have helped the patients' nausea. Yet the staff who worked with him, and who kindly agreed to continue with me, were deeply warm, kind, and professional. They still are. When the doctor proudly asked me, "Well, what do you think of the office?" I said, "The carpets have got to go!" With that, the staff and I knew we could work together.

MAKING IT OKAY

He comes early to stand outside my office, well before the first patient arrives.[7] He always dresses the same—fatigue coat in the spring and fall, black coat in the winter. He carries no sign. He walks back and forth deliberately, when he is alone, looking around, sometimes praying. He scares me. If there are pro-choice female escorts, he notices their legs, the length of their skirts. He talks about what they do sexually, how they "stick their knees in each other's vagina [sic!]." He does not approach patients if they are with a man, or if they look strong. If they are alone and scared, however, he comes up to them with a quiet, understanding voice and says, "Please. I can help you. I just need you to listen to me for a minute." She looks around to see if anyone is watching, maybe someone will help her. There is no one. She approaches him. "Don't kill your baby. You don't know what it's like in there. You don't know what they will do to you. You'll never have children. Never." She starts to cry and back away. He gets louder. "Don't kill your baby! I have your license number. I'll find you." Now she knows that something bad has happened. She feels invaded and dirty. It isn't the first time. She rushes into the office, scared and crying hard. She gets some tissues and takes some time to recover. By the time she enters the counselor's office, she is really angry. "You really should do something about that guy out there," she orders.

The receptionist, a great-grandmother who has been working in abortion-providing offices since 1971, first tries to dispel some of the woman's fear and anger. She tries to make the patient feel safe. The counselor then goes about the difficult job of preparing the woman for an abortion. The counselor begins, "You may not believe us, since that guy out there oozes charm out of every pore, but we didn't invite him here." "You could still get rid of him." "Well," says our counselor, "I'll tell it the way I see it. I take my life in my hands coming in here. I make sure I am up-to-date on birth control information. We go to conferences to learn the latest about the procedure. I trust this doctor to take care of you. I have enough to do. You will have to find someone else to sweep the sidewalks." Finally, a smile and a beginning. I have to get rid of my anger before I talk to her or touch her. (I don't know if I'm angrier at the protester or her, and then I think I'm not a real feminist, wanting to take it out on the patient, who is all too used to feeling shame.) We talk about her life, and what she will do for birth control. I perform the procedure and reinforce her need for good birth control. I want her to leave the office feeling a lot more peaceful than when she came in. She does.

I was determined to remake the office so that it looked like we cared. In fact, it was a challenge and a joy to design a warm space for women who expect to be treated poorly. It couldn't look cheap or thrown together. It couldn't look overdesigned. I wanted the office decor to be undramatic but pretty and comfortable. There is so much going on when a woman comes for an abortion that the surroundings shouldn't be intrusive. For months I painted swatches in the far hall to find just the rosy buff color that disappears into the walls. I brought artwork from home. I called a seventy-eight-year-old former patient who is a photographer and purchased her exquisite color photographs of nature for the waiting room. We arranged the couches so that people can avoid each other when they want to. I stocked entertainment videos for the TV. *Thelma and Louise* was the only video that disappeared—spirited away by an ardent admiring patient or a disgruntled boyfriend, I'll never know. I hung pictures on the wall next to shamelessly feminist propaganda and poetry. The setting isn't a good one for plants, but a huge peace plant from my mother celebrating our opening is flourishing six years later in the waiting room. We keep aromatic vases of eucalyptus leaves so that the office does not have the scary smell of the dentists' offices around me. When women lie down on the exam table, they look up at bird mobiles, not fluorescent lights. We wear uniforms, however, to affirm our role in mainstream medicine. Other practices choose casual clothes, to disassociate themselves from authoritarian medicine. In all of these design and environmental decisions, we've aimed to welcome, to soothe, and to affirm our respect for the patients.

We applied the same care to our choice of background music and found this more difficult than arranging furniture. We went through many kinds of music: jazz, country, rap, soft and sappy. I originally piped in classical music, but even my favorite, the Bach Unaccompanied Cello Concertos, palled pretty quickly. I realized I couldn't use anyone's favorite music; who wants *that* played during their abortion? After some months, we settled on nature sounds with only a hint of new-age music in the background—just enough for the patients to know that the birds aren't stuck in the vents, and the gurgling brook is neither broken pipes nor the toilet running over. We have been listening to the same CDs for five years, and they are still a comfort to us. After all, we have to relax and breathe to offer good services too.

Even before I saw my first abortion patient, I felt the emotional climate of the office. The incredibly lovely staff I acquired (along with the awful furniture) brought a peace and professionalism to a fearful procedure. When I decided to do abortions, one of my first tasks was to make sure I had an outstanding counselor. I wanted someone who could do cut-to-the-quick therapy and offer a medical perspective. The person I had in mind was a nurse I had worked with for years—someone who really loved to laugh. She was a specialist in alcohol and drug rehabilitation, an expertise we knew we needed. Now a grandmother, she was a Catholic mother of nine who took in foster children with her own family. When a patient was in her room crying uncontrollably, she asked, "Why are you crying so hard?" "I'm Catholic," answered the patient. "Oh, honey, that's a good reason to cry. I'm Catholic, too." She taught us about substance abuse, so that we could bring this knowledge to our patients and affected family members. It was hard but enlightening working with a part-time saint. We saw her vulnerabilities. The protesters targeted her and her family harder than me. They knew they could hurt her, not only because of her Catholicism but also because she had a child and a grandchild living with her. They made her life a living hell, surrounding her home many times a week, calling her name as she walked into the office, stalking her. She never wavered.

She died after three years with us, from a cancer she probably had when she came. The protesters, of course, accused us of causing her death through our sins. Our present counselor was also brought up Catholic and can relate to our many Catholic patients, but she is remarkably different. She is a genius at discerning active problems and discussing the difficult issues of sex, substance abuse, violence, and incest in the crisis counseling time. I often hear laughter behind her closed door. "How are you?" she asks, ushering the patient into her room. "Fine," lies the patient. "Oh, I suppose you've had one or two better days in your life," the counselor suggests. A smile. Another beginning. Most of our patients are relatively at ease by the time I see them. There is more laughter in our office than most.

One of our goals for the counseling session is to learn enough about the woman for us to make the procedure as comfortable as possible, and to learn enough about her life to find out what failed—that is, what created her need for an abortion in the first place—and help correct it. We are continually working on a counseling form, which includes questions on sexual history, contraception history (most of our patients are not using contraception when they get pregnant), social history (including parental alcohol use), and incest and other abuse history. We ask only questions we have the time and ability to address.[8]

We calm incest survivors and women who have been otherwise abused when we understand that they might find a pelvic exam and instrumentation frightening. We soothingly explain that this is not weakness but a realistic reaction to terrible things that have happened in the past. I never do a pelvic exam without having met and spoken to our patient when she was upright and dressed. The jelly and instruments are warmed on an ancient wedding-present hot plate. Our patients remark that we are different from other doctors who become impatient and yell, "*Just relax!*" when they stiffen during pelvic exams. For the most affected, those who are used to dissociating, the simple request to stay in the room and not dissociate often helps the procedure go easily. And if a patient stiffens and starts to writhe or say, "No!" I stop the procedure, have her sit up, cover her up, and start talking to her again. Face to face. Usually, she insists on "getting it over with," but I insist on finding out what the block was about. Then the procedure goes uneventfully. Once every few months a patient may decide that today is not the right day for the procedure and ask to leave, or we decide she is not ready. Almost all return another day for a relaxed and altogether different procedure. A woman should not have to be on the abortion table to learn that being frightened during pelvic instrumentation is not her fault. Many patients leave our office having learned that they have much more control over their reactions than they ever thought—a benefit of having had the abortion.

And when we are frightened, receive death threats, have loud scary protests, or have patients who are so fragile we are afraid for them, what do we do? We know that the potential for complications during the procedure is higher, because both the patient and the physician are more nervous. First, we admit our rage and fear. Second, we take more time, talking and laughing together. We are all very good at laughter. If the patients have been affected, we do this together. Third, we eat a lot of chocolate.

It is very important to me to know that I am not alone doing abortions. Many people have asked, "How can you do this in the face of so much hatred?" It's easy. Patients stop for a hug on the way home. Women stop me in the supermarket and, with tears in their eyes, thank me for what I do. Last week in the beauty parlor a woman jumped up from her chair, cut hair flying from the plastic smock, to thank me. Many patients choose to come to me as their regular physician, since they feel most comfortable in our office. And I know, even being hated, that I'm in good company. I recently heard folk singer Oscar Brand on the radio, talking about the McCarthy years. He said, "Well, you know there's a whole country hating your guts out there!" If I'm with my 1950s folk heroes, I'm in good company.

I am an abortion practitioner because of my utmost respect for motherhood, which I refuse to believe is punishment for a screw. I do what I do because I am convinced that being a mother is the hardest job there is. Women know they have to gather their strengths if they choose to become mothers. Even more than performing a religious ritual, being a mother requires precise abilities, arrangements, resources, and a community of support. Motherhood, then, is the true sacrament, and helping make it so is the essence of my work.

WHAT ABOUT THE FUTURE?

My great joy now is going to medical schools and teaching first- and second-year medical students what I have just told you—why and how I do abortions. I rarely teach third- or fourth-year students because most have already been made suspicious and stodgy by an abusive system. I have been invited to all parts of the country by medical students, not by medical schools, and have been honored to watch the birth and development of an amazingly strong grassroots political-medical organization—Medical Students for Choice. Over three thousand medical students have signed petitions asking their schools to teach more about abortion. In cases where the school doesn't oblige them quickly enough, I show up with video, latex pelvis model, and good cheer. I love to teach these incredible people, younger than my children. So I can tell you that there is more than hope. There is a new generation—smarter, better educated, more savvy, more fun, and more involved than we are—ready to take care of you and your daughters and granddaughters. I think we will be all right.

NOTES

1. See Rickie Solinger, *The Abortionist* (New York: Free Press, 1994), especially chapters 7 and 8, for sexual descriptions of abortion facilities in both the media and trials of the 1950s. For example, "Describe for us, Ann, how you were positioned on the doctor's table? Were your legs raised and your knees spread wide apart?" This woman had been brutally raped by her cousin, but the trial did not investigate or prosecute the rapist. The sexual crime had to be the abortion (200–201).

2. For a more sympathetic view of physicians' response to women's health requests, see Judith Walzer Leavitt, *Brought to Bed: Childbearing in America, 1750–1950* (New York: Oxford University Press, 1986).

3. "Prior to the formation of the American Medical Association in 1847, opposition to abortion was scattered and largely ineffective. . . . Once the AMA came to speak for a large part of the 'respectable' medical community, it became a force capable of controlling abortion policy in the United States. (The AMA was steadfastly committed to outlawing the 'irregulars' and the pharmacists while saving the 'therapeutic exception' for themselves. . . . In 1869 Bishop Spaulding of Baltimore set forth what was to remain the official Catholic position for the next hundred years: 'No mother is allowed, under any circumstances, to permit the death of her unborn infant, not even for the sake of preserving her own life' " (Patricia Miller, *The Worst of Times* [New York: Harper Perennial, 1993], 314).

The 1873 Act for the Suppression of Trade in and Circulation of Obscene Literature and Articles for Immoral Use, pushed by Anthony Comstock, effectively outlawed contraception at the same time (ibid., 315).

4. Carole Joffe, *Doctors of Conscience: The Struggle to Provide Abortion before and after Roe v. Wade* (Boston: Beacon Press, 1995), 46.

5. Ibid., 47.

6. Interestingly, from the time I started doing abortions in 1990, none of our friends in the legislature have asked me to testify. We are seen as a danger by our friends, too.

7. He is a composite of separate abortion protesters in separate cities. The description is accurate, however.

8. We are constantly reevaluating and changing our counseling form. It is presently undergoing another metamorphosis. We would like to know more about parental sexual attitudes, since so many of our patients get pregnant at the same age as their mothers. Our present working form is available on request.

13

■■■

Jane E. Hodgson

THE TWENTIETH-CENTURY GENDER BATTLE

Difficulties in Perception

We live life forward;
we comprehend it backward.

Anonymous

How much sexual discrimination was there in the first half of the twentieth century? Was I disadvantaged because of my gender? Have I been aware of sexism throughout my medical career?

In June 1993 Dr. Frances K. Conley, a neurosurgeon on the Stanford Medical School faculty, resigned from her tenured position because of sexual harassment and discrimination over a twenty-five-year period. Even though she later withdrew her resignation after concessions from the administration, her action touched off a national debate on the subject of sexism. Coming on the heels of the hearings for the appointment of Clarence Thomas to the U.S. Supreme Court, Conley's revelations outraged many people and received media attention. The consciousness level of American society has been raised to new heights in regard to the injustice of sexism, and thankfully, some things will never be the same.

It is difficult to recognize social changes while living in the midst of them. No one ever spoke of sexual harassment or discrimination in my youth. The word *feminist* was not in our vocabulary, and the term *sexual harassment* was first used in a legal case in 1976. It did not come into popular usage until the mid-1980s.

I was slow to perceive the abortion struggle as a gender battle over reproductive control. Rather, in 1945, when I began the practice of obstetrics and gynecology, I accepted the restrictive abortion laws as something inevitable, probably necessary to protect the "sanctity of life." I had been carefully taught that invasion of a pregnant uterus was extremely dangerous as well as immoral. Every textbook said so. Even though I might question this principle, I never believed that abortion laws would change in my lifetime. A model of social and professional conformity, I had never, during the first half of my life, espoused a cause, broken a law, or even indulged in politics.

But frustration over Minnesota's archaic abortion law and its effect on women's health finally drove me to an act of civil disobedience in 1970, after several years of legislative testimony and numerous editorials had proved of no avail. I performed an abortion and became a convicted felon until I was rescued by *Roe v. Wade* in 1973. One week following the Supreme Court's decision, my conviction was overturned, and Minnesota's abortion law was repealed.

My purpose in struggling against the Minnesota abortion law was simply to provide better health care for women. I had no interest in the nascent gender war against the male medical and religious hierarchy; I even feared it might become a handicap if our voices were too strident. When asked to explain the absence of male medical leadership in the new pro-choice cause, I naively defended the male doctors. In early 1970 I wrote that the apparent indifference, even opposition, of my male colleagues to abortion law reform arose not from a lack of caring for patients, but from other reasons, such as inadequate exposure to problem pregnancies and a rigid training to preserve life at all costs. I believed that once they were fully informed, few male physicians would disregard their moral obligation to provide the best possible health care to a patient, or to at least refer her elsewhere.

Today, no one can rationally argue that legalized abortion does not result in better health care for women. All the statistics prove it. But admittedly, my defense in 1970 of the male medical establishment for its apparent indifference to the pro-choice cause now seems weak, and probably naive. But let me start at the beginning.

BORN INTO A SOCIAL REVOLUTION

I was born in 1915, the younger of two girls. My father was a family physician, dedicated and humble; my spirited, independent mother had been a schoolteacher. Certainly I felt no sexual discrimination in such a predominantly female family. I recall overhearing remarks to the effect that my father probably would have favored a son over a second daughter. If he felt that way, he never showed it. Instead, he taught me how to fish, shoot a gun, drive a car, and tramp the woods. As a hunting and fishing partner, he preferred my company to that of his older buddies—or so, at least, he made me feel.

At an early age I accompanied Dad on house calls and hospital rounds. As the county physician, he frequently visited the jail to care for the prisoners or town prostitutes. His concern for their plight was apparent to me as a child, and I came to share his attitude. During his days in surgery, I even worried about whether the operations would go well. But there was never any mention of my becoming a doctor. I had no female role models in medicine other than nurses, and I doubt that Dad ever entertained any thoughts of a medical career for me. Certainly I didn't at the time.

The only times I incurred my father's disapproval were because of late-night parties, especially ones with dancing. Local travel during sub-zero winters in northern Minnesota was accomplished almost entirely by foot, as automobiles were scarce and usually frozen. I still recall my extreme mortification when I would spot him trudging through the snow to meet me, *and my date,* if we were late (according to his standards).

The importance of scholastic achievement was never emphasized; instead, I was repeatedly warned against studying too hard, as "good health is more important than good grades—B's are fine." I happily complied with that directive, but because of a then-popular trend toward accelerated education, I found myself pushed ahead by enthusiastic teachers to graduate from high school shortly after my fifteenth birthday.

So the first fifteen years of my life left me self-confident and imbued with the feeling that being female was no handicap whatsoever in any endeavor I should care to undertake. I was unaware that my mother and other women had only obtained the right to vote when I was four years of age. I was unaware that she could not sign a contract or establish credit at a store without her husband's signature, and that job opportunities for women were few indeed except for teaching school. It didn't occur to me that school superintendents were always men, women's wage scales pitiful, child labor and compulsory education laws inadequate. I would learn later that I had been born into a social revolution. The first victory had been women's winning the vote.

I REMAIN UNAWARE

Because of my relative youth, Mother wanted me to attend a women's college. I preferred coeducation and finally won my father to my side with the argument that the scholastic standards would be higher at a coed school. One of my few recollections of sexual discrimination at Carleton College was the 7:30 P.M. nightly curfew (10:00 P.M. on Saturdays) for freshman women, while men had none. Smoking resulted in prompt expulsion for women, while men smoked with few restrictions. No career counseling was offered to women, the majority of whom accepted marriage as their major role after college. Those women remaining single usually earned teacher's certificates or took up social work. The men went on to professional schools, usually law or medicine. I was intrigued when I met a woman physician for the first time. She was employed at the college health service; her physician director was male, of course, as were all other department heads.

Strangely enough, I accepted these differences without questioning their fairness. It was the world into which I had been born. I majored in mathematics and chemistry simply because I liked those fields, while unconsciously fulfilling the requirements for medical school. Realizing in my senior year that I would have to acquire a teaching certificate if I wanted a job after graduation (marriage seemed like the end of everything), I took the dull but necessary education courses required for a certificate to teach high school.

But the year was 1934, the depth of the Depression. There was a surplus of unemployed teachers, and men were preferred for the science slots. Wearing a hat and white gloves, I rode the train to many small Minnesota towns, applying for almost any vacant position. The typical job included not only teaching high school chemistry, mathematics, and physics, but glee club, orchestra, and debating as well. My heart wasn't in it, and only one school board was willing to take a chance on a nineteen-year-old female—even for $75 a month. Prevailing opinion was that preference should be given to men with families. Because I had supportive parents at home, I never questioned the justice of this concept, not stopping to think of other women who might need a job as desperately as a man.

Thus my teaching career was short-lived, and I moved to Chicago, almost one thousand miles from home, working for $85 a month as a secretary for a large drug company (Winthrop Chemical). My boss, Dr. Hebert, was a physician in charge of the research in the pharmaceutical division, and his wife was a physician-turned-housewife. A gentle, kindly man, Dr. Hebert was very tolerant of an inexperienced secretary who faked her shorthand and was trying to learn to type at night school. Like the other secretaries, I made the usual coffee and stayed at the lower end of the company's wage scale, but if there was other sexual discrimination here, I was oblivious to it. In less than one year I had absorbed most of the company's pharmaceutical literature and had decided to apply to medical school. My boss encouraged me and wrote letters of recommendation for my admission to medical school, and years later, more letters to help me obtain postgraduate training.

On the whole, my first job experience, while lonely, was characterized by little sexual harassment or discrimination. As a middle-class white woman, I belonged to the privileged few who escaped to professional school. I was still nurtured and protected by circumstances from perceiving the harsh realities of sexism, racism, and classism. Later, my patients would reeducate me.

My father never questioned my new career decision, and he assumed he should provide financial support, although he was at retirement age and far from wealthy. My mother, however, was somewhat dubious. She foresaw a future for me that she liked to depict gloomily as "smelling of antiseptics and having to wear low-heeled oxfords." But in spite of her pessimism, I felt she was secretly proud of her physician daughter, for whom she regularly provided medical advice until her death at age eighty-seven, long after I had completed a fellowship at the Mayo Clinic.

A FIRST GLIMPSE AT THE GLASS CEILING

Following my application to Northwestern University School of Medicine, I received a polite reply from the admissions office to the effect that their quota of four women, four Jews, and four blacks had already been filled. I have often wished I had saved that letter. But neither dismayed nor surprised, I applied to the University of Minnesota and was promptly accepted—one of eight women in a class of one hundred fifty, an unusually high percentage of women for 1935.

Northwestern's quota system was an example of how the establishment controlled access to power. Such a quota system was not uncommon then. I was to learn eventually that the higher one climbed the ladder, whether social, economic, or academic, the more the establishment felt threatened, and the more often the ugly *isms* appeared: racism, sexism, classism. It was my first glimpse of the glass ceiling.

Four hardworking but wonderful years followed. We eight women students protected and nurtured one another, both literally and figuratively, sharing our funds and our lunches with anyone in the group who was unable to come up with her quarterly tuition payment. I was so happy to be in medical school—in fact, we all were—that we ignored the occasional sexual joke or put-down, accepting mild harassment as something we could never change. We knew and accepted that one professor was reputed to have never given a woman student a grade higher than C. This was a male world we inhabited, without any evidence of female authority. I can recall no woman professor, teacher, or even laboratory assistant throughout our four years, from 1935 to 1939. There was no mention of contraceptives, and female sterilizations, we were told, were rarely performed and required the husband's permission. Induced abortion was mentioned only to be condemned for both moral and medical reasons.

Even sixty years later there are few women who chair medical school departments in this country. While women medical students are conspicuous in the classroom, comprising 50 percent or more of the students in several medical schools, women faculty are still in the minority.

Little wonder that we women students realized intuitively that we would have to work a little harder than the men if we wanted a desirable internship or residency after medical school. Sensing that specialization in medicine was becoming increasingly important, I had abandoned the idea of becoming a general practitioner. But at that time there were relatively few accredited residencies in any of the specialties and competition was very keen. Therefore, before leaving Minnesota in 1939 for New Jersey (where I had a rotating internship at Jersey City Medical Center), I had applied, and was accepted for, a future Mayo Graduate School residency in internal medicine, to begin in July 1941. So I left Minnesota with a sense of security, knowing I would have a stimulating three years of training upon my return. If Dad had held any expectations that I would return home to work with him, he never expressed it. He proffered no advice—just encouragement and financial aid, without obligation.

SURVIVAL IN A POLITICAL MACHINE

Jersey City Medical Center had been my first choice for an internship. A huge modern medical facility, it provided free medical care on demand to each and every one of Mayor Hague's constituents. That it served as a political machine for a big-city boss was of little concern to me. I simply sought the diversity of clinical experience offered by a large metropolitan hospital in an area distant from the academia of the University of Minnesota and the Mayo Graduate School of Medicine. This 800-bed institution included a large emergency room and six ambulances in constant twenty-four-hour service. The new Margaret Hague Maternity Center, named after Mayor Hague's wife, was an impressive part of the complex.

Women interns were quartered in small single rooms, originally intended for patients, on the twentieth floor of a hospital wing. The male interns had the luxury of small apartments separated from the hospital. Their building also housed the medical director and some of the permanent unmarried staff—all male, of course—as well as a large dining room for the hundred or more interns, residents, and staff physicians.

It was necessary for the women interns to walk outside for two blocks to reach this dining room, which was the only place where food was available. Strangely, the women were assigned to special tables, segregated from the men. I found this rule applied even after I married Frank, another intern: we were forced to limit our mealtime socializing to waving across the large dining room. It didn't matter if it was a holiday or a day off.

Our indoctrination into the tough politico-medical system was necessarily rapid. Any complaints or suggestions were to no avail. We knew that our intern appointments were highly sought after by medical students. The medical director, Dr. George O'Hanlon, often reminded us that it was far easier to replace an intern than it was to hire an elevator operator, and we believed him. We received no salary for our services, just room, board, laundry, and uniforms. Because accredited internships were few and hard to get in 1939, no one complained.

My memories of Jersey City are hazy, probably because of the chronic fatigue from overwork, as well as financial worries, which characterized that period. Frank and I got married six months into our internships. I had known and seriously considered marrying several men before in my life, but the feeling that marriage would be a handicap to my medical career had always restrained me. But this young intern from the University of South Georgia was different from the others. I took my chances with him because not only did he possess all the virtues I considered important, as well as a smooth south Georgia accent, but he also convinced me that he valued my medical career as much as his own. Our partnership has lasted happily for over fifty years. Needless to add, he is a true feminist.

The hospital had no living arrangements for married couples, so Frank and I remained in our separate dormitories. A rented apartment was a financial impossibility, and we were on call most of the time anyway. The little money we spent was borrowed, as neither of us accepted financial help from home. My original wardrobe had to last throughout my five years of training, with the exception of silk stockings. (Women interns had to wear stockings with uniform jackets and skirts—no pants were allowed.) So I was obliged to replace my stocking supply, and every run in my sock caused a major financial crisis. Except for the joys of learning and working with patients, life was on the grim side. Constantly surrounded by dirty tenements, we longed for even a city park, but none was available. A nickel ferry ride served as a meager source of recreation.

Some of my most enduring memories of Jersey City concern the jovial (but armed) Irish policemen who drove the ambulances. Chivalrous and protective, one was always at my side, trudging up tenement stairs with me, accompanying me to the waterfront and the red-light districts, where I stumbled on accidents, suicides, homicides, and other crimes. For someone as inexperienced as I was, the cops' advice and help were invaluable. They taught a very green intern about the diagnosis and treatment of acute asthma, heart attacks, diabetic coma, epilepsy, and shock. I still possess the brass buttons from a Jersey City policeman's uniform—a parting gift.

In midwinter, after three hard months of ambulance service, I contracted a strep throat, which developed into a peritonsillar abscess. The only antibiotic in use in 1940 was sulfanilamide, and it was not very effective. Eventually I underwent hospitalization and surgery, but fortunately I recovered with no permanent damage.

What I experienced during my two years at Jersey City was more exploitation than sexism. Except for their superior living quarters, the male interns were exploited as much as the women. The pay men and women received was exactly the same—room, board, laundry, and uniforms.

The threat of war during our second year at Jersey City probably improved the status of female doctors, none of whom could be drafted. The sudden depletion of male physicians made it possible for me to obtain a job at a small private hospital in Summit, New Jersey, as resident physician for $100 a month. I enjoyed a little financial security, and the work seemed relatively easy in contrast to that at the medical center.

RESIDENCY AND WAR YEARS

In June 1941 we packed our few belongings into an secondhand 1936 Chevy, purchased for $200 with my earnings from Summit, and we headed for the Midwest. I went to Rochester, Minnesota, to begin my fellowship at the Mayo Clinic, while Frank, temporarily deferred from military service, continued his surgical training at the University of Minnesota in Minneapolis. Separated by ninety miles, we managed to find enough gas ration coupons to meet on rare weekends. I received the magnificent salary of $85 a month, Frank earned $50 at the university, and we were each expected to provide our own board and room.

My first assignment was to perform initial history-taking and examinations on new patients on one of the general medical floors devoted to women. The dress code prohibited wearing hospital uniforms outside the hospitals. When working in the clinic buildings, residents were expected to wear street clothes. The temperature that July was over ninety degrees, and air-conditioning, if any, was primitive indeed. I worried about what to wear, as the only lightweight clothing I owned were the hospital "whites" I'd lived in for the past two years. I finally found a wrinkle-proof, rust-colored, linen-rayon-mixture suit for $8.95. It apparently passed inspection, and I wore that suit so long that fifty years later I can still see every detail of it in my mind.

During our second summer in Minnesota, Frank was finally able to transfer from the university to Rochester to continue his surgical residency at the Mayo Clinic. After two and one-half years of separate quarters, we rented our first apartment together.

The first successful women doctors to serve as real role models for me were two women on the staff of the department of obstetrics and gynecology. They were excellent teachers, clinicians, and researchers, and they became my mentors of a sort. At the beginning of my second year at Mayo, the administration suggested I might like to change my specialty from internal medicine to obstetrics and gynecology. I readily accepted this option, and never regretted doing so. I firmly believe that this specialty is distinctly advantageous for women.

The small prairie town of Rochester was truly isolated during the war years. The war seemed far away and affected us very little. Excellent teaching conferences and libraries, along with congenial and stimulating people, made for a peaceful environment in which to work and study.

Even after Pearl Harbor, the Mayo Clinic obtained draft deferments enabling most of the male residents to complete their medical training. Frank's deferment expired in July 1944, and he left for training at Carlisle Barracks, Pennsylvania. I remained behind only long enough to complete a master's thesis.

At Mayo the men did not seem to have special privileges; we all performed the same work. That women physicians were greatly outnumbered was perceived not as being discriminatory but rather as reflecting the smaller number of qualified female applicants. That all the department chairs, as well as the governing board members, were male caused little comment, although I suspect that more assertive women physicians probably left in later years because of the lack of female leadership. The only inequity of which I was aware was a difference in the salaries of young staff members, depending on marital status, whether the wife worked, and number of dependents. As the typical female staff doctor was single during those war years, her salary was lower than that of the average male. At the resident level, however, the stipends were equal.

A REEDUCATION

My entrance into private practice in 1945 marked the beginning of my real medical education. At that time my perception of sexual harassment or discrimination was about as limited as that demonstrated by the Senate Judiciary Committee at the Clarence Thomas hearings. As an obstetrician/gynecologist I began to listen to thousands of stories from patients, many of whom were poor, handicapped, or nonwhite. I heard tales of sexual abuse and of physical and financial hardship. I learned about the many tragedies associated with unplanned pregnancies, sexual discrimination and harassment, child abuse, incest, the inequities of the divorce laws. I was reeducated by the pregnant teen-ager, the single welfare mother, the cancer patient, the drug addict, the menopausal mother.

I also served on six tours of foreign duty for Project Hope, a volun-teer medical organization that provides health care and medical educa-tion around the world. Working in third-world countries, I came to realize how women are disproportionately represented among the poor, illiterate, and unemployed, and how their status is directly related to their ability to control their reproduction. I was reeducated to perceive a reality from which I myself had been sheltered by circumstance, and by 1965 I had become a strong activist for reproductive rights for all women. My level of sensitivity to women's health problems rose. I knew intuitively when my warnings of the dangers of illegal abortion would go unheeded, and the frantic patient would leave, to return later with serious complications. I believed this to be horrible health care, totally inconsistent with the principles I had been taught in public health class in medical school. I had become convinced that abortion must be a safe, humane procedure, rather than a felony.

The sexism of the health care system had finally become very clear.

BATTLING LEGALIZED SEXISM

Written in 1851, at a time when it was illegal to give an anesthetic or a smallpox vaccination, Minnesota's abortion law (M.S. 617.18) was one of the harshest in the country. Both physician and patient were liable to imprisonment for two to four years if found guilty of involvement in an abortion for *any reason other than to save the life of the mother.* Encouraged by the relaxation of abortion laws in a handful of states (Colorado, Georgia, Maryland, California, and New York), and unable to persuade the Minnesota legislature to initiate any type of legislative reform, I naively hoped that a test case might illustrate the cruelty of the abortion law and result in a declaratory judgment as to its unconsti-tutionality. On April 16, 1970, I petitioned a three-judge federal court for a declaratory judgment that Minnesota's abortion law was unconsti-tutional, and asked for permission to perform an abortion on a twenty-four-year-old homemaker, mother of three children, then ten weeks pregnant. She gave a documented history of having contracted German measles during the fourth week of her pregnancy, and she feared the possibility of congenital defects. I requested an early decision from the court in order to avoid doing a procedure any later than twelve weeks. When two weeks had passed without any decision from the court, I performed the procedure openly in the hospital, with consultation from five medical authorities as to the advisability of the surgery. The following day the federal court voted 2–1 against granting jurisdiction, stating that I was in no jeopardy. But indictment from the state court followed the next day, so I returned to federal court, where I was again refused help, 2–1, because the case was now under the jurisdiction of the state district court. Arraignment, trial, and conviction followed in September. My sentence was thirty days in the county jail, one year probation, with sentence suspended pending my appeal to the Minnesota Supreme Court. If my conviction were to be upheld by the Minnesota Supreme Court, my medical license would be in jeopardy.

Polarization of the public and the medical world followed. I was condemned by some of my colleagues and praised by others. I lost some friends but made many new ones.

It would be two and one-half years before the Minnesota Supreme Court handed down a decision. Weary of working in a state of limbo, I left my medical practice and family in early 1972 to assume the medical directorship of an innovative, freestanding abortion clinic—Preterm Clinic in Washington, D.C. Performing 1,500 abortions a month, we became the largest abortion clinic on the East Coast, outside of New York City. I realized the importance of establishing a safety record for the new technique of performing suction abortions under local anesthesia instead of using the formal operating-room procedures under general anesthesia with which most physicians were familiar. Therefore, we strove to maintain careful records, to publish our results, and to teach.

Our goal was to provide safe, low-cost ($125), humane abortion and contraception services, along with one-to-one counseling of the patient. Situated just a few blocks from the White House, we were regularly asked to demonstrate the procedure for foreign visitors referred from the State Department, such as British and African physicians, psychologists, and counselors. Even the anthropologist Margaret Mead spent two days looking over my shoulder.

Those were heady but frightening years from 1971 to 1973, working in a gray area, both medically and legally. The safety of a new type of delivery of medical care had to be established. We were uncertain what degree or type of complications we might encounter. One safeguard for emergencies was the installation of a shiny new ambulance in the

basement of the old Medical Arts Building, where we occupied the entire second floor (along with Trisha and Julie Nixon's dentist). Fortunately, the ambulance was never needed.

On January 22, 1973, women won a tremendous and unexpected
victory. The United States Supreme Court announced its *Roe v. Wade*
decision, which legalized abortion throughout the country. For me, it
was an especially welcome decision, for one week later the Minnesota
Supreme Court reversed my conviction. More generally, the necessity
for legal uniformity had become very obvious to me, as I witnessed the
confused and guilt-ridden patients arriving at our Washington clinic
from states with varying laws.

DEFENDING *ROE* AND FIGHTING FOR
ITS IMPLEMENTATION

After abortion suddenly became legal, maternal and infant mortality
rates promptly declined. But anti-abortion forces formed coalitions,
pressed for restrictive laws, began to politicize. Organized medicine re-
acted with a surprising lack of enthusiasm, and it was obvious that
many male physicians disliked having to relinquish their traditional role
as decision makers. Doctors debated the proper place for abortions to
be performed—in hospitals, offices, or freestanding clinics. Abortion
clinics rapidly multiplied throughout the country, as hospital boards
voted to close their doors to the newly legalized procedure.

By 1980 the number of abortions performed each year stabilized at
around 1.6 million. Women were now better able to control their destinies and their reproductive lives, to carve their own careers, develop
their talents, obtain higher education, perform their own home pregnancy tests, use effective contraception, and obtain an abortion or sterilization. True equality for women seemed almost at hand.

But the victories of the 1970s, when the courts defended *Roe v.
Wade,* began to fade during the 1980s, chiefly because of the lack of
support from a pro-natalist government. With the Reagan and Bush
administrations in control in the 1980s, a gradual setback occurred in
the field of reproductive health care. By the end of the decade, over 50
percent of the federal judges had been replaced by conservative Reagan
or Bush appointees. Hundreds of restrictive abortion laws were introduced by state legislators. Denial of reproductive rights to women, as
manifested by the refusal to introduce RU 486 into this country, the

decreasing accessibility of contraceptives and abortion services, denial of abortion funding for welfare women, and the insulting gag rule were all examples of the worst type of sexual harassment. Women felt propelled to organize and to enter politics and professions in rapidly increasing numbers. Ironically, the medical profession remained so engrossed in health care reform and economic issues that its members ignored the fact that reproductive health care was inaccessible to one-third of the women in our country.

As the Clarence Thomas hearings unfolded in October 1991, we watched the struggle over abortion rights change into a battle over sexual harassment. And the biggest stumbling block to peace and harmony between the two sexes was a difference in perception. Nowhere has this difference been more aptly illustrated than by the Senate Judiciary Committee, which seemed so helpless in evaluating women's problems with sexual harassment in the workplace. They just didn't get it! Why didn't Anita Hill report the harassment sooner? Why didn't she document it in writing? Why should she continue to maintain a cordial relationship with Clarence Thomas?

I was reminded of the fact that for the previous twenty-five years we had tried to explain the difficulties that women face with a problem pregnancy, particularly teenagers, but very few men seemed capable of genuine empathy. Even the questions were similar: Didn't she know she was pregnant? Why did she wait so long? Why did she get pregnant? Why didn't she use contraception? Why not just say "no"?

To me, the most appalling and significant affront toward women by the Senate Judiciary Committee was its ignoring the possibility that a black woman's accusations could be true, as well as its attempts to discredit Anita Hill in order to save the nomination of Clarence Thomas. The old boys' club was truly shaken by this accurate depiction of sexual harassment in the workplace of America for what it truly is—an assertion of power and the desire to control by making women vulnerable.

The long-standing debate over the issue of abortion in the United States continued to escalate. The peaceful picketing of the early 1980s developed into a war of angry epithets and inflammatory rhetoric. By the end of 1994 the casualties for a six-month period totaled five murders and six woundings, along with numerous clinic bombings and death threats to doctors in particular. Abortion clinics, which had been legal for almost twenty-two years, were being forced to become armed fortresses or to close their doors. Physician providers were retiring or deceased, and medical schools and residency training programs were failing to replace them.

In 1993 the pro-choice movement was temporarily buoyed up by the inauguration of the first president to promise support for women's reproductive rights. While some of the optimistic forecasts materialized, such as passage of the Freedom of Access to Clinic Entrances (FACE) Act, the new Republican Congress elected in November 1994 threatened to overturn President Clinton's previous reform efforts, such as his removal of the gag rule, instituting abortion services in military hospitals overseas, facilitating the importation of RU 486, and voiding the Mexico City policy. The new Congress even threatened to overturn *Roe v. Wade* itself.

THE SILENCE OF ORGANIZED MEDICINE

In the last decade over thirty-five countries have liberalized their abortion laws, and currently 75 percent of the women in the world live in countries where abortions are permitted for broad social and economic reasons. In contrast, in the United States during the last fifteen years we have seen increasing restrictions on abortion, fewer doctors willing to perform them, and increasing efforts by our government to eliminate this medical procedure. I have long puzzled over why the American Medical Association and even my own specialty organization, the American College of Obstetrics and Gynecology (ACOG), are so reluctant to take a definite position of leadership on such an important health issue. The World Health Organization has proclaimed population control, including easy access to abortion and contraception, to be the number-one health problem in the world today. But organized medicine in the United States is afraid to speak out and demand free access to contraception and abortion services for women of all ages.

As fewer abortions are performed in hospitals, currently less than 10 percent, reproductive health care remains outside the mainstream of medical care, resulting in less residency training. Research in this field is essentially ignored; the subject of abortion is rarely discussed in medical journals, in the *AMA News,* or at medical meetings, except in an adversarial manner. Clinic doctors are labeled "abortionists," even though they may be certified in some other specialty. Abortion services have been marginalized, and abortion providers are rapidly decreasing in number due to harassment, death, or old age.

Medical Students for Choice, a national organization of medical and health professional students, has prodded the AMA and ACOG to require that accredited residencies include training in abortion techniques. But Congress has stepped in and recently passed a law prohibiting such a training requirement. While the press generally decries such congressional maneuvering, it usually fails to mention one important point, namely, the long and ongoing silence of organized medicine. Both AMA and ACOG have seemed very reluctant to take a position on this congressional attempt to legislate medicine, just as the AMA refused to speak out during Margaret Sanger's lifetime on behalf of contraception, or against Dr. Jocelyn Elder's dismissal from the surgeon general's position, or against denying Dr. Henry Foster a hearing for nomination to that post.

SHARING THE POWER AND
COMMON PERCEPTIONS TO ACHIEVE THE PEACE

A new stage in this social revolution or gender battle has begun—a period of reeducation for many men and some women. And brave women, such as Anita Hill and Hillary Rodham Clinton, will teach them. As Hill recently told a group of female legislators, women "must capture their rage and turn it into positive energy. Making the workplace a safer and more productive place for ourselves and our daughters is, and should be, on each of our agendas."

How long will it take to achieve the peace? Women are gaining strength. By 1991, for the first time, women comprised 54 percent of all physicians entering a first-year ob-gyn residency. Of the total membership (31,000) of the American College of Obstetrics and Gynecology, women represented 21 percent.

The numbers of women in all fields of medicine are increasing. It would seem inevitable that some young activists among them will eventually become chairwomen of departments, tenured professors, and medical policy makers in government administrative roles.

The subject of reproductive control deserves recognition at medical meetings, as well as in the medical journals. Medical leaders should speak out regarding the effect of reproductive control upon women's health and economic status. American society's bitter debate over reproductive choice will come to an end much sooner if organized medicine will properly assume its moral obligation to provide better reproductive health care, improved contraceptive research, and education. Clinics should be accessible to all women of all ages, providers should receive moral support instead of stigmatization, and training programs must be guaranteed for medical students and residents.

Government, too, has a moral responsibility to provide funding for the poor and the young, early sex education in the schools, and health clinics in high schools. The judiciary will increasingly need to defend the availability of late abortions in selected cases where genetic defects are discovered late in pregnancy or serious medical complications arise. The mother's rights should not be held secondary to those of a fetus. Laws restricting access to health care, such as mandatory parental notification, waiting periods, and denial of funding for low-income women, should be repealed.

Despite recent setbacks, I find reason for hope that this power struggle will end and we can move on. Many new technologies will develop rapidly in the twenty-first century to arouse new controversies. Laws may be changed overnight, but social customs and attitudes change very slowly. Prejudices must be overcome, and a gigantic medical delivery system must be developed to deliver early, safe, and low-cost reproductive health care to rich and poor alike.

Tolerance and understanding must narrow the gulf between men and women, who differ so widely in their perceptions of the relationships between the sexes. Only then will sexism fade away.

14

Warren M. Hern

LIFE ON THE FRONT LINES

The first abortion I performed was for a seventeen-year-old high school student. She told me, as I talked to her before the operation, that she wanted to be a doctor and an anesthesiologist. I was terrified, and so was she. She cried after the operation in sadness and relief. Her tears and the immensity of the moment brought on my tears. I had helped her change her life. I was relieved that this young woman was safe to go on with her life and realize her dreams. I felt I had found a new definition of the idea of medicine as an act of compassion and love for other human beings, an idea that I gained from learning about Albert Schweitzer. I had followed that ideal by working as a medical student at a Schweitzer-inspired hospital in the Peruvian Amazon in 1964 and later as a Peace Corps physician in Brazil. It was a long way from a primitive hospital in the steaming jungles of Peru to the operating room at Preterm Clinic in Washington, D.C., in 1971. But to me, this was a renewed and compelling expression of that fundamental commitment in medicine that comes to us from Hippocrates and Galen, through Maimonides, the Jewish physician in twelfth-century Spain, who wrote, "And let me only see the suffering person, my fellow human being in pain." [1]

That moment in Preterm, the first freestanding abortion clinic in the nation's capital, led me to the tumultuous experience of providing abortion services through a time of a great upheaval over this issue in our nation's history. I was working at the time at the Office of Economic

Opportunity to change federal government restrictions on abortion funding,[2] and I began corresponding with various abortion rights groups such as the National Association for the Repeal of Abortion Laws (NARAL) and the Women's National Abortion Action Coalition. I was privileged to hear the Supreme Court arguments in the *Vuitch, Roe v. Wade,* and *Doe v. Bolton* cases and to know the doctors and lawyers involved with the cases. Although I was keenly interested in the public health and social justice aspects of abortion, I did not see myself providing services or even practicing clinical medicine.

After returning to Colorado, I worked part-time as the medical director of a family-planning training program under private contract with the U.S. Department of Health, Education, and Welfare. Bringing doctors in the Rocky Mountain region information about new abortion methods was part of my work. In April 1973 I was asked if I would be interested in helping to start a nonprofit abortion clinic in Boulder. I said I would because I now saw the main challenge before us as implementing the Supreme Court's *Roe v. Wade* decision. The freedom to choose a safe and legal abortion meant nothing without someone willing to do it. I thought it would be a valuable thing to do while I was preparing to go back to do graduate work in epidemiology. It allowed me to put my beliefs about the need for this service into action. I did not feel highly prepared, but I felt confident of my basic surgical and medical skills.

After meeting with the group in Boulder and coming to an agreement about the project, I responded to their request that I write a program plan and set up the clinic. I made myself medical director reporting to the executive director, a sociology graduate student, and the board of directors, which was composed of dedicated individuals who were deeply concerned with safe abortion.

In trying to establish relationships with the Boulder medical community, I applied for privileges at Boulder Community Hospital, to be able to admit patients with complications. The chairman of the obstetrics-gynecology staff had been one of my attending physicians when I was in medical school in Denver. He was deeply opposed to abortion, which I discovered at the first obstetrics-gynecology staff meeting I attended several days before we opened the clinic in November 1973. The conversation stopped as I entered the meeting area that had been set off by sliding screens in the hospital cafeteria. Several other staff doctors were also opposed to abortion. Other physicians on the staff, who regarded abortion as a menial operation but one that must be performed by someone specially trained in obstetrics and gynecology, did not think someone like myself, without that residency training, should do abortions. There were one or two who were silent and raised no opposition. They proved to be my allies in a long struggle.

About this time a local newspaper reported attacks by the newly formed Fight the Abortion Clinic Committee (FTACC) in Boulder, which demanded that the city council close the clinic as a "clear and present danger" to community health. We were accused of "corrupting the youth" because the clinic was only a block from a public junior high school and a Catholic school. I thought of Socrates and felt solace.

The FTACC requested a special meeting of the Colorado Board of Health, to which the FTACC alleged that we were virtually running a butcher shop. I came to the meeting prepared with the statistics, including complication rates and follow-up rates, for our first month's patients. I also informed the board that regulations requested by the FTACC would probably violate the *Doe v. Bolton* companion decision to *Roe v. Wade*. The meeting was widely (and favorably, from our point of view) covered by the regional news media. The board decided to leave us alone.

At the November meeting of the Boulder County Medical Society, a group of anti-abortion doctors formed a committee with the purpose of getting the society to pass a resolution asking the state and county health boards to declare the clinic a "clear and present danger" to public health and requesting the boards to shut down the clinic. One of my classmates from medical school recommended an investigation of the clinic before deciding on the resolution. On the day of the December meeting, we were visited by a delegation from the committee, two anti-abortion physicians (including the hospital obstetrics-gynecology department chairman). I took them on a guided tour and explained our procedures. At the meeting that evening, the committee chairman, to the astonishment and dismay of our opponents, announced that our standards of medical care were "exemplary and commendable" and "equal to the highest standards of medical care in the community." The resolution opposing us was derailed by a friendly pediatrician.

In December, the day after the Colorado Board of Health meeting and the week after the medical society meeting, I went to a quarterly meeting of the Boulder Community Hospital medical staff, where my request for hospital privileges would be decided. A rancorous debate over my privileges went on for forty-five minutes. The anti-abortion department chief argued against my staff appointment on several grounds. He said I lived too far away to see a sick patient in an emergency, which was necessary before a consultant would see her. Someone pointed out that this had not been a problem for a neurosurgeon from Denver who had requested and received privileges the year before. The debate ended when an obstetrician-gynecologist whom I had met, and who was strongly pro-choice, stood up and guaranteed his consultation if I needed it at any time. My appointment was approved by a narrow majority.

When we started in the first week of November 1973, we were the only freestanding abortion clinic in Colorado. The pickets began. The Boulder Valley Right to Life Committee sent out lurid brochures covered with pictures of dismembered fetuses to every household in the county. I began to get threatening phone calls at home, every night I was home, all night. I was afraid to get out of my car when I got home. I got a rifle and kept it by my bed. Two nights a week, in order to be available for patients who might have problems from the first day of laminaria insertion to the next day of abortion procedure, I slept on one of the cots in the clinic's recovery room. In the evenings I worked on charts and wrote letters to people who referred patients. I knew hardly anyone in Boulder and had no friends in town except for a couple of classmates from medical school, and our lives were very different. They had normal medical practices and were already leaders in the community.

When the weekend came, I went to my mountain home to relax. It did not seem to me that the people I met in Boulder, save those at the clinic, were very supportive of what we were doing, although they may have been more supportive than I knew. I just saw the hate letters and got the threatening phone calls.

Picketers would walk in front of the clinic during work hours from time to time. I would go out in my green scrub suit and ask them what they were doing. Sometimes I would just make pleasant remarks. They carried signs saying I was a murderer. It gave me some satisfaction for a time to know that I was irritating them.

In the summer of 1974 a Denver television station decided to have a major program on abortion set up as a debate. I debated a family doctor who was head of the Boulder Valley Right to Life Committee. Each of us was flanked by two supporters. I have no idea how many people saw the program, but it seemed to help make me a target of opprobrium for the anti-abortion fanatics. After a subsequent debate, I had to be taken out the back door to escape the anti-abortion mob that threatened to come up over the desk separating the speakers from the audience.

That summer of 1974, the Denver chapter of the National Organization for Women held an outdoor rally at East High School in Denver to honor those who had helped women's rights and progress. I was one of those they chose to honor. At the rally, the anti-abortion fanatics showed up shouting my name and calling me a murderer. They had numerous signs showing my name and various descriptions of me, none of them flattering. As I began to speak, they began to shout. I spoke above them. It was a little frightening but exhilarating, and I was all but overcome with emotion. There was really something fearsome about people who hated me so much and who would go after me in a personal way. I spoke of the need for safe and legal abortions for the sake of women and their families. I said we would not return to back-alley abortions for the same reasons that we would not go back to slavery, public flogging, and the bubonic plague. That barbaric time in history is over. I felt defiant. But I also felt afraid of what those people might try to do to me. It was a defining moment.

At the end of our first year of operation, it was clear that those who held power at Boulder Valley Clinic and I had very different ideas about what we were doing and why.[3] They wanted no one person in charge of the clinic, nor did they want a medical director. Among other things, they abolished my job and title but not my responsibilities. After long weeks of painful debate, I resigned.

I felt by this time that providing abortion services was the most important thing I could do in medicine. I took my last week's salary and used it as a deposit on a small office space, being careful not to tell the lease manager that I planned to do abortions. I knew that revealing this would make it impossible to find office space in Boulder. I went to a local bank to look for help. The banker expressed the view that my former employer, the abortion clinic, had brought a lot of "undesirables" into town. I didn't know if he thought or realized that I was one of the "undesirable" elements to whom he referred, but I did not go to pains to explain to him the objectives of my medical practice. I borrowed $7,000, remodeled the office, and saw three patients on the second anniversary of *Roe v. Wade*. Four years later, when the doctors upstairs moved to their own new building, I took over their space, and with more loans, I bought the building so I could not be kicked out later by an anti-abortion owner.

Now we faced the street across from the hospital. The picketers began to make regular visits to my office. By this time, I had to change my home phone number and have it unlisted. On one occasion, I went out to the parking lot to write down the license numbers of cars whose owners were picketing and harassing my patients. One of the picketers got in his car and tried to run over me in the parking lot. At the time I was running about five miles a day and I could escape the car's path, but it was frightening because I could see him coming after me. I reported this incident to the Boulder police, but there was no prosecution. The man was a regular demonstrator at my office.

The patients came from all over—first Colorado, then all of North America. Their stories were compelling. We gave each patient careful individual attention. I found that getting to know the patients and their families was the most rewarding part of the experience, and it was gratifying to see what a positive event this was for them. Each day, each patient, some more than others, convinced me of the absolute need for the service we were providing and the need for it to be of as high a quality as we could make it.

We did not just provide a medical service. We had to solve important problems for individuals and families that frequently had nowhere else to turn. We dealt with problems of acute emotional need and suffering, acute family and social disorganization, frequently under circumstances of severe economic deprivation and social injustice, individual grief and loss, occasional psychiatric disorder, and wrenching religious and philosophical issues, all in a context of public controversy.

In my own way, I worked to find better ways of *doing* abortions safely, especially second-trimester abortions, because they seemed difficult to obtain and more dangerous than early abortions.[4] In 1984 my textbook, *Abortion Practice,* was published. The publisher was deluged with hate mail and threats of boycott. In 1989 the publisher destroyed more than 300 of the remaining 350 books and took it out of print. The next year I formed my own publishing company and published the book in a paperback edition to keep it in print.[5]

The attacks on abortion rights had begun to escalate from civilized debates to personal and legislative attacks. Colorado was led by a strong pro-choice governor, Dick Lamm, who had successfully introduced the nation's first abortion reform law, passed in 1967. But the Colorado legislature was increasingly controlled by those who were not pro-choice.

On November 5, 1980, the day after his election as president, Ronald Reagan held his first press conference. The very first thing he said was that he intended to make abortion illegal.[6] After he took office and lent the power of the presidency to the anti-abortion fanatics, the violent attacks on clinics increased dramatically.[7] The demonstrators were literally on our doorsteps. Threats on my life and harassment of all kinds increased. The fetus became a fetish object for the anti-abortion fanatics, a moral symbol that justified their actions.

By this point I had decided that my only option for taking the high moral ground was to place my own life and body on the line. I decided that I had to risk my life for the cause by continuing to provide safe abortion services in the face of these threats and attempts to intimidate. For those of us involved in providing abortions, only our own moral courage in doing what we see as right and ethical could be an effective counterpoise to the anti-abortion movement.

Two dozen abortion clinics were completely destroyed in the year 1984 alone. The head of the FBI, William Webster, declared that violence against abortion clinics was "not terrorism" because the FBI didn't know the identities of the perpetrators.[8]

On October 19, 1985, a rock was thrown through the front window of my clinic, hurled by a follower of Joseph Scheidler, head of the Pro-Life Action League of Chicago, who was due to arrive in Boulder the following week. Scheidler, whose six-foot, four-inch bulk towered over me, told me to my face in 1984 that he was coming to Boulder to "shut down" my clinic. He was now about to attempt to deliver on his threat. He was scheduled to speak at the University of Colorado at the invitation of a right-wing group and to work with the local right-to-life group to close my office.[9]

On the following Monday, the glass company was due to replace the plywood covering the empty window frame with new glass. I canceled the repair job, and when I got to the office, I made a hand-lettered sign, all in capital letters: "THIS WINDOW WAS BROKEN BY THOSE WHO HATE FREEDOM." The sign was at Scheidler's back as he spoke to the television cameras that afternoon.

Several months later, I was sued for slander by the anti-abortion groups for publicly stating that they had created "an atmosphere of violence and confrontation,"[10] but I was defended free of charge by some of the best constitutional lawyers in Colorado, and the anti-abortion groups had to pay attorney's fees.

The connection between attacks on abortion by Ronald Reagan and other high officials and anti-abortion harassment and terrorism was increasingly plain for anyone to see,[11] but it did not seem to be of much concern to the public or to opposition political leaders. On February 6, 1988, the day Ronald Reagan announced the "gag rule" and the day after Pat Robertson spoke to the New Hampshire legislature and accused Planned Parenthood of trying to create a "master race" by providing abortion services, five bullets were fired through the front windows of my waiting room with a high-powered rifle.[12] The next day, I held a press conference on my front lawn to denounce the criminals who did it, and offered a reward of $5,000 for information leading to their arrest. We installed bulletproof windows and electronic security systems at a cost of tens of thousands of dollars.

The gunshots fired into my office occurred in the same week that my divorce became final. The two events were not unrelated, because the anti-abortion harassment had a disastrous effect on my marriage of six years. The juxtaposition of the two events did nothing positive for my self-esteem.

On September 25, 1988, while campaigning for the presidency, George Bush expressed the view that doctors who do abortions should be imprisoned. He was elected by a landslide.

On October 10, 1990, Joseph Scheidler's protégé, Randall Terry, national head of Operation Rescue, stood with his followers in front of my clinic and prayed for my death. CBS's 60 Minutes showed a tape of Terry's prayer on their broadcast concerning the "Lambs of Christ" on February 2, 1992.

As of March 1, 1993, there had been 1,285 acts of violence against abortion clinic facilities and doctor's offices, and over 100 facilities had been completely destroyed.

On March 10, 1993, Dr. David Gunn was assassinated by an anti-abortion demonstrator in Pensacola, Florida. The murder was tacitly condoned by anti-abortion leaders and condemned by President Bill Clinton, in office for six weeks. Congressional leaders and Janet Reno, U.S. attorney general, called for federal protection for abortion clinic workers.

What did Dr. Gunn represent to the anti-abortion fanatic who killed him? He represented individual dignity. He represented opportunity for women to become full citizens and participants in our society. He represented social change. He represented the value of the individual adult human being as opposed to state control of individual lives and fascist totalitarianism. He represented a thought. The man who killed Dr. Gunn tried to kill a thought.

Dr. Gunn's crime was not that he killed children, which he did not, but that he brought liberty and health to women. He saved their lives and futures. That's why every doctor in America who does abortions lives under a death threat.

On August 13, 1993, Randall Terry of Operation Rescue went on National Christian Radio Broadcasting and, identifying me by name, invited his listeners to assassinate me. The next day, the Reverend David Trosch of Birmingham, Alabama, announced that killing doctors who do abortions is "justifiable homicide." The day after that, August 15, the doctor who replaced Dr. Gunn at the Pensacola clinic was murdered in Birmingham with money in his pocket. The next week, on August 19, 1993, Rachelle Shannon, an Oregon woman active in anti-abortion activities, tried to assassinate Dr. George Tiller in Wichita. She shot Tiller in both arms, but he returned to see his patients the next day.

In November 1993 both houses of Congress passed legislation making it a federal crime to assault patients and health workers at abortion clinics. The bill was signed into law by President Clinton in May 1994.

One of Trosch's supporters, Paul Hill, assassinated Dr. John Britton and his volunteer bodyguard, James Barrett, in July 1994. The assassinations were applauded by anti-abortion leaders, who set up a defense fund for Hill.

In October 1994 Dr. Gary Romalis was critically wounded in his own dining room during an assassination attempt carried out with an assault weapon, which was fired at close range through the rear window of Dr. Romalis's home near Vancouver, British Columbia.

In the elections of November 1994, the Republican Party swept to an overwhelming majority in both houses of Congress. Speaker Newt Gingrich declared that this was a sign of voters' approval of the "Contract with America," which contained strong anti-abortion language and proposed restrictions on abortion.

On December 30, 1994, John Salvi shot five clinic workers at two women's centers providing abortion services in Brookline, Massachusetts, killing two, Shannon Lowney and Leanne Nichols. The shootings and assassinations were applauded by anti-abortion leaders.

On January 22, 1995, representatives of the American Coalition of Life [sic] Activists held a press conference and announced a hit list of the first thirteen abortion service physicians they wanted eliminated. I was on the list, and so was Dr. Tiller. All thirteen physicians were placed under the twenty-four-hour protection of armed U.S. marshals for several days. The Republican congressional leadership later declared that federal anti-crime funds could not be used for implementation of the Freedom of Access to Clinic Entrances (FACE) law.

In February 1995 I was asked to speak briefly at a candlelight vigil for those murdered by anti-abortion assassins. The meeting was to be held in front of the city hall in Boulder, Colorado, where the city council had passed an ordinance protecting women and clinic workers from anti-abortion harassment. Since an anti-abortion demonstrator who had indicated he wished to kill me had just been released from jail that week, I was brought to the rear of the building under heavy security provided by the SWAT team of the Boulder police department. I wore a bulletproof vest and was held in a secure area until I was introduced, and I was brought back to the secure area immediately after speaking. Several armed plainclothes detectives walked throughout the crowd and observed the perimeter. Law enforcement officials expected someone to attempt to assassinate me.

The question that I asked my pro-choice friends at that meeting was: "Is it possible for a physician who performs abortions in the most pro-choice community in the country to walk a few blocks from his medical office without an armed security escort to the front of the city hall to speak to a publicly announced peaceful assembly of his fellow citizens about this matter without a serious risk of being assassinated? The answer to that question is, No. Think about what that means for your country."

In July 1995, declaring it "payback time" for the anti-abortion religious right's help in winning the 1994 elections, Republican congressional leaders advanced thirteen anti-abortion measures in the U.S. House of Representatives and Senate. For the first time in U.S. history, Congress voted to prohibit a specific surgical procedure, which had not been described in the medical literature but which congressional leaders called "partial birth abortion." Legislators described portions of a late-abortion procedure in lurid terms on the floor of both houses. Doctors who perform the procedure were singled out for criminal penalties. Lost and ignored in the political rhetoric were the hundreds of individual tragedies experienced by women carrying desired but deeply problematic pregnancies that sometimes threatened their own lives. Surrounded by some of these women, who had been treated and sometimes saved from death by the late Dr. James McMahon, President Clinton vetoed the "Partial Birth Abortion" Act in early 1996.

By the end of 1995, I had experienced hundreds of hours of harassment organized by the Denver man who had issued death threats against me since the previous October, and whose harassment caused an outstanding and dedicated nurse to leave her position on my staff. He had stalked me to my home in a remote area of the Colorado mountains, and he had followed me closely about town in his vehicle, requiring me to evade him on more than one occasion. At my request, he was served with a permanent restraining order on January 2, 1996. His fellow demonstrators, at least one of whom served prison time for armed robbery and assault, continued their harassment of my patients and staff.

Not a bullet has been fired at any of the thirteen doctors targeted by the American Coalition of Life Activists since ACLA issued its hit list on January 21, 1995, as far as I know, but speaking as one of those physicians, I can testify that such an announcement goes a long way toward destroying the target's life. That, of course, is the intended effect. The announcement ruined much of my life in 1995 and 1996, and its effect has continued.

I am grateful for the protection of federal marshals who were assigned to me and my colleagues after this announcement. But why should it be necessary for doctors who help women to be protected by armed guards?

Why should I have to accept as routine the fact that the first thing I do when I walk out of my medical office is to look for snipers in the new parking garage overlooking my office? Why should I routinely have to ask the county sheriff to inspect my house and surroundings for assassins before I approach it? Why should I expect assassination at any moment?

What is more at stake than the lives of a few doctors is the issue of whether Americans now accept the level of violence and terrorism embraced by the anti-abortion movement as a means of political expression. When the anti-abortion movement gets through with us, who's next? People who write books? People who read them?

We must surely ask whether it is beyond the limits of free speech that a group operating under the laws of the United States can stand up at a press conference, identify targets among people who belong to a category already marked for assassination by ideological colleagues of the announcing group, and then sit back and wait for the inevitable results. In a society pervaded by the glorification of violence, notorious for unlimited access to lethal military weapons, and diffused with people suffering from untreated severe mental illness, the probabilities are excellent that one or more of us will be assassinated. It is a new form of electronic fascism. Assassination has been a tool of tyrants for thousands of years. The technology and the degree of "plausible deniability" have improved over time. But things have not really changed much since the times of Julius Caesar.

Neither the American Coalition of Life Activists nor those they hope to inspire care about me as a person or about the women whose lives I save as a physician. What they care about is power. So does the Republican Party, which has been the chief beneficiary of twenty years of anti-abortion rhetoric leading to this terrorism. The anti-abortion movement is the face of fascism in America, and its chief public sponsor is the Republican Party.

How many more doctors, receptionists, and other abortion clinic workers have to be killed before the American people and their government step in and stop this insanity? When will Americans see that the anti-abortion ideology is a collective psychosis masquerading as religion that has become a political force threatening democratic society?

More to the point, when will Americans hold their political leaders accountable for demagoguery that breeds this fascism?

NOTES

An earlier version of this essay appeared in *Women's Health Issues* 4, no. 1 (1994): 48–54; it is reprinted with permission of the Jacobs Institute of Women's Health.

1. Maimonides, "Oath and Prayer," in *Great Adventures in Medicine,* ed. S. Rapport and H. Wright (New York: Dial Press, 1952).

2. G. Contis and W. M. Hern, "U.S. Government Policy on Abortion," *American Journal of Public Health* 61 (1971):1038.

3. W. M. Hern, M. Gold, and A. Oakes, "Administrative Incongruence and Authority Conflict in Four Abortion Clinics," *Human Organization* 36 (1977):376–83.

4. W. M. Hern, "Laminaria in Abortion: Use in 1368 Patients in First Trimester," *Rocky Mountain Medical Journal* 72 (1975):390–95; W. M. Hern and A. Oakes, "Multiple Laminaria Treatment in Early Midtrimester Outpatient Suction Abortion," *Advances in Planned Parenthood* 12 (1977):93–97; W. M. Hern, W. A. Miller, L. Pain, and K. D. Moorhead, "Correlation of Sonographic Cephalometry with Clinical Assessment of Fetal Age Following Early Midtrimester D & E Abortion," *Advances in Planned Parenthood* 13 (1978):14–20; W. M. Hern, "Outpatient Second-Trimester D & E Abortion through 24 Menstrual Weeks' Gestation," *Advances in Planned Parenthood* 16 (1981):7–

13; W. M. Hern, "Serial Multiple Laminaria and Adjunctive Urea in Late Outpatient Dilatation and Evacuation Abortion," *Obstetrics and Gynecology* 63 (1984):543–49.

5. W. M. Hern, *Abortion Practice* (Boulder: Alpenglo, 1990 [Philadelphia: Lippincott, 1984]).

6. D. E. Kneeland, "Triumphant Reagan Starting Transition to the White House," *New York Times,* November 7, 1980, A1, A14.

7. D. Clendinen, "President Praises Foes of Abortion, *New York Times,* January 23, 1985; P. Brown, "Reagan Tells Abortion Foes He's with 'Em," *Rocky Mountain News,* January 23, 1986; Associated Press, "Abortion Clinic and Two Doctors' Offices in Pensacola, Florida, Bombed," *New York Times,* December 26, 1984.

8. W. M. Hern, "The Antiabortion Vigilantes," *New York Times,* December 21, 1984, op-ed page.

9. C. Brennan, "Anti-abortion Leader Targets Boulder Clinic," *Rocky Mountain News,* October 22, 1985.

10. L. Horsley, "Abortion Opponent Sues Hern," *Daily Camera,* January 18, 1986.

11. W. M. Hern, "Must Mr. Reagan Tolerate Abortion Clinic Violence?" *New York Times,* June 14, 1986, op-ed page; W. M. Hern, "Abortion Clinics under Siege," *Denver Post,* November 1, 1988; M. McKeegan, *Abortion Politics: Mutiny in the Ranks of the Right* (New York: Free Press, 1992).

12. "Shots Shatter Front Window of Boulder Abortion Clinic," *Daily Camera,* February 5, 1988. R. Robey, "Shots Fired at Boulder Abortion Clinic," *Denver Post,* February 6, 1988.

15

Carole Joffe, Patricia Anderson,
and Jody Steinauer

THE CRISIS IN ABORTION PROVISION
AND PRO-CHOICE MEDICAL ACTIVISM
IN THE 1990S

The relationship of organized medicine to abortion has long been a
complex one. In the nineteenth century, physicians in the newly organized American Medical Association (AMA) were among the leading
forces pushing for the criminalization of abortion. In the twentieth century, pro-choice physicians were among the most articulate voices calling for the legalization of abortion.[1] Since the landmark *Roe v. Wade*
decision in 1973, a strong majority of physicians, including obstetri-
cians/gynecologists, report that they support legal abortion.[2] Yet historically there has been noticeably little support from mainstream medicine
for the establishment of abortion services, and even less support for that
embattled minority of physicians who actually provide abortions. But
the "loud silence," as one observer has characterized organized medicine's stance toward abortion since *Roe*,[3] showed signs of ending in the
1990s. In the familiar pattern of radical social movements spawning
"countermovements,"[4] it is evident that the extremism of anti-abortion
activity—both at clinic sites and in Congress—has led to an unusual
degree of pro-choice activism within medical circles.

ORGANIZED MEDICINE AND
ABORTION SINCE *ROE V. WADE*

In the years leading up to the *Roe* decision, many physicians actively
worked for the legalization of abortion in the United States. They held

several high-profile conferences on abortion, pushed to liberalize hospital policies governing sanctioned abortions, and in numerous cases risked their medical licenses and personal freedom to provide illegal abortions to women they felt incapable of refusing. The prime motivating forces for many of those doctors who lobbied for legal abortion were their emergency-room experiences with incompetently performed illegal abortions—either attempts at self-abortion by desperate women or the work of inept abortionists.[5] In 1970 the House of Delegates of the AMA—which more than a century earlier had led the fight to criminalize abortion—passed a resolution supporting legal abortion.[6]

Yet after the *Roe* decision, organized medicine was conspicuous for its *lack* of effort to incorporate abortion into routine medical care. With the notable exception of a handful of medical groups, such as the American Public Health Association, most of the medical establishment made no statement on abortion—issuing neither guidelines nor standards of care, as would normally be expected from such groups as the Association of American Medical Colleges, the Joint Commission on Accreditation of Hospitals, and the National Board of Medical Examiners.[7] Many hospitals did not establish abortion services—even if they had no religious affiliation. (Some of the hospitals that did acted only when threatened by lawsuits from pro-choice physicians.) In 1973, immediately after *Roe,* hospitals performed about half of all abortions in the United States, with the rest being done at freestanding clinics and doctors' offices; but hospitals steadily withdrew from this level of abortion provision, and by 1992 hospitals accounted for only 7 percent of all abortions.[8] Similarly, ob/gyn residencies did not consistently move to incorporate abortion training, and in the years since *Roe* there has actually been a steady decline in the number of residencies that require this training. By the early 1990s, only 12 percent of ob/gyn residencies routinely required training in first-trimester abortion procedures.

The reluctance of mainstream medical institutions to become involved in abortion has led to a situation in which the vast majority of abortions in the United States are performed in freestanding clinics.[9] These clinics are themselves a proud creation of the pro-choice movement, originating in the early 1970s, when abortion was legal in a handful of states, and women flew in from all over the country for outpatient services. These clinics have amassed a superb safety record and have been a chief factor in keeping the costs of abortion low.[10] But there have also been downsides to this innovation—most notably, the further marginalization of abortion services from the rest of medicine. The clinic founders' original vision—that these institutions would have strong, ongoing relationships with dominant medical institutions in the community, particularly hospitals—has not, for the most part, been realized. Teaching hospitals have not typically used clinics as training sites, leading obstetricians/gynecologists in many communities have not chosen to work several hours per week at a clinic or to conduct research there, and so on. A major indicator of the marginality of these clinics is the increasing need to bring abortion-providing physicians in from out of town—often at great cost—because local doctors refuse to work in these facilities.[11]

Because organized medicine has distanced itself from abortion, individual doctors who *do* perform abortions often find themselves professionally isolated and stigmatized by their medical colleagues. Abortion providers have recounted incidents of being refused hospital privileges, asked to leave group practices, passed over for expected positions of medical leadership, snubbed by medical societies, and so on.[12] And as anti-abortion terrorism began to intensify dramatically in the late 1980s, the silence of mainstream medicine in the face of harassment and physical attacks on abortion-providing colleagues has been particularly dismaying.[13]

This seeming contradiction—that most physicians voice support for legal abortion, while abortion services and, above all, abortion providers are professionally marginalized—has several explanations. As discussed elsewhere at greater length,[14] these reasons include the complicated legacy of the pre-*Roe* era, when the "abortionist," both lay and physician, was perceived by the medical profession as the embodiment of greed and ineptness. Another factor is what some professionals see as a "de-skilling" of medical ability, in which a healthy woman makes the "diagnosis" of an unwanted pregnancy and the abortion-providing doctor then serves as a mere technician. In addition, there is the tendency of a conservative, conflict-averse profession to avoid issues so thoroughly entwined with gender politics, on the one hand, and the extremism of the anti-abortion movement, on the other.

Medicine's refusal to incorporate abortion into routine health care delivery in the years since *Roe* has contributed to a genuine crisis in the availability of abortion. By the early 1990s, some 84 percent of U.S. counties did not have an abortion facility.[15] Furthermore, those facilities that did exist faced an ever more beleaguered environment. In the late 1980s anti-abortion violence began to rise dramatically. And several Supreme Court decisions, most notably the *Webster* decision in

1989, permitted states to impose major restrictions on abortion services.[16] It was in this highly politicized atmosphere that the events we describe below occurred.

A SYMPOSIUM ON THE ABORTION PROVISION CRISIS

In the late 1980s the National Abortion Federation (NAF)—a professional membership association of abortion providers—began to receive an increasing number of calls from clinic members asking for the organization's help in locating physicians who could provide abortion services on a full- or part-time basis. Some clinic administrators reported losing physicians who had worked for many years in this field and were now retiring; other administrators simply could not find replacements for regular providers who wanted to take vacations or personal leaves. The difficulties faced by its members spurred NAF to seek foundation funding to explore the "physician shortage." The goal was to identify the key reasons underlying the lack of available abortion providers and to develop strategies to address this situation.

In the fall of 1990 support from the Ford and the Gund foundations made possible a pivotal meeting of physicians, physician assistants, clinic administrators, researchers, and medical association representatives in Santa Barbara, California. The symposium was noteworthy as much for who was present as for what was said. The American College of Obstetricians and Gynecologists (ACOG) agreed to cosponsor the meeting with NAF and sent a representative. The Accreditation Council of Graduate Medical Education (ACGME) and the Council on Resident Education in Obstetrics and Gynecology (CREOG) also sent representatives to the meeting. (ACGME and CREOG are directly involved with establishing educational standards and evaluating and accrediting ob/gyn residency programs in the United States.) It was the first time that any of these groups had participated in NAF-originated events or had actively advocated changes related to abortion access and training. As it turned out, the representatives from these groups would continue to keep the issues of the symposium alive before their associations and eventually serve as crucial allies in the battle to increase access to abortion.

Participants at the symposium explored various factors contributing to the shortage of physician abortion providers. Among those noted were the "graying" of abortion providers who had come of age in the pre-*Roe* era and had seen the ravages of illegal abortion, increasing anti-abortion harassment and violence, inadequate economic incentives for abortion work, and the social stigma and professional isolation that commonly accompanied abortion work. The symposium issued a number of recommendations to address these problems, including improved working conditions for providers and incorporation of "med-level" clinicians—physician assistants, nurse practitioners, and nurse mid-wives—into abortion provision. Most fundamentally, however, the symposium concluded that "obstetrics and gynecology residency programs fall short of meeting their responsibility to train physicians in abortion and contraceptive services."[17] In what was to prove the most consequential of all the statements issued from the Santa Barbara meeting, the attendees recommended "the integration of abortion care as a required component of ob/gyn residency training through curriculum guidelines, minimum training standards, and integration of abortion proficiency assessments into board examinations and residency reviews."[18]

In the immediate aftermath of the symposium, NAF, along with allies in ACOG, began a political campaign to gain widespread support for the findings and recommendations, especially the one pertaining to residency requirements and abortion training. *Who Will Provide Abortions?*, the document resulting from the symposium, was widely disseminated, and sympathetic organizations, within and without medicine, joined in the call to make abortion training a routine part of ob/gyn residency. The American Civil Liberties Union, the American Public Health Association, the Center for Reproductive Law and Policy, Planned Parenthood Federation of America, and the newly founded Medical Students for Choice were among the allies at this stage of the campaign.

Shortly after the 1990 symposium, several well-regarded studies by physician researchers appeared, giving further visibility to the crisis in abortion training. Trent McKay, then at the University of California, Davis, Medical School, surveyed all U.S. ob/gyn residency programs and found that only 12 percent routinely required training in first-trimester abortion techniques (in contrast to the 22 percent found in a 1985 survey) and only 6 percent trained physicians to perform second-trimester abortions. Similarly, Carolyn Westoff and her colleagues at Columbia University Medical School found that nearly half of all graduating ob/gyn residents had completed their studies without ever performing a first-trimester abortion.[19] These studies and the continuing publicity from the NAF-ACOG symposium spurred a number of articles in both the medical and popular press about the "provider shortage" in abortion.[20]

The early 1990s also saw a steady escalation in abortion-related harassment and violence. In 1992 almost two hundred "violent" incidents were recorded at abortion facilities (including clinic or office invasions, acts of vandalism, arson, and bombings), and nearly three thousand incidents of "disruption" (hate mail, harassing calls, bomb threats, and picketing). In 1993 the worst fears of abortion providers materialized when one of their colleagues, Dr. David Gunn, was shot down in front of a clinic in Pensacola, Florida, by an anti-abortion zealot. Later that year in Kansas, another abortion provider was shot, though not seriously wounded, and during this same year there were nearly two hundred reports of the "stalking" of abortion staff and their family members, at workplaces, homes, and churches. In 1994 tragedy again struck the abortion-providing community. That summer, John Britton—the physician who had assumed some of David Gunn's duties in Pensacola—was murdered, along with James Barrett, a retired air force colonel, who had been acting as his voluntary escort. And in late December of that year, Shannon Lowney and Leanne Nichols, receptionists at two different clinics in Brookline, Massachusetts, were killed, and several others wounded, when a gunman walked in and started shooting randomly.[21]

NEW STANDARDS FOR ABORTION TRAINING

Against this backdrop of increasing abortion-related turbulence, ACGME undertook a periodic review of ob/gyn residencies in 1993, a process that involved discussions with all the program directors of these residencies nationwide. Some of the participants forcefully argued for the adoption of an abortion-training requirement, as recommended by the NAF-ACOG symposium. Those on the ob/gyn residency review committee acknowledged that the previous educational standard, which required "clinical experience in family planning," was intended to include education in abortion techniques but was, quite obviously, not explicit enough—in view of the evidence of the lack of routine abortion training.[22] After extensive consultation with residency program directors and relevant organizations, such as the AMA, ACOG, the American Board of Obstetrics and Gynecology, and the various member organizations of ACGME, the council in February 1995 approved new standards for ob/gyn residencies, requiring training in abortion and the management of abortion-related complications. The standards permitted an opt-out clause for residents with religious or moral objections to abortion. Institutions with objections to abortion, such as Catholic hospitals, were not required to provide such training on site but were obliged to arrange for off-site training of residents.[23]

Predictably, the new training requirements stimulated immediate opposition from anti-abortion forces. Various organizations strongly denounced them, and the Catholic Health Association objected to the participation of Catholic hospitals in making any arrangements for abortion training—even off-site training. In Congress, where the anti-abortion movement had picked up considerable strength in the fall 1994 elections, various anti-abortion legislators in both the House and the Senate announced plans to hold hearings on the new requirements—an unprecedented level of congressional interference in the workings of the ACGME. The House Subcommittee on Oversight and Investigations ultimately held these hearings in June 1995.

This congressional assault on abortion training remobilized the medical community, and representatives from numerous organizations, including the AMA, ACOG, the Association for American Medical Colleges, Medical Students for Choice, the Society of Physicians for Reproductive Choice and Health, and the American Medical Women's Association, spoke or submitted statements on behalf of the ACGME's revised standards. The medical representatives defended the revised standards on medical grounds—explaining the health risks to American women if physicians were not trained in abortion and the management of abortion complications—but they also spoke forcefully against congressional interference in the ACGME's internal affairs. As ACOG clearly stated:

> Congressional override of the ACGME requirements would represent an unprecedented involvement in the private educational accreditation process. Never before has an override of educational standards been proposed and such a proposal represents an unwarranted intrusion into the ability of the medical profession to determine the appropriate level of training and education required for the practice of medicine. The implications of such an override are not insignificant. Congress is simply not equipped to make decisions about what is or is not appropriate medical care and training.

In a similar vein, the statement from the American Medical Women's Association voiced "outrage that the U.S. House of Representatives would consider legislative meddling into a private accrediting body." [24]

In response to the furor over its new standards, the ACGME announced in June 1995 that it had amended its training requirements. Under the revised standard, hospitals with religious or moral objections would not have to participate in arranging or scheduling abortion training for residents who wished to learn abortion procedures. On the other hand, they could not impede residents in their programs from obtaining this training elsewhere. This concession notwithstanding, the House appropriations committee in July 1995 voted for an amendment intended to nullify the ACGME's action. [25]

As of early 1997, it is not clear what the ultimate resolution of this struggle will be. The congressional actions taken in 1995 have been further modified by subsequent legislative actions. It seems fairly certain, irrespective of what happens in Congress, that some hospitals, especially those affiliated with the Catholic Church, will continue to resist any imposition of abortion training, even off-site training. We can predict with confidence, moreover, that abortion training will remain a central issue for both sides in the abortion conflict, given its consequence for the future of abortion services. Whatever the outcome, it is clear that the events surrounding the ACGME's revision of abortion standards did mobilize much of the medical establishment, at least partly overcoming the "long-standing lethargy of organized medicine" with respect to abortion. [26]

MEDICAL STUDENTS FOR CHOICE

We turn now to Medical Students for Choice (MSFC), a new organization of pro-choice medical students that may signify a changing tide in attitudes of mainstream medicine toward abortion care. MSFC initially came into being as a result of two incidents in March 1993: the mailing of the notorious "Bottom Feeders" pamphlet, a compilation of vulgar and inflammatory anti-abortion jokes that was sent to the homes of many medical students across the country by a radical anti-abortion group, and shortly thereafter, the murder of Dr. David Gunn. Outrage and shock spurred pro-choice activism on U.S. medical school campuses. Students sympathetic to abortion became increasingly aware not only of the strength of the anti-abortion movement but of the marginalization of abortion within mainstream medical training, as they examined the curricula of their own schools and saw, in most cases, the omission of abortion from the core curriculum.

In several instances, students responded to the "Bottom Feeders" mailing by raising funds for pro-choice organizations, while publicly "thanking" Life Dynamics (the group that distributed the pamphlet) for providing the inspiration to support such organizations. On other campuses students organized panels and forums with titles such as "Providing Abortion: The Personal, Political and Ethical Dilemmas" and "The Death of Dr. Gunn: A Response to the Killing of a Health Care Provider." At some campuses, students formed groups to help place their members as volunteers in freestanding abortion clinics, where they were able to observe abortion procedures. At the University of Pennsylvania, students, with the support of sympathetic faculty, were able to organize electives on abortion for second- and fourth-year students.

In the summer of 1993, one of the authors (Jody Steinauer), then a second-year medical student at the University of California, San Francisco, decided to intern at the National Abortion Federation, working on projects stemming from the 1990 NAF-ACOG symposium. That internship facilitated a process of networking with activist medical students from all over the country, many of whom had been newly politicized by the events of the spring. Steinauer and other activists began to see the need for a national organization of pro-choice medical students to fill in the gaps created by the omission of abortion from medical education. Two Columbia students, Hillary Kunins and Sara Cade, eventually cofounded the new student organization with Steinauer.

The founders decided that this new organization—Medical Students for Choice—must work closely with existing medical student organizations to avoid marginalization and isolation from their peers. They contacted student leaders in organizations such as the American Medical Women's Association (AMWA) and the American Medical Students Association (AMSA); they held regional meetings in New York and Washington, D.C., and conducted conference calls with student leaders across the country. The group's first national project was a petition campaign to encourage the ACGME to adopt revisions requiring abortion training in ob/gyn residencies. This campaign was highly successful, ultimately gathering more than three thousand signatures from over forty medical schools.

During the 1993–94 academic year this fledgling movement engaged in a variety of activities, such as publishing the "Abortion Action

Guide,"[27] a collection of ideas based on the actual organizing efforts from students across the country during the spring of 1993; establishing an electronic mailing list with student contacts at over ninety campuses; and conducting outreach to students attending the meetings of organizations such as AMWA and AMSA. Members of the new group held numerous interviews with the media, receiving coverage in the *New York Times, Ms., The Progressive, Mademoiselle,* and other periodicals. MSFC established mentorship and internship programs, placing students in the offices of veteran abortion providers as well as in the national office of the organization.

MSFC held its first official annual meeting in conjunction with the spring 1994 annual meeting of NAF in Cincinnati. This meeting offered many of the students in attendance their first opportunity for in-depth discussion of issues pertaining to abortion services—both with other medical students and with abortion-providing physicians. Students engaged in frank discussions with their senior colleagues about the gratifications and risks of abortion work and were seemingly quite moved by the physicians' unwavering commitment to abortion provision, in spite of the undeniable stresses.[28] This first annual meeting also offered workshops in techniques of first-trimester abortion provision, as well as abortion counseling, with NAF members serving as faculty.

In fall 1994 MSFC launched three new projects: a drive among family-practice residency programs and accreditation organizations to include abortion in residency training, a curriculum resource project to collect outstanding examples of women's health curricula to aid MSFC members in curriculum reform drives on their home campuses, and a response to the "No Place to Kill" campaign launched at that time by the anti-abortion group Operation Rescue of California. That group had announced plans to target, with aggressive picketing and media appearances, two medical schools, Stanford and UCLA, for allegedly training medical students to do abortions. MSFC activists responded to this anti-abortion initiative by pointing out that neither school teaches abortion techniques to medical students (an activity confined to ob/gyn residencies) and that, in fact, these schools were *deficient* in the abortion information given to medical students. Stanford students used the publicity generated by the "No Place to Kill" campaign to organize an educational forum on abortion. Pro-choice students on both campuses contacted the deans of their schools and received assurances that the activities of Operation Rescue would not influence school policies.

By early 1995 MSFC had incorporated and had received a three-year start-up grant from an anonymous donor. The group hired an executive director (Patricia Anderson) and two part-time staff members. MSFC quickly established contacts in over one hundred U.S. medical schools.

MSFC, it should be stressed, represents future physicians who will eventually choose an array of medical specialties for their professional practice. Not all current members will become obstetricians/gynecologists or family practitioners (the two main groups now involved in abortion), nor all provide abortion services. However, the members of MSFC are united in their efforts to legitimize and normalize abortion provision. These medical students will soon graduate and ultimately join such organizations as ACOG, AMA, AMWA, the American Academy of Family Physicians, and so on. Hence, the changing perspective on abortion already under way among mainstream medical organizations presumably will be given additional force by the infusion of this pro-choice cohort.

CONCLUSION

Just as scholars have argued that the *Roe v. Wade* decision in 1973 created the "right to life" movement in the 1970s,[29] so we can argue that recent anti-abortion violence and political extremism have led to a surge of pro-choice activism within U.S. medicine in the 1990s. Speaking as pro-choice partisans, we are, to be sure, encouraged by these developments, yet we do not wish to overstate our optimism. The legislative assault on abortion services and the physical assault on abortion providers and their patients will no doubt continue. Furthermore, within medicine itself, there continue to be effective groupings of anti-abortion physicians, committed to blocking any advances in abortion delivery made by pro-choice doctors. Within the leading medical organizations, in spite of the recent developments we have chronicled, there still exist powerful forces urging the profession to minimize its engagement with such a controversial and divisive issue as abortion. Many of the pro-choice medical students we have described will doubtless encounter equally well-organized groups of "pro-life" students on their campuses. It is certainly understandable that some within the abortion-providing community, after more than twenty difficult years on the front lines of abortion delivery, may view organized medicine's recent actions as the proverbial "too little, too late."

We acknowledge the uncertain future of abortion provision in the

United States, and how much more needs to be done by mainstream medicine to assure a stable place for abortion services within routine health care. However, the increasing visibility of women within the medical profession (particularly in the field of obstetrics/gynecology)[30] and the mobilization of a large cohort of medical students, politicized not only by anti-abortion excesses but also by the ideas of gender equality that have permeated U.S. campuses in the last twenty-five years, offer hope that American women will continue to have access to needed abortion services.

NOTES

1. On nineteenth- and twentieth-century physician involvement in abortion campaigns, see Kristin Luker, *Abortion and the Politics of Motherhood* (Berkeley: University of California Press, 1984); James Mohr, *Abortion in America: The Origins and Evolution of National Policy, 1800–1900* (New York: Oxford University Press, 1978); Rosalind Petchesky, *Abortion and Woman's Choice,* rev. ed. (Boston: Northeastern University Press, 1990); and David Garrow, *Liberty and Sexuality: The Right to Privacy and the Making of Roe v. Wade* (New York: Macmillan, 1994).

2. In 1971, shortly before *Roe,* a poll of the members of the American College of Obstetricians and Gynecologists revealed that 83 percent of those responding agreed that "elective abortions should be performed under some circumstances," and only 13 percent disagreed. When this poll was repeated in 1985, the numbers were virtually unchanged. See "ACOG Poll: Ob-Gyns Support for Abortion Unchanged Since 1971," *Family Planning Perspectives* 17 (1985): 275.

3. Anna Quindlen, "A Very Loud Silence," *New York Times,* August 3, 1994, A21.

4. Clarence Lo, "Countermovements and Conservative Movements in the Contemporary U.S.," *Annual Review of Sociology* 8 (1982): 107–34.

5. Such emergency-room experiences are described in Carole Joffe, *Doctors of Conscience: The Struggle to Provide Abortion Before and After Roe v. Wade* (Boston: Beacon Press, 1995), chap. 3.

6. Petchesky, *Abortion and Women's Choice,* 124.

7. Frederick Jaffe, Barbara Lindheim, and Philip Lee, *Abortion Politics: Private Morality and Public Policy* (New York: McGraw-Hill, 1981), 46–47.

8. Stanley Henshaw and Jennifer Van Vort, "Abortion Services in the United States, 1991 and 1992," *Family Planning Perspectives* 26 (1994): 104.

9. Ibid., 105.

10. David Grimes, "Clinicians Who Provide Abortions: The Thinning Ranks," *Obstetrics and Gynecology* 80 (1992): 719–23. With respect to the cost of clinic abortions, Grimes points out: "In 1972, a first-trimester abortion in a clinic in New York City cost approximately $147; in 1989 dollars, that

would translate into about $588. . . . However, the average cost of such abortions in 1991 was below $300. Thus, the true cost of an abortion is about half that in the early 1970s" (721).

11. For an account of one physician's commute to perform abortions, see Cynthia Gorney, "Hodgson's Choice: A Long, Cold Abortion Fight," *Washington Post*, November 29, 1989, B1, B6–9.

12. Such incidents are discussed in Joffe, *Doctors of Conscience*, chap. 6.

13. One journalist recounted a terrorist campaign against Elizabeth Karlin, an abortion provider in Wisconsin:

> In 1993, a postcard was mailed throughout Madison with her photograph on it and the words FOR YOUR INFORMATION . . . ELIZABETH KARLIN [here the card gave both her home and office addresses] IS AN ABORTIONIST. "The president-elect of the American Women's Medical Association wrote letters," Karlin told me, "to the deans of the two medical schools in Wisconsin, saying 'One of the doctors is being treated poorly because of a legal medical procedure. What are you doing?' They said, 'We don't have to [do anything].' It never occurred to them that something very bad was happening and they were folding. I got a visceral reaction: okay, now I know how Hitler did it, how you absolutely paralyze a thinking society. I saw these thugs coming and frightening a medical school. This medical establishment, no matter what they say, would have to believe that women who have abortions are a little kinda dirty, a little kinda whorish; otherwise they wouldn't be able to fold" [Verlyn Klinkenborg, "Violent Certainties," *Harper's*, January 1995, 51].

14. Joffe, *Doctors of Conscience*, chap. 2.

15. Henshaw and Van Vort, "Abortion Services in the United States," 100.

16. *Webster v. Reproductive Health Services*, 109 U.S. 3040 (1989).

17. *Who Will Provide Abortions? Ensuring the Availability of Qualified Practitioners* (Washington, D.C.: National Abortion Federation, 1991), 6.

18. Ibid.

19. H. Trent McKay and Andrea P. McKay, "Abortion Training in U.S. Obstetrics and Gynecology Residency Programs: A Follow-up Study," *Family Planning Perspectives* 27 (1995): 112–15; Carolyn Westhoff, Frances Marks, and Allan Rosenfeld, "Residency Training in Contraception, Sterilization, and Abortion," *Obstetrics and Gynecology* 81 (1993):311–14.

20. Gina Kolata, "Under Pressures and Stigma, More Doctors Shun Abortion," *New York Times*, January 8, 1990, A1, B8; Sandra Boodman, "Abortion Foes Strike at Doctors' Home Lives," *Washington Post*, April 8, 1993, A1, A17; Helene Cooper, "Medical Schools, Students Shun Abortion Study," *Wall Street Journal*, March 12, 1993, B1, B3; Felice Belman, "Abortion Training Is Harder to Come By," *Boston Globe*, January 12, 1995, A1, A7.

21. National Abortion Federation, Washington, D.C., "Incidents of Violence and Disruption Against Providers, 1992, 1993." The increasing turn to violence by the anti-abortion movement is discussed in Dallas Blanchard, *The Anti-Abortion Movement and the Rise of the Religious Right* (New York: Twayne, 1994).

22. Statement of Robert D'Alessandri, chair-designate of the Accreditation Council of Graduate Medical Education, before the Subcommittee on Oversight and Investigations, Committee on Economic and Educational Opportunities, U.S. House of Representatives, June 14, 1995.

23. James Baron, "Group Requiring Abortion Study," *New York Times,* February 15, 1995, A1, A10.

24. Statement of Dr. Frank Ling on behalf of the American College of Obstetricians and Gynecologists, and statement of the American Women's Medical Association, on the ACGME Requirements for Abortion Training for Residents in Obstetrics-Gynecology, before the Subcommittee on Oversight and Investigations, Committee on Economic and Educational Opportunities, U.S. House of Representatives, June 14, 1995.

25. Jerry Gray, "Senate Approves Cutback in Current Federal Budget," *New York Times,* July 22, 1995, A7.

The summer and fall of 1995 saw the beginnings of yet another congressional intervention into abortion provision—this one concerning an abortion method, used in the second and third trimesters, known as intact "D&X" (dilation and extraction) or, as termed by anti-abortionists, "partial birth abortion." In this rarely used procedure, the fetus is delivered feet first and then the skull is partly collapsed in order to extract an intact fetus. In 1996 both the House and Senate passed legislation banning this procedure (and imposing stiff penalties, including imprisonment, on those physicians who perform it), but the bill was vetoed by President Clinton. In explaining his controversial veto, Clinton reported that he was deeply moved by encounters with women (some of them staunch right-to-lifers) whose doctors had concluded that the D&E procedure offered these patients the best chance to preserve future fertility. As of early 1997, anti-abortion forces are preparing yet another vote on this procedure. As with the ACGME regulations, this controversy also mobilized many sectors of the medical community, who again raised questions about the unprecedented nature of congressional intervention into medical affairs. See Tamar Lewin, "Bill to Ban a Type of Late-Term Abortion Could Have Much Wider Impact, Doctors Say," *New York Times,* November 6, 1995, A14, and Melody Petersen, "Cardinal Calls on President to Shift View," *New York Times,* March 10, 1997, A12.

26. Jane E. Hodgson, "Violence Versus Reproductive Health Care," *British Medical Journal* 310 (1995): 548.

27. Jody Steinauer, *Abortion Action Guide: Medical Students for Choice* (Washington, D.C.: National Abortion Federation, 1993).

28. See Joffe, "Afterword," *Doctors of Conscience,* for an account of this meeting between students and physicians.

29. See, for example, Luker, *Abortion and the Politics of Motherhood.*

30. Carol Weisman, Constance Nathanson, Martha Ann Teitelbaum, Gary Chase, and Theodore King report that "recently trained female obstetrician-gynecologists in active practice have more favorable attitudes toward abortion than do recently trained male ob/gyns, and the former are more likely to provide abortions" ("Abortion Attitudes and Performance among Male and Female Obstetricians-Gynecologists," *Family Planning Perspectives* 18 [1986]:67).

PART FIVE

REINTERPRETING ABORTION RIGHTS OVER TIME

None of the three essays in this last section could have been written at an earlier point in the struggle for abortion rights. Each reflects the theoretical, experiential, and political fruits of many decades of contestation. Philosopher Alison Jaggar revisits two influential 1970s essays supporting abortion rights, one of which she wrote. In rethinking her earlier arguments for abortion rights, she reinforces her original commitment to the centrality of gender in any adequate theory of abortion rights and now promotes a theory of privacy that encompasses principles of social obligations along with principles safeguarding the individual rights of women.

Psychologists Sharon Gold-Steinberg and Abigail Stewart assess the reports of women who obtained abortions under four different circumstances, in three different eras: pre-*Roe* illegal abortions and hospital-based therapeutic abortions, early legal abortions (1970s and early 1980s), and more recent legal abortions in the context of violence and clinic harassment. Gold-Steinberg and Stewart provide vivid frontline reports, and they contrast the stresses and possibilities for abortion with dignity and safety under various conditions.

Finally, Marsha Saxton's essay describes the recent emergence of a disability rights perspective on abortion politics. Like Dorothy Roberts (in Part Two), Saxton insists that reproductive rights must go beyond the right to have an abortion and must include the right of women to have a child. She explains the danger to all women when pregnancy is governed by marketplace concepts like quality control and the commodification of children. Saxton's essay models the possibility of simultaneously exposing the limits of pro-choice politics while espousing a profoundly pro-rights stance.

16

<hr>

Alison M. Jaggar

REGENDERING THE
U.S. ABORTION DEBATE

At a 1994 conference on abortion issues, my colleague Michael Tooley and I were asked to reevaluate our individual articles on abortion from twenty-some years earlier.[1] While Tooley and I both contended that abortion should have no legal restrictions, the style and content of our arguments were strikingly different. Contemplating these differences has reinforced my own belief in the centrality of gender in discussions of abortion. Since gender as we know it is a system of dominance as well as difference, I contend that we must address the relationship between abortion access and the social status of women.[2] My early article addressed this relationship to some extent, but I now raise a number of additional gender issues.

CONTRASTING A FEMINIST WITH A
NONFEMINIST ARGUMENT FOR ABORTION RIGHTS

Michael Tooley's influential 1972 article, "Abortion and Infanticide," was a classic example of a gender-blind treatment of abortion. It made no reference to the varying social expectations, norms, and sanctions that provide different life options for men and women, while assigning differing meanings to apparently similar choices. Briefly, Tooley argued that fetuses, while obviously human, did not have the moral status of full persons because they lacked what he regarded as the necessary and sufficient conditions for personhood, including the capacity to conceive of a continuing self, the capacity to envision a future for such a self, and the capacity for self-consciousness. Since fetuses were not persons, Tooley contended, they did not possess a "serious" right to life, and so he concluded that there was no moral justification for legal restrictions on abortion.

Denying the moral status of full personhood to the fetus is a standard move in the philosophical literature on abortion; indeed, it has often been thought indispensable to reaching a pro-choice conclusion. Tooley's article became famous, however, because it went on to argue that newborn infants as well as fetuses failed to meet the conditions of personhood; from this conceptual claim Tooley drew the startling moral conclusion that infanticide was permissible, at least for infants in the first week of life.

My own article "Abortion and a Woman's Right to Decide," published in 1975, also argued in favor of legalizing abortion, but my rationale was very different from Tooley's. I contended that because prevailing gender norms assigned women the primary responsibility for the welfare of their offspring, the birth of children affected the lives of their mothers far more significantly than it affected the life of anyone else and thus gave women the moral authority to decide whether to carry their pregnancies to term. I argued that this moral authority should be formalized in a legal right. Because this right would derive primarily from mothers' socially assigned responsibility for child rearing, I suggested that it might conceivably be limited in a society that did not place the entire burden of child rearing on mothers. However, I noted that pregnant women's wishes should still be accorded special weight because their bodies were uniquely involved.

Despite the fact that Tooley and I made virtually identical recommendations regarding abortion law, there were striking contrasts in the ways that we framed the issue:

1. Tooley focused on the fetus and its moral status, ignoring the pregnant woman; I focused on the pregnant woman, virtually ignoring the fetus except to assume that its right to life was not so strong that abortion was always morally prohibited.
2. Whether the fetus was located inside or outside the woman's body was a matter of moral indifference for Tooley. For me, by contrast, the location of the fetus inside or outside the woman's body was a crucial element of the situation; indeed, my article had an adden-

dum specifically denying that my arguments might be extended to justify killing fetuses not located inside women (i.e., infanticide).

3. Tooley's argument was not anti-feminist, but it made no mention of gender or feminist issues. By contrast, my article was overtly gendered because it focused on the fact that men and women were situated differently with respect to procreation—not primarily because of differences in their reproductive physiology but most significantly because gendered social norms assigned them different responsibilities in child rearing. As well as being gendered, my article was also feminist because it was concerned to alleviate women's subordination.

4. Tooley argued that all abortions were morally permissible, but I did not assume this. Although I insisted that pregnant women should be legally empowered to decide whether to abort, I acknowledged that women were fallible and might make a decision that was morally wrong. I agreed, however, with the bumper-sticker assertion that if a woman was mature enough to be a mother, she was also mature enough to decide not to be one.

5. Because his argument was primarily conceptual, Tooley asserted a right to abortion that was universal, holding in all worlds where creatures resembling humans began life with immature rational faculties. For me, by contrast, an unrestricted right to abortion held contingently, depending on a social context of privatized childbearing and child rearing; if the context changed, the right might be limited.

6. Tooley's argument was much cleaner and neater than mine since, although he left open some questions about animal rights, he offered a straightforward answer to most moral and legal questions about abortion. My own argument offered no guidance concerning the moral justification of abortion, and while it aimed to close the legal question for societies similar to the contemporary United States, it left open questions about the legal regulation of abortion in societies that were very different, especially societies that made more extensive public provision for pregnant and birthing women and their children.

7. Tooley's discussion was conducted entirely in terms of rights. I appealed to rights, too, but much of my argument revolved around the notion of responsibilities. As noted in 5 above, my argument was also much more responsive than Tooley's to the moral salience of differing social contexts. In these ways, my thinking resembled

that of the U.S. women contemplating abortion in the mid-1970s, whose reasoning was discussed in psychologist Carol Gilligan's well-known work.[3]

While I have never been an advocate of the ethics of care described by Gilligan, it is surely not by chance that there are some striking parallels in the ways that Gilligan's subjects and I addressed the issue of abortion. This coincidence suggests to me that the contrasts between Tooley's and my approaches reflect not only differences between feminist and non-feminist priorities but also differences between moral sensibilities and styles of reasoning that, in Anglo-American cultures, are coded feminine and masculine.[4]

ABORTION AS A PRIVATE RIGHT: 1990S REFLECTIONS ON MY 1970S ARGUMENT

Two decades later, I continue to endorse the main line of argument pursued in my 1975 article, but I now see a need to clarify and even modify several aspects of it.

Separating the Legal from the Moral

Some critics have charged that, by avoiding the issue of the fetus's moral status, I beg the central question of the abortion controversy. How far this is a valid criticism depends in part on one's primary concerns in entering the debate. My article was not directed toward establishing the circumstances in which abortion was and was not morally permissible; instead, I aimed to determine who should be legally empowered to make abortion decisions and what legal limits, if any, should be imposed on those decisions. I believed that I could provide answers to these political questions while withholding commitment on the moral ones.

I now think that my argument for assigning women the legal right to abortion conceals more substantive moral and political assumptions than I realized twenty years ago. Specifically, it assumes not only that abortion is at least sometimes morally justifiable but also that making a morally unjustified decision on this issue is not such an indisputably egregious wrong as to deserve legal penalty. This assumption needs more support than I offered in 1975, but I would still like to defend it on grounds that are primarily political, continuing to avoid the vexed question of fetal moral status.

The issue of the proper relationship between morality and law is difficult and contested, but liberal democratic, secular, and culturally diverse nations like the United States explicitly reject the idea that law should function simply to enforce morality. Instead, law is regarded as providing a just framework (a public morality) that maximizes all citizens' opportunities to pursue their varying conceptions of the good life (their private moralities) while itself remaining neutral between those conceptions. How to distinguish between justice and the good life or between public and private morality is itself contestable, however, and here the line must be drawn by politics.[5]

One way of understanding the contemporary U.S. controversy over abortion is to see it as a disagreement over whether abortion should be categorized as an issue of justice or the good life—of public or private morality. Those who insist that the fetus is a person, so that even early abortions are the moral equivalent of murder, clearly regard abortion as an issue of justice to fetuses and thus as a matter for state regulation. By contrast, those who regard even late abortions as being on a moral par with tooth extraction obviously take abortion simply to be a matter of personal preference or at most of private morality on which the state should remain neutral.

Despite deep disagreement regarding the moral significance of abortion, an "overlapping consensus"[6] does exist in the United States that abortion is at least occasionally permissible. Although this claim is in principle open to challenge, in practice it has been accepted by virtually all participants in the U.S. debate over the past twenty years; even those who wish to set very tight legal limits on abortion are generally prepared to permit abortions not only for pregnancies that threaten the life or health of the woman but also for those resulting from rape or incest or involving damage to the fetus. The widespread consensus on the permissibility of abortion at least in those circumstances suggests that even people who speak of abortion as murder regard fetal rights as weaker or more easily annulled than the rights of full-fledged persons. After all, they presumably would not regard it as morally acceptable to kill children or adults conceived through rape or incest or suffering from disabilities.[7]

In the absence of any consensus on whether abortion is a matter of public justice or private morals, I contend that it is undemocratic and illiberal to categorize abortion decisions as matters of justice to fetuses that are properly subject to legal constraints. The general consensus that abortion is permissible on some occasions, coupled with the conspicuous lack of consensus about which occasions those are, provides a democratic justification for leaving the decision whether to abort up to individual women.

In a society where women's heterosexual encounters are frequently manipulated and coerced and in which mothers remain primarily responsible for the welfare of their children, I continue to believe that it is important to separate the issue of when, if ever, abortion is morally permissible from the issues of who should be empowered to make abortion decisions and how, if at all, they should be legally regulated. My personal view is that not all abortions are morally justified even in the first trimester, but I nevertheless insist that abortion must be an option legally available to all women.[8] Indeed, I believe that the importance of having this option available is increasing in the 1990s as welfare nets disintegrate almost everywhere. Certainly a pregnant woman may make a morally wrong decision concerning abortion, but the fact that she knows her own desires, capacities, and circumstances better than anyone else means she is more likely than anyone else to make the right decision. Those who advocate severe legal constraints on abortion frequently postulate women aborting in order not to spoil vacations abroad, suggesting that women's reasons for abortion are typically selfish and frivolous, but I believe there is ample evidence, including the reflections reported by Carol Gilligan, demonstrating that women in general do not make the abortion decision lightly. Women who seek abortions generally have excellent reasons for their decisions, and as a feminist, I believe that their diverse reasons should be respected.

Although so far I have contended only that the right to abortion is a matter of private rather than public morality, I do not think this is all that needs to be said. I shall now argue that, because abortion decisions have public as well as private significance, there is justification for some public measures designed to influence those decisions.

Making the Right to Abortion Contingent

My 1975 article has troubled not only nonfeminists but also some feminists, who have worried that tying the right to abortion to women's contingent social situation would open the door to limiting that right as women's situation changed, raising the specter of forced abortions and forced motherhood. This concern is understandable, even though my article did assert that pregnant women's voices should always carry special weight. In what John Rawls calls the ordinary circumstances of justice, I cannot imagine how it could ever be justified to override a pregnant woman's wishes, but my 1975 article left open the possibility that there might be some extreme circumstances in which this could be envisioned. I did not specify those circumstances, but I had in mind women in communities facing catastrophes such as genocide, mass starvation, or mass infertility.

Twenty years later, I should like to develop this thought in a direction more salient to the circumstances of everyday life in nations where extreme conditions do not obtain for most people, where population size, health care, and sexual inequality are matters of concern but not of such immediate and overwhelming urgency as to outweigh all other considerations. In these more normal circumstances, I believe that women should have a legal right to abortion that cannot be overridden, but I also believe that it is legitimate in principle to shape public policies in ways designed to influence their abortion decisions. To regard these two beliefs as incompatible would be to ignore the fact that individual decisions are always made in the context of options that are socially constructed. Birth has consequences for the society at large as well as for individual women, and I see no reason in principle why policy makers considering the probable outcomes of various policies should not also take into account their likely consequences for women's abortion decisions.

This principled claim does not justify any and all social incentives designed to achieve any and all abortion outcomes. Which abortion decisions should be encouraged and which incentives are impermissibly coercive or otherwise inappropriate is open to debate; for example, in wealthy nations like the United States I can see no justification for measures that penalize poor families in which women refuse abortion. The intuition embodied in my 1975 assertion that the right to abortion is contingent on the social context recurs here in the thought that developing appropriate answers to the questions of which incentives are permissible in motivating which abortion decisions requires reference especially to the social supports available to pregnant women, mothers, and children. When more of the responsibility for the care and well-being of children is underwritten by the society as a whole rather than being left to individual mothers, it seems to me that, other things being equal, the society is justified in creating stronger incentives to encourage women either to terminate or to retain their pregnancies. In this context, it should be noted that a multitude of factors other than direct regulation influences rates of abortion: these factors include not only the availability of contraception, health care, and social supports for child rearing but also the level of women's education, their employment prospects, and whether girl babies are valued as much as boys.

Even though I continue to believe that women's rights to abortion may be limited in some extraordinary circumstances, I have now reevaluated the general suspicion of individual rights that I expressed in 1975. That suspicion reflected the dream of a nonadversarial community in which individual rights at best were features of a transitional morality, destined to lose their function when structural conflicts of interest were reconciled. I now think that the dream of ultimate social harmony not only is utopian in the sense of being unrealizable but may also often be the thin end of the wedge of totalitarianism. Today I believe that individual rights must be a permanent feature of any society that we can reasonably foresee—though I would not give metaphysical grounding to such rights and I think that their content will vary. In a time when some conservatives are appropriating the rhetoric of community to attack individual rights, including abortion rights, it becomes more incumbent on feminists to defend them.

Despite the utopian speculation that appeared in its conclusion, the overall spirit of my 1975 article was firmly practical in pointing to the political realities of existing gender inequities. I think my early insistence on the contingency of the right to abortion was valuable in focusing attention on some of those inequities, but it is now necessary to address further gender-related issues, omitted from my 1975 article, which have become more evident and urgent in the intervening years.

ABORTION ACCESS AS A PUBLIC RESPONSIBILITY: MAKING GENDER CONCERNS EXPLICIT

Gender is invisible in many mainstream philosophical discussions of abortion; gender-blindness like Michael Tooley's is the rule rather than the exception.[9] Feminists have often noted, however, that in gender-structured societies that situate men and women differently, ignoring gender is as likely to lead to gender injustice as to gender equity. One striking example is the notorious 1976 U.S. Supreme Court decision in the case of *Gilbert v. General Electric,* in which the Court ruled that excluding pregnancy from health insurance coverage was not a form of sex discrimination because any man who became pregnant would be similarly excluded. Abortion is one example of an issue in which gender-blind thinking has generated gender-biased outcomes.

Current abortion law in the United States derives from the landmark 1973 Supreme Court decision in the case of *Roe v. Wade*. This decision justified the right to first-trimester abortions in terms of a constitutional right to privacy attributed to all citizens—and to pregnant women under the guidance of their physicians. In the second trimester, *Roe* ruled that the state might regulate the procedure in ways reasonably related to the pregnant woman's health, and in the third trimester it allowed abortion to be restricted and even prohibited, except where the woman's life or health was at stake, because the state was said to have an interest in protecting the fetus after it had become viable.

The decision in *Roe* represented first-trimester abortion as an exclusively individual matter of gender-neutral privacy, recognizing no specifically gendered links between abortion access and women's social status or freedom. A number of authors have noted, however, that grounding the right to abortion in a right to privacy has mixed implications from a feminist perspective. On the one hand, the appeal to privacy supports women's reproductive autonomy by shifting the decision-making authority away from the state and toward the pregnant woman (and her physician); on the other hand, privacy invokes a legal tradition of noninterference in marriage that has operated historically to reinforce male dominance in the family by denying women legal redress from economic, physical, and sexual abuse by their fathers, brothers, husbands, and other men in their families.[10] More generally, the doctrine of privacy protects individual liberties while obscuring recognition of community responsibilities. In addition to its ambiguous symbolic significance, the *Roe* judgment has had several practical consequences that are unsatisfactory from a feminist perspective insofar as they have opened the door to various restrictions on women's right to abort even in the first trimester.

It is noteworthy that the judgment in *Roe* involved physicians, not only in carrying out abortions, but also in making abortion decisions. The inclusion of physicians in a decision-making capacity suggests that the 1973 Supreme Court was concerned at least as much with protecting the privacy of physician-patient relationships as with protecting women's reproductive freedom. However, unless decisions whether to abort are made on medical grounds—which, in the overwhelming majority of cases, they are not—compulsory physician involvement in decision making infringes in principle on women's autonomy. Women's right to make their own abortion decisions was finally recognized by the U.S. Supreme Court in the 1977 case of *Whalen v. Roe*.

Women's autonomy is infringed on, in practice as well as principle, by the fact that *Roe v. Wade* relates the permissibility of abortion to the length of pregnancy. Anxious to secure at least some abortion rights, activists in the early 1970s acquiesced in restrictions on later abortions, including a virtual prohibition on third-trimester abortions—which, of course, are most likely to be needed by the most vulnerable women: young, poor, mentally disabled, abused or abandoned by their partners. Acceding to the principle that abortion was subject to state regulation not only permitted women's rights to be limited as pregnancy progressed but also opened the door for limitations even on first-trimester abortions. Since 1973 the U.S. Supreme Court has accepted a series of restrictions on women's right to abort. In 1979 the Court upheld a Massachusetts "squeal-rule" law requiring minors to notify both their parents or obtain their consent for an abortion; it argued that the requirement of parental consent or notification did not infringe on a minor's right to privacy if the minor could bypass the parents by obtaining judicial consent.[11] In the 1980 cases of *Harris v. McRae* and *Williams v. Zbaraz*, the Court upheld the right of Congress and state legislatures to refuse to pay even for *medically necessary* abortions for poor women. This decision upheld the 1976 Hyde Amendment, which had prohibited Medicaid funding for abortion except where the woman's life was at risk; it was followed by campaigns in many states to prohibit state funding of abortion, and today only a small minority of U.S. states continue to fund abortions on the same basis as other medical procedures.[12]

Ironically, despite its involvement of physicians in abortion decisions, *Roe*'s privacy rationale fails to conceptualize abortion as a matter of public health, regardless of the health hazards associated with both pregnancy and illegal abortions. This failure is unfortunate because conceptualizing abortion as an issue of health would have provided a rationale for demanding the provision of abortion services as a necessary aspect of health care. Without this, *Roe* has permitted abortion access to be restricted by cost as well as in the ways mentioned above.

The problems inherent in the *Roe* decision suggest that feminists should explore alternative justifications for the right to abortion, alternatives that will make the gender dimensions of the issue more explicit. My 1975 article offered one gendered rationale for abortion choice, but its main concern was to argue that abortion should be a private right—at least in societies that relegated pregnancy, birth, and child rearing to the private realm of maternal responsibility. In insisting that abortion was a private right, I neglected to consider the conditions necessary for exercising that right. In light of the withdrawal of most public funding for abortion since the early 1970s, as well as the increasing restrictions on even first-trimester abortions, it has now become evident that my argument for making abortion legally available needs to be supplemented by an argument that abortion should also be practically available—supplied when necessary by public provision. At a minimum, this provision should take the form of paying for abortions for indigent women, but in areas where anti-abortion terrorism has forced the closure of abortion facilities, publicly funded abortion clinics should also be established.

At least two possible lines of thought lend themselves to this conclusion. One is to recognize abortion access as indispensable to women's health, since the unavailability of safe and affordable abortions often leads women who seek to terminate their pregnancies to resort to practitioners or methods that threaten their health and even their lives. Framing abortion as a health care issue would, as I suggested above, open the way to justifying the public provision of abortion services. Alternatively or perhaps complementarily, abortion may be seen as necessary to equal opportunity for women, since the denial of abortion access clearly has a disparate impact on women's possibilities for full social participation. Insofar as government has a responsibility to equalize opportunities, this rationale, too, can justify a social obligation to provide abortion services. Lack of abortion access has an especially severe impact on poor women, including women of color (who in the United States are disproportionately poor). Poor women have much greater difficulty in finding the money for private—let alone illegal—abortions, and unwanted pregnancy also imposes a greater health, economic, and employment burden on poor women. For this reason, the public provision of abortion services is a matter of class and race as well as gender justice.

Arguing that gender equity requires the government to make abortion services practically available to all women moves the issue out of the realm of private morality into that of public justice—at which point it appears to run counter to my earlier argument that abortion should be a private decision. How can it be claimed simultaneously that abortion is a matter of private morality, on which the state should be neutral, *and* that it is a public matter of gender justice, whose availability should be guaranteed by the state?

The apparent contradiction between these two claims vanishes when ones notes the distinction between abortion decisions and the context in which they are made. There is no contradiction between asserting that abortion decisions should be private rights in societies that privatize pregnancy, childbearing, and child rearing and simultaneously insisting that justice requires a guarantee of the conditions in which those decisions may be genuine choices. If the state has a responsibility to enable the exercise of private rights, it is arguable that the first claim is not only compatible with the second but actually presupposes it. What constitutes a genuine choice is always debatable, of course, but it is hard to see how a woman could be said to have a real choice to abort if she has no way of reaching an abortion facility or paying for abortion services.

Resolving the logical dilemma unfortunately does not solve the political one. Even though feminists may agree that abortion access is indispensable to gender equity, there is no more public consensus on this issue in the contemporary United States than there is on the question of whether abortion decisions are matters of justice for fetuses. In the absence of consensus, the same reasoning that finds it illiberal and undemocratic to permit abortion to be legally prohibited entails that it is equally illiberal and undemocratic to require that abortion access be publicly supported.

Until a consensus emerges regarding the justice of abortion access, the dilemma may be addressed by challenging conventional conceptualizations of public neutrality, which is not necessarily achieved by making abortions available only to those who can afford them.[13] Rather than interpreting the refusal to make abortions available to women who cannot afford to pay for them as public neutrality on the issue, it is at least as plausible to interpret it as *de facto* support for the view that abortion is unjust. After all, those who regard abortion as morally prohibited are not compelled to avail themselves of abortion services, just as some people refrain on moral grounds from accepting other medical services, such as blood transfusions, organ transplants, or life-support systems. Health care workers who are reluctant on moral grounds to participate in abortion procedures could have alternatives made available to them, just as alternatives should be available for scientists-in-training who oppose animal vivisection or for draftees who oppose militarism. If abortion access is indeed a means to the achievement of goods such as health and equity that are public as well as private, the refusal to make this means universally available demonstrates not public neutrality but public endorsement of a status quo in which women are not equal citizens.

Objectors to public funding for abortion may argue that making tax money available for such highly controversial purposes forces taxpayers who are morally opposed to abortion to violate their consciences. But abortion is not uniquely controversial when compared with many other purposes for which tax money is spent, including support for various research programs, construction projects, and military adventures. It is always open to those who feel strongly enough about the injustice of a public expenditure to oppose it through the political process or even engage in the civil disobedience of tax resistance.

Acknowledging the centrality of gender to abortion has the potential for disrupting the apparent consensus in the United States that the state has a right, even a duty, to regulate abortion in ways that go far beyond its regulation of comparably simple and inexpensive medical procedures. Disrupting this consensus would create a space in which feminists could again raise the 1960s call to repeal all laws singling out abortion as a special medical procedure. The demand for the repeal of all laws specifically regulating abortion was eventually compromised away in the effort to secure first the passage of abortion rights in New York in 1970 and later the *Roe v. Wade* decision, and it is now a part of U.S. feminist history that has been almost forgotten.[14] Today, the idea of repealing all abortion laws is virtually never raised in public discourse, which focuses almost exclusively on which restrictions on abortion may be justified, never questioning the whole idea of regulation. Recasting the abortion debate as being about gender rather than about fetal life would encourage questions about why abortion is singled out for special regulation instead of being simply subject to the same health and safety provisions imposed on other medical procedures. Once the gender issues underlying the abortion debate are revealed, a discursive space is opened for giving them the attention they deserve.

Making the gender implications of abortion more explicit would also have the advantage of broadening the focus of abortion debates. For instance, it would encourage questions about why half of all U.S. pregnancies are aborted, when most women in the United States, unlike many men, want at least one child. Other gendered questions relevant to abortion include:

- What kinds of pressure are brought to bear on women in the sexual encounters that initiate unplanned pregnancies?
- Why do women not insist on contraception? Are they deprived of information about it, unable to afford it, or simply not in a position to insist?
- Why is contraception women's responsibility, anyway? Why are most methods directed at women's rather than men's bodies? And why, when so many other methods involve unpleasant or dangerous side effects, do so many men refuse to use condoms?
- When it takes two to conceive a child, why are women primarily responsible for child rearing?
- Why is there so little public support for children, in terms of familial services, housing, health care, and child care?
- Why do full-time employed women still earn about two-thirds of what full-time employed men make? Why is the minimum wage too low to support a family?

Raising these questions obviously leads away from a tunnel-vision focus on abortion as involving simply "parents," fetuses, and (perhaps) physicians, toward examining the wider social conditions that produce so many unwanted pregnancies and then turn them into crises for individual women. It also leads toward developing a vision of full reproductive freedom for women that goes far beyond making abortion legally or even practically available.

ABORTION RIGHTS TRANSFORM FAMILY RELATIONS

My 1975 paper on abortion was written while I was enjoying a planned pregnancy with my second child. At the time I remember being pleased that the experience of pregnancy had not changed my views by stimulating some overwhelming maternal instinct and even thinking that the timing of my paper constituted a counterexample to the crude biological determinisms that were around at the time, including a lot of talk about so-called raging hormones. (Actually, all attempts by pregnant women to secure abortions constitute counterexamples to such determinisms.) Although being pregnant did not stimulate some visceral horror of abortion, my own experiences of pregnancy have enriched my views on this subject, and since feminists are characteristically unwilling to separate the personal from the political, I want to conclude by relating what I have learned from these experiences.

Two of my children were unplanned. One was conceived in 1972, the other in 1986, and the timing of both was terrible. In 1972 I had just been appointed as the first female faculty member in a university philosophy department and felt I had to prove myself in what was then almost exclusively a man's world. In 1986 my partner had decided to make a midlife career change and arranged to train in a city three hundred miles from our home, leaving me with our two teenagers. The 1972 pregnancy was due just two days before the academic year began; the 1986 one was due just a few days before my partner was leaving on a one-chance-in-a-lifetime trip to China.

The first unplanned pregnancy was prior to *Roe v. Wade* but after the legalization of abortion in New York; with the second, abortion was easily available in my home state. On both occasions I considered abortion but each time decided to have the child. Even though I chose not to end either of my unplanned pregnancies, those experiences taught me two important lessons about abortion.

The first lesson was that unplanned pregnancies can always occur, even to women holding Ph.D.s. While we can certainly reduce the number of unwanted pregnancies, we are unlikely to eliminate them entirely; abortion must therefore always remain available, not only as a backup method of birth control but also so that women can change their minds about giving birth if their life circumstances unexpectedly change in the course of their pregnancies.

The second lesson I learned from my two unplanned pregnancies was that the right to abortion is extremely important even to those women who do not choose to exercise it. My life was enormously difficult after the birth of both unplanned children, and I am sure I would have resented the babies, not to mention their father, if I had not been able to make a deliberate decision to carry the pregnancies to term. The fact that I had chosen rather than been forced to give birth provided quite a different and much more positive meaning to the birth experience and certainly made me and my family much happier than we would have been if abortion had not been a real option.

Conservatives charge abortion activists with undermining so-called family values, even, as Rickie Solinger has put it, with "killing motherhood." By contrast, I believe that abortion access is necessary to making motherhood—and fatherhood and childhood—more fully human. The availability of abortion is certainly insufficient alone to transform family life in all the ways that feminists would like, but it can definitely make a significant contribution to improving the quality of the family lives that we lead already.

NOTES

1. The 1994 conference was "Abortion: New Issues for the 90s," sponsored by the Center for Values and Social Policy, University of Colorado at Boulder, April 1994. The two articles Tooley and I were asked to reevaluate at the conference are Michael Tooley, "Abortion and Infanticide," *Philosophy and Public Affairs* 2, no. 1 (Fall 1972), and Alison M. Jaggar, "Abortion and a Woman's Right to Decide," *Philosophical Forum* 5, nos. 1–2 (Winter 1975). I should like to thank my colleague Ann Davis, who organized the conference, as well as Karuna Jaggar, Linda Nicholson, James Nickel, Karsten Struhl, Michelle Wilcox, and Jessica Wilson, who commented on drafts of this essay.

2. Catharine A. MacKinnon, "Difference and Dominance: On Sex Discrimination," in *Feminism Unmodified: Discourses on Life and Law*, ed. Catharine A. MacKinnon (Cambridge, Mass.: Harvard University Press, 1987).

3. Carol Gilligan, *In a Different Voice: Psychological Theory and Women's Development* (Cambridge, Mass.: Harvard University Press, 1982).

4. Of course, this is not the same as postulating differences in the working of male and female brains.

5. Seyla Benhabib, *Situating the Self: Gender, Community, and Postmodernism in Contemporary Ethics* (New York: Routledge, 1992).

6. John Rawls, *Political Liberalism* (New York: Columbia University Press, 1993).

7. The rape/incest/fetal damage exceptions are interesting from a feminist point of view because they suggest that those who oppose the legalization of abortion may be motivated less by a conviction of the sanctity of fetal life than by a desire to control women's sexuality. If fetal life is indeed sacrosanct, it seems immaterial whether it was conceived through rape or incest or whether it suffers some disability. The unspoken subtext of the exemptions is that women cannot be held responsible for these misfortunes and so should not be made to deal with the consequences. The unspoken comes closer to being spoken when women carrying damaged fetuses or pregnant as a result of rape or incest are described as innocent or "blameless," thereby implying that other pregnant women are in some sense blameworthy and deserve the punishment of having to bear a child.

8. Somewhat analogously, I believe that eating meat in the circumstances of the contemporary United States tends to promote injustice to animals, but without much more consensus than presently exists on this issue, I do not think that eating meat should be outlawed.

9. For instance, Bruce Ackerman offers a two-page discussion of abortion formulated strictly in the gender-neutral terms of parents and their offspring (Ackerman, *Social Justice in the Liberal State* [New Haven: Yale University

Press, 1980], cited in Susan Moller Okin, *Justice, Gender, and the Family* [New York: Basic Books, 1989], 12).

10. Rhonda Copelon, "From Privacy to Autonomy: The Conditions for Sexual and Reproductive Freedom," in *From Abortion to Reproductive Freedom: Transforming a Movement,* ed. Marlene Gerber Fried (Boston: South End Press, 1990).

11. Girls who withhold from their parents the information that they are pregnant generally have good reason for doing so, and enforcing parental notification may result in such girls being coerced or abused by their parents. Attempting to exercise the option of obtaining judicial consent can be a logistical as well as legal ordeal for girls who wish to keep their pregnancies secret.

12. In 1989, in the case of *Webster v. Reproductive Health Services,* the Court upheld a Missouri law permitting the state to prohibit "public facilities" (i.e., hospitals with public funding) and "public employees" from being used to perform or assist abortions not necessary to save the life of the woman and requiring that whenever a woman appeared to be at least twenty weeks pregnant, the physician must conduct tests to determine viability. In its 1992 *Casey* decision the Court accepted Pennsylvania's requirement that a woman seeking abortion must listen to a physician deliver information on the status of the fetus and then wait twenty-four hours before the procedure could be performed.

13. Similarly, public neutrality on the issue of vegetarianism is generally thought to require that public schools and military dining halls make both meat and vegetable dishes available, not that they refuse to serve any meat.

14. Ninia Baehr, *Abortion without Apology: A Radical History for the 1990s* (Boston: South End Press, 1990). NARAL is the largest U.S. pro-choice organization; when it was founded in 1969, its name was an acronym for National Association for the *Repeal* of Abortion Laws—not, as it has since become, the National Abortion and Reproductive Rights Action League.

17

Sharon Gold-Steinberg and
Abigail J. Stewart

PSYCHOLOGIES OF ABORTION

Implications of a Changing Context

Abortion is at once a personal and a political event. Women often talk about abortion as a personal choice. Typically, women recount having had an abortion as a vivid and significant episode in their reproductive histories. It occurs in their bodies. Yet, when the government controls access to abortion, terminating a pregnancy can become a political event as well. In fact, the legal, moral, and logistic context for abortion deeply influences a woman's experience of abortion: How easy or difficult is it to arrange? Who else must be involved in the decision? How far will she need to travel? How much will it cost? How dangerous will the procedure be? Will she need to break the law? How will others construe her decision? Furthermore, recognizing that someone else is determining the parameters of her choice to have an abortion often motivates a woman to a new political analysis of her status in relationship to men and to the state.[1]

Ultimately both personal and political factors affect the psychology of abortion. This chapter explores how these two factors have interacted to shape women's experiences of abortion in the United States over the last thirty years. We begin by providing a brief history of how the political, legal, and moral definitions of abortion have changed. We then review the findings from psychology about the personal and interpersonal factors likely to affect a woman's experience of abortion, regardless of the legality of the procedure. Our emphasis, then, is on how women have coped with abortion under four different sets of political-legal circumstances: illegal abortions, therapeutic abortions, legal abortions in the 1970s and early 1980s, and legal abortions in the context of protest, harassment, and threats of violence.

THE HISTORY OF POLITICAL CHANGES

In the last century the political climate surrounding abortion in the United States has taken a number of dramatic turns. During the second half of the nineteenth century, after about one hundred years of largely ignoring the issue of abortion, every state imposed laws stating that only "therapeutic" abortions—those needed to preserve the life of the mother—could be performed legally. Both eugenic concerns (hopes that middle- and upper-class women would have more babies) and the professionalization of medicine (leading to the definition of abortion as a strictly medical procedure) contributed to these policy changes.[2] Moral or ethical concerns about abortion neither informed nor motivated this change in legal policy.

An important shift in how doctors defined therapeutic abortion became prominent in the 1940s. Psychiatrists, as a specialty group within the medical community, were increasingly called upon to determine whether an individual woman could be granted a therapeutic abortion. As physical threats to a pregnant woman's life became less common, therapeutic abortions could be obtained only if a psychiatrist—or medical board—deemed that continuing the pregnancy would lead to suicide.[3] In the late 1960s fourteen states liberalized their laws to permit access to therapeutic abortions in cases of fetal deformity, rape, incest, or more broadly defined threats to a woman's mental health than suicide.[4]

Also in the late 1960s, in the course of the "second wave" of the women's movement, feminists sought to define abortion as covered by the individual's right of privacy. Four states legalized first-trimester abortions in 1970. The Supreme Court decision in the case of *Roe v. Wade* guaranteed this right nationally in 1973. Beginning in the late 1980s, however, a number of states again began legislating restrictions on access to abortion, including waiting periods, parental consent for teens, and prohibitions on Medicaid funding. These legislative actions reflected growing conservative political pressure about the moral implications of abortion. Even in states that have not restricted access to first-trimester abortions, women frequently confront protesters and the threat of violence or harassment, as they approach or enter clinics where abortions are performed.

FACTORS AFFECTING COPING WITH ABORTION

There is much political debate about the psychological effects of abortion, and controversy surrounds the methodological issues involved in research on this topic.[5] Those studies that are more methodologically rigorous have generally concluded, however, that the risk of negative psychological effects, at least in the short term, is quite low and not unlike the risks associated with childbirth.[6] Typically, researchers have found that stress is highest before the abortion procedure, whereas relief is the predominant emotion in the hours and weeks following an abortion.[7] This pattern suggests that many women experience abortion as a resolution to the crisis of an unwanted pregnancy; it is the pregnancy, then, that is the primary stressor.[8] Evidence suggests that a woman copes best with abortion when she experiences a low degree of ambivalence or conflict about her decision, receives support from significant others, and has positive expectations about her ability to cope with the abortion.[9]

Nonetheless, researchers have identified a number of factors that can contribute to the negative psychological outcomes documented in a small minority of abortion cases.[10] For instance, experiencing greater difficulty or conflict in deciding to terminate a pregnancy is associated with poorer adjustment after the abortion. A woman's decision may be made more difficult by such factors as value conflicts, an initially planned or wanted pregnancy, the length of the pregnancy, and a partner who does not support her choice.[11] Blaming herself for the pregnancy and having negative expectations before the abortion also may contribute to adjustment problems.[12] Finally, life events after an abortion, such as later infertility or a change in values or religious orientation, may lead a woman to reevaluate her decision.[13]

Most of the empirical research on the psychological effects of abortion has been conducted since the legalization of abortion and has focused on the contextual features of women's lives and circumstances that affect coping. Studies of therapeutic abortion generally were more methodologically flawed and addressed the narrower question of whether psychiatric illness predicted negative outcomes of abortion.

Complicating the study of this issue was the fact that the legal restrictions on abortion may have resulted in women fabricating or exaggerating psychiatric symptoms in order to be granted a therapeutic abortion.[14] Interestingly, studies on therapeutic abortion, like those on legal abortion, generally concluded that the psychological outcome for most women was benign.[15]

Prospective studies of coping with illegal abortions or abortions in clinics picketed by protesters have not been conducted, to our knowledge. Nonetheless, it has been asserted that "more than most medical procedures, abortion is embedded in a social context that has implications for psychological reactions of patients."[16] To learn more about the impact of abortion under different legal circumstances, we asked women engaged in women's organizations and political activities to recount their experiences of abortions between 1962 and 1978.[17] Although such retrospective accounts may be subject to unknown distortion, our interest was in the psychological impact of abortion, which can be legitimately evaluated from retrospective accounts, even without data about pre-abortion personality. Moreover, it seemed crucial to collect even limited retrospective data when there is so little data on which to base an understanding of the psychological implications of legal changes in abortion policy.

We tried to limit the period during which the abortion occurred in order to keep fairly constant the larger sociopolitical environment in which the abortions occurred, while at the same time sampling from before and after the *Roe v. Wade* decision. The 1960s and 1970s do, in retrospect, seem to have had a certain unity of activist spirit, animated by a tone of hope and idealism. Although there were some important indications of social crisis, including urban rioting, a growing drug problem, the assassination of a president, and Watergate, it was a period dominated by such social causes as civil rights, the war on poverty, opposition to the Vietnam War, and women's rights. It was a period of relative affluence and of increasing rights and opportunities for those traditionally limited and excluded (chiefly women and nonwhites). The advancement of women's rights certainly contributed to changes in legal access to abortion. Nonetheless, a consistent theme that emerges from our research is that women's reproductive experiences continued to take place in a context in which other parties controlled and structured the range of choices.

Ninety-nine women who had had abortions—illegal (36), therapeutic (10), or legal (53)—during this period completed lengthy questionnaires, including narrative accounts of their experiences and reflections on the abortion's impact on them. Several women also participated in lengthy interviews about their experience of abortion and its sequelae. On average, the women were just under twenty-three years old when they had their abortions. All the participants were European American. Most had attended college, and many held advanced degrees. The majority identified themselves as pro-choice. The homogeneity of the sample certainly limits the generalizability of the conclusions, especially as these were all women already involved in women's organizations or political activities; at the same time, it allows for comparison of the women's different abortion experiences.[18]

Although each woman's experience was different, we did find some common features for each of four types of abortion experiences: illegal, therapeutic, legal, and legal under siege. Our account is derived from quantitative and qualitative analysis of the data from our research project, from a review of the psychological literature, and from reading contemporary accounts of women confronting protest or violence at clinics where abortions are provided.

Illegal Abortion

For women who sought illegal abortions, finding someone to perform the procedure was a monumental and all-consuming task. As one woman who had an abortion in 1968 explained:

> The decision was 100 percent simple. The solution was difficult, because abortionists were too expensive or too "sleazy." Good doctors were afraid of prosecution or blacklisting. . . . I followed leads from other friends who'd had abortions. I used a secret password, met in a darkened office after hours, paid about $200 just to be examined and told it was too late. I talked to about ten different abortionists.

Eventually, this woman self-induced an abortion with knitting needles.

Women repeatedly told us that they contacted anyone—pharmacists, members of left-wing political groups, friends on the police force, and prostitutes—who they imagined might help them locate an abortionist. On average, it took women in our sample almost four weeks to arrange for an illegal abortion, compared with one and one-half weeks for a legal abortion. The delay meant that women were on average just shy of twelve weeks pregnant when they succeeded in obtaining an illegal abortion. It also meant they spent an additional two and one-half to three weeks suffering pregnancy-related discomforts (or, in some cases, risks to their health), as well as increased anxiety about whether they could find someone to perform an abortion, especially before the end of their first trimester. Forty-four percent of these women considered self-induced abortion or actually attempted to self-induce an abortion, the major cause of septic abortions in the illegal era.[19]

Women in our sample who had had an illegal abortion had dreaded the experience, even if they could arrange it. Compared with women in the other groups, they reported the highest level of worries before their abortions: worries that they might die, become sterile, be molested, get arrested, or be hurt. "I had heard horror stories," recounted one woman who had an illegal abortion in 1968, "of women whose abortions were botched up in Mexico or back alleys. I thought that I would be arrested. I thought I'd die on a table in a dirty garage."

Another woman emphasized that the illegality of abortion "made the experience much more difficult, because I had to cope with the thought of possible arrest." A third woman underlined the fear of "literally giving your life over to strangers."

The circumstances in which the abortions took place and the secrecy surrounding them contributed to the women's anxiety. Illegal abortions occurred largely outside of sterile medical settings. Women in our sample described a variety of locales, including private homes, a theater building, the back room of a drug store, and a kitchen table in an apartment with bedsheets used as stirrups. Except in rare circumstances, counseling was not provided to help the woman make her decision or to inform her about what to expect during the procedure. (This was no doubt sometimes the result of the need for secrecy, quiet, and speed in completing the procedure.) Most women said they did not know the qualifications of the person who performed the abortion.

Contrary to our expectations, the fact that abortion was illegal did not increase the women's sense of shame about seeking an abortion. If anything was shameful, it was being pregnant as an unmarried teenager or young adult in the 1960s or 1970s. The major impact of abortion being illegal was, as we have described, that it was difficult to arrange and frightening. It was also, in objective terms, dangerous.

In our sample women who had illegal abortions waited longer, paid more, and traveled farther than women who had legal abortions. Half of these women who had illegal abortions reported medical complications afterward, including excessive hemorrhaging, infection, and sterility. Some of these women confronted significant obstacles in obtaining treatment for these conditions, stemming from the illegality of the abortion procedure. The fear and dangers associated with illegal abortion contributed, we believe, to feelings of helplessness, powerlessness, anger, and for too many women, trauma.

In addition, these circumstances led many women to become aware, in a very personal sense, of their political oppression. They described feeling resentful that they, and not their male partners, suffered the risks and consequences of unwanted pregnancy. They also came to feel that the government had placed them in jeopardy by restricting access to safe and legal medical care. In these ways, illegal abortion contributed to a personal event being experienced as a political one.

Therapeutic Abortion

"Therapeutic" abortions, those allowed to save the life of the woman or in other rare circumstances, were available to some women in the era before *Roe v. Wade*. Many women who secured therapeutic abortions described themselves as having been intent on finding a legal option. They knew well the dangers of illegal and self-induced abortions. They were, on average, twenty-six years old, older than the women in our sample who had either legal or illegal abortions. Perhaps they had better connections as well. Yet they were also determined, for a variety of reasons, to end their pregnancies. As one woman stated, "My only decision was how to find someone to give me a legal abortion."

Qualified physicians performed these procedures in hospitals. Counseling about contraception and about what to expect during the procedure was sometimes provided. Yet physicians or hospital ethics boards controlled women's access to these procedures. The focal concern of women seeking therapeutic abortions was not physical danger or arrest, but the humiliation and powerlessness of having to convince someone in power of their legitimate need for a legal abortion. Some women acknowledged feigning symptoms of depression and suicidal tendencies; on the other hand, one woman reported that her doctor did not believe she genuinely intended to kill herself.

One woman detailed the steps in her ordeal to obtain a therapeutic abortion when she was twenty-four years old and single. She first asked the doctor who diagnosed her pregnancy for information on obtaining a therapeutic abortion. Instead of complying, he encouraged her to be happy about keeping the baby and tried to dissuade her from a self-induced abortion. Ultimately, he agreed to call her with the information. After three weeks passed, the woman sent the doctor an angry letter. He finally responded and arranged for her to meet with two psychoanalysts. She prepared for these meetings by reading psychology texts. She "worked up an act" of a suicidal depression. The doctor who performed the abortion did so with an unnecessary C-section, leaving the woman with a long vertical scar on her abdomen.

Other women in our sample reported similar accounts of hostility and unreasonable demands from physicians. Women commonly reported delays in learning whether the hospital would grant the request for a therapeutic abortion. Three women in our sample said that sterilization was a requirement of receiving a therapeutic abortion.[20] For example, one thirty-eight-year-old mother of three who was in the midst of a divorce discovered she was pregnant at the end of the first trimester. She was made to wait until she was sixteen weeks pregnant for her abortion. She was then placed in a waiting area with women trying to save their pregnancies, and she had to undergo a tubal ligation as part of her agreement with the gynecologist who performed the abortion.

A review of physicians' writings about their role in the therapeutic abortion process offers insight into an ambivalence that may have affected their approach to their patients. Some psychiatrists were sympathetic to the women they evaluated. For example, Theodore Lidz publicly acknowledged that he endorsed phony diagnoses of suicidal depression out of sympathy for women's personal or socioeconomic circumstances.[21] Many other physicians appeared to feel uncomfortable with their assigned role in determining when legal exceptions could be made to the laws against abortion. They reported feeling manipulated by the women,[22] or revealed great insensitivity to the circumstances of women's lives. For instance, some construed women's social conditions, such as being made "pregnant by men who used and abused them," as evidence of sadomasochism.[23] Further evidence of some physicians' categorical judgments of their pregnant patients can be found in Mary Calderone's conclusion that in circumstances of therapeutic abortion "we are in effect confronted both with a sick person and a sick situation."[24]

A number of researchers in fact expressed concern about the deleterious effects of staff hostility toward women terminating pregnancies.[25] The stress sometimes involved in obtaining permission for a therapeutic abortion led one doctor to conclude that the process was not therapeutic at all. In fact, he believed it served to create the anxiety and depression it assessed.[26]

In general, women who had therapeutic abortions appeared grateful, in part, that they were spared what they imagined to be the worse fate of an illegal abortion. One woman expressed relief that "someone cared about whether or not I lived or died." Another woman articulated, "The fear of infection, sterility, violation were reduced. There was a professional, qualified medical staff caring for me. I was not breaking the law." While some risks were "reduced" by therapeutic abortion, the risk of feeling exploited was not. Many women described the patronizing attitudes of the doctors they encountered. For these women, the physicians personified the control that the government held over their bodies and reproductive freedom. Their anger, as well as their gratitude, was focused on the doctors. Their experiences of abortion, though personal, were very much constrained by the political context that defined the relationship between them and their physicians. Though these women found a loophole that allowed them access to legal abortion, they still did not control either their fate or what happened to their bodies.

Legal Abortion

Our data regarding legal abortion come from two groups of women: those who had legal abortions in their home states between the years 1973 and 1978 (N = 37), and those who traveled to other states or countries to obtain legal abortions before abortion was legalized where they lived (N = 16). What is most striking to us is the matter-of-factness of these women's accounts of their abortion experiences in contrast to the accounts of the two groups previously described. These women gave far fewer descriptions of emotionally traumatizing experiences than did women who had illegal or therapeutic abortions. This finding was true even for the women who had to travel out of state for their abortions. The only additional anxiety some of these women described involved finding their way around a new city. A woman described how, age twenty-one and single in 1971, she was scared to travel from the Midwest to New York for a legal abortion: "It would have been easier if I had been home with a friend, or even alone. But going to an unknown area, alone, was the worst." Another woman who traveled out of state to obtain an abortion in 1972 commented, "It was safe, and I knew so ahead of time. My concerns were emotional, not physical. There was no question about being arrested or butchered. It was illegal where I lived, so I was discreet."

After 1973 most women were able to locate a clinic that performed abortions in their home states by opening the phone book. Most women received counseling, which in part helped them to predict and understand the medical procedure. One woman told us: "It was so well described beforehand to prepare me and answer all questions, that it's almost as if it wasn't memorable. . . . The fact that I trusted the staff and felt comfortable placing my life in their hands prevented the kind of fear that would have made it a bad experience."

Counseling typically also addressed the decision-making process, though the choice to terminate the pregnancy was their own, and it felt that way to them. Although these women remember the details of their legal abortion experiences vividly, they recount them as they might another significant medical event in their lives. One woman provided the following step-by-step account for her legal abortion in New York in 1972:

> I remember being counseled as part of the intake procedures. The options I had were explained to me, as were birth control methods. Next a urine sample was taken to confirm the pregnancy along with other tests, such as blood type and pressure. I was then taken into a room and the procedure [vacuum aspiration] was completely explained to me. I remember feeling completely supported by the staff. The abortion procedure took place and was over more quickly than I expected. I felt a good deal of cramping afterward. I was taken to a recovery area and allowed to lie down for about an hour. Then I was released with instructions.

As the logistics of arranging for a legal abortion became less complicated, and the procedure itself became less mysterious, we suspect that at least some women were better able to attend to the psychological meaning of the abortion.[27] Personal reflection is a luxury that is not available in a stressful or traumatic situation. Though unwanted pregnancy may be experienced as a crisis in and of itself, the easy availability of safe abortion defused some of these crisis dynamics. With legal access to abortion, women focused more on the personal than the political aspects of their decisions. Nonetheless, many women in these early years of legal abortion remember drawing direct comparisons with their impressions of an earlier period. For example, one woman wrote about her legal abortion: "My risk of death, infection, etc., was almost zero. I was not subjected to emotional, physical, or sexual abuse by the abortion provider. I was scared, but not completely terrified [as] my grandmother was [when she had an illegal abortion]. I didn't have to risk arrest or prosecution for murder. I could easily call and make an appointment within a week or so."

Despite the legality of abortion, some women reported encountering forms of exploitation. For instance, one woman said she was forced to use contraception, without her consent. Another woman, who was an investigative reporter, discovered clinics that falsified pregnancy results so that women would purchase their services even though they were not in fact pregnant. Though abortion procedures became safer and more accessible in this era, women's awareness of the possibility of being exploited persisted.

Legal Abortion under Siege

Because the women in our study had their abortions between 1962 and 1978, none had been harassed or intimidated by anti-abortion protesters. Throughout the 1980s and into the 1990s, legal abortions have increasingly been performed under such conditions. Accounts of women's experiences of legal abortion under protest often come, not from the women themselves, but from employees at clinics providing abortions, who witness the women's harassment. One gynecologist in Milwaukee, for example, described how his clinic instituted schedule modifications to avoid the afternoon protesters who blocked the entrance with their bodies and harassed anyone driving into the parking lot.[28]

A similar account was contained in testimony before the Subcommittee on Civil and Constitutional Rights of the House Judiciary Committee, in hearings on abortion clinic violence in 1985–86:

> The number of demonstrators varies from 5 to 100. I have personally observed women's arms being grabbed when they have refused to acknowledge the picketers or pleaded with them to be left alone. Their arms are grabbed as these picketers are screaming within inches of their faces, "Don't murder your baby. They'll rip your baby's eyes out." I have seen [demonstrators] block the entrance to the parking lot of the clinic until the person in the car was going to roll down the window of her car and allow them to force their antiabortion literature into the window. . . .
>
> Although patients are advised of the picketing, many times they will drive up to the clinic and see what is happening to women entering the building and will drive away and reschedule their appointment until a later point when they believe that picketing will not occur, thus increasing their health risk by delaying the termination of their pregnancies.[29]

One parent of a young woman whose life was jeopardized by her pregnancy described what happened when she accompanied her daughter to her abortion because of the likely presence of picketers:

When we arrived at the clinic, we realized our decision to accompany Kate was important, as about 12 men and only 1 woman were doing much more than peacefully picketing. The group as a whole [was] yelling obscenities to the patients as they approached the door. The five of us got out of the car, unsure of what our reactions to these people would be.

. . . [A]s soon as the picketers discovered that we were actually going into the clinic, they gathered around us, thrusting their signs in our faces and yelling. For example, one man approached within 6 inches of my face and yelled, "Baby killer." The other, and the only woman, said nothing but "Auschwitz." When I attempted to ask her a question, she just replied, "Auschwitz." Then, while inside the clinic, the screams of the protesters continued to be heard.[30]

An employee of a different clinic said that each of her clients "has to go through all that and then she gets to have an abortion."

When a patient shows up, she walks briskly across the street, surrounded by a circle of green-bibbed escorts and accosted in turn by a circle of adult anti-abortionists shouting, "Don't let them take the life of your child. This is a mistake you'll have to live with the rest of your life. It will haunt you. It will haunt you the rest of your life. They're baby butchers." When she reaches the front door, she is lifted up by escorts, over the heads of the blockaders, and sheltered by still more escorts as she enters the clinic.[31]

What is the psychological impact of this new experience of abortion? One abortion provider in Wisconsin stresses the women's sense of guilt and responsibility: "All of these women feel they're doing something wrong by being here, all of them, 100 percent."[32] A journalist-observer concurred that he "saw how deeply [the women] anticipated judgment of some kind, perhaps even more than the possibility of pain itself."[33]

Abortion in an atmosphere of siege carries a renewed threat of danger, but now the danger derives, not from the state or the illegality of the procedure, but from the hate and certainty of protesters who oppose legal abortion and from the failure of the state to stop the harassment. It carries, in addition, a new moral stigma, a new and profound burden of social judgment, expressed very directly—often six inches away from their faces—by angry protesters.

While some women must face angry protest and harassment, others have bizarre, almost surreal experiences when they arrive at clinics falsely advertised as providing abortions. These agencies deliver "pro-life" propaganda and often impede women's steps to find reputable abortion providers. One thirty-one-year-old woman testified about her encounter with such a clinic, where she went with a friend—also pregnant, in her early twenties, and "a bit more confused about her situation." Both women were shown a graphic slide show as part of their "counseling." The clinic personnel later confessed they did not actually provide abortions and refused to give a referral to a clinic that did. The younger woman was so shaken by the experience that her friend believes she delayed making a decision. In the end she traveled out of state to have a very late, dangerous, and expensive abortion.[34]

CONCLUSION

Certain characteristics of women's psychological experiences of abortion appear to be consistent regardless of whether they have had a legal,[35] illegal, or therapeutic abortion. In our study, women concurred in their reports that feelings of anxiety were a prominent feature of the period prior to the abortion and were highest just before the procedure, decreasing once the abortion was complete. Relief was the emotion rated most highly after abortion.

Many women described feeling that abortion was their only alternative. Many concluded that having an abortion secured or preserved important opportunities for them, and led them to reconsider their role and status as women. A number of women commented that abortion had not changed their lives; rather, it allowed them to continue their lives. Thus, their focus was on the danger to their lives posed by an unwanted pregnancy. The disproportionate responsibility they carried for this pregnancy, when compared with their male partners, was quite obvious to them, and often led them to consider the nature of women's "gender burdens" in a new light.

Although there have been changes in legal policies regarding abortion since the 1960s, social and political factors continue to constrain women's rights and reproductive freedoms. The risk of exploitation, for instance, has been a recurrent theme in the recent history of abortion in the United States. Women who sought illegal abortions felt that government restrictions on access to safe and legal abortion subjected them to physical and emotional harm. Though some illegal abortion providers were skilled and compassionate, others were motivated by profit and inflicted unnecessary pain and damage. Women who had therapeutic abortions resented the physicians who held the power to decide their fate. Even after the legalization of abortion, exploitation of women seeking abortions did not end. Since the 1980s, anti-abortion protesters have instilled fear in women seeking abortions and tried to exploit their feelings of shame or guilt to further the protesters' own political agenda.

Similarly, the theme of stigmatization occurs repeatedly in the recent history of abortion. Women who had illegal abortions may have felt stigmatized by having to go outside of the law to secure reproductive freedom. Women who sought therapeutic abortions all too frequently were humiliated by members of medical boards. In the current political climate, women are vulnerable to being stigmatized by those who construe the choice to have a legal abortion as being morally wrong.

Brenda Major and Catherine Cozzarelli have concluded that a woman's expectation about how she will cope with having an abortion is the most important predictor of her short-term psychological adjustment after an abortion.[36] It is necessary then to consider how the legal and political context of abortion can affect women's beliefs about their capacity to cope with an abortion. In this light, illegal abortion may be most challenging psychologically because it interferes with a woman's sense that her destiny is manageable and rests in her hands. Women's expectations about their capacity to cope with illegal abortion appear to have been low, given the many worries they recall experiencing before the abortion. Perhaps these expectations were realistically low. The hurdles and dangers they confronted were real. Their options were constrained by the government, and their fate was determined in large part by the skill and goodwill of those to whom they turned for help. Faced with the illegality of abortion, women felt relatively powerless. A sense of lack of control of their fate was also experienced by women who applied for permission to have a therapeutic abortion. Though these women expected that the procedure would be medically safe, they first had to interact with medical professionals who had the power to permit or deny their request. Though legal abortion offers the optimal circumstances for enhancing women's coping expectations, fear of harassment now threatens to undermine women's belief that they will be safe. Anti-abortion protesters deliberately attempt to increase the difficulty or conflict a woman may experience in choosing to end a pregnancy. Such obstacles have been shown to predict greater difficulty in coping with abortion. Similarly, laws that dictate the involvement of parents, partners, or judges in abortion decisions may, in many instances, serve to increase the level of conflict or difficulty involved in a woman's decision about whether to terminate a pregnancy.

In short, some legal abortions in the 1990s are like those in the period immediately following *Roe vs. Wade:* medically safe and surrounded by rational discussion of the woman's alternatives and decision. Other abortions today involve violent harassment, deception, and pressure. Since all women are aware that this harassment, deception, and pressure exist, even the most benign abortion experience is now freighted with political controversy, social disapproval, and moral judgments. It is our best guess that this climate not only reminds women of the extra responsibilities they bear for pregnancy, but also, as with illegal abortions, reminds them of their vulnerability and of the unwillingness of the state to protect them, and, as with therapeutic abortions, forces them into an infantilizing dependency on the kindness of strangers. In psychological, if not medical, respects, abortion experiences today include the worst aspects of all previous abortion experiences. In our study the strains associated with illegal and therapeutic abortions were vividly described by women who were mostly adult, white, middle class, and well educated. How much more dangerous, frightening, and humiliating these experiences must have been for women who did not have the same age, race, class, and educational advantages. Similarly, the strains associated with contemporary abortions are most intense for those with the fewest buffers and privileges, particularly adolescents and women living in poverty.

Postscript

As if to highlight our point, on September 25, 1995, an article in the *New York Times* described what happened to a fifteen-year-old girl when she told her parents she was pregnant. Though her family helped her arrange for the abortion she wanted, "their house was violently invaded by the boyfriend, his parents and friends; their daughter was taken from them in the middle of the night by law-enforcement officers determined to stop her from having an abortion; she was put into foster care, and finally, she was ordered by a judge not to abort the pregnancy."[37] In this case, a sixteen-year-old boy and his family were able to use the law to separate a teenage girl from her family and to force her to give birth to a child she did not feel ready or able to raise. This case and others like it suggest that at least for the most vulnerable females, who cannot maintain their right to legal abortions, we are moving into an era of childbirth under protest. It is not difficult to project the painful consequences for women—denied the ability to control their bodies and their lives—as well as for the unwanted children they are forced to bear.[38]

NOTES

1. A. J. Stewart and S. Gold-Steinberg, "Women's Abortion Experiences as Sources of Political Mobilization," in *Myths about the Powerless: Contesting Social Inequalities*, ed. M. B. Lykes, A. Banuazizi, and R. Liem (Philadelphia: Temple University Press, 1996).

2. See K. Luker, *Abortion and the Politics of Motherhood* (Berkeley: University of California Press, 1984), and R. P. Petchesky, *Abortion and Women's Choice: The State, Sexuality and Reproductive Freedom* (Boston: Northeastern University Press, 1984).

3. See A. F. Guttmacher, "The Shrinking Non-psychiatric Indicators for Therapeutic Abortion," in *Therapeutic Abortion*, ed. H. Rosen (New York: Julian Press, 1954), 12–21; also see P. H. Gebhard, W. B. Pomeroy, E. Clyde, and C. V. Christenson, *Pregnancy, Birth and Abortion.* (New York: John Wiley, 1958).

4. R. Tatalovich and B. W. Daynes, *The Politics of Abortion: A Study of Community Conflict in Public Policy Making* (New York: Praeger, 1981).

5. G. Wilmoth, M. de Alteriis, and D. Bussell, "Prevalence of Psychological Risks Following Legal Abortion in the U.S.: Limits of the Evidence," *Journal of Social Issues* 48 (1992): 37–66.

6. B. Major and C. Cozzarelli, "Psychosocial Predictors of Adjustment to Abortion," *Journal of Social Issues* 48 (1992): 121–42; Wilmoth, Alteriis, and Bussell, "Prevalence of Psychological Risks," 37.

7. See J. Osofsky and H. Osofsky, "The Psychological Reactions of Patients to Legalized Abortion," *American Journal of Orthopsychiatry* 42 (1972): 48–60; also see A. Lazarus, "Psychiatric Sequelae of Legalized Elective First Trimester Abortion," *Journal of Psychosomatic Obstetrics and Gynecology* 4 (1985): 141–50.

8. E. M Smith, "A Follow-up Study of Women Who Request Abortion," *American Journal of Orthopsychiatry* 43 (1973): 574–85.

9. C. M. Friedman, R. Greenspan, and F. Mittleman, "The Decision-Making Process and the Outcome of Therapeutic Abortion," *American Journal of Psychiatry* 31 (1974): 1332–37; D. T. Moseley, D. R. Follingstad, H. Harley, and R. V. Heckel, "Psychological Factors That Predict Reaction to Abortion," *Journal of Clinical Psychology* 37 (1981): 276–79; B. Major, P. Mueller, and K. Hildebrandt, "Attributions, Expectations, and Coping with Abortion," *Journal of Personality and Social Psychology* 48 (1985): 585–89; also see Major and Cozzarelli, "Psychosocial Predictors," 137.

10. Major and Cozzarelli, "Psychosocial Predictors," 121.

11. See M. B. Bracken, M. Hachamovitch, and G. Grossman, "The Decision to Abort and Psychological Sequelae," *Journal of Nervous and Mental Disease* 158 (1974): 154–62; see also J. P. Lemkau, "Emotional Sequelae of Abortion: Implications for Clinical Practice," *Psychology of Women Quarterly* 12 (1988): 461–72; see also Major, Mueller, and Hildebrandt, "Attributions," 585–89; and Major and Cozzarelli, "Psychosocial Predictors," 124–36.

12. Major and Cozzarelli, "Psychosocial Predictors," 126–30.

13. Lemkau, "Emotional Sequelae," 461–72.

14. B. Sarvis and H. Rodman, *The Abortion Controversy* (New York: Columbia University Press, 1974).

15. See N. Simon, A. Senturia, and D. Rothman, "Psychiatric Illness Following Therapeutic Abortion," *American Journal of Psychiatry* 15 (1967): 378–89; see also N. Simon, D. Rothman, J. Goff, and A. Senturia, "Psychological Factors Related to Spontaneous and Therapeutic Abortion," *American Journal of Obstetrics and Gynecology* 104 (1969): 799–808.

16. N. Adler, "Abortion: A Social-Psychological Perspective," *Journal of Social Issues* 35 (1979): 100–119.

17. See S. Gold-Steinberg, "Legal and Illegal Abortion: Coping with the Impact of Social Policies on Women's Lives," Ph.D. diss., University of Michigan, Ann Arbor, 1991. Also see S. Gold-Steinberg, "Personal Choices in Political Climates: Abortion," in *Women Creating Lives: Identities, Resilience and Resistance,* ed. C. Franz and A. J. Stewart (Boulder: Westview, 1984), 263–72.

18. Detailed accounts of the procedures used to collect and analyze the data are contained in Gold-Steinberg, "Legal and Illegal Abortion," 62–96.

19. See R. Solinger, *The Abortionist* (New York: Free Press, 1994), xi.

20. For further discussion of this issue, see R. Solinger, " 'A Complete Disaster': Abortion and the Politics of Hospital Abortion Committees, 1950–1970," *Feminist Studies* 19 (1993): 259–61.

21. T. Lidz, "Reflections of a Psychiatrist," in *Therapeutic Abortion,* ed. H. Rosen (New York: Julian Press, 1954), 276–83.

22. See N. R. Bernstein and C. B. Tinkham, "Group Therapy Following Abortion," *Journal of Nervous and Mental Disease* 152 (1967): 303–14; S. Bolter, "The Psychiatrists' Role in Therapeutic Abortion: The Unwitting Accomplice," *American Journal of Psychiatry* 119 (1962): 312–16; see also T. Wolff and J. Caldwell, "Psychiatric Aspects of Therapeutic Abortion," *Florida Medical Association Journal* 52 (1965): 95–98.

23. Simon, Senturia, and Rothman, "Psychiatric Illness," 378–89. For similar examples, see C. V. Ford, P. Castelnuevo-Tedesco, and K. D. Long, "Women Who Seek Therapeutic Abortion: A Comparison with Women Who Complete Their Pregnancies," *American Journal of Psychiatry* 129 (1972): 546–52; and R. S. Mumford, "Interdisciplinary Study of Four Wives Who Had Induced Abortions," *American Journal of Obstetrics and Gynecology* 87 (1963): 865–76.

24. M. Calderone, ed., *Abortion in the United States* (New York: Hoeber & Harper, 1958).

25. For examples, see G. M. Burnell, W. A. Dworsky, and R. L. Harrington, "Postabortion Group Therapy," *American Journal of Psychiatry* 129 (1972):

220–23; W. F. Char and J. F. McDermott, "Abortions and Acute Identity Crises in Nurses," *American Journal of Psychiatry* 128 (1972): 952–57; F. J. Kane, M. Feldman, S. Jain, and M. Lipton, "Emotional Reactions of Abortion Services Personnel," *Archives of General Psychiatry* 28 (1973): 409–11; and L. Marder, "Psychiatric Experience with a Liberalized Therapeutic Abortion Law," *American Journal of Psychiatry* 126 (1970): 1230–36.

26. Z. Lebensohn, "Abortion, Psychiatry, and the Quality of Life," *American Journal of Psychiatry* 128 (1972): 946–51.

27. See Gold-Steinberg, "Personal Choices in Political Climates," 271.

28. V. Klinkenborg, "Violent Certainties," *Harper's,* January 1995, 37–52.

29. See U.S. House Subcommittee on Civil and Constitutional Rights, "Abortion Clinic Violence," *Oversight Hearings before Subcommittee on Civil and Constitutional Rights of Committee on Judiciary, House of Representatives,* 115 (1987): 5–6.

30. Ibid., 13.

31. Klinkenborg, "Violent Certainties," 49.

32. Quoted in ibid., 44.

33. Ibid.

34. U.S. House Subcommittee on Civil and Constitutional Rights, "Abortion Clinic Violence," 324.

35. Because of the time frame of our study, we have not addressed the now more common practice of post-screening selective abortion of desired pregnancies.

36. Major and Cozzarelli, "Psychosocial Predictors."

37. Tamar Lewin, "Nebraska Abortion Case: The Issue Is Interference," *New York Times,* September 25, 1995, A6.

38. For an account of the psychological and social costs of denial of abortion, see H. P. David, Z. Dytrych, Z. Matejcek, and V. Schuler, eds., *Born Unwanted: Developmental Effects of Denied Abortion* (New York: Springer, 1988).

18

Marsha Saxton

DISABILITY RIGHTS AND
SELECTIVE ABORTION

Disability rights activists are now articulating a critical view of the widespread practice of prenatal diagnosis with the intent to abort if the pregnancy might result in a child with a disability. Underlying this critique are historical factors behind a growing activism in the United States, Germany, Great Britain, and many other countries, an activism that confronts the social stigmatization of people with disabilities.

For disabled persons, women's consciousness-raising groups in the 1960s and 1970s offered a model for connecting with others in an "invisible" oppressed social group and confirming the experience of pervasive social oppression. ("That happened to you, too?") Participants in such groups began to challenge a basic tenet of disability oppression: that disability *causes* the low socioeconomic status of disabled persons. Collective consciousness-raising has made it clear that stigma is the cause.

Effective medical and rehabilitation resources since the 1950s have also contributed to activism. Antibiotics and improved surgical techniques have helped to alleviate previously fatal conditions. Consequently, disabled people are living longer and healthier lives, and the population of people with severely disabling conditions has increased. Motorized wheelchairs, lift-equipped wheelchair vans, mobile respirators, and computer and communication technologies have increased the mobility and access to education and employment for people previously ostracized because of their disabilities.

Effective community organizing by blind, deaf, and mobility-impaired citizen groups and disabled student groups flourished in the late 1960s and resulted in new legislation. In 1973 the Rehabilitation Act Amendments (Section 504) prohibited discrimination in federally funded programs. The Americans with Disabilities Act of 1990 (ADA) provides substantial civil rights protection and has helped bring about a profound change in the collective self-image of an estimated 45 million Americans. Today, many disabled people view themselves as part of a distinct minority and reject the pervasive stereotypes of disabled people as defective, burdensome, and unattractive.

It is ironic that just when disabled citizens have achieved so much, the new reproductive and genetic technologies are promising to eliminate births of disabled children—children with Down's syndrome, spina bifida, muscular dystrophy, sickle cell anemia, and hundreds of other conditions. The American public has apparently accepted these screening technologies based on the "commonsense" assumptions that prenatal screening and selective abortion can potentially reduce the incidence of disease and disability and thus improve the quality of life. A deeper look into the medical system's views of disability and the broader social factors contributing to disability discrimination challenges these assumptions.

REPRODUCTIVE RIGHTS IN A DISABILITY CONTEXT

There is a key difference between the goals of the reproductive rights movement and the disability rights movement regarding reproductive freedom: the reproductive rights movement emphasizes the right to have an abortion; the disability rights movement, the right *not to have to have* an abortion. Disability rights advocates believe that disabled women have the right to bear children and be mothers, and that all women have the right to resist pressure to abort when the fetus is identified as potentially having a disability.

Women with disabilities raised these issues at a conference on new reproductive technologies (NRTs) in Vancouver in 1994.[1] For many of the conference participants, we were an unsettling group: women in wheelchairs; blind women with guide dogs; deaf women who required a sign-language interpreter; women with scarring from burns or facial anomalies; women with missing limbs, crutches, or canes. I noticed there what we often experience from people who first encounter us:

averted eyes or stolen glances, pinched smiles, awkward or overeager helpfulness—in other words, discomfort accompanied by the struggle to pretend there was none.

It was clear to me that this situation was constraining communication, and I decided to do something about it. I approached several of the nondisabled women, asking them how they felt about meeting such a diverse group of disabled women. Many of the women were honest when invited to be: "I'm nervous. Am I going to say something offensive?" "I feel pretty awkward. Some of these women's bodies are so different!" One woman, herself disabled, said that she'd had a nightmare image of a disabled woman's very different body. One woman confessed: "I feel terrible for some of these unfortunate disabled women, but I know I'm not supposed to feel pity. That's awful of me, right?"

This awkwardness reveals how isolated the broader society and even progressive feminists are from people with disabilities. The dangerous void of information about disability is the *context* in which the public's attitudes about prenatal diagnosis and selective abortion are formed. In the United States this information void has yielded a number of unexamined assumptions, including the belief that the quality and enjoyment of life for disabled people is necessarily inferior, that raising a child with a disability is a wholly undesirable experience, that selective abortion will save mothers from the burdens of raising disabled children, and that ultimately we as a society have the means and the right to decide who is better off not being born.

What the women with disabilities were trying to do at the Vancouver conference, and what I wish to do in this essay, is explain how selective abortion or *eugenic abortion*, as some disability activists have called it, not only oppresses people with disabilities but also hurts all women.

EUGENICS AND THE BIRTH CONTROL MOVEMENT

The eugenic interest that stimulates reliance on prenatal screening and selective abortion today has had a central place in reproductive politics for more than half a century. In the nineteenth century, eugenicists believed that most traits, including such human "failings" as pauperism, alcoholism, and thievery, as well as such desired traits as intelligence, musical ability, and "good character," were hereditary. They sought to perfect the human race through controlled procreation, encouraging those from "healthy stock" to mate and discouraging reproduction of those eugenicists defined as socially "unfit," that is, with undesirable traits. Through a series of laws and court decisions American eugenicists mandated a program of social engineering. The most famous of these was the 1927 U.S. Supreme Court ruling in *Buck v. Bell*.[2]

Leaders in the early birth control movement in the United States, including Margaret Sanger, generally embraced a eugenic view, encouraging white Anglo-Saxon women to reproduce while discouraging reproduction among nonwhite, immigrant, and disabled people. Proponents of eugenics portrayed disabled women in particular as unfit for procreation and as incompetent mothers. In the 1920s Margaret Sanger's group, the American Birth Control League, allied itself with the director of the American Eugenics Society, Guy Irving Burch. The resulting coalition supported the forced sterilization of people with epilepsy, as well as those diagnosed as mentally retarded and mentally ill. By 1937, in the midst of the Great Depression, twenty-eight states had adopted eugenics sterilization laws aimed primarily at women for whom "procreation was deemed inadvisable." These laws sanctioned the sterilizations of over 200,000 women between the 1930s and the 1970s.[3]

While today's feminists are not responsible for the eugenic biases of their foremothers, some of these prejudices have persisted or gone unchallenged in the reproductive rights movement today.[4] Consequently, many women with disabilities feel alienated from this movement. On the other hand, some pro-choice feminists have felt so deeply alienated from the disability community that they have been willing to claim, "The right wing wants to force us to have defective babies."[5] Clearly, there is work to be done.

DISABILITY-POSITIVE IDENTITY VERSUS SELECTIVE ABORTION

It is clear that some medical professionals and public health officials are promoting prenatal diagnosis and abortion with the intention of eliminating categories of disabled people, people with Down's syndrome and my own disability, spina bifida, for example. For this reason and others, many disability activists and feminists regard selective abortion as "the new eugenics." These people resist the use of prenatal diagnosis and selective abortion.

The resistance to selective abortion in the disability activist community is ultimately related to how we define ourselves. As feminists have transformed women's sense of self, the disability community has reframed the experience of having a disability. In part, through developing a sense of community, we've come to realize that the stereotyped notions of the "tragedy" and "suffering" of "the disabled" result from the *isolation* of disabled people in society. Disabled people with no connections to others with disabilities in their communities are, indeed, afflicted with the social role assignment of a tragic, burdensome existence. It is true, most disabled people I know have told me with certainty, that the disability, the pain, the need for compensatory devices and assistance can produce considerable inconvenience. But the inconvenience becomes minimal once the disabled person makes the transition to a typical everyday life. It is discriminatory attitudes and thoughtless behaviors, and the ensuing ostracism and lack of accommodation, that make life difficult. That oppression is what's most disabling about disability.

Many disabled people have a growing but still precarious sense of pride in an identity as "people with disabilities." With decades of hard work, disability activists have fought institutionalization and challenged discrimination in employment, education, transportation, and housing. We have fought for rehabilitation and Independent Living programs, and we have proved that disabled people can participate in and contribute to society.

As a political movement, the disability rights community has conducted protests and effective civil disobedience to publicize our demand for full citizenship. Many of our tactics were inspired by the women's movement and the black civil rights movement in the 1960s. In the United States we fought for and won one of the most far-reaching pieces of civil rights legislation ever, the Americans with Disabilities Act. This piece of legislation is the envy of the international community of disability activists, most of whom live in countries where disabled people are viewed with pity and charity, and accorded low social and legal status. Disability activists have fought for mentor programs led by adults with disabilities. We see disabled children as "the youth" of the movement, the ones who offer hope that life will continue to improve for people with disabilities for generations to come.

In part because of our hopes for disabled children, the "Baby Doe" cases of the 1980s caught the attention of the growing disability rights movement. These cases revealed that "selective nontreatment" of disabled infants (leaving disabled infants to starve because the parents or doctors choose not to intervene with even routine treatments such as antibiotics) was not a thing of the past. In this same period, we also took note of the growing number of "wrongful birth" suits—medical malpractice suits brought against physicians, purportedly on behalf of disabled children, by parents who feel that the child's condition should have been identified prenatally.[6] These lawsuits claim that disabled babies, once born, are too great a burden, and that the doctors who failed to eliminate the "damaged" fetuses should be financially punished.

But many parents of disabled children have spoken up to validate the joys and satisfactions of raising a disabled child. The many books and articles by these parents confirm the view that discriminatory attitudes make raising a disabled child much more difficult than the actual logistics of care.[7] Having developed a disability-centered perspective on these cases, disabled adults have joined with many parents of disabled children in challenging the notion that raising a child with a disability is necessarily undesirable.

The attitudes that disabled people are frightening or inhuman result from lack of meaningful interaction with disabled people. Segregation in this case, as in all cases, allows stereotypes to abound. But beyond advocating contact with disabled people, disability rights proponents claim that it is crucial to challenge limiting definitions of "acceptably human." Many parents of children with Down's syndrome say that their children bring them joy. But among people with little exposure to disabled people, it is common to think that this is a romanticization or rationalization of someone stuck with the burden of a damaged child.

Many who resist selective abortion insist that there is something deeply valuable and profoundly human (though difficult to articulate in the sound bites of contemporary thought) in meeting and loving a child or adult with a severe disability. Thus, contributions of human beings cannot be judged by how we fit into the mold of normalcy, productivity, or cost-benefit. People who are different from us (whether in color, ability, age, or ethnic origin) have much to share about what it means to be human. We must not deny ourselves the opportunity for connection to basic humanness by dismissing the existence of people labeled "severely disabled."

MIXED FEELINGS: DISABLED PEOPLE
RESPOND TO SELECTIVE ABORTION

The disability *activist* community has begun to challenge selective abortion. But among disabled people as a whole, there is no agreement
about these issues. After all, the "disability community" is as diverse as
any other broad constituency, like "the working class" or "women."
Aspects of this issue can be perplexing to people with disabilities because of the nature of the prejudice we experience. For example, the
culture typically invalidates our bodies, denying our sexuality and our
potential as parents. These cultural impulses are complexly intertwined
with the issue of prenatal testing. Since the early 1990s, disability rights
activists have been exploring and debating our views on selective abortion in the disability community's literature.[8] In addition, just like the
general population's attitudes about *abortion,* views held by people
with disabilities about *selective abortion* relate to personal experience
(in this case, personal history with disability) and to class, ethnic, and
religious backgrounds.

People with different kinds of disabilities may have complex feelings
about prenatal screening tests. While some disabled people regard the
tests as a kind of genocide, others choose to use screening tests during
their own pregnancies to avoid the birth of a disabled child. But disabled people may also use the tests differently from women who share
the larger culture's anti-disability bias.

Many people with dwarfism, for example, are incensed by the idea
that a woman or couple would choose to abort simply because the fetus
would become a dwarf. When someone who carries the dwarfism trait
mates with another with the same trait, there is a likelihood of each
partner contributing one dominant dwarfism gene to the fetus. This results in a condition called "double dominance" for the offspring, which,
in this "extra dose of the gene" form, is invariably accompanied by
severe medical complications and early death. So prospective parents
who are carriers of the dwarfism gene, or are themselves dwarfs, who
would readily welcome a dwarf child, might still elect to use the screening test to avoid the birth of a fetus identified with "double dominance."

Deafness provides an entirely different example. There is as yet no
prenatal test for deafness, but if, goes the ethical conundrum, a hearing
couple could eliminate the fetus that would become a deaf child, why
shouldn't deaf people, proud of their own distinct sign-language cul-

ture, elect for a deaf child and abort a fetus (that would become a hearing person) on a similar basis?

Those who challenge selective or eugenic abortion claim that people with disabilities are the ones who have the information about what having a disability is like. The medical system, unable to cure or fix us, exaggerates the suffering and burden of disability. The media, especially the movies, distort our lives by using disability as a metaphor for evil, impotence, eternal dependence, or tragedy—or conversely as a metaphor for courage, inspiration, or sainthood. Disabled people alone can speak to the women facing these tests. Only we can speak about our real lives, our ordinary lives, and the lives of disabled children.

"DID YOU GET YOUR AMNIO YET?": THE PRESSURE TO TEST AND ABORT

How do women decide about tests, and how do attitudes about disability affect women's choices? The reproductive technology market has, since the mid-1970s, gradually changed the experience of pregnancy. Some prenatal care facilities now present patients with their ultrasound photo in a pink or blue frame. Women are increasingly pressured to use prenatal testing under a cultural imperative claiming that this is the "responsible thing to do." Strangers in the supermarket, even characters in TV sit-coms, readily ask a woman with a pregnant belly, "Did you get your amnio yet?" While the ostensible justification is "reassurance that the baby is fine," the underlying communication is clear: screening out disabled fetuses is the right thing, "the healthy thing," to do. As feminist biologist Ruth Hubbard put it, "Women are expected to implement the society's eugenic prejudices by 'choosing' to have the appropriate tests and 'electing' not to initiate or to terminate pregnancies if it looks as though the outcome will offend."[9]

Often prospective parents have never considered the issue of disability until it is raised in relation to prenatal testing. What comes to the minds of parents at the mention of the term *birth defects?* Usually prospective parents summon up the most stereotyped visions of disabled people derived from telethons and checkout-counter charity displays. This is not to say that all women who elect selective abortion do so based on simple, mindless stereotypes. I have met women who have aborted on the basis of test results. Their stories and their difficult decisions were very moving. They made the decisions they felt were the only ones possible for them, given information they had been provided by doctors, counselors, and society.

Indeed, some doctors and counselors do make a good-faith effort to explore with prospective parents the point at which selective abortion may seem clearly "justifiable," with respect to the severity of the condition or the emotional or financial costs involved. These efforts are fraught with enormous social and ethical difficulty. Often, however, unacknowledged stereotypes prevail, as does a commitment to a libertarian view ("Let people do whatever they want!"). Together, these strains frequently push prospective parents to succumb to the medical control of birth, while passively colluding with pervasive disability discrimination.

Among the most common justifications of selective abortion is that it "ends suffering." Women as cultural nurturers and medical providers as official guardians of well-being are both vulnerable to this message. Health care providers are trying, despite the profit-based health care system, to improve life for people they serve. But the medical system takes a very narrow view of disease and "the alleviation of suffering." What is too often missed in medical training and treatment are the *social factors* that contribute to suffering. Physicians, by the very nature of their work, often have a distorted picture of the lives of disabled people. They encounter disabled persons having health problems, complicated by the stresses of a marginalized life, perhaps exacerbated by poverty and race or gender discrimination, but because of their training, the doctors tend to project the individual's overall struggle onto the disability as the "cause" of distress. Most doctors have few opportunities to see ordinary disabled individuals living in their communities among friends and family.

Conditions receiving priority attention for prenatal screening include Down's syndrome, spina bifida, cystic fibrosis, and fragile X, all of which are associated with mildly to moderately disabling clinical outcomes. Individuals with these conditions can live good lives. There are severe cases, but the medical system tends to underestimate the functional abilities and overestimate the "burden" and suffering of people with these conditions. Moreover, among the priority conditions for prenatal screening are diseases that occur very infrequently. Tay-Sachs disease, for example, a debilitating, fatal disease that affects primarily Jews of eastern European descent, is often cited as a condition that justifies prenatal screening. But as a rare disease, it's a poor basis for a treatment mandate.

Those who advocate selective abortion to alleviate the suffering of children may often raise that cornerstone of contemporary political rhetoric, *cost-benefit*. Of course, cost-benefit analysis is not woman-centered, yet women can be directly pressured or subtly intimidated by both arguments. It may be difficult for some to resist the argument that it is their duty to "save scarce health care dollars," by eliminating the expense of disabled children. But those who resist these arguments believe the value of a child's life cannot be measured in dollars. It is notable that families with disabled children who are familiar with the actual impact of the disabilities tend not to seek the tests for subsequent children.[10] The bottom line is that the cost-benefit argument disintegrates when the outlay of funds required to provide services for disabled persons is measured against the enormous resources expended to test for a few rare genetic disorders. In addition, it is important to recognize that promotion and funding of prenatal tests distract attention and resources from addressing possible environmental causes of disability and disease.

DISABLED PEOPLE AND THE FETUS

I mentioned to a friend, an experienced disability activist, that I planned to call a conference for disabled people and genetics professionals to discuss these controversial issues. She said, "I think the conference is important, but I have to tell you, I have trouble being in the same room with professionals who are trying to eliminate my people." I was struck by her identification with fetuses as "our people."

Are those in the disability rights movement who question or resist selective abortion trying to save the "endangered species" of disabled fetuses? When this metaphor first surfaced, I was shocked to think of disabled people as the target of intentional elimination, shocked to realize that I identified with the fetus as one of my "species" that I must try to protect.

When we refer to the fetus as a *disabled* (rather than defective) fetus, we *personify* the fetus via a term of pride in the disability community. The fetus is named as a member of our community. The connection disabled people feel with the "disabled fetus" may seem to be in conflict with the pro-choice stance that the fetus is only a part of the woman's body, with no independent human status.[11]

Many of us with disabilities might have been prenatally screened and aborted if tests had been available to our mothers. I've actually heard people say, "Too bad that baby with [*x* disease] didn't 'get caught' in prenatal screening." (This is the sentiment of "wrongful birth" suits.) It is important to make the distinction between a pregnant woman who chooses to terminate the pregnancy because she *doesn't want to be pregnant* as opposed to a pregnant woman who *wanted to be pregnant* but rejects a particular fetus, a particular potential child. Fetuses that are wanted are called "babies." Prenatal screening results can turn a "wanted baby" into an "unwanted fetus."

It is difficult to contemplate one's own hypothetical nonexistence. But I know several disabled teenagers, born in an era when they could have been "screened out," for whom this is not at all an abstraction. In biology class their teachers, believing themselves to be liberal, raised abortion issues. These teachers, however, were less than sensitive to the disabled students when they talked about "eliminating the burden of the disabled" through technological innovation.

In the context of screening tests, those of us with screenable conditions represent living adult fetuses that didn't get aborted. We are the constituency of the potentially aborted. Our resistance to the systematic abortion of "our young" is a challenge to the "nonhumanness," the nonstatus of the fetus. This issue of the humanness of the fetus is a tricky one for those of us who identify both as pro-choice feminists and as disability rights activists. Our dual perspective offers important insights for those who are debating the ethics of the new reproductive technologies.

DISENTANGLING PATRIARCHAL CONTROL AND EUGENICS FROM REPRODUCTIVE FREEDOM

The issue of selective abortion is not just about the rights or considerations of disabled people. Women's rights and the rights of all human beings are implicated here.

When disability rights activists challenge the practice of selective abortion, as we did in Vancouver, many feminists react with alarm. They feel "uncomfortable" with language that accords human status to the fetus. One woman said: "You can't talk about the fetus as an entity being supported by advocates. It's too 'right to life.' " Disabled women activists do not want to be associated with the violent anti-choice movement. In the disability community we make a clear distinction between our views and those of anti-abortion groups. There may have been efforts to court disabled people to support anti-abortion ideology, but anti-abortion groups have never taken up the issues of expanding resources for disabled people or parents of disabled children, never lobbied for disability legislation. They have shown no interest in disabled people after they are born.[12]

But a crucial issue compels some of us to risk making people uncomfortable by discussing the fetus: we must clarify the connection between control of "defective fetuses" and the control of women as vessels or producers of quality-controllable products. This continuum between control of women's bodies and control of the *products of women's bodies* must be examined and discussed if we are going to make headway in challenging the ways that new reproductive technologies can increasingly take control of reproduction away from women and place it within the commercial medical system.

A consideration of selective abortion as a control mechanism must include a view of the procedure as a wedge into the "quality control" of all humans. If a condition (like Down's syndrome) is unacceptable, how long will it be before experts use selective abortion to manipulate—eliminate or enhance—other (presumed genetic) socially charged characteristics: sexual orientation, race, attractiveness, height, intelligence? Pre-implantation diagnosis, now used with in vitro fertilization, offers the prospect of "admission standards" for all fetuses.

Some of the pro-screening arguments masquerade today as "feminist" when they are not. Selective abortion is promoted in many doctors' offices as a "reproductive option" and "personal choice." But as anthropologist Rayna Rapp notes, "Private choices always have public consequences."[13] When a woman's individual decision is the result of social pressure, it can have repercussions for all others in the society.

How is it possible to defend selective abortion on the basis of "a woman's right to choose" when this "choice" is so constrained by oppressive values and attitudes? Consider the use of selective abortion for sex selection. The feminist community generally regards the abortion of fetuses on the basis of gender—widely practiced in some countries to eliminate female fetuses—as furthering the devaluation of women. Yet women have been pressed to "choose" to perpetuate their own devaluation.[14] For those with "disability-positive" attitudes, the analogy with sex selection is obvious. Oppressive assumptions, not inherent characteristics, have devalued who this fetus will grow into.

Fetal anomaly has sometimes been used as a *justification* for legal abortion. This justification reinforces the idea that women are horribly oppressed by disabled children. When disability is sanctioned as a justification for legal abortion, then abortion for sex selection may be more easily sanctioned as well. If "choice" is made to mean choosing the "perfect child," or the child of the "right gender," then pregnancy is turned into a process and children are turned into products that are perfectible through technology. Those of us who believe that pregnancy and children must not be commodified believe that real "choice" must include the birth of a child with a disability.

To blame a woman's oppression on the characteristics of the fetus is to obscure and distract us from the core of the "choice" position: women's control over our own bodies and reproductive capacities. It also obscures the different access to "choice" of different groups of women. At conferences I've been asked, "Would I want to force a poor black woman to bear a disabled child?" That question reinforces what feminists of color have been saying, that the framework of "choice" trivializes the issues for nonprivileged women. It reveals distortions in the public's perception of users of prenatal screening; in fact, it is the middle and upper class who most often can purchase these "reproductive choices." It's not poor women, or families with problematic genetic traits, who are creating the market for tests. Women with aspirations for the "perfect baby" are establishing new "standards of care." Responding to the lure of consumerism, they are helping create a lucrative market that exploits the culture's fear of disability and makes huge profits for the biotech industry.

Some proponents argue that prenatal tests are feminist tools because they save women from the excessive burdens associated with raising disabled children.[15] This is like calling the washer-dryer a feminist tool; technological innovation may "save time," even allow women to work outside the home, but it has not changed who does the housework. Women still do the vast majority of child care, and child care is not valued as real work. Rather, raising children is regarded as women's "duty" and is not valued as "worth" paying mothers for (or worth paying teachers or day-care workers well). Selective abortion will not challenge the sexism of the family structure in which women provide most of the care for children, for elderly parents, and for those disabled in accidents or from nongenetic diseases. We are being sold an illusion that the "burden" and problems of motherhood are being alleviated by medical science. But using selective abortion to eliminate the "burden" of disabled children is like taking aspirin for an ulcer. It provides temporary relief that both masks and exacerbates the underlying problems.

The job of helping disabled people must not be confused with the traditional devaluing of women in the caregiver role. Indeed, women can be overwhelmed and oppressed by their work of caring for disabled family members. But this is *not caused by the disabilities per se*. It is caused by lack of community services and inaccessibility, and greatly exacerbated by the sexism that isolates and overworks women caregivers. Almost any kind of work with people, if sufficiently shared and validated, can be meaningful, important, joyful, and productive.

I believe that at this point in history the decision to abort a fetus with a disability even because it "just seems too difficult" must be respected. A woman who makes this decision is best suited to assess her own resources. But it is important for her to realize this "choice" is actually made under duress. Our society profoundly limits the "choice" to love and care for a baby with a disability. This failure of society should not be projected onto the disabled fetus or child. No child is "defective." A child's disability doesn't ruin a woman's dream of motherhood. Our society's inability to appreciate and support people is what threatens our dreams.

In our struggle to lead our individual lives, we all fall short of adhering to our own highest values. We forget to recycle. We ride in cars that pollute the planet. We buy sneakers from "developing countries" that exploit workers and perpetuate the distortions in world economic power. Every day we have to make judgment calls as we assess our ability to live well and right, and it is always difficult, especially in relation to raising our own children—perhaps in this era more so than ever—to include a vision of social change in our personal decisions.

Women sometimes conclude, "I'm not saintly or brave enough to raise a disabled child." This objectifies and distorts the experience of mothers of disabled children. They're not saints; they're ordinary women, as are the women who care for spouses or their own parents who become disabled. It doesn't take a "special woman" to mother a disabled child. It takes a caring parent to raise any child. If her child became disabled, any mother would do the best job she could caring for that child. It is everyday life that trains people to do the right thing, sometimes to be leaders.

DISABLED WOMEN HAVE A
LEGITIMATE VOICE IN THE ABORTION DEBATE!

Unfortunately, I've heard some ethicists and pro-choice advocates say that disabled people should not be allowed a voice in the selective abortion debate because "they make women feel guilty." The problem with this perspective is evident when one considers that there is no meaningful distinction between "disabled people" and "women." Fifty percent of adults with disabilities are women, and up to 20 percent of the female population have disabilities. The many prospective mothers who have disabilities or who are carriers of genetic traits for disabling conditions may have particular interests either in challenging or in utilizing reproductive technologies, *and* these women have key perspectives to contribute.

Why should hearing the perspectives of disabled people "make women feel guilty"? The unhappy truth is that so many decisions that women make about procreation are fraught with guilt and anxiety because sexism makes women feel guilty about their decisions. One might ask whether white people feel guilty when people of color challenge them about racism. And if so, doesn't that ultimately benefit everyone?

Do I think a woman who has utilized selective abortion intended to oppress *me* or wishes I were not born? Of course not. No more than any woman who has had an abortion means to eliminate the human race. Surely one must never condemn a woman for making the best choice she can with the information and resources available to her in the crisis of decision. In resisting prenatal testing, we do not aim to blame any individual woman or compromise her individual control over her own life or body. We *do* mean to offer information to empower her and to raise her awareness of the stakes involved for her as a woman and member of the community of all women.

A PROPOSAL FOR THE
REPRODUCTIVE RIGHTS MOVEMENT

The feminist community is making some headway in demanding that women's perspectives be included in formulating policies and practices for new reproductive technologies, but the disability-centered aspects of prenatal diagnosis remain marginalized. Because the technologies have emerged in a society with entrenched attitudes about disability and illness, the tests have become embedded in medical "standards of care." They have also become an integral part of the biotech industry, a new "bright hope" of capitalist health care and the national economy. The challenge is great, the odds discouraging.

Our tasks are to gain clarity about prenatal diagnosis, challenge eugenic uses of reproductive technologies, and support the rights of all women to maintain control over reproduction. Here are some suggestions for action:

- We must actively pursue close connections between reproductive rights groups and disabled women's groups with the long-range goal of uniting our communities, as we intend to do with all other marginalized groups.

- We must make the issue of selective abortion a high priority in our movements' agendas, pushing women's groups and disability and parent groups to take a stand in the debate on selective abortion, instead of evading the issue.

- We must recognize disability as a feminist issue. All females (including teenagers and girls) will benefit from information and discussion about disability *before* they consider pregnancy, so they can avoid poorly informed decisions.

- Inclusion of people with disabilities must be part of the planning and outreach of reproductive rights organizations. Inclusion involves not only use of appropriate language and terminology for disability issues but also *involvement of disabled people* as resources. Women's organizations must learn about and comply with the Americans with Disabilities Act (or related laws in other countries). If we are going to promote far-reaching radical feminist programs for justice and equality, we must surely comply with minimal standards set by the U.S. Congress.

- We must support family initiatives—such as parental leave for mothers and fathers, flex- and part-time work, child care resources, programs for low-income families, and comprehensive health care programs—that help *all* parents and thus make parenting children with disabilities more feasible.

- We must convince legislatures, the courts, and our communities that fetal anomaly must never be used again as a justification or a defense for safe and legal abortion. This is a disservice to the disability community and an insupportable argument for abortion rights.

- We must make the case that "wrongful life" suits should be eliminated. "Wrongful birth" suits (that seek damages for the cost of caring for a disabled child) should be carefully controlled only to protect against medical malpractice, not to punish medical practitioners for not complying with eugenic policy.

- We must break the *taboo* in the feminist movement against discussing the fetus. Getting "uncomfortable" will move us toward clarity, deepening the discussion about women's control of our bodies and reproduction.

- In response to the imperative from medical providers to utilize reproductive technologies, we can create programs to train "NRT peer counselors" to help women to learn more about new reproductive technologies, become truly informed consumers, and avoid being pressured to undergo unwanted tests. *People with disabilities must be included as NRT peer counselors.*

- We can help ourselves and each other gain clarity regarding the decision to abort a fetus with a disability. To begin with, we can encourage women to examine their motivations for having children, ideally before becoming pregnant. We can ask ourselves and each other: What needs are we trying to satisfy in becoming a mother? How will the characteristics of the potential child figure into these motivations? What opportunities might there be for welcoming a child who does not meet our ideals of motherhood? What are the benefits of taking on the expectations and prejudices of family and friends? Have we met and interacted meaningfully with children and adults with disabilities? Do we have sufficient knowledge about disability, and sufficient awareness of our own feelings about disabled people, for our choices to be based on real information, not stereotypes?

Taking these steps and responding to these questions will be a start toward increasing our clarity about selective abortion.

CARING ABOUT OURSELVES AND EACH OTHER

Here are some things I have learned while working to educate others on this issue. I try to be patient with potential allies, to take time to explain my feelings. I try to take nothing for granted, try not to get defensive when people show their confusion or disagreement. I must remember that these issues are hard to understand; they run contrary to common and pervasive assumptions about people and life. I have to remember that it took me a long time to begin to understand disability stereotyping myself. At the same time, I have very high expectations for people. I believe it is possible to be pushy but patient and loving at the same time.

To feminist organizations attempting to include disabled women in discussions of abortion and other feminist issues: forgive us for our occasional impatience. To disabled people: forgive potential allies for their ignorance and awkwardness. At meetings we disabled people hope to be heard, but we also perceive the "discomfort" that nondisabled people reveal, based on lack of real information about who we are. *There is no way around this awkward phase.* Better to reveal ignorance than to pretend and thereby preclude getting to know each other as people. Ask questions; make mistakes!

I sometimes remember that not only have I taken on this cutting-edge work for future generations, but I'm doing this *for myself now.* The message at the heart of widespread selective abortion on the basis of prenatal diagnosis is the greatest insult: some of us are "too flawed" in our very DNA to exist; we are unworthy of being born. This message is painful to confront. It seems tempting to take on easier battles, or even just to give in. But fighting for this issue, our right and worthiness to be born, is the fundamental challenge to disability oppression; it underpins our most basic claim to justice and equality—we are indeed worthy of being born, worth the help and expense, and we know it! The great opportunity with this issue is to think and act and take leadership in the place where feminism, disability rights, and human liberation meet.

NOTES

1. *New reproductive technologies* is the term often used to describe procreative medical technologies, including such prenatal diagnostic tests as ultrasound, alpha fetal protein (AFP) blood screening, amniocentesis, chorionic villi screening (CVS, a sampling of a segment of the amniotic sac), and the whole host of other screening tests for fetal anomalies. NRTs also include in vitro fertilization and related fertility-enhancing technologies. The conference, "New Reproductive Technologies: The Contradictions of Choice; the Common Ground between Disability Rights and Feminist Analysis," held in Vancouver, November 1994, was sponsored by the DisAbled Women's Network (DAWN), and the National Action Council on the Status of Women (NAC).

2. David J. Kevles, *In the Name of Eugenics* (New York: Knopf, 1985).

3. Not long after eugenics became a respectable science in the United Sates, Nazi leaders modeled state policies on their brutal reading of U.S. laws and practices. After their rise to power in 1933 the Nazis began their "therapeutic elimination" of people with mental disabilities, and they killed 120,000 people with disabilities during the Holocaust. See Robert J. Lifton, *The Nazi Doctors: Medical Killing and the Psychology of Genocide* (New York: Basic Books, 1986).

4. Marlene Fried, ed., *From Abortion to Reproductive Freedom: Transforming a Movement* (Boston: South End Press, 1990), 159.

5. Michelle Fine and Adrienne Asch, "The Question of Disability: No Easy Answers for the Women's Movement," *Reproductive Rights Newsletter* 4, no. 3 (Fall 1982). See also Rita Arditti, Renate Duelli Klein, and Shelley Minden, *Test-Tube Women: What Future for Motherhood?* (London: Routledge and Kegan Paul, 1984); Adrienne Asch, "The Human Genome and Disability Rights," *Disability Rag and Resource*, February 1994, 12–13; Adrienne Asch and Michelle Fine, "Shared Dreams: A Left Perspective on Disability Rights and Reproductive Rights," in *From Abortion to Reproductive Freedom*, ed. Fried; Lisa Blumberg, "The Politics of Prenatal Testing and Selective Abortion," in *Women with Disabilities: Reproduction and Motherhood*, special issue of *Sexuality and Disability Journal* 12, no. 2 (Summer 1994); Michelle Fine and Adrienne Asch, *Women with Disabilities: Essays in Psychology, Culture, and Politics* (Philadelphia: Temple University Press, 1988); Laura Hershey, "Choosing Disability," *Ms.*, July/ August 1994; Ruth Hubbard and Elijah Wald, *Exploding the Gene Myth: How Genetic Information Is Produced and Manipulated by Scientists, Physicians, Employers, Insurance Companies, Educators and Law Enforcers* (Boston: Beacon Press, 1993); Marsha Saxton, "The Politics of Genetics," *Women's Review of Books* 9, no. 10–11 (July 1994); Marsha Saxton, "Prenatal Screening and Discriminatory Attitudes about Disability, in *Embryos, Ethics and Women's Rights: Exploring the New Reproductive Technologies*, ed. Elaine Hoffman Baruch, Amadeo F. D'Adamo, and Joni Seager (New York: Haworth Press, 1988); Marsha Saxton and Florence Howe, eds., *With Wings: An Anthology by and about Women with Disabilities* (New York: Feminist Press, 1987).

6. Adrienne Asch, "Reproductive Technology and Disability," in *Reproductive Laws for the 1990s: A Briefing Handbook*, ed. Nadine Taub and Sherrill Cohen (New Brunswick, N.J.: Rutgers University Press, 1989).

7. Helen Featherstone, *A Difference in the Family: Life with a Disabled Child* (New York: Basic Books, 1980).

8. To my knowledge, Anne Finger was the first disability activist to raise this issue in the U.S. women's literature. In her book *Past Due: Disability, Pregnancy, and Birth* (Seattle: Seal Press, 1990), which includes references to her earlier writings, Finger describes a small conference where feminists and disability activists discussed this topic. German and British disability activists and feminists pioneered this issue.

9. Ruth Hubbard, *The Politics of Women's Biology* (New Brunswick, N.J.: Rutgers University Press, 1990), 197.

10. Dorothy Wertz, "Attitudes toward Abortion among Parents of Children with Cystic Fibrosis," *American Journal of Public Health* 81, no. 8 (1991).

11. This view must be reevaluated in the era of in vitro fertilization (IVF), where the embryo or a genetically prescreened embryo (following "pre-implantation diagnosis") can be fertilized outside the woman's body and frozen or can be implanted in another woman. Such a fetus has come to have legal status apart from the mother's body: for example, in divorce cases where the fate of these fetuses is decided by the courts.

12. Many "pro-life" groups support abortion for "defective fetuses." Most state laws, even conservative ones, allow later-stage abortions when the fetus is "defective."

13. Rayna Rapp, "Accounting for Amniocentesis," in *Knowledge, Power, and Practice: The Anthropology of Medicine in Everyday Life*, ed. Shirley Lindenbaum and Margaret Lock (Berkeley: University of California Press, 1993).

14. Suneri Thobani, "From Reproduction to Mal[e] Production: Women and Sex Selection Technology," in *Misconceptions: The Social Construction of Choice and the New Reproductive Technologies*, vol. 1, ed. Gwynne Basen, Margaret Eichler, and Abby Lippman (Quebec: Voyager Publishing, 1994).

15. Dorothy C. Wertz and John C. Fletcher, "A Critique of Some Feminist Challenges to Prenatal Diagnosis," *Journal of Women's Health* 2 (1993).

Contributors

Patricia Anderson is the executive director of Medical Students for Choice, a grassroots organization dedicated to improving abortion and reproductive health education in medical schools nationwide. She previously served as director of the Abortion Access Initiative for the National Abortion Federation and organized NAF's ground-breaking symposium on the abortion provider shortage. Anderson's employment history includes extensive work in educational settings with curriculum development on women's health issues. She holds an M.P.H. from the University of California at Berkeley.

Marie Bass is a principal in the public policy and political consulting firm of Bass and Howes, Inc., which specializes in women's and health issues. Before founding the firm in 1986, Bass spent two decades in senior political posts, including several years as the director of political action for the National Abortion Rights Action League.

Marlene Gerber Fried is the director of the Civil Liberties and Public Policy Program at Hampshire College and associate professor of philosophy. She is a longtime activist with the Boston Reproductive Rights Network and the Abortion Rights Fund of western Massachusetts, and president of the National Network of Abortion Funds. She is the editor of *From Abortion to Reproductive Freedom: Transforming a Movement* (South End Press, 1990).

Faye Ginsburg has been studying activists on both sides of the abortion debate since the early 1980s, on film (*Prairie Storm*) and in print, notably in her book *Contested Lives: The Abortion Debate in an American Community* (University of California Press, 1989). She is on the advisory board of the Common Ground Network for Life and Choice and teaches at New York University, where she is a professor of anthropology.

Sharon Gold-Steinberg is a clinical psychologist in private practice in Ann Arbor, Michigan. In addition, she is a faculty supervisor at the University of Michigan Center for the Child and the Family and a lecturer in the department of psychology.

Dr. Warren M. Hern, a physician and epidemiologist, is director of the Boulder Abortion Clinic. He has provided abortion services on a full-time basis in Boulder since 1973. He was a founding board member of the National Abortion Federation and is the author of the medical textbook *Abortion Practice* (Lippincott, 1984).

In 1970 **Dr. Jane E. Hodgson** became the first and only obstetrician/gynecologist in the United States to be convicted of performing an abortion in a hospital following proper consultation. As a deliberate and open challenge to Minnesota's harsh abortion law, she pled guilty. It took almost three years and the *Roe v. Wade* decision for the Minnesota Supreme Court to reverse her conviction (February 2, 1973) and to change Minnesota's old abortion law. As a health provider, educator, and abortion advocate, Dr. Hodgson continues to testify in courtrooms, classrooms, and legislative meetings on the deleterious effect of restrictive abortion legislation upon the health of women and children.

Alison M. Jaggar is professor of philosophy and women's studies at the University of Colorado at Boulder and director of the women's studies program there. She was formerly Wilson Professor of Ethics at the University of Cincinnati and has also taught at the University of Illinois at Chicago, the University of California at Los Angeles, and Rutgers University, where she held the Laurie New Jersey Chair in Women's Studies. She has been a visiting professor at Victoria University in New Zealand and the University of Oslo. Her most recent books are *Morality and Social Justice,* coauthored with James P. Sterba et al. (Rowman and Littlefield, 1994), and *Living with Contradictions: Controversies in Feminist Social Ethics* (Westview, 1994).

Carole Joffe is a professor of sociology and women's studies at the University of California at Davis. She is the author of *Doctors of Conscience: The Struggle to Provide Abortion Rights Before and After Roe v. Wade* (Beacon Books, 1995) and *The Regulation of Sexuality: Experiences of Family Planning Workers* (Temple University Press, 1986).

Laura Kaplan was a member of Jane and is the author of *The Story of Jane: The Legendary Underground Feminist Abortion Service* (Pantheon, 1996). She cofounded a women's health center and a battered women's shelter. She has been a rural lay midwife and an advocate for nursing-home residents.

After living in Tanzania and England, **Dr. Elizabeth Karlin** had two children before starting medical school at the University of Wisconsin, which she thought would be easier than being a full-time mother. It was. She is certified by the American Board of Internal Medicine and has practiced as an internist. For the last six years she has specialized in reproductive health (which is not a recognized specialty), including abortions. She is a coauthor of the American Medical Women's Association Reproductive Health Curriculum. She lectures to medical students and writes on the joy and angst of being an abortion provider.

Amy Kesselman is professor of women's studies at the State University of New York at New Paltz. She is the author of *Fleeting Opportunities: Women Shipyard Workers in Portland and Vancouver during World War II and Reconversion* (SUNY Press, 1990) and one of the editors of *Women: Images and Realities, a Multicultural Anthology* (Mayfield, 1995), and is currently working on a study of the women's liberation movement in New Haven, Connecticut, 1967–75.

Kathryn Kolbert, vice president of the Center for Reproductive Law and Policy, has twice argued abortion-related cases before the U.S. Supreme Court.

Andrea Miller is communications director for the Center for Reproductive Law and Policy.

Dorothy E. Roberts is a professor at Rutgers University School of Law–Newark, where she teaches courses on criminal law and family law. She has written and lectured extensively on the interplay of race, gender, and poverty in legal issues concerning reproduction and poverty. She is completing a book on race and reproductive freedom.

Loretta J. Ross is the executive director of the National Center for Human Rights Education, the USA Project of the People's Decade of Human Rights Education. Before founding the center in 1996, Ross was the national program research director (1991–95) for the Atlanta-based Center for Democratic Renewal, the program director for the National Black Women's Health Project, and director of Women of Color programs for the National Organization for Women.

William Saletan is a columnist for *Slate* and a contributing writer to *Mother Jones.* He designed and was the original editor of *The Abortion Report,* a nonpartisan daily digest of abortion news widely read by activists and the media. His book on the politics of abortion is forthcoming from the University of California Press.

Marsha Saxton is a disability rights and women's health activist. She is currently a researcher at the World Institute on Disability and teaches disability studies at the University of California. She serves on the Council for Responsible Genetics and the NIH Ethical, Legal, Social Implications (ELSI) Working Group of the Human Genome Initiative.

Rickie Solinger, a historian, is the author of *Wake Up Little Susie: Single Pregnancy and Race before Roe v. Wade* (Routledge, 1992) and *The Abortionist: A Woman Against the Law* (Free Press, 1994).

Jody Steinauer is founder and board president of Medical Students for Choice. She grew up in Omaha, Nebraska, and received her B.A. in biology from the University of California at Santa Cruz. She graduated from the University of California at San Francisco Medical School in May 1997 and is pursuing a residency in obstetrics-gynecology.

Abigail J. Stewart is professor of psychology and women's studies at the University of Michigan. She is also director of the newly established Institute for Research on Women and Gender on that campus. Her research focuses on the intersection of personality development, social history, and women's lives.

Marcy J. Wilder is the legal director of the National Abortion and Reproductive Rights Action League (NARAL) in Washington, D.C., where she specializes in federal and state legal and legislative issues related to women's reproductive rights and health. She is a graduate of Stanford University Law School. She currently serves on the board of the National Abortion Federation, and she is a past recipient of a Women's Law and Public Policy Fellowship from the Georgetown University Law Center.

Index

Abele, Janice, 53
Abele v. Markle, xiii, 43, 53–54, 60–61
abortion: African Americans and, 51,
161–201; attitudes toward, xi, xii, 33,
37, 86, 112, 116, 190–91, 199, 253;
availability of, 40, 49, 62, 74, 86, 95,
97, 105, 177, 201, 208–24, 304, 322,
331, 349, 353; cost of, 56, 213, 300,
321; civil disobedience and, 229, 291;
class and, 281, 370; constitutional ban
on, 80; delayed access to, 213–14; disability rights and, 183, 374–91; drug
use and, 134–35; exploitation of
women and, 368–69; federal employees and, xv, 97; federal prisoners and,
xv, 123; feminist model of, 38–39; fetal anomaly and, 385–86, 389; forced,
344; gender and, 290–91, 339–54,
368; genetic defects and, 306; genocide
arguments and, 84, 165–66, 180, 190,
345; in harassing context, 366–68; historical perspective on, xi–xvi, 2–7; in
hospitals, 304, 321; as human rights issue, 164, 219, 223; insurance and, 86,
122, 123; judicial rulings on, 55–56,
59–60, 74, 322; late, 306, 316; legalization of, 16, 49, 73, 183, 357; lesbians
and, 277; media and, 111, 169, 277;
medical model of, 38–39; medical opposition to, 308–9; methods of, 286,
301, 308, 312; "mills," 233, 235, 239;
military hospitals and, xv, 123, 304;
moral significance of, 89–90, 341–43,

mortality rates and, 302; as murder,
73, 76, 81, 83, 91, 209, 242, 274, 343;
myths concerning, 3–5; as negative
right, 99; nonsurgical, 267; philosophy
of, 339–54; physicians' views of, 271–
333; political context and, 111–23,
252–53; 349–51, 356, 364, 369–70;
poor women and, 97–98, 123, 142,
254, 345, 349; post-viability, 98; prenatal diagnosis and, 374, 381–82; as private moral issue, 343–44, 349–50; as
private privilege, 146, 349; psychological impact of, 25, 356–71; public funding for, xiv, 74, 80, 97, 98, 99, 103–4,
112, 113, 114, 118–21, 163, 211–14,
254, 259, 303, 306, 308, 348, 349–51,
356–71; as public health issue, 102;
348–49; as public justice issue, 343–
44, 349; as public right, 146; rates of,
73, 210, 302; recriminalization of,
191, 201, 210, 216, 241, 313; reducing need for, 76, 87; reporting requirements, 85; residency training and,
304–5; as resistance, 6, 19; restrictions
on, xvi, 74, 75, 97, 102, 112, 118–21,
123, 211, 233, 302–4, 316, 321–23,
351, 357; safety of, 56, 208; selective,
375–78, 382, 389–90; self-hatred and,
275, 278; self-induced, 4, 201, 208–9,
213, 257, 275, 321, 360–62; sex selection and, 385; sexualization of, 276;
shame and, 284; silence about, 279,
281–82; social context of, 341,344,

401

abortion *(continued)*
349–50, 356; state legislatures and,
xiv, xvi, 85, 86, 96, 97, 102, 302; stigmatization of, 216–18, 277, 369; stress
and, 258; vocabulary of, 2–3, 219;
women's health and, 220, 291, 349;
young women and, 97, 104, 215, 222
abortion, illegal, 1, 4, 33–39, 52, 357,
360–62; and abortifacients, 175; African-American women and, 161, 169,
173; arrests for, 18, 291; "back alley,"
4, 20, 23, 56, 73, 77, 95, 361; complications from, 174, 280, 361; cost of
34–35, 174, 178; counseling for, 33–
41, 261; criminal trials, 18–20; danger
of, 178, 300; as deviance, 19, 25; foreign venues for, 77; in legal era, 86,
209; procedures, 36–37; as public
health problem, 77, 174, rates of, xi,
178; referrals, 45–46, 178; self-induced, 174–75, 178; studies of, 359;
291
abortion clinics, 41, 208, 233, 285, 301,
365, 367; administration of, 311;
blockades of, xiv, 81, 82, 106, 193,
211, 227–28, 231–32, 234, 235; bombings of, 209, 231; client demographics
of, 282; community opposition to,
309; counseling ban and, 121; creation
of, 63, 308; decor of, 283–84; defense
of, 211, 228, 234, 236; falsification of
pregnancy tests and, 366; freestanding,
321; landlords of, 311; law enforcement and, 228, 312; multiplication of,
302; music at, 285; murder of employees at, xv, 82, 209–10, 237, 315; picketing of, 310, 312, 325; public funding
and, 349; rescues, xiii, 228, 231; safety
records of, 301, 321; security, 210,
233, 314; staffing of, 285; stress and,
286–87; terrorism and violence at, xiv,
xv, 74, 81, 82, 84, 209–10, 214, 228–
29, 230, 231, 236, 237, 254, 277, 281,
303, 313–15, 325, 349, 358, 366
abortion counseling, xiv, 41, 52, 283–86,
312, 365; ban on, 121; mandatory and
biased, xv, 40, 74, 97, 98, 99, 101; *see
also* Jane
Abortion Counseling Service of Women's
Liberation. *See* Jane
abortion decision, 73, 339–54; legal vs.
moral considerations, 342–44, 350;
physician's role in, 96, 347
abortion practitioners, 304, 273–318; African-American women as, 185–86;
birth control and, 278; death threats
against, 81, 303, 310, 315, 317, 318;

decreasing number of, 84, 254, 304;
economic incentives for, 324; FBI harassment of, 277; federal protection of,
315–17; female, 185–86, 276, 279;
feminist, 273–88; geographical distribution of, 214; gratifications of, 329;
hospital privileges and, 309–10, 322; illegal, 1,4, 6, 16–20, 28, 34–35, 169,
172, 173, 174, 198, 321, 322, 368–69;
inadequate number of, xiv, 74, 214,
237, 323–25; lay and safety records of,
105; murder of, 74, 81, 209, 228–29,
236, 277; physical assaults on, 330; retirement of, 323; stigmatization of, 17,
40, 76, 306, 322, 324; training of, 74,
105, 215, 237, 254, 273, 287–88, 304,
306, 324–25; vulnerablitity of, 20, 28,
41, 74, 84, 106, 209–10, 214, 235,
237, 274, 277, 281–82, 291, 313, 315,
317, 318
abortion rights and abortion rights movement, 1–9, 87, 185, 224, 252–54, 302–
6, 314; access issues and, 208–24,
346–52; African-American women
and, 161–201; civil rights movement
and, 163, 185; in Connecticut, 42–63;
conservative message strategy of, 111–
23; demonstrations, 99, 192–93, 236;
disabled persons and, 374–91; legal
strategies, 86–87, 95–110, 279; medical students and, 327–30; race and, 51,
103–4, 124–50, 161–201; 211, 220–
24; reframing arguments, 73–91, 339–
54; RU 486 and, 256–68; social status
of women and, 339–54; *see also* reproductive rights, *Roe v. Wade, specific
abortion rights groups*
Accreditation Council of Graduate Medical Education, 323
Adolescent Family Life Act, xiv
adoption, 29, 51, 278
affirmative action, 163, 195, 224
African Americans, 51, 58; attitudes toward abortion, 181, 190–91, 199; children, 135; churches, 166, 171, 181,
196, 198; male opinion of abortion,
180; population growth rate of, 163,
167, 169; student activists, 197
African-American women, 126, 138,
148, 161–201; abortion rates of, 165;
birth control and, 162, 167–68; club
movement of, 162, 167–70, 172; feminist movement and, 184, 185, 187–88;
illegal abortions and, 161, 169, 173;
leadership, 182–200; mothers, 126,
130, 132–34, 137, 139, 141, 143, 148,
149, 167; professional organizations

of, 187–88; self-definition and, 140; sexuality of, 165–67; sororities, 187–88, 196; sterilization and, 177, 218
African American Women for Reproductive Freedom, 164, 191, 195–96
AIDS, 166, 195, 222, 263, 267–68
Aid to Families with Dependent Children (AFDC), 213, 217
Alabama, 115, 132
Alliance Against Women's Oppression, 186
Alpha Kappa Alpha, 196
American Academy of Family Physicians, 330
American Bar Association, xii, 54
American Birth Control League, 171, 377
American Board of Obstetrics and Gynecology, 325
American Center for Law and Justice, 83
American Civil Liberties Union (ACLU), 117, 197, 324; Reproductive Freedom Project of, 198, 200
American Coalition of Life Activists (ACLA), 229, 237, 238, 315, 317–18
American College of Obstetrics and Gynecology (ACOG), 304–5, 323, 325, 330
American Council for Graduate Medical Education (ACGME), 215, 325–28
American Eugenics Society, 377
American Independent Movement (AIM), 44
American Law Institute (ALI), xi, xii, 77
American Medical Association (AMA), xi, xii, 17, 84, 279, 304–5, 320, 321, 325, 326, 330
American Medical Students Association (AMSA), 328, 329
American Medical Women's Association (AMWA), 326, 328, 329, 330
American Public Health Association, 321, 324
Americans United for Life, 80–81
Americans with Disabilities Act of 1990 (ADA), 375, 378
Anderson, Don, 82
Anderson, Patricia, 320–33, 395
anti-abortion rights movement, 54, 57, 73, 84, 91, 99, 121, 215, 227–42, 312, 313; abortion training and, 326; African-American support of, 166; "campaign of terror," 106; "direct action" of, 83, 228, 230, 233; disabled women and, 384–85; fascism and, 318; hate mail from, 209, 325; inception of, 6, 79, 229; legislative strategies of, 101–

2, 120, 210–11; media and, 228, 231, 232, 238–39; militia movement and, 237; murder and, 81, 106, 210, 236, 277, 325; "permissible" violence and, 230; "pro-life" clinics of, 368; on RU 486, 255; on Supreme Court appointments, 80; tactics of, 74, 81, 208–20, 227–42, 277, 312, 313; violence by, xiv, 7, 40, 74, 90, 106, 209, 210, 215, 238, 280, 303, 313–17, 322, 325
anti-abortion statutes, 4, 16, 44, 77, 351, 357; impact of, 43, 52–53, 57, 60, 77, 96; litigation and, 46–49, 52–53, 59; professionalization of medicine and, 357; reform of, xii, 42, 45, 48, 77, 96, 300, 304, 312; repeal of, xii, 42, 45, 49, 54, 56, 78, 351
anti-choice movement. See anti-abortion rights movement
anti-poverty programs, dismantling of, 181
anti-Semitism, 180
Arkansas, 114, 115, 121, 187
Asian Americans, 222
Association of American Medical Colleges, 321, 326
Association to Repeal Abortion Laws (Calif.), xii
Atlanta, "siege of," 231–32
Avery, Byllye, 185–86, 190, 192, 196

"Baby Doe" cases, 378–79
Baggish, Michael, 57
Ballard, Janet, 196
Bambara, Toni Cade, 183, 186
Baraka, Amiri, 180
Barrett, James, xv, 82, 236, 315, 325
Barrett, June, 82
Barrow, Willie, 191, 196
Bass, Marie, 8, 251–68, 395
battered women's shelters, 185
Beal, Frances, 183, 186
Beasley, Joe, 174
Beijing, 222–23
Bell, Becky, xiv, 86, 220
Bennett, William, 90
birth control. See contraception
birth control clinics: African Americans and, 162, 168, 180, 182; Planned Parenthood, 182; race and, 132, 142
Birth Control Federation of America, 77, 132, 168, 171
birth control movement, 168, 170; African-American women and, 162, 168, 181–84; eugenics and, 377; nativism and, 170–71; racism and, 170–72
"blacklash," 201

Blackmun, Harry, 60, 84
Black nationalism, 51, 169, 180, 193, 197
Black Panther Party (New Haven), 47, 51
Black Power, 150
Black Women's Liberation Committee of the Student Nonviolent Coordinating Committee, 183, 186
Black Women's Liberation Group (Mt. Vernon, N.Y.), 183–84
Bond, Julian, 193
Bork, Robert, 115–16, 256
Boston Women's Health Book Collective, 260
Boulder Community Hospital, 308, 309
Boulder County Medical Society, 309
Boulder Valley Right to Life Committee, 310
Bowen v. Kendrick, xiv
Brand, Oscar, 287
Brazile, Donna, 191, 195
breast cancer, 256
Bridefare, 217
Britton, John, xv, 82, 236, 315, 325
Brookline (Mass.), xv, 82, 210, 237, 315
Brown, Dorothy, 182, 190
Buchanan, Patrick, 4, 122
Buck, Carrie, 144
Buck v. Bell, 144, 377
Burch, Guy Irving, 171, 377
Bush, George, 115, 121, 193, 302; anti-choice stance of, 82, 259, 314; Supreme Court appointments of, 86

Cade, Sara, 328
Caesar, Julius, 318
Cage, Maggie, 281
Calderone, Mary, xi, 363
California, xi, xii, 105, 186, 192, 200, 300
Camp, Sharon, 257–58, 261, 263
Campbell, Bebe Moore, 190
Catholic Church, 2, 45, 56, 58–59, 97, 169, 176, 182, 209, 223, 254, 265, 285, 327
Catholics for Free Choice, 256
Catholic Health Association, 326
Catholic hospitals, 56, 107, 326
Center for Constitutional Rights, 43
Center for Reproductive Law and Policy (CRLP), 7, 117, 324
Center for Women's Development (Medgar Evers College), 197
child abuse, 217, 299
childbearing, 212, 386; coercion and, 58, 371; right to, 218, 220

child care, 49, 62, 87, 222, 345, 346, 352, 386–87
child pornography, 242
childrearing. *See* child care
China, and RU 486, 265
Chisholm, Shirley, 183, 184, 186, 191, 192, 196
choice: authenticity of, 350, 385; as constitutional right, 73, 95–99, 140; meaning of, 62, 119, 196, 200–1; 356, 386, 387; privacy and, 60, 146 (*see also* privacy doctrine); of procreation, 138–41, as term, 9, 219; women of color and, 137–43, 165; *see also* abortion rights, reproductive rights
Christensen, Dennis, 282
Christian Coalition, 87
Christian Defense Council, 235, 242
Christian leadership institutes, 229
Christian ideology, 229, 232, 238, 240
Chung, Mary, 222
circumcision, female, 282
Citizens for Human Abortion Laws, xi
civil disobedience, 234, 351, 378
civil libertarians, 112
Civil Liberties and Public Policy Program, 222
civil rights movement, 1, 34, 77, 187, 193, 359; abortion rights movement and, 163, 185; anti-abortion rights movement and, 237; disability rights movement and, 378
Civil Rights Restoration Act of 1988, 188, 194–5
Clarie, Emmett, 53–54, 55, 56, 60
clergy, 17, 45, 83, 181, 233
Clergy Consultation Service on Abortion (New York City), xii, 178
Clinton, Bill, 75, 88, 117, 122, 123, 268, 277, 304, 314, 315; on abortion, xvi, 224, 228, 236, 316; as governor, 114, 121
Clinton, Hillary, 277, 305
Clothesline Project, 222
Coalition of 100 Black Women, 194, 196
Coalition to End Sterilization Abuse, 125
Coffee, Linda, 78
Collins, Cardiss, 193, 196
Colorado, xii, 300, 308, 312
Columbia University Medical School, 324
Combahee River Collective, 185
Committee for Abortion Rights and Against Sterilization (CARASA), 186
condom, female, 263
Congressional Black Caucus, 196
Conley, Frances, 290

Connecticut, xii, xiii, 42–63, 259
Connecticut Civil Liberties Union, 59
Connecticut Medical Society, 44, 57
consciousness-raising, 44, 374
contraception, xii, 16, 36, 87, 88, 170–72, 200, 222, 280, 301, 305; access to, 142, 177, 304, 346, 352; African-American women and, 161, 165, 167, 168, 177; attacks on, 220; coercion and, 212, 366; counseling, 136; emergency, 267; IUD, 263; long-term, 218; medical profession and, 48, 263–64, 273; middle class women and, 281; oral (the Pill), 262–66, 276; population control and, 264–65; post-coital, 263; RU 486 and, 255, 256; unmarried persons and, 139; as women's responsibility, 352; see also birth control clinics, birth control movement
Contraceptivefare, 217
Cook, Constance, 78
Cook, Rebecca, 258
Coolidge, Calvin, 170
Coombs, Joan, 211
Council on Resident Education in Obstetrics and Gynecology, 323
Cozzarelli, Catherine, 369
crack cocaine, 124, 127–29
Crenshaw, Kimberle, 127
cryptoporn, 19
Cuomo, Mario, 254
cystic fibrosis, 382

Dalkon Shield, 260
Davies, Marvin, 180
Davis, Angela, 167, 180, 192
"Deadly Dozen," 237, 315
Dean, Cindy, (Mrs. Randall Terry), 231
Defensive Action Pledge, 209
Delta Sigma Theta, 194, 196, 197
Democratic Party, 121, 191–92, 231, 234
Depo Provera, 218, 262
Depression, 19, 169, 293, 377
DES (diethylstilbestrol), 260
Diamond, Sarah, 238
dilation and evacuation, 102
dilation and extraction, xv, 102; see also "partial birth" abortion
disability rights movement, 374–91; conference on, 375–76; international efforts of, 374; mentoring programs of, 378; response to "Baby Doe" cases, 378–79; on right to reproduce, 375; on selective abortion, 380; on technological advances, 374
disabled fetus, 383–84
disabled infants, 378–79

disabled persons, 378, 379, 382, 388, 391; diversity of, 380; elimination of, 375, 377, 383; feminist perceptions of, 376–77; quality of life, 376; self-image of, 375; stereotypes of, 379, 381, 391
divorce laws, 300
Djerassi, Carl, 256
Doe v. Bolton, xiii, 60, 308, 309
Dole, Robert, 123
domestic violence, 222; centers, 97
Douglas, William O., 144–45
Down's Syndrome, 375, 377, 379, 382, 385
Draper Fund, 175
drug-addicted mothers: infant screenings and, 128; prosecution of, 124–50; protective incarceration and, 129; race and, 124–50; sentencing, 134; treatment programs, 134–36
Du Bois, W. E. B., 171, 180, 182
Dukakis, Michael, 115, 259
due process clause, 55, 148
dwarfism, 380

Edelin, Kenneth, 184–85
Eisenstadt v. Baird, 139
Elders, Joycelyn, 187, 305
Elim Bible Institute, 231
Emery, Noemie, 90
Emmett, Kathryn, 52
endometriosis, and RU 486, 255
England, and RU 486, 265 2, 265
Epic/MRA-Mitchell opinion poll, 123
Equal Employment Opportunity Commission (EEOC), 192
equal protection doctrine, 52, 142, 145
Equal Rights Amendment (ERA), 96, 192
eugenics, 125, 143–44, 169–71, 177, 376–77; African-American women's opposition to, 162–63
euthanasia, 242

Falk, Gail, 51
Falkenberg, Nanette, 254, 256–57
Faludi, Susan, 239
Falwell, Jerry, 232, 235, 241
family caps, 217, 218
Family Life Bureau (Bridgeport, CT), 57
family-planning programs, 174–77, 187
"family values," 113, 218
Favorite, Gloria, 185
Federal Bureau of Investigation (FBI), 209, 277, 313
federal courts, xiii, 49, 84, 101
feminism, 35, 41, 44, 77, 112, 346, 347; African-American women and, 162, 164, 183, 185, 187, 189–90; anti-

feminism *(continued)*
abortion rights movement and, 233;
disability rights and, 374–91; medicine
and, 274
feminist health centers, xiii, 97, 185
feminist legal theory, 126–27, 148
Feminist Majority Foundation, 261
feminist movement, 77, 117, 184, 230;
racism of, 187, 191; reproductive
rights and, 193
Feminist Women's Health Center (Los
Angeles), xiii
Ferraro, Geraldine, 191, 254
fertility control, and African-American
women, 163, 169, 167, 171, 172, 177,
181, 183–84, 186
fetal anomaly, 77, 213
fetal rights, 74, 125, 131, 199
fetal surgery, 142
fetal viability, 2–3, 96
fetus, 2, 3, 21, 25, 60, 102, 135, 149,
381, 384, 385, 390; disabilities of,
375, 380, 383–84; drug exposure and,
124, 131; harm to, 134, 143; justice
for, 350; moral status of, 242–43; as
person, 73, 83, 91, 149, 339–40, 343–
44, 383; protection of, 56, 125, 131;
right to life of, 74; women's constitutional rights and, 61; *see also* unborn
child
Fight the Abortion Clinic Committee
(Boulder), 309
Finkbine, Sherri, xi
First Amendment, 235
First National Conference on Abortion
Laws, xii, 78
First National Conference on Black Wom-
en's Health, 190
First National Conference on Women of
Color and Reproductive Rights, 193,
196
Florida, xv, 105, 116, 124, 180, 186,
209, 210
Florio, James, 119
Food and Drug Administration, 259–60,
265
Ford Foundation, 323
Foster, Henry, 88, 305
Fourteenth Amendment, 55, 60, 139
Fourth World Conference on Women
(Beijing), 222
Fox Valley Reproductive Center (Apple-
ton, Wis.), 281–82
fragile X, 382
France, and RU 486, 254, 256, 257
Freedman, Ann, 62
Freedom of Access to Clinic Entrances

Act (FACE), xv, 84, 106, 214, 228,
237, 303, 316
Freedom of Choice Act, 122
Fried, Charles, 211
Fried, Marlene Gerber, 5, 208–26, 395
fundamentalism, Christian, 3, 176, 241;
activism of, 233–35, 239–40; misogyny and, 276; tradition of, 240, 242; violence and, 277, 280

"gag rule," xiv, 194, 211, 303–4, 314; Af-
rican-American women and, 197–98
Gainesville Women's Health Center
(Fla.), 186
Galen, 307
Garcia, Inez, 185
Garrow, David, 237
Garvey, Marcus, 169, 180
Gates, Jacqui, 196
gay and lesbian liberation, 222
Gelb, Marjory, 52
Georgia, 96, 121, 161, 300
German measles (rubella), xii, 183, 300
Gidding, Lee, 79
Gilbert v. General Electric, 346–47
Gilbertson, Betsy, 45, 46–47, 50
Gillespie, Marcia, 195
Gilligan, Carol, 342, 344
Gingrich, Newt, 122
Ginsburg, Faye, 3, 227–50, 396
"glass ceiling," 294–95
Goeas, Ed, 123
Gold-Steinberg, Sharon, 356–73, 396
gonorrhea, 282
Gordon, Linda, 172
Gore, Albert, 121
Gray, William, 193
Greenberg, Stan, 123
Gregory, Dick, 180
Griffin, Michael, 209
Grimes, David, 255
Griswold v. Connecticut, xii, 47, 55–56,
177
group dynamics, 260, 268
guilt, benefits of, 388
Gund Foundation, 323
Gunn, David, xv, 81, 82, 83, 209, 236,
314–15, 325, 327
Guttmacher, Alan, 23, 77, 279
Guttmacher (Alan) Institute, 194, 256

Haden, William "Bouie," 180, 182
Hague, Frank, 296
Hamer, Fannie Lou, 177, 188
Harlem, 135
Harlem Hospital, 187
Harmon, Sasha, 49

Harris, Angela, 127, 140
Harris v. McRae, xiii, 146–47, 348
Harvey, Jacqueline, 185
Hatch, Orrin, 80
Hawaii, xii, 49
Height, Dorothy, 192, 196
Helms, Jesse, 80, 253
Henderson, Georgia, 182
Hern, Warren M., 307–19, 396
Hernandez, Aileen, 192
heterosexism, 185
Hickman, Harrison, 114–16
Hill, Anita, 199, 303, 305
Hill, Ann, 45, 50
Hill, Paul, xv, 210, 236, 315
Hippocrates, 307
Hirsch, Michael, 83
Hispanics, 218, 241, 251
Hodgen, Gary, 255
Hodgson, Jane, xiii, 290–306, 396
Hodgson v. Minnesota, xiv
Hoechst AG, 260, 265
Hoffman, Abby, 239
Holland, 275
Holmes, Janet Linda, 173
Holmes, Oliver Wendell, 144
Holocaust, 240
home birth, 40
Homewood-Brushton Citizens Renewal Council (Pittsburgh), 182
homophobia, 164, 220
homosexuality, 166
hooks, bell, 166, 188
hospital abortion boards, xi, 6, 16, 20–26, 28, 44, 59, 77, 279, 302, 357, 362–63
Howard University, 197
Howes, Joanne, 254, 256–58, 261–62
Hubbard, Ruth, 381
Huggins, Ericka, 47
Hulton, Jill, 62
Human Life amendment, xiii, 79
Hunter, James Davison, 239, 241
Hurley, LaBrentha, 173
Hurston, Zora Neale, 140
Hyde Amendment, xiii, xv, 97, 103–4, 122, 163, 186, 194, 212–13, 348
hysterectomy, 213

Ifill, Sherrilyn, 197
illegitimate children, 27, 28
imaging technology, 21
immigrants, 170, 208, 224
incest, xv, 77, 104, 123, 211, 217, 286, 299, 343
Indiana, 86
infanticide, 242, 340

infant mortality, 165, 187–88, 194, 223, 302; race and, 135, 146, 189
intelligence testing, 163
International Conference on Population and Development (Cairo), 222
International Ladies' Garment Workers' Union, 192
International Monetary Fund, 189
in vitro fertilization, 385

Jackson, Jesse, 191, 193
Jacob, John, 193
Jaggar, Alison M., 7, 339–55, 396–97
Jane, xii, 33–41, 178–79, 185
Jefferson, Mildred, 79
Jersey City Medical Center, 295–96
Jews, 241, 382
Jim Crow laws, 170
Joffe, Carole, 320–33, 397
Johnson and Johnson, 255
Johnson, Jennifer Clarise, 124, 134
Johnson, Lyndon Baines, 176
Joint Commission on Accreditation of Hospitals, 321
Joint Committee on Public Health and Safety (Conn.), 57–58
Jones Institute for Reproductive Research, 255
Jordan, Barbara, 193
Joseph, Annie, 185
Joseph, Gloria, 187, 200
Joyner, Brenda, 162, 186

Kansas, 208, 325
Kaplan, Laura, 8, 33–41, 179, 397
Karlin, Elizabeth, 273–89
Katz, Harriet, 62
Keemer, Edward, 172–73
Kennedy, Flo, 184, 192
Kennedy, Ted, 254
Kesselman, Amy, 5, 42–67, 397
King, Martin Luther, Jr., 177
Kinsey, Albert, xi
Kolbert, Kathryn, 7, 95–110, 397
Ku Klux Klan, 170, 278
Kunins, Hillary, 328

Lader, Lawrence, 59
Lake, Celinda, 123
Lambs of Christ, 236, 314
Lamm, Richard, 77, 312
LaRue, Linda, 182
Latinas, 218, 251
Learnfare, 217
Ledbetter, Brownie, 114
Lewis, Jill, 187
Lewis, John, 193

Lidz, Theodore, 363
Life Dynamics, 214, 328
Little, Joann, 185
Logan-White, Judy, 198
Lorde, Audre, 201
Louisiana, 161, 174, 176, 181, 185, 187
Lowery, Joseph, 193
Lowney, Shannon, xv, 237, 315, 325
Lumbard, Edward, 55
lynchings, 169
Lysol, 88

MacKinnon, Catharine, 141, 146–47
Mafia, 238
Maginnis, Pat, xi
Maimonides, 307
Major, Brenda, 369
Major, Naima, 200
managed health care, 107
Marable, Manning, 198
March for Women's Lives (1986), 191
Margaret Hague Maternity Center (Jersey City), 296
Marshall, Thurgood, 56
Martinez, Luz Alvarez, 263
Maryland, 300
Massachusetts, 43, 139, 209, 211, 154, 277
maternal instinct, 352
Matsuda, Mari, 138
Mayo Clinic, 298–99
Mayo Graduate School of Medicine, 295–96
McCabe, Jewell, 196
McCarthy, Joseph, 282
McKay, Trent, 324
McKenna, George, 90
McMahon, James, 316
Mead, Margaret, 301
Medicaid, 54, 98, 103, 176, 348; abortion-funding ban and, xiii, 40, 163, 254; family caps, 218; Norplant and, 133; restrictions, 97, 104, 123, 211, 348, 357
medical profession, 18, 40, 48, 57, 273–318, 326–27, 331, 382; attitudes toward abortion, xii, 302, 308, 320–22, 330; attitudes toward disabled, 381–82; birth control and, 170, 263, 273; family-planning programs and, 176; feminism and, 273–88; legal profession and, 22; reproductive health services and, 304, 305–6; rights of, xiv, 52; on RU 486, 255; sexism and, 290–306; sterilization abuse and, 125
medical schools, 74, 287–88; abortion rights activism in, 327–28; abortion

training in, 324, 327–28; females in, 295–96; quotas in, 294–95
Medical Students for Choice (MSFC), xv, 288, 305, 324, 326–30
Meharry Medical College, 183
menopause, 300
"menstrual extraction," xiii
Meskill, Thomas, 56–60; Meskill bill, xiii
methotrexate, 267
Mexico City Policy, 194, 304
Michelman, Kate, 86, 87, 114–15
Michigan, 120
midwives 105, 173, 174, 324
mifepristone. See RU 486
militia movement, 237
Miller, Andrea, 7, 95–110, 397
Miller, Zell, 121
Milstein, Barbara, 52
Minnesota, 291–93, 294, 300; Supreme Court, 301, 302
Minorfare, 217
misogyny, 29, 217, 239, 276, 280
Mississippi, xv, 100
Mondale, Walter, 191
Montana, 105
Moral Majority, 241
mother(hood): abortion and, 278, 353; for disabled women, 387; forced, 344; privatization of, 350; race and, 130–33, 137; responsibilities of, 340, 344; rights of, 125, 306; single, 15, 26–27, 217–18; social context of, 345–46, 387; see also drug-addicted mothers
Mount Sinai Hospital (New York City), 23, 57
Moynihan, Daniel Patrick, 133–34
Murray, Pauli, 192
muscular dystrophy, 375

Nairobi, 188–89
NARAL, xii, xiii, xv, 75, 79, 86, 87, 88, 113, 114–17, 121, 173, 186, 195, 199, 252–54, 256, 260, 261, 262, 308
National Abortion and Reproductive Rights Action League (NARAL), xv, 75, 87, 88, 199
National Abortion Federation (NAF), 256, 323–25, 328
National Abortion Rights Action League (NARAL), xiii, 75, 79, 86, 113, 114–17, 121, 195, 199, 252–54, 256, 260, 261, 262
National Asian Women's Health Organization, 220–21, 222, 251
National Association for Perinatal Research and Education, 127

National Association for the Advancement of Colored People (NAACP), 168–69, 177, 180, 194, 197
National Association of Colored Women, 167
National Association of Negro Business and Professional Women's Clubs, 196, 197
National Association to Repeal Abortion Laws (NARAL), xii, 75, 79, 173, 186, 308
National Board of Medical Examiners, 321
National Black Feminist Organization (NBFO), 184–5
National Black Women's Health Project, xiii, xv, 185, 190, 193, 196, 200, 212, 220–21, 251, 262–63
National Christian Radio Broadcasting, 315
National Conference for Women (1977), 188
National Conference of Catholic Bishops, 80
National Council of Negro Women, 194, 196
National Institutes of Health, 255
National Latina Health Organization, 220–21, 263
National Lawyers Guild, 47
National Network of Abortion Funds, xiv, 208, 221–22
National Organization for Women (NOW), xii, 117, 192–93, 199, 238, 311; Women of Color Program, 191–92, 198
National Political Congress of Black Women, 191, 196
National Right to Life Committee, 74, 79, 80, 227, 238
National Urban Coalition, 194, 197
National Urban League, 168–69, 180, 194
National Welfare Rights Organization, 182
National Welfare Rights Union, 252
National Women's Health Network, xiii, 190, 251
National Young Women's Day of Action, 222
Nation of Islam, 180
Native American women, 213, 218, 251
Native American Women's Health and Education Resource Center, 220
Nazis, 125, 239
"Negro Project," 132, 171
New Hampshire, 314

New Jersey, 43, 116, 119, 172, 295
Newman, Jon, 55, 56, 57, 60–61
new reproductive technologies (NRTs), 142, 252, 260, 262, 381, 389, 390; disabled persons and, 375, 388; eugenics and, 376; limits of, 252; market for, 381, 386; politicization of, 200, 251–52; women of color and, 252;
New York, xii, 23, 43, 44, 49, 52, 60, 178, 186, 227, 230, 235, 254, 300, 301, 328, 353, 364
Nichols, Leanne, xv, 237, 315, 325
Ninth Amendment, 55
Nixon, Richard, 176, 181
nonsurgical abortion, 103
Nordic-Teutonic population, 169
Norplant, 133, 200, 217, 218, 265
Norsigian, Judy, 260
North Carolina, xii, 120
North Dakota, 84, 251
Northwestern University School of Medicine, 294
Norton, Eleanor Holmes, 184, 191
nurse-practitioners, 105, 324

Oakland Feminist Health Center, 281
obstetrics and gynecology, 282, 291, 299, 309, 324–26; abortion training in, 321, 325–26; women practitioners of, 305
O'Connor, John, 254
O'Connor, Sandra Day, 85
Office of Economic Opportunity (OEO), 176, 181, 307–8
O'Hanlon, George, 296
Ohio, xv, 102
Oklahoma Habitual Criminal Sterilization Act, 145
Operation Goliath, 235
Operation Push, 196, 197
Operation Rescue, xiv, 3; 81, 82, 83, 193, 223, 227–42, 314–15; clinic blockades, 234, 242; lawsuits against, 234–36; on murder, 236–37; "No Place to Kill" campaign, 329
Oregon, 120, 315

parental consent laws, xiv, 40, 74, 86, 97, 112, 113, 120–21, 211, 215–16, 220, 306, 348, 357; court hearings and, 104; judicial bypass provision of, 215, 348; rulings on, 105, 118, 119
Paltrow, Lynn, 198
Paris, France, 257–58, 261
Parish, Mary, 260, 268
Parks, Rosa, 193

"partial birth" abortion, xv, xvi, 102, 316
pelvic exams, 278, 286
Pennsylvania, xv, 43, 98
Pennsylvania Abortion Control Act, 85, 215
Pensacola (Fla.), 81, 314, 325
Perez, Leander, 176, 176
pharmaceutical companies, 255–56
pharmacists, 279
physicians. *See* medical profession
Pipel, Harriet, 43
Pitt, Terry
Planned Parenthood Federation, xi, 59, 117, 168, 177, 182, 185, 187, 196, 251, 254, 256, 261, 263, 267, 314, 324; of Connecticut, 47, 59; of Philadelphia, 211; of Texas, 238
Planned Parenthood v. Casey, xv, 75, 85–86, 90, 98, 99, 100, 101, 103, 107, 112, 117, 121
Pope John Paul II, 209
Population Action International, 263
population control, 42, 51, 175, 263, 304; Black women's resistance to, 162; racialization of, 125, 164, 175
Population Council, 175, 251, 255; and RU 486, 261, 266
Population Crisis Committee (Population Crisis International), 257
Population Reference Bureau, 171
pornography, 241, 242
Powell, Adam Clayton, 168
Powell, Colin, 121
pregnancy: as choice, 25, 353; defined, 21, 25; drug use and, 124–50; falsification of, 366; feelings about, 352, 358; health insurance coverage of, 346–47; medical-commercial control of, 385; reproductive technologies and, 381; state control of, 138; unplanned, 73, 87, 299, 353; unwanted, 352, 358, 368; unwed, 51, 361
prenatal care, 87, 200, and poverty, 142; and race, 135, 189
prenatal screening, 375–76, 381–82, 383, 385, 386
pre-*Roe v. Wade* era, 4, 15, 28, 37, 291, 322, 324, 362; legalization efforts during, 42, 300–1
Preterm Clinic (Washington, D.C.), 301, 307
Priddy, Albert, 144
Princeton University, 177
privacy doctrine, xii, 7, 52, 56, 60, 95, 96, 103, 115, 127, 137, 139, 147, 149, 219, 224, 342–46; drug use and, 142,

146; Fourteenth Amendment and, 139; feminism and, 357; feminist critique of, 146, 347; poor women and, 147; as right, 146–48; trimester framework and, 347; women of color and, 126, 138, 140–41, 143, 146, 148
pro-choice movement. *See* abortion rights
Pro-Life Action League, 230, 238; of Chicago, 313
pro-life movement. *See* anti-abortion rights movement
procreation, 143–46; criminalization of, 139; right to, 138–41, 145, 375, 385, 386
Project Hope, 300
psychiatrists, 17, 22, 25, 257–58
Puerto Ricans, 51, women and illegal abortions, 161
Puerto Rico, 178, 263, 265

Quayle, Dan, 121, 259

racism, 29, 51, 142, 161–64, 167, 169–71, 177, 185, 187, 199, 200, 217–18
Racketeer Influenced and Corrupt Organizations (RICO), xv, 238
rape, xv, 44, 77, 104, 119, 123, 164, 185, 208, 211, 217, 343; of slaves, 167
rape crisis projects, 97, 185
Rapp, Rayna, 385
Rawls, John, 345
Reagan, Ronald, 82, 189, 193, 211, 252, 253, 259, 302, 314; against reproductive rights, 194, 312–13; Supreme Court and, 74, 80
Redstockings, xii, 44
Rehabilitation Act Amendments (1973), 375
Religious Coalition for Abortion Rights, xiii, 196, 198. 199, 220
religious right, 228–29, 233, 234, 238, 240, 241, 268, 276
Reno, Janet, xv, 238, 314
Reproductive Health Technologies Project, xiii, 251–68; accomplishments of, 260, 266–68; racial issues and, 262, 265
Reproductive Justice Coalition, 198
reproductive rights, 7, 43, 51, 63, 141–42, 185, 220, 303; African-American women and, 161–201; disability issues and, 374–91; drug prosecutions and, 124–50; global perspective on, 223, 300; race and, 26–27, 127, 142, 146, 148; *see also* abortion rights, RU 486
reproductive technology. *See* new reproductive technologies

Republican Party, xiii, xv, 28, 120, 122, 176, 191, 238, 315, 316; on abortion issue, 90, 80, 119, 121, 218
Rescue America, 83, 238
right-to-life movement. *See* anti-abortion rights movement
Rio de Janeiro, 222, 258
Roberts, Dorothy E., 5, 7, 8, 124–50, 397–98
Robertson, John, 142
Robertson, Pat, 83, 241, 314
Rodriguez-Trias, Helen, 263
Rodrique, Jesse, 168
Roe v. Wade, xiii, 5, 29, 33, 40, 43, 60, 63, 73, 76, 80, 86, 90, 210, 229, 308, 311, 347, 353, 357, 359; civil rights groups and, 195; as compromise, 224; erosion of, 85–86, 97, 98, 111, 211, 218; impact of, 302; implementation of, 308; licensed physicians and, 105; medical support for, 279, 320; as negative right, 99; oral arguments in, 54; period following, 62, 186, 212; privacy rights and, 95, 347; right-to-life movement and, 330; *stare decisis* and, 103; as victory, 78–79, 302; vulnerability of, xiv, 74–75, 84, 111, 115, 195, 252, 259, 304
Romalis, Gary, xv, 315
Roosevelt, Theodore, 169
Roraback, Catherine (Katie), 46–48, 52, 54–55, 58, 61
Ross, Loretta J., 3, 5, 161–207, 398
Roussel Uclaf, 255, 257, 258, 261, 265–66
RU 486, xiv, xvi, 251, 254–68, 302; approval process, 254, 267; availability of, 259, 265, 304;
Ruffin, Josephine St. Pierre, 167
Rust v. Sullivan, xiv, 121
Rutherford, Charlotte, 197

Sakiz, Edouard, 257
Saletan, William, 8, 11–23, 398
Salvi, John, III, 83, 210, 237, 315
Sanders, Marion, 183
Sanger, Margaret, 170–72, 266, 305, 377
Saxton, Marsha, 7, 374–93, 398
Scalia, Antonin, 195
Schaeffer, Francis, 229
Scheidler, Joseph, 230, 231, 238, 313, 314
Schweitzer, Albert, 307
Scott, Julia, 262
Searle, 255
Seichter, Marilyn, 52, 60
sex education, 87, 88, 189, 200

sexism, 47, 161–64, 180, 185, 198, 217, 292, 297, 306, 388; in health care system, 300; in medical profession, 290; in prenatal screening, 386–87; selective abortion and, 386–87
sex selection, 85, 385
sexual abuse, 136, 222, 299
sexual harassment, 199, 290, 299, 303
sexual preference, 200
sexually transmitted disease, 88, 222, 263, 267–68
sex workers, 251
Shalala, Donna, 266
Shannon, Rachelle, 236, 315
sickle cell anemia, 375
sign-language culture, 380–81
single mothers, 15, 26–27; attacks on, 217–18
Sioux, 251
Sistereach Project, 221
Skinner v. Oklahoma, 145
slavery, 124, 133, 140, 162, 167, 178, 185, 196; birth control and, 166–67; legacy of, 162; reproduction and, 132, 139, 149, 164
Sloan, Margaret, 184
Smeal, Eleanor, 261
Smith, Barbara, 185
Smith, Beverly, 196
Smith, Joan, 187
Smith, Lois (pseud.), 179
Smith, Wilbur, 58
Society of Physicians for Reproductive Choice and Health, 326
Socrates, 309
Solinger, Rickie, 1–9, 15–32, 173–74, 353, 398
South Dakota, 84, 208
Southern Christian Leadership Conference, 193, 194
speak-outs, 44, 46, 61
Speidel, Joseph, 257
Spelman College, 190, 196, 197
spina bifida, 375, 377, 382
spousal-consent laws, 85, 97, 98
"Spring of Life," demonstrations, 236
"squeal rule," 348
Stanford University, 256; medical school, 329
State v. Johnson, 137
Stearns, Nancy, 42, 43, 52, 60
Steinauer, Jody, 320–33, 398
sterilization, 170, 177, 178, 377; African-American women's resistance of abuse, 163, 185; as choice, 177, 201; coerced, 125, 145–46, 189, 217; of disabled persons, 377; eugenics and, 144,

sterilization *(continued)*
171, 377; federally funded programs,
132–33, 181; race and, 27, 51, 125,
132, 139, 143, 165
Stewart, Abigail J., 356–73, 398
Stokes, Louis, 193
strict scrutiny standard, 95, 98
Sunnen Foundation, 255

Tallahassee Feminist Women's Health
Center (Fla.), 186
Tay-Sachs disease, 382
teenagers: pregnancy of, 88, 188, 194,
195, 215, 300; programs for, 193–94;
sexuality of, 166
Tennessee, 121, 183
terrorism, 234, 237, 254, 317, 349
Terry, Randall, xiii, 4, 16, 81, 86, 227–
42; lawsuits against, 234–36; tac-
tics of, 231–32, 235, 239
Tervalon, Melanie, 189
Texas, 78, 96, 120
thalidomide, xi, 260
therapeutic abortion, 21, 52, 362–64,
369, 385; indications for, 20–21, 357;
psychiatric grounds for, xii, 22, 257,
358
Third World Women's Alliance, 186
Thomas, "Able" Mable, 198
Thomas, Cal, 83
Thomas, Clarence, 86, 199, 290, 299,
303
Thornburgh v. American College of Ob-
stetricians and Gynecologists, 111,
113, 116
Tiller, George, 236, 315
Tooley, Michael, 339–42, 346
Toure, Nkenge, 181
Treshman, Don, 83
Tribe, Laurence, 147
trimester framework, 62, 96
Trosch, David, 315
Truth, Sojourner, 168, 188
tubal ligation, 280
Tubman, Harriet, 185, 187, 188
Tucker, C. Delores, 191
Tynes, Emily, 195, 262
Tyson, Pat, 196

unborn child, 56, 59, 60, 232; *see also*
fetus
Underground Railroad, as model for
Jane, 178
"undue burden" standard, 85, 98, 100,
102
United Movement for Progress, 180

United Nations, 222; Decade for Women,
188, 189, 194
United States Agency for International
Development, 189
United States Congress, 80, 113, 183,
252, 366, 389; on abortion bans, xvi,
102, 316; on clinic violence, 106, 228,
315; conservative victory and, 122,
220; on family-planning programs,
176; on health care reform, 107; on
Hyde Amendment, 212–13; on medical
profession, 215, 304, 305, 326–27; reli-
gious right and, 211; *see also* United
States Senate
United States Constitution, 79, 80, 143
United States Department of Health, Edu-
cation, and Welfare, 97, 308
United States Department of Justice, 82,
106, 210
United States Department of State, 301
United States House of Representatives,
252, 326–27, 366
United States Senate, 120, 181, 252;
Judiciary Committee of, 299,
303
United States Taxpayers Party (USTP),
229
United States v. Vuitch, 308
University of California, 324, 328, 329
University of Colorado, 313
University of Connecticut, 57
University of Minnesota Medical School,
294–95, 298
University of Pennsylvania, 328
University of Southern California, 255
University of South Georgia, 297
Upjohn, 255

vasectomy, 145
Vaughn, Brenda, 129
Vermont, 105
Vietnam war, 34, 77, 359
violence, 8, 217, 224, 279, 318; against
women, 185, 190, 222; glorification
of, 317; *see also* terrorism
Virginia, 114, 116, 119, 144, 255
Virginia State Epileptic Colony, 144
vivisection, morality of, 350
Voting Rights Act of 1964, 176

waiting periods, xv, 40, 74, 85, 86, 97,
98, 99, 211, 306, 357; challenges to,
101; effects of, 100
Walker, Alice, 161, 184, 188
Wallace, Michele, 187
Ward, Robert, 235
Washington, xii, 54

Waters, Maxine, 191, 193
Watson, Diane, 192
Wattleton, Faye, 187, 195, 196, 216
Webster, William, 313
Webster v. Reproductive Rights Services,
    xiv, 42, 84, 99, 112, 115, 120, 188,
    233, 259; aftermath, 116–18, 195,
    234, 322–33; backlash against,
    120
Weddington, Sarah, 78
Weiker, Lowell, 259
Weisz, Erik (Houdini), 282
welfare, 27, 132, 185, 300; abortion and,
    63, 213, 218, 303; abuse, 165; attacks
    on, 211, 217; procreation and, 125;
    reform, 163, 217, 220, 224; rights,
    199
Wells, Ida B., 188
"We Remember: African American
    Women for Reproductive Freedom,"
    195, 197, 200
West, Robin, 89, 148
Westoff, Carolyn, 324
Whalen v. Roe, 348
white supremacy, 16, 27, 28, 167, 278
Wichita, xiv, 82, 228, 236, 315
Widdicombe, Judith, 120, 254–55
Wilder, Douglas, 114, 119–20
Wilder, Marcy J., 8, 73–94, 398–99
Wilkens, Roger, 193
Williams, Lizzie, 124
Williams v. Zbaraz, 348
Wills, Gary, 240–41
Winthrop Chemical Co., 293
Wisconsin, 49, 281, 367
Wise, Leah, 193
Wolf, Naomi, 89
Women of African Descent for Reproduc-
    tive Justice, 198

Women's Democratic Club of Darien,
    CT, 62
Women's Health Collective (New York
    City), 43, 46
women's health movement, 40, 185, 193,
    281; and centers, 281
Women's Health Resource Center (Chi-
    cago), 281
Women's Health Services (New Haven),
    63
women's liberation movement, 34–35,
    40, 42–47, 49, 57, 61, 62, 63, 77, 187,
    219
Women's National Abortion Action Co-
    alition, 308
Women's Political Association of Harlem,
    168
women's rights, 87, 113–14, 119, 137,
    189, 198, 292, 302; abortion and, 219,
    220, 224, 348, 384 (see also abortion
    rights); contraception and, 171–72; fe-
    tal rights vs., 74, 149; international,
    223, 258; limitations on, 348; see also
    reproductive rights
women's rights movement, 29, 359, 378;
    see also feminism
Women versus Connecticut, xiii, 47–55,
    57–63
Workfare, 217
World Bank, 189
World Decade for Women, 188
World Health Organization, 304
Wright, Doris, 184
"wrongful birth" suits, 379, 380
Wyatt, Addie, 192

Yale University, 46, 197
Young, Andrew, 121, 193
Young, Whitney, 180

Design:	Nola Burger
Composition:	Maple-Vail Manufacturing Group
Text:	10/13 Sabon
Display:	Franklin Gothic Book and Demi
Printing and binding:	Maple-Vail Manufacturing Group